Reform
Judaism
Then
and
Now

SYLVAN D. SCHWARTZMAN, PH.D.

Reform Judaism

Then and Now

*Union of American Hebrew Congregations
New York*

By Sylvan D. Schwartzman

Rocket to Mars (1953)

The Story of Reform Judaism (1953)

Reform Judaism in the Making (1955)

Once Upon a Lifetime (1958)

Meeting Your Life Problems, with David S. Hachen (1959)

Into the Underground Kingdom (1960)

An Orientation to God, Prayer and Ethics (1961)

An Orientation to the Religious School, the Temple and the Jewish Home (1961)

The Commitments of Confirmation (1961)

The Living Bible, with Jack D. Spiro (1962)

Our Religion and Our Neighbors, with Milton G. Miller (1963)

Casebook: The Non-Text Sermon (1965)

Rocket to Mars [Sephardic Edition]. (1969)

Reform Judaism—Then and Now (1971)

Library of Congress Catalogue Card No. 161900
Copyright 1971
by the
Union of American Hebrew Congregations
New York, N.Y.

Published in the United States of America

To Lori Ann and Daniel Jay
and Their Generation of Reform Jews

FOREWORD

THIS BOOK AND REFORM JUDAISM ITSELF BELIE THE STORY OF A BOY WHO WAS ASKED WHETHER HE was Catholic, Protestant, or Jewish, and he answered: "I'm Reform." Reform Judaism is not a sect or a denomination, although it has been incorrectly interpreted as both. A statement from rabbinic literature (Sifré, Devarim 306) captures the essential nature of Reform Judaism: "Rabbi Jacob, son of Rabbi Chaninah, said to Rabbi Yehudah: 'Come, let us investigate the laws again and again that no rust may gather upon them.'"

Reform Judaism is not a novel offshoot of traditional Judaism; it is, rather, a Judaism of the ages which strives to be contemporary and to respond to the needs of every generation. As the rabbinic statement indicates, Jewish tradition should never become intransigent or immobile. The history of Judaism reveals manifold changes and reforms. The *shalshelet kabalah* (chain of tradition) has continued to grow through the millennia, each generation adding a new link of understanding forged on the anvil of contemporary conditions under which Jews have lived.

Reform Judaism dramatizes the dynamic character of Jewish tradition. It unfolds the creative principle of Jewish history working for the continuous relevance of Judaism, the dynamic force intended to keep the tradition alive and the chain unbroken. Judaism, then and now, has been and must be its own vital source of renewal and growth.

Possibly the most significant innovation of Reform Judaism is its approach to change itself. Not always content with the natural process of change, Reform has pioneered in creating accelerated forms of change—not as a result of impatience but for the sake of creative survival and revitalization. This idea of conscious and actuated progression is the key to an understanding of Reform Judaism.

Reform Jews have responded to every issue and problem with the conviction that adaptation, rather than immutability, will assure the continuation of Jewish values.

The author explores the character of Reform Judaism—its history and theology, its social dynamics and personalities—by introducing each chapter with a contemporary problem related to the past. We learn that Reform, by its very nature, is basically a problem-solving approach to the issues which have confronted and continue to challenge Jews involved in the realities of the contemporary world.

Jack D. Spiro

PREFACE

FOR NEARLY A QUARTER OF A CENTURY, MY EARLIER WORK, *The Story of Reform Judaism,* SERVED to inform thousands of Reform young people about the origins, development, principles, and practices of their faith. During this period, however, a series of unparalleled events in human history occurred. For these were the years that witnessed the catastrophe of Hitler and World War II, the establishment of the State of Israel, and the birth of the atomic, computer, and space ages.

The consequence of sweeping change has led to vastly different patterns of life and thought and to a Reform Judaism caught up in critical conflict over most of the current problems besetting modern man as well as those confronting the acculturated Jew in the open society of the West. Meanwhile, the movement has also been called upon to respond to an expanding membership whose desires range from neo-traditionalism to agnosticism and radical freedom.

Hence the need for a new text on Reform Judaism, designed not merely to update the facts or to accommodate the sensibilities of our more sophisticated Reform young people today but to expose them to some of the religious perplexities confronting their faith in the latter third of the twentieth century.

But in a movement such as ours, no single pedagogical approach—be it historical, topical, or problem-centered—will satisfy everyone. The treatment of fact is also bound to be questioned by those who prefer more emphasis on theology, sociology, psychology, or something else. And it is hardly a secret that among us not even a description of current Reform ideology or practice is accepted at face value.

Still, the conviction that Reform young people are entitled to know something of their faith has helped me persevere, and this volume is the result. For continuity and clarity, it follows a semi-historical approach. Yet, with the needs of the younger reader in mind, I have also sought to provide added motivation and relevance by introducing each chapter with a contemporary problem relating to the past; and, in line with current trends in history instruction, I have placed at the end of the chapter a series of significant documents for further student interest and enrichment. Therefore the teacher is free to conduct the class with any of three main approaches: formal history instruction, problem-solving, or historical self-discovery—or a combination of these.

In an effort to be objective—though I confess to a strong partisanship for Reform—I have drawn upon a wide variety of sources, both old and new, that reflect many different Reform and non-Reform points of view. They are far too numerous to mention by name, but I sincerely acknowledge my debt to all of them and express my appreciation for permission to quote those documents as well as brief selections from works appearing in the bibliography.

I would also like to express my sincere gratitude to the editor, Rabbi Jack D. Spiro, and the members of the Reading Committee, Rabbis Bernard J. Bamberger, Leonard S. Kravitz, Harold

Preface

Silver, Dr. Robert Sperber, and Heinz Warschauer for their valuable criticisms, suggestions, and comments, many of which have been incorporated in this work. To Ralph Davis for the impressive and attractive format of this volume, and to Mrs. Rose Zamonski for the distinctive art work. To the late Mrs. Sam Spivak, my secretary, for her careful and devoted preparation of the typescript. To the UAHC copy editing department headed by Josette Knight.

My thanks go to the organizations and individuals for the photographs used in the text.

Finally, to those rabbis, educational directors, and teachers whose suggestions over the years have proved so personally helpful in preparing this and other volumes.

I earnestly hope that *Reform Judaism — Then and Now* will help our young people to grasp the purposes to which they are committed as Reform Jews and to grapple courageously with the issues of their day so that they may ultimately reap the blessings of a living faith.

S. D. S.

Hebrew Union College-Jewish Institute of Religion
Cincinnati, Ohio

CONTENTS

Reform Judaism Then and Now

A LIVE ISSUE

In the course of its development, Reform Judaism has had to contend with many problems. A good number trouble the movement today, and chief among them are various "live issues" about which there is considerable difference of opinion.

Every chapter in this book deals with at least one "live issue" to which you, as a Reform Jew, are asked to give some thought. At the very least, you are expected to form an opinion about where you stand on the question.

One such "live issue" is touched on in this chapter. From the data supplied about the religious affiliation of American Jews, you will observe that a great many have no formal association with Judaism. Nevertheless, most regard themselves as loyal Jews, who believe in the preservation of the Jewish people and identify themselves with various Jewish organizations and causes. They are generally referred to as "secular" Jews.

The Basic Problem: In contrast to those who subscribe to Judaism, the secular Jew claims to have no need for religion. Whatever his arguments, he usually insists that it is possible to maintain Jewish life in the United States without Judaism. Most Reform Jews strongly dispute this and believe it is necessary to win over the "unaffiliated" to religious life.

Some Important Questions: (1) Is it possible for Jewish life to survive in America without the existence of synagogues and religious schools? (2) Can the individual rear his children as worthwhile Jews without religious beliefs and practices? (3) Is participation in non-religious Jewish causes and organizations enough to sustain the individual as a Jew? (4) What more does Judaism offer toward the preservation of Jewish life?

What Do You Think? What conclusions do you come to about the position of the secular Jew? To what extent do you find Judaism necessary for the preservation of Jews? Why? Should the Reform movement therefore make even greater efforts to attract the unaffiliated to the temple?

1. WHAT IS REFORM JUDAISM?

Reform in the News

Reading an American Jewish newspaper these days, you often come across headlines like these:

REFORM LEADER URGES MORE REGARD FOR TRADITIONAL LAW

MERGER WITH REFORM MOVEMENT PROPOSED BY CONSERVATIVE RABBI

REFORM LEADERSHIP DEBATES MODERN SABBATH OBSERVANCE

ISRAELI RABBINATE REFUSES TO ACCEPT REFORM CONVERSION

Each of these, you note, has something to do with Reform Judaism.

You need not be surprised to find Reform so much in the news. This has been true ever since it began, and you can be sure that it will continue. As in the past, some among the Orthodox will vigorously oppose it, while from time to time proposals will be made for a merger with the Conservatives. And within the Reform movement itself, many issues will arise on which disagreements occur.

Why all this happens is part of the Reform story. So, to be able to follow the news calls for good knowledge of Reform Judaism.

But that is only a small part of it. There are far more important reasons that involve you directly.

Matters That Concern You

Suppose, for instance, someone asked you to tell him something about yourself. Eventually you would get around to mentioning the fact that you are a Reform Jew.

"What's a Reform Jew?" he might ask.

That should be easy for you to answer. After all, you belong to a Reform congregation and attend a Reform religious school. Well, what would you reply?

Does this start you thinking? It should, because if you are a Reform Jew you certainly ought to know what it means.

But here are some additional facts worth considering:

—Being a Reform Jew should be a matter of your own personal choice, not simply your family's. In today's world, that is your right. Why, then, do you prefer being Reform, rather than something else?

—What sort of a Reform Jew can you possibly be without knowing what it demands? It is like trying to play basketball without understanding how the game is played or what the rules are.

—We constantly face situations in life where religion can be of help—for example, when dealing with personal problems or social issues like poverty, discrimination, and war. Wouldn't some knowledge of Reform Judaism be helpful here?

—As people mature, they face some of the deeper questions of life such as its purpose, the existence of God, values by which to live, and others. Undoubtedly Reform Judaism has something of importance to say here, but do you know what?

—Life is changing rapidly these days, and religion with it. We observe this among both the Roman Catholics and Protestants who have already made many modifications in worship and Church structure. Reform is likewise in the process of reexamining some of its own beliefs and practices. But without sufficient knowledge, can you make an intelligent judgment about the changes that are needed?

All of this simply adds up to one conclusion: A Reform Jew needs to know something about Reform Judaism.

This Matter of Observance

To be sure, you already possess certain information. You know, for instance, that Reform is part of Judaism, and that it is different from Orthodoxy and Conservatism. Thus, you attend services at temple, but some of your friends go to *shul* (a Yiddish word for synagogue), where they worship somewhat differently. Nor do you, as a Reform Jew, observe in quite the same way that they do the Sabbath, the Jewish holidays, and various other rites, such as a *Berit Milah* (בְּרִית מִילָה covenant or ceremony of circumcision) or marriage.

Many Jews think that these are the only real differences, and they even joke about it. They will say that what distinguishes the Reform, Conservative, and Orthodox Jew is how far from the synagogue each parks his car on Yom Kippur. Everybody knows, of course, that traditional Jews are not supposed to ride at all on the Day of Atonement, though many do and conceal it.

So when people talk about the various forms of Judaism, they generally concentrate on differences in observance. Reform Jews, they say, keep only seven days of Passover, while the Orthodox and Conservative observe eight; or the temple uses a different prayer book than the *shul*.

This is true, though all religious Jews share much more in common than we often realize. Nevertheless, practices do differ, and that is one way of distinguishing Reform from the others. But that is by no means the only difference, or even the most important. It goes much deeper than that.

A Different Approach to Judaism

Actually it involves a different approach to Judaism and, to help you understand what this means, suppose we consider a Friday

4

evening service at a typical temple. Here are some of the things that generally take place:

—Families sit together.

—The men worship bareheaded.

—The rabbi wears a rabbinical robe.

—He calls a woman to the pulpit to light the candles, after which the cantor chants the *Kiddush.*

—The rabbi, cantor, and congregation read prayers in English and Hebrew from the *Union Prayer Book.*

—A choir of men and women, accompanied by the organ, joins with the cantor in singing the responses.

—The rabbi takes the Torah from the Ark, reads and translates it.

—The rabbi preaches a sermon.

—The congregation joins in a final hymn from the *Union Hymnal* or *Union Songster.*

All of this tells us something about Reform's outlook on Judaism. In the first place, some of the rites, though traditional, such as lighting the candles and reading from the Torah, would never be permitted in an Orthodox synagogue on a Friday night. Hence we learn that though Reform draws upon Jewish tradition for many of its practices it is not necessarily bound by traditional rules and regulations.

Furthermore, the use of the organ and mixed choir—both prohibited by traditional Judaism—confirms the fact that Reform considers itself free to introduce new elements into the worship. It also explains why Reform congregations were the first to permit the wearing of a rabbinical robe, the reading of portions of the service in English, the delivery of a weekly sermon, the seating of men and women together, and many other things.

REFORM RABBI. Here, wearing his rabbinical robe and *atarah,* this Reform rabbi conducts the service.

Finally, incorporated within the service itself are certain basic Reform principles. The fact that men worship without hats, for example, reveals Reform's conviction that Judaism must adapt itself to modern life where respect is shown by removing one's hat, as when viewing the flag or greeting a lady. The participation of women in the service grows out of Reform's belief in their religious equality, and the recitation of some prayers and hymns in English affirms the Jew's right to worship in the vernacular, the language of his country.

A Reform service, then, is more than simply a matter of different observances. It also represents a considerably different approach to Judaism.

An Organized Movement—and More

But the service tells us other things as well. It reminds us, for example, that Reform is a movement made up of people and organizations. Not only have you, your family, and others joined together to maintain a congregation, but the very worship itself indicates the existence of certain other Reform organizations.

For instance, when you pray from the *Union Prayer Book* or sing hymns from the *Union Hymnal* or *Union Songster,* you are using materials prepared by the Reform rabbinate through its Central Conference of American Rabbis. The beautiful engraved silver *kiddush* cup which the cantor holds aloft is a ceremonial object produced by the Union of American Hebrew Congregations, a body made up of all Reform congregations in North America. And when the rabbi and cantor officiate, you are observing men trained by a Reform seminary, the Hebrew Union College–Jewish Institute of Religion.

Each temple, then, draws upon the resources of an organized movement that came into being over a considerable period of time through the efforts of a great many people. How and why the movement began is an important part of the Reform story. So is what Reform hopes to achieve, how it has developed its beliefs, practices, and structure, and the very problems it has encountered in the process.

Attending a Friday evening service at temple, therefore, gives us much to think about. At the very least, it confirms the fact that when we speak of Reform Judaism we are dealing with:

—a particular approach to Judaism

—various principles and beliefs

—numerous religious practices

—many individuals and organizations

—a movement with a past

—an assortment of problems.

Understanding Reform Judaism, therefore, means that we are familiar with these and something more—certain fundamental facts about the movement, such as its name, its size, where its congregations are located, and how old it is.

A Movement with Several Names

Suppose, then, we start with some of this more basic information. Take the name of the movement, for instance. You may be surprised to learn that "Reform" is not its only name. In France, Holland, and Switzerland, Reform congregations are always called "Liberal." So are some in England where there are particular differences between "Liberal" and "Reform" temples.

Congregations in Ireland, South Africa, and Italy prefer the name "Progressive." So does the international organization of Reform Jews, which calls itself the World Union for Progressive Judaism.

Actually "Reform" is the oldest term, and it originated in Germany where those advocating changes in Judaism were known as "reformers." At first they referred to their movement as "Reform*ed*," that is, "changed," but they eventually switched to "Reform" to emphasize the fact that theirs was a continuing program of religious change.

The terms "Liberal" and "Progressive" appeared somewhat later. The dictionary defines a "liberal" religion as "a faith not bound by permanently established forms," and a "progressive" religion as one "capable of making progress through regular and gradual improvement." Thus all three names refer to a religion that develops through a process of change.

Often the three terms are used interchangeably, but sometimes people use one or the other to distinguish between different types of Reform. Thus, in England, "Reform" congregations are much more traditional than the "Liberal," while in the United States some of the more moderate congregations in the movement call themselves "Liberal" or "Progressive" in contrast to those that are less traditional, or "Reform," in practice. Nevertheless, "Reform" is the term that is most widely accepted, particularly in America, as indicated by the fact that the name recently chosen for the movement's annual campaign for funds is the Reform Jewish Appeal.

How Many Congregations? And Where?

Figures can also supply valuable information. For instance, looking at the map, Reform Judaism in the World—1968, we discover how small a movement Reform really is. It has only 796 congregations in the entire world.

Notice that though Reform congregations are found in twenty-seven countries, 688, or about 86 percent, are located in the United States. Significantly, most of the remaining 108 congregations are located in other English-speaking countries. Second in size to the American movement is that found in the British Isles, where 43 congregations are distributed throughout England, Ireland, Scotland, and Wales. Another 36 English-speaking congregations are located in Canada, South Africa, Australia, and New Zealand. The rest exist chiefly in Western and Central Europe and Central and South America.

The map confirms the fact, then, that Reform Judaism flourishes mainly where democracy and Western culture prevail, which, as we shall see, is scarcely accidental.

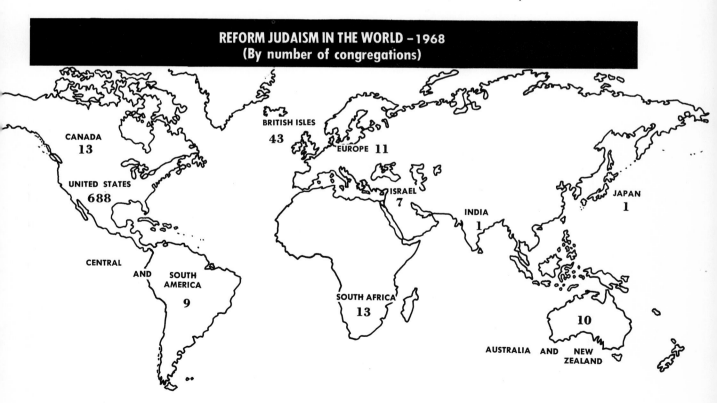

REFORM JUDAISM IN THE WORLD – 1968
(By number of congregations)

CANADA
13

BRITISH ISLES
43

EUROPE 11

UNITED STATES
688

ISRAEL
7

INDIA
1

JAPAN
1

CENTRAL
AND SOUTH AMERICA
9

SOUTH AFRICA
13

AUSTRALIA AND NEW ZEALAND
10

How Reform Compares in Size

All told, there are only about one million, one hundred thousand Reform Jews, which is just a tiny fraction of 1 percent of the entire population of the world.

But how does the movement compare in size among the Jews as a whole? The two following charts provide the answer. In the first, Comparative Size of the Reform Movement, the figures on the left compare Reform membership with the total number of Jews in the world; the figures on the right present the facts in the United States.

Again we observe how small a movement Reform really is. Still, in terms of American Jewry, it begins to represent a sizable number. When we realize how influential the American Jewish community is today, the size of the Reform movement here makes it of much greater significance.

This is certainly so when it comes to religious life. For about half of all religious Jews live in the United States and, among them, as we observe from the second chart, Comparative Size of American Reform Jewry, the Reform membership is a large proportion.

Indeed, in view of its concentration in the United States, the Reform movement becomes far more important than its limited membership might lead us to believe.

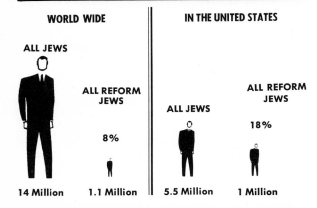

COMPARATIVE SIZE OF THE REFORM MOVEMENT

WORLD WIDE — IN THE UNITED STATES

ALL JEWS

ALL REFORM JEWS

8%

14 Million — 1.1 Million

ALL JEWS

ALL REFORM JEWS

18%

5.5 Million — 1 Million

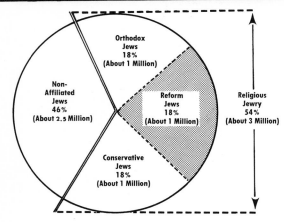

COMPARATIVE SIZE OF AMERICAN REFORM JEWRY
(All American Jews, About 5,500,000)

Orthodox Jews 18% (About 1 Million)

Non-Affiliated Jews 46% (About 2.5 Million)

Reform Jews 18% (About 1 Million)

Religious Jewry 54% (About 3 Million)

Conservative Jews 18% (About 1 Million)

How Old Is Reform?

How old, finally, is the Reform movement? That is a difficult question to answer for two reasons. One is the fact that we have no way of pinpointing just when it started. No dramatic episode, special meeting, or written resolution marks the beginning. Reform simply emerged gradually over half a century in Central and Western Europe as a result of certain changes in Jewish life.

Second, some people would also argue that Judaism itself has always been a "reform" movement in the sense that it has constantly undergone change. So a leading Reform scholar insists when he writes:

> . . . **Our present Reform Judaism is not the first movement of its kind in Jewish history. The name may be new and applied for the first time, but the movement itself is old, as old as Judaism; in fact, it *is* Judaism, the very soul . . . of Judaism; it is historic Judaism.**

Again and again, in the course of its four thousand years of history, Judaism has reformed itself—formed or formulated itself anew, as the term implies—reshaped itself, restated its principles, redefined its content and philosophy, reorganized its ritual practice, made itself over more or less completely; yet in every case and through all the centuries it has remained Judaism.

Nevertheless, as a distinct religious movement, Reform can be traced back to the early nineteenth century, which means that it is really not very old, as we note from the time-chart, The Historical Development of Judaism.

Note at what point Reform finally appears. It comes long after the Bible and the Talmud, the period of the *Geonim* (plural of גָּאוֹן, excellency, the leading Babylonian scholars who interpreted the Talmud), and the Golden Age in Spain, with such eminent figures as Moses ibn Ezra and Maimonides. It is still later than the age of Jewish mysticism, known as Kabalah (קַבָּלָה, tradition), and Joseph Karo, who wrote the *Shulchan Aruch* (שֻׁלְחָן עָרוּךְ, Prepared Table), the basic code-book of traditional law and practice. Even Chasidism, a popular form of Judaism among the East European masses of the eighteenth century, is older.

In fact, Reform was not even in existence at the time of either the American Revolution or the adoption of the Constitution.

Why the Need for Reform?

Here, then, are four important things we have learned from Reform's vital statistics:

—As its various names indicate, it views Judaism as a changing and improving faith in line with the developments of the times.

—Located in many parts of the world, the Reform movement exists largely where Western culture prevails and Jews enjoy a high degree of equality.

—Comparatively few in number, Reform members are concentrated in the United States where they exert considerable influence upon Judaism and Jewish life throughout the world.

—Reform is a relatively new movement in Jewish history and is the outgrowth of nearly thirty-eight hundred years of previous development in Judaism.

Perhaps you may be wondering why, in view of the fact that all through the ages Judaism underwent change, a Reform movement was

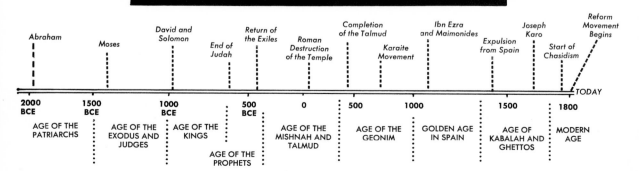

THE HISTORICAL DEVELOPMENT OF JUDAISM

9

even necessary. For the answer, we will have to look into the conditions of Jewish life some two centuries ago.

QUESTIONS FOR DISCUSSION

1. In view of the fact that the Reform Jew does not observe Judaism as tradition demands, is he a "good" Jew? Who determines what a "good" Jew is, and on what basis?

2. Since many Conservative and Orthodox congregations have adopted various Reform practices, is there need any longer for a distinct Reform movement? What arguments can you give both for and against a merger of all three groups?

3. What particular problems do you believe present-day Reform Judaism faces as a result of new conditions today? What changes in Reform Judaism would you therefore recommend?

4. How do you account for the fact that most of world Jewry today is not Reform? How do you explain the similar situation in the United States?

5. Why has Reform Judaism been so much more successful in the English-speaking countries than elsewhere? What additional reasons can you give for the movement's concentration in the United States?

6. What justification is there for saying that Judaism has always been "reform"? How does this make the modern Reform movement a truer expression of the Jewish religion than other interpretations?

SIGNIFICANT DOCUMENTS

Reform, Not "Reformed" or "Liberal" Judaism

. . . Thus . . . Reform Judaism became the name expressive of the principle of Reform and Progress as justified by history, in contrast to the stability of Orthodoxy, which claimed the immutability of the

DR. KAUFMANN KOHLER. This leading American Reformer made his way from Germany to the United States in 1869. He was the guiding force in the creation and adoption of the Pittsburgh Platform of 1885. Author of many important works on Jewish theology, he served as president of the Hebrew Union College for eighteen years.

Torah both in its written form and its oral interpretation as having come down from Mount Sinai. It is, accordingly, utterly erroneous to speak, as so many do, of a "reform*ed*" Judaism, as if the Reform leaders had ever intended to create a schism, a new system of religion or creed fixed and final. . . .

Neither can the name Liberal Judaism, which is now in vogue, be accepted as a substitute. It is altogether too vague and arbitrary . . . In the one case it makes allowance for the old synagogal prayers for the restoration of the Temple with its sacrificial cult and for the resurrection of the Jew, though they belie the conviction of the enlightened modern Jew. In the other case [where the term "Liberal Judaism" is used], concessions are made to a [Christian] creed which totally differs from our monotheistic faith, and which for more than eighteen hundred years stood out as a hostile force to Jew and Judaism, sowing hatred instead of fostering the spirit of justice, of love, and humanity in the name of God, the Father of mankind.

Reform Judaism stands firmly and positively for principles, the principle of liberalism and loyalty, for progress and steadfast continuity with the past, for the One Revelation of God as recorded in our Scriptures and the one undivided humanity which is finally to share in our truth, for the God of righteousness and the God of love but, above all, for the covenant of Sinai which never grows *old!* Liberal Judaism [as the term is used], however, often wavers and halts between the two sides.

—From Kaufmann Kohler,
"A Revaluation of Reform Judaism,"
*Central Conference of
American Rabbis Yearbook,*
Vol. 34 (1924), pp. 223–224.

Reform and Change

. . . These four or five generations of Reform Judaism have been generations of constant change. The practice and observance in Reform Judaism varied and developed in response to the changing feelings and the attitudes of the people. The rabbis have expressed certain principles, certain theological ideals, but the people themselves by their rejections and their acceptances, by their neglects and by their observances, have largely determined their own religious practices. Reform Jewish practice is not fixed. It is still changing . . .

Some of its practices, such as Confirmation, the late Friday evening services, the abolition of the woman's gallery, have been adopted by other branches of Jewry.

DR. SOLOMON B. FREEHOF. Noted Reform rabbi of Pittsburgh, he has written extensively on the subject of Reform practice. Much of his writing has taken the form of "responsa," or replies to queries about what constitutes appropriate Reform practice. For many years he was chairman of the Commission on Jewish Education. (HUC, American Jewish Archives)

Some are looked upon by the Conservative and Orthodox Jews as extreme and unjustified changes. But all the Reform practices together form a fairly harmonious unity and represent the summation of . . . the effort by one branch of Jewry to adjust itself to modern life . . .

It has been the consistent attitude of Reform that practices should be modified to meet the needs of the times, that the ethical and spiritual ideals of Judaism are eternal but they must find new modes of ceremonial expression from time to time. Therefore, Reform itself does not consider its present practice as definite and fixed. It is consciously seeking new and better ways in which Jewish observances may inculcate Jewish ideals. Therefore many

Reform Judaism—Then and Now

new practices develop constantly. Often they are a modification of some older Jewish practice which had hitherto been entirely neglected and which now it is felt can be reconstructed and serve to instruct and inspire.

—From Solomon B. Freehof,
Reform Jewish Practice,
Vol. 1 (1944), pp. 13–14.

Reform, a Constant Process in Judaism

Reform Judaism is a Jewish religious movement originating in Germany in the 18th century. It has sought and continues to seek so to interpret Judaism that it may meet the religious needs of the Jew in modern times. It clings to the basic concepts of historical Judaism. But it has made changes in some of the customs and ceremonies which have come to us from the past. In doing this, Reform Judaism remained true to the spirit and practice of traditional historic Judaism which, be it remembered, has always been both adaptable and progressive.

When we speak of Reform Judaism we are not speaking of a new kind of Judaism. It was only the name that was new as it came into being near the end of the 18th century in Germany. This name has become the label of that interpretation of Judaism which recognizes and emphasizes the dynamic character of the Jewish religion—*dynamic,* which is the opposite of arrested or static Judaism. Reform Judaism emphasizes what is inherent in all Judaism, the principle of progression in the concepts and forms of the Jewish religion. Reform has its roots in the past! It proudly acknowledges the glory, the dignity, the validity of Jewish tradition. It chooses to continue to identify itself with the tradition and it refuses to admit that Jewish tradition is something which is petrified, the crystallization of any one moment or era of Jewish religious thought

DR. ABRAHAM J. FELDMAN. A well-known Reform rabbi who served for many years as rabbi in Hartford, Connecticut. He is the author of many articles on Reform Judaism. He was also one of the leading advocates of the new Reform platform, the Guiding Principles of Reform Judaism, adopted in 1937. (HUC, American Jewish Archives)

and experience. This idea of a progressive Jewish tradition is not new. The Jewish tradition always was progressive. . . .

Thus Reform is classical Judaism asserting anew the right and the duty of accelerating the process of progress and change where changes seem to be necessary. If some customs and practices are no longer meaningful, then they are no longer useful, and to cling to them mechanically or to acknowledge them as valid whilst they are largely neglected is to endanger the very survival of Jews and Judaism. The absence of an authoritative legislative body continuing to function would compel us to wait for the slow process of *Halachic* [from הֲלָכָה, the way; here it refers to the "legal" rules prescribed by Judaism]. This would come about through responsa [written opinions by rabbinic authorities stated "in response" to particular questions about Jewish law], which often takes generations, and would therefore expose the patient to danger. Therefore, Reform's principal contribution is the decision to keep Judaism forever contemporary, and to keep it responsive to the religious needs of successive generations. . . .

Reform insists that changes be made *when* they are needed, *in* and *by* the generation that needs them, rather than wait generations or even centuries before any perceptible adjustments occur. Our generations today and the generations tomorrow have the right and, we think, the duty to keep Judaism alive by keeping it contemporary, and responsive to their spiritual needs. . . .

—From Abraham J. Feldman,
Reform Judaism:
A Guide for Reform Jews
(1956), pp. 5, 7.

OTHER THINGS TO READ

Bamberger, Bernard J., *The Story of Judaism:* Chap. 1, "Seeds and Roots"; Chap. 2, "Growth of a National Religion"; Chap. 3, "The Great Revolution"; Chap. 4, "The Great Revolution (continued)"; Chap. 5, "The Beginnings of Torah"; Chap. 6, "Exile"; Chap. 7, "Hopes and Disappointments"; Chap. 8, "Judaism Is Complete"; Chap. 9, "Universalism and Particularism"; Chap. 10, "Did the Jews Borrow Their Religion?"; Chap. 13, "The End of the World"; Chap. 14, "The Struggle for Religious Democracy"; Chap. 15, "Judah and Hellas: Alexandria"; Chap. 17, "Judah and Rome"; Chap. 18, "The World of the Rabbis"; Chap. 19, "The Way of the Law"; Chap. 20, "The Ideals of Rabbinic Judaism"; Chap. 21, "The Torah Returns to Babylon"; Chap. 22, "New Paths"; Chap. 23, "New Paths (continued)"; Chap. 24, "The Golden Age"; Chap. 25, "An Age of Reason"; Chap. 26, "An Age of Reason (con-

tinued)"; Chap. 27, "War Among the Theologians"; Chap. 29, "The Cabala"; Chap. 33, "Dreams,"; Chap. 34, "Nightmares"; Chap. 35, "The Rebirth of Joy"; pp. 420–422 (religion in Israel); pp. 434–438 (American Jewry); pp. 445–449 (Reform today).

Edidin, Ben M., *Jewish Community Life in America:* Chap. 2, "From Immigrants to Community"; Chap. 5, "Synagogue and Community."

Feldman, Abraham J., *Reform Judaism: A Guide for Reform Jews* (pamphlet).

Feuer, Leon I., *Jewish Literature since the Bible,* I: pp. 15–21 (The Mishnah); pp. 40–56 (The Talmud); pp. 57–62 (The Midrash); pp. 119–128 (Maimonides).

Feuer, Leon I., and Azriel Eisenberg, *Jewish Literature since the Bible,* II: pp. 3–106 (Chasidism and Mysticism).

Freehof, Solomon B., *Recent Reform Responsa* or *Responsa Literature:* Introduction.

Freehof, Solomon B., *What Is Reform Judaism?* "Popular Studies in Judaism" series.

Gittelsohn, Roland B., *Modern Jewish Problems:* Chap. 1, "What Is a Jew?"; Chap. 2, "What Keeps Jews Together?"

Hertzberg, Arthur, "The American Jew and His Religion," Chap. 5 in Oscar I. Janowsky (ed.), *The American Jew: A Reappraisal.*

Jewish Encyclopedia: "Abraham," Vol. 1, pp. 83–87; "Abraham ben David of Posquieres," Vol. 1, pp. 103–105; "Ba-al Shem Tov," Vol. 2, pp. 383–386; "Deuteronomy," Vol. 4, pp. 538–543; "Moses," Vol. 9, pp. 44–57; "Moses ben Maimon (Maimonides)," Vol. 9, pp. 73–86; "Pharisees," Vol. 9, pp. 661–666; "Prophets and Prophecy," Vol. 10, pp. 213–219; "Reform Judaism from the Point of View of the Reform Jew," Vol. 10, pp. 347–352; "Saadia ben Joseph," Vol. 10, pp. 579–585; *She'elot u-Teshubot* (Responsa)," Vol. 11, pp. 240–250.

Levinger, Lee J., *A History of the Jews in the United States:* Chap. 28, "How American Jews Are Organized for Many Purposes"; Chap. 29, "American Jews and World Jewry"; Chap. 32, "The Future of the American Jew."

Reform Judaism—Then and Now

Mandelbaum, David G., "Change and Continuity in Jewish Life," in Marshall Sklare (ed.), *The Jews*, pp. 509–519.

Noveck, Simon (ed.), *Great Jewish Personalities in Ancient and Medieval Times:* Editor's Introduction; Chap. 1, "Moses"; Chap. 3, "Jeremiah the Prophet"; Chap. 4, "Philo of Alexandria"; Chap. 5, "Akiba"; Chap. 6, "Saadia"; Chap. 7, "Judah Halevi"; Chap. 8, "Moses Maimonides"; Chap. 11, "Ba-al Shem Tov"; Chap. 12, "Vilna Gaon."

Pilch, Judah, *Fate and Faith:* Chap. 1, "Jews in Numbers"; Chap. 2, "The Rights of Jews"; Chap. 3, "The Rights of Jews (continued)"; Chap. 6, "The Jew and His Religion."

Plaut, W. Gunther, *The Growth of Reform Judaism:* pp. 359–362 (growth of Reform outside America).

Plaut, W. Gunther, *The Rise of Reform Judaism:* Introduction.

Polsky, Howard, "A Study of Orthodoxy in Milwaukee," in Marshall Sklare (ed.), *The Jews,* pp. 325–335.

Reichler, Max, "Reform Judaism and World Jewry," in *Reform Judaism: Essays by Hebrew Union College Alumni.*

Sachar, Howard M., *The Course of Modern Jewish History:* Chap. 24, "The Growth of the American-Jewish Community"; pp. 551–557 (religion in Israel).

Schwartzman, Sylvan D., *Reform Judaism in the Making:* Chap. 1, "Reform and the Jewish Future."

Sherman, C. Bezalel, "Demographic and Social Aspects," Chap. 2 in Oscar I. Janowsky (ed.), *The American Jew: A Reappraisal.*

Sklare, Marshall (ed.), *The Jews:* "Aspects of Religious Worship in the Contemporary Synagogue," pp. 357–366.

Standard Jewish Encyclopedia: "Abraham," pp. 10–11; "Ba-al Shem Tov," pp. 208–209; "Conservative Judaism," pp. 479–480; "Deuteronomy," p. 551; "Judaism," pp. 1077–1080; "Moses," pp. 1359–1360; "Moses ben Maimon (Maimonides)," pp. 1361–1364; "Orthodoxy," pp. 1460–1461; "Pharisees," pp. 1497–1498; "Prophets, Prophecy," pp. 1546–1547; "Reconstructionism," p. 1583; "Reform Judaism," pp. 1584–1586; "Responsa," pp. 1595–1596; "Saadia Gaon ben Joseph," pp. 1631–1632; "Saducees," pp. 1638–1639.

Universal Jewish Encyclopedia: "Abraham," Vol. 1, pp. 35–38; "Abraham ben David of Posquieres," Vol. 1, p. 41; "Ba-al Shem Tov," Vol. 2, pp. 3–5; "Deuteronomic Code," Vol. 3, pp. 549–550; "Judaism in America," Vol. 6, pp. 238–246; "Maimonides," Vol. 7, pp. 287–295; "Moses," Vol. 8, pp. 1–8; "Pharisees," Vol. 8, pp. 473–475; "Prophets and Prophecy," Vol. 8, pp. 658–664; "Reform Movement," Vol. 9, pp. 101–103; "Responsa and Decisions," pp. 137–139; "Saadia ben Joseph," Vol. 9, pp. 289–291.

Weisberg, Harold, "Ideologies of American Jews," Chap. 12 in Oscar I. Janowsky (ed.), *The American Jew: A Reappraisal.*

World Union for Progressive Judaism, *Directory* (latest edition).

SUGGESTED ACTIVITIES

1. Visit an Orthodox synagogue (one of the less modern type, if possible). Then prepare a magazine article on the subject of Jewish worship today, in which you compare your own with what you have observed there.

2. Have every member of the class prepare a list of arguments favoring the use of the terms "Reform," "Liberal," and "Progressive" to describe the movement. Then, on the basis of a thorough discussion, conduct a debate on the subject: "*Resolved,* that the name 'Reform' should be abandoned."

3. Using the current list of member congregations and their sizes (found in the *Annual Reports of the Union of American Hebrew Congregations,* latest edition), prepare a map of the United States showing the locations and sizes of Re-

form congregations. On the basis of this, where are the major centers of Reform Judaism in this country? How does this serve to confirm the importance of the Reform movement today?

SUBJECTS FOR RESEARCH

1. What are some of the more important differences in practice between the ''Liberal'' and ''Reform'' congregations in England? How does the use of these terms differ in the United States?

2. Investigate present-day Orthodox Judaism. What different groups do you find within it today? How does each differ from one another? From Reform?

3. What varieties of Conservative Judaism are there? What, for instance, is Reconstructionism, and where does it differ from the official Conservative position? From Reform?

4. What particular groups in the present-day American Jewish community are included among the ''non-affiliated'' Jews? To what various interpretations of Jewish life do they subscribe, and how do these differ from those of religious Jews?

5. The statistical information in this chapter is for the year 1968. How has it changed since then? On the basis of population figures given in the latest *American Jewish Yearbook* and the information about Reform membership secured from the World Union for Progressive Judaism, prepare a revised chart showing the location of Reform Jews and their percentage of world Jewry. What progress does the movement seem to be making, and where?

FILMSTRIPS TO SEE

Within the Family of Liberal Judaism (UAHC), picturing Reform Judaism as a movement and the relationship of the local temple to its national organizations.

The Leo Baeck School in Israel (UAHC), portraying the activities of this Liberal Jewish secondary school in Haifa.

Judah the Prince: Teacher of Law (UAHC), describing the life and times of the editor of the Mishnah and an overview of the contents of this important work that established the foundations of rabbinic Judaism.

Rav and Samuel: Teachers of Talmud (UAHC), tracing the careers of two great Babylonian scholars who helped produce the Talmud as a further stage in Judaism's development.

Saadia Gaon: Teacher of Science and Faith (UAHC), picturing the life of this famous tenth-century Jewish scholar and philosopher and his contributions to Judaism.

Maimonides (Jewish Education Committee of New York), presenting the highlights of the career of this great Jewish philosopher of the Middle Ages and his contributions to the advancement of Judaism.

Baal Shem Tov: The Teachings of the Hasidim (UAHC), illustrating the beliefs of Chasidism as viewed through the lives of its followers.

The Jewish Home (Jewish Education Committee of New York), portraying the customs and ceremonies observed among present-day Orthodox and Conservative Jews.

A LIVE ISSUE

In the city of New York and elsewhere, a sizable number of ultra-Orthodox Jews carry on a way of Jewish life much like that described in this chapter. Not only do they attempt to isolate themselves as much as possible from the outside world, but they claim that this is something Judaism requires.

On the other hand, the great majority of American Jews—and that includes the members of Reform congregations—prefer to live in an ''open society'' where they can involve themselves in the affairs of the community-at-large. In fact, the Reform Jew maintains that his religion insists upon it.

The Basic Problems: The main issue here hinges upon where Judaism puts its emphasis. If, as with the ultra-Orthodox, religion involves the continual observance of a great many traditional laws and rites, then ghetto life makes this much more feasible. But where greater emphasis is put on moral and ethical relationships with one's fellow men, as in the case of Reform, ghettos become barriers to the practice of Judaism. Which position historically seems more reasonable?

Some Important Questions: (1) How did the isolation of Jews in the ghetto originally come about? (2) To what extent did the Jews view it as a means of carrying out the demands of their religion? (3) How and why did life in the ghetto tend to reinforce the ultra-Orthodox emphasis in Judaism? (4) In what ways do the circumstances under which American Jews live refute or support their claim today? (5) How do they lend validity to the Reform view?

What Do You Think? In reading this chapter, to what extent are you persuaded that the essential purposes of Judaism are better carried out within a ghetto than in an open society? Why do you come to that conclusion?

2. THE YEARS BEFORE REFORM

Why No Reform Judaism?

If you are wondering why Reform Judaism was so late in making its appearance, there are two good reasons for it.

First, within a religion that repeatedly underwent change, there was no need for reform. Almost from the beginning, Judaism experienced changes. Some are reflected within the Bible itself, where, for instance, the prophets stressed moral and ethical conduct over the earlier emphasis on ritual and observance; and where the conception of God during the time of Moses was enormously refined and expanded during the Babylonian Exile, about a thousand years later.

Similarly, the rabbis who produced the Talmud modified many former biblical beliefs and practices. For example, they converted the law of ''an eye for an eye and a tooth for a tooth'' (Exodus 21:24 and elsewhere) into monetary compensation for damages, and they established detailed procedures for the Jewish marriage ceremony. And Judaism continued to change at the hands of those who interpreted the Talmud, the various commentators, writers of responsa, and codifiers, as well as the philosophers and leaders of particular movements within Judaism itself, such as Kabalah, or Jewish mysticism.

Yet, in the seventeenth and eighteenth centuries, the process appeared to stop and Judaism seemed rigid and no longer capable of significant change. By now, Joseph Karo's great code of Jewish law, the *Shulchan Aruch,* prescribed the whole of the Jew's practice, and the organization of the Jewish community regulated most other phases of Jewish life. Only now was Reform Judaism necessary.

Second, it was not until the start of the nineteenth century that conditions in Europe made such a movement possible. Reform, as we have already noted, seems to prosper only where equality for Jews and a high degree of Western culture prevail, and prior to the late 1700's neither of these conditions existed. On the contrary, up until then one of the main features of life was the Jews' exclusion from the general society. Not that they desired it; rather, the peoples of Europe insisted upon isolating and even oppressing them.

The Situation in Frankfort

Typical was the experience of those who lived in Frankfort-on-the-Main (River), a large city in southeastern Germany. The following passage from a biography, which, though fictional, is based on historical fact, gives us a glimpse of what Jews endured there:

> From time to time, I heard my great grandfather talk about our family in Germany. He could trace it back, he said, to 1175 when some of the first Jews settled in Frankfort-on-the-Main.

What dreadful times they went through there! In the year 1349, for instance, a plague called the "Black Death" swept through the city and took thousands of lives. Everyone suffered, but none more than the Jews for, in addition to their own losses, they were also accused of having caused the plague. Mobs started to attack them and finally destroyed every Jewish

EUROPE IN THE MID-1700's

FINLAND
St. Petersburg
RUSSIA
KINGDOM OF DENMARK AND NORWAY
KINGDOM OF SWEDEN
SCOTLAND
KINGDOM OF GREAT BRITAIN
North Sea
Baltic Sea
Vilno
LITHUANIA
PRUSSIA
IRELAND
NETHERLANDS
Hamburg
PRUSSIA
KINGDOM OF POLAND
ENGLAND
Berlin
Warsaw
London
Brussels
Cologne
UKRAINE
Atlantic Ocean
Frankfort
Paris
HOLY ROMAN EMPIRE
KINGDOM OF FRANCE
SWITZERLAND
KINGDOM OF HUNGARY
Bordeaux
Milan
Adriatic Sea
OTTOMAN EMPIRE
Toulouse
PAPAL STATES
KINGDOM OF SPAIN
PORTUGAL
CORSICA
Rome
KINGDOM OF SICILY
Madrid
Mediterranean Sea
Naples
BALEARIC ISLANDS
KINGDOM OF SARDINIA
0 100 200 300 400 500
MILES...
Jefferson

home in the city. Those who could fled for their lives, and for fifteen years no Jew was permitted to return to Frankfort.

A century passed. Then, in 1458, all of the Jews were moved into a ghetto, a Jewish quarter that occupied a single curved street that followed the bend of the Main River and was walled in on the landside. The three gates that connected it with the city were always locked on Sundays and during Easter when the townspeople were reminded that the Jews had killed Jesus.

Though the number of residents constantly increased, the area of the ghetto remained the same. To provide more room, the Jews filled in an old moat that lay within the Jewish quarter and even added extra stories to their houses, until some were five and six floors high. Eventually, as many as four thousand were living in the 190 houses, and the city government decided to intervene. It now permitted only six new families to settle there a year and limited all Jewish marriages to just twelve.

Fire and disease were constant threats within the ghetto, but far worse was the danger of attack. Though the walls offered some protection, once the mob broke through, the Jews were trapped inside. This occurred in 1614 during the riots created by Vincent Fettmilch, the leader of a religious group that was hostile to the City Council. To show his power, he got his supporters to storm the ghetto. The Jews resisted fiercely, but the mob soon breached the walls and poured inside, setting fire to the synagogue, ripping up Torahs, and smashing the gravestones in the Jewish cemetery. Wild looting followed.

Some of the townspeople tried to protect the ghetto-dwellers and even sheltered them in their homes. However, expecting to be killed, most of the Jews fled to the cemetery where the mob surrounded them. Fortunately, the authorities were able to persuade Fettmilch to let them be expelled rather than massacred.

When they were eventually readmitted, they were put under further restrictions which barred them now from trading in new goods and even owning property . . .

This story was repeated time and again. In fact, down until the 1800's, most Jews of Europe shared similar experiences.

The Jews as Outsiders

To a large extent their situation grew out of the feudal system under which medieval society operated and which automatically ex-

JEWS SWORN IN COURT. Special oaths were often required of medieval Jews testifying in court.

Major Developments in Judaism,

Important World Events	Key Events in Jewish History	Developments in Judaism
About 30 C.E.—Execution of Jesus.	**66 C.E.**—Jewish revolt in Palestine leading to the destruction of Jerusalem in 70.	Yochanan ben Zakkai founds school at Yavneh. Temple destroyed. Growing rivalry between Christianity and Judaism.
Around 100—Early growth of Roman (Catholic) Church.	**135**—End of Bar Kochba's revolt against Rome. Growth of the Diaspora.	By now, the Writings section of the Bible and basic liturgy established. Beginnings of the Mishnah.
		About 200—Mishnah completed. Start of *Gemara* and sermonic *Midrash*. Growth of Babylonian academies.
311—Constantine's Edict of Tolerance, enabling Christianity to become the official religion of Rome.		
476—Fall of Rome.		**About 500**—Babylonian Talmud completed. Continuing development of Jewish law.
	590—Special enactments against the Jews by Pope Gregory I.	
622—Mohammed's flight from Mecca. Start of the Moslem conquest of Syria and Palestine.	**629**—Start of Jewish expulsions from France.	
711—Widespread Moslem conquests begin in Spain.		**767**—Anan ben David leads Karaite revolt against the Oral Law. Growth of responsa literature.

cluded non-Christians. Hence feudal Europe looked upon the Jews as "outsiders," which in turn led to their great disadvantage.

They were barred from agriculture, not only because the Church owned many of the larger estates, but also because, in order to work the land, farmers were expected to swear an oath of loyalty as Christians to their noble or king. Jews were likewise ineligible for membership in the various Christian guilds that carried on

from the Common Era to Chasidism

Important World Events	Key Events in Jewish History	Developments in Judaism
800—Charlemagne crowned Emperor of the Holy Roman Empire.		
		935—Saadia's *Belief and Opinions.* Growth of philosophic interpretation of Judaism.
	About 1000—Start of the "Golden Age" of Spain.	1040—Birth of Rashi, famous commentator.
1054—Split between the Eastern Orthodox and Roman Catholic Churches.		
	1096—Start of intensified persecution of Jews with First Crusade, leading to forced conversions and expulsions.	
		About 1200—Maimonides' *Guide to the Perplexed.* Kabalah appears in Europe. Appearance of intense mysticism and false messiahs.
1215—Magna Carta granted in England.		
1492—Discovery of America by Columbus.	1492—Jews expelled from Spain.	
1517—Start of the Protestant Reformation by Luther.		1567—Karo's *Shulchan Aruch,* code of Jewish practice.
1620—Pilgrims land at Plymouth.	1648—Massacres in Poland.	
	1654—Jews settle in New Amsterdam.	1665—Sabbatai Zevi proclaims himself Messiah.
1681—William Penn founds Pennsylvania.	About 1700—Birth of Israel Ba-al Shem Tov.	About 1735—Start of Chasidism.

most of the manufacturing and commerce. Thus they were forced to turn largely to petty trade, small shopkeeping, and moneylending, an occupation prohibited to Christians by Church law.

Any benefits of citizenship were also denied them. With few exceptions Jews were looked upon as aliens who, as a source of income, became the "property" of some nobleman or city council. Not only were heavy annual taxes

21

demanded of them, but they had to endure all sorts of special assessments. So, in Spain, as one writer points out:

> . . . The Jews, among other things, had to pay for the king's dinner; they were subjected to a hearth tax, a coronation tax, a tax on meat and bread—but it would be impossible to enumerate all the . . . [annoying] dues extracted from Jews everywhere throughout the Middle Ages.

> . . . At one time or another the Jews had to pay for every act of their lives—for leaving or entering towns, for passing through gates or traversing bridges, for crossing the frontiers of . . . [each small] state, for buying or selling, for marriage or burial . . .

For financial reasons, it was to the ruler's advantage to grant them permission to reside in his territory and protect them. Occasionally, however, he was caught unprepared by a mob bent on plunder, and the Jews suffered. Or, if at times they were unable to pay what he demanded, he would order them out of the country. In France alone, the kings expelled the Jews three times in less than ninety years.

Christianity and the Jews

Another factor in the situation of the Jew was the Church, which was not only religiously supreme in medieval Europe but a powerful political and economic force as well. From earliest times it had looked upon the Jews as stubborn and even wicked for remaining loyal to Judaism and rejecting the New Testament, or "new revelation" that with the coming of Jesus the Christians had replaced them as God's Chosen People. But the Church's fear of heresy, or false doctrines, also led it to view the Jews' teachings as an ever-present threat and to try in every way to limit Christian contact with them.

Thus, as far back as 312 C.E., the Council of Elvira in Spain prohibited Christians from eating with Jews, and, when the Roman Empire adopted Christianity as an official religion, it forbade Jews from employing Christian servants. Then, in the thirteenth century, the Fourth Lateran Council required Jews to wear a special form of dress—a yellow badge or certain type of hat—to set them off from the rest of society.

The final act was the establishment of the ghetto, a term traced back to the Italian word for "foundry," a facility supposedly found within the Jewish quarter of Venice. With the creation of the ghetto of Rome in the sixteenth century, the practice quickly spread throughout the whole of Europe, effectively sealing off most of the Jews.

Hope for improvement in their situation was raised with the appearance of Protestantism in 1517 under Martin Luther, who at first seemed sympathetic to them. They soon discovered, however, that he was simply out to convert them; and, when he proved unsuccessful, he likewise turned against them, even sanctioning persecution.

The Consequences of Isolation

The isolation of the Jews promoted even greater suspicion and fear of them, with the result that all sorts of sinister tales about them were spread throughout Europe. They were said to use Christian blood in celebration of Passover, a charge known as "blood libel" or "ritual murder," for which hundreds were imprisoned or killed. In 1144, for instance, the Jews were brutally attacked for the supposed ritual murder of William of Norwich, an English boy later made a saint by the Church. Some years later, thirty-one Jewish men and women in a small French town were burned to death on a similar charge.

According to another evil legend, Jews

were also said to steal into churches and stab the holy wafer, which represents the body of Jesus for Christians, thereby "killing Christ" once more. One such accusation by a notorious thief in fifteenth-century Bavaria caused the execution of ten Jews. Word likewise spread that Jews were responsible for poisoning wells and spreading disease, so that when the Black Death, a bubonic plague carried by rats, swept away some twenty-five million Europeans in the fourteenth century, many Swiss and German Jews were massacred.

Such relentless propaganda of hatred directed against them, fed by fears of possible economic competition as well, made the Jews a convenient scapegoat. Those in debt to Jewish moneylenders incited mobs against them, and kings faced with popular uprisings would divert attention to them, with the added promise of rich booty to those who attacked them. Even the Catholic Church, frightened by the Protestant revolt in the sixteenth century, threw the blame on the Jews and ordered the Talmud burned.

For some fourteen hundred years, then, the Jews were the outcasts of European society, and not without reason did Shakespeare in *The Merchant of Venice* have Shylock account for his humiliation simply by saying, "I am a Jew."

How the Jews Managed to Survive

The Jews could do little about the outside world. They had no choice but to bear the heavy taxes and the numerous indignities because they knew from bitter experience in England, France, Spain, and elsewhere how frightful expulsion could be, with no country willing to accept them and plunderers eager to do away with them.

That they managed to survive is due largely to the satisfying life they developed inside the ghetto, where they generally were given the

right to conduct their own affairs. To understand how the Jewish community operated, we return to our fictional biography describing the situation in Frankfort-on-the-Main:

From information I gathered later on, I found out still other things about our family's life in Frankfort. For example, I learned that several members served on the Jews' governing council of twelve elected officials that conducted the affairs of the ghetto. They represented their people before the authorities, collected taxes, and maintained the important institutions within the Jewish community.

Among these were the courts, presided over by the rabbis who operated according to the laws of the Talmud, other Jewish codes, and local community regulations. Through the use of the *cherem* (חֵרֶם, excommunication), any Jew found guilty of a serious breach of the law or endangering the safety of fellow Jews could be expelled, thus forcing him to live in the hostile community outside.

Within the ghetto, the main institution was the synagogue where, in addition to worship, education devoted to the study of the Bible and Talmud was carried on. But the community possessed many other facilities, including the cemetery, bakery, slaughter-house, social hall, combination hospital and poor-house, bath-house, and fire-station. Special societies also existed to provide aid to the poor, the transient, and the bereaved, to arrange for the burial of the dead, and to supply dowries for poor brides.

The ghetto even had a language of its own, Judeo-German. It was a dialect of German and Hebrew, written in Hebrew characters, that was the forerunner of what finally became "Yiddish."

It was the practice of Judaism, however, that did most to sustain the spirit of the

23

> people. The men would come to the synagogue for morning and evening services, and everyone joined in the observance of the Sabbath and holidays, when all the shops were closed.
>
> What joy reigned during the festivals, and especially on Purim when there was masquerading, carnivals, and humorous dramatics. In contrast, deep solemnity prevailed during the High Holy Days and various fast days like the Ninth of *Av* (אָב, the fifth month of the Hebrew calendar) when the Temple was destroyed.
>
> A wedding, *Berit, Bar Mitzvah* (בַּר מִצְוָה, literally "a son of [the] commandment," or the observance marking the boy's thirteenth year when he assumed adult religious responsibilities), all called for widespread celebration in the ghetto. . . .

In this respect, too, Frankfort was typical of the ghettos everywhere in Europe.

A Source of Pride—and Hope

Life within the ghetto not only insured the Jews' self-preservation but enabled them to achieve a special sense of pride. For when they compared their own situation with what went on outside, they realized some of the advantages they enjoyed. Their emphasis upon learning, for example, made them far better educated. Almost every Jew was able to read and write whereas, outside the ghetto, learning was reserved chiefly for the privileged few—usually only the clergy and nobility—so that the masses were totally illiterate.

The standard of conduct among the Jews was also much higher. Outside, robbery and murder were common; so were promiscuous relations between the sexes and desertion and ill-treatment of wives and children. In con-

trast, serious crime and immorality were quite rare among the Jews. This seemed to confirm their belief that they were indeed God's "Chosen People," especially blessed and entrusted with a responsibility to be a "light," an example, to the other peoples on earth.

Along with this belief came hope of ultimate deliverance. They felt that their suffering was not without meaning; nor had God forsaken them. Though they were presently being punished for their sins, some day they would be forgiven and restored to the Promised Land in Palestine.

First, however, as the Talmud predicted, conditions would have to become even worse:

> . . . Scholars become few in number; and, as for the rest of the people, their eyes fail through sorrow and grief. Multitudes of trouble and evil happenings will occur, with each new evil quickly coming before the other has ceased.

Only then would the prophet Elijah appear and announce the coming of the Messiah (from מָשִׁיחַ, the anointed one), the all-powerful descendant of King David, who would deliver the Jews out of their exile. In triumph they would return to the Holy Land where, after rebuilding the sacred city of Jerusalem and its Temple and restoring the ancient sacrificial rites, they would forever enjoy peace, freedom, and prosperity. Eventually, seeing their triumph, the rest of the world would come to worship the one true God and enjoy all the blessings of His Kingdom on earth.

When the Messiah would come was, of course, known only to God, but some who subscribed to Kabalah sought to discover the secret through various mystical techniques that included *gematria,* the conversion of Hebrew words into numbers, from which they believed they could calculate the exact date of his appearance. Often such predictions stimulated certain individuals, such as Sabbatai Zevi in 1665, to proclaim themselves the Messiah, to the ultimate disappointment and despair of those who believed in them.

For the most part, however, the Jew took comfort in his belief in a hereafter, known as the *olam haba* (עוֹלָם הַבָּא, the world-to-come), where he would be amply rewarded for all his suffering. After death, asserted his religion, the souls of the righteous who had faithfully lived according to the Torah would ascend to the heavenly "Garden of Eden" where God himself dwelt. There He would reward them in keeping with their deeds, with the greatest blessings reserved for martyrs and diligent students of the Torah.

A dreadful fate, on the other hand, awaited the wicked, among whom were those who afflicted the Jews. Their souls would descend to a place of terrible punishment known as *Gehinnom*, named after "the Valley of Hinnom" (גֵּיא הִנֹּם), where people once burnt children alive as sacrifices to the Canaanite gods. There, the Talmud promised, the wicked would be tormented with unceasing fire.

No Need for Change

Such was the nature of Jewish life at the start of the eighteenth century. For by then the patterns of the ghetto and its particular religious beliefs and practices were thoroughly established.

True, there were those who were not entirely satisfied with the way Judaism had developed. As far back as the early 1600's, a

THE GHETTO OF FRANKFORT. It consisted of a single curved street. Note the extra stories on the houses. (Hebrew Union College Museum)

25

Dutch Jew named Uriel Da Costa (sometimes written "Acosta") expressed strong objection to some of the teachings of the Talmud, especially those dealing with the resurrection of the dead and promise of reward and punishment after death, but he was promptly excommunicated and forced to retract his statements.

Shortly after Da Costa's death, the Amsterdam community also proceeded to excommunicate Baruch (Benedict) Spinoza, who ultimately became one of the outstanding philosophers of modern times and the father of the scientific study of the Bible as well. Emphasizing the use of reason in the quest for truth, Spinoza took issue with some of the teachings of the Bible—among them those relating to angels—and a number of traditional interpretations, including the one that held Moses to be the sole author of the entire Torah.

And a century and a half later, others, notably the supporters of Chasidism, voiced their own disapproval of the prevailing form of Judaism from which they felt they derived too little religious satisfaction.

Still, during much of the eighteenth century, most Jews seemed content. But certain events were already taking place in Europe that were destined to make an increasing number dissatisfied with the Judaism of the times.

QUESTIONS FOR DISCUSSION

1. How do the attitudes of Roman Catholicism and Protestantism toward the Jews today differ from those of the Middle Ages? How do you explain this in view of their treatment of the medieval Jew? In what ways has the Jewish attitude toward Christians and Christianity also undergone change?

2. How does Jewish experience justify keeping religion from interfering in government and vice versa (usually referred to as "separation of Church and State")? What attempts are being made today to obtain government aid for religion? What attitude do you think Jews should take toward these?

3. How does the experience of the Jews in the Middle Ages still affect you? The Jewish community? How do you account for this?

4. In what respect did Judaism sustain the Jews of the ghetto? What advantages do you enjoy today by reason of the fact that you are a Jew? How do these compare with those prized by the Jews of the Middle Ages?

5. Contrast your own beliefs about the hereafter and the Messianic Age with those of the Jews in the ghetto, beliefs incidentally that traditional Judaism continues to hold. How do you account for the differences?

6. Why did Reform Judaism not arise during the ghetto period? On the basis of your answer, what changes in the conditions of Jewish life would you assume to be necessary for the existence of a liberal interpretation of Judaism?

SIGNIFICANT DOCUMENTS

From the Decrees of the Fourth Lateran Council of the Roman Catholic Church, 1215

1. Concerning the Interest Taken by Jews

The more the Christian religion is restrained in the exaction of interest so much more does the knavery of the Jews in this matter increase, so that in a short time they exhaust the wealth of Christians. Wishing therefore to provide for Christians in this matter lest they be burdened excessively by the Jews, we ordain through synodal [church council] decree that if they hereafter extort heavy and unrestrained interest, no matter what the pretext be, Christians shall be withdrawn from association with them until the Jews give adequate satisfaction for their unmitigated oppression. Also the Christians shall be compelled, if necessary, through Church punishment, from which an appeal will be disregarded, to abstain from business relations with the Jews . . .

2. That Jews Should be Distinguished from Christians in Dress

In some provinces a difference in dress distinguishes the Jews or Saracens [Moslems] from the Christians, but in certain others such a confusion has grown up that they cannot be distinguished by any difference. Thus it happens at times that through error Christians have relations with the women of Jews or Saracens, and Jews or Saracens with Christian women.

Therefore, that they may not, under pretext of error of this sort, excuse themselves in the future for the excesses of such prohibited intercourse, we decree that such Jews and Saracens of both sexes in every Christian province and at all times shall be marked off in the eyes of the public from other peoples through the character of their dress. Particularly, since it may be read in the writings of Moses [a reference to Numbers 15:37–41] that this very law has been enjoined upon them . . .

Moreover, during the last three days before Easter and especially on Good Friday, they [the Jews] shall not go forth in public at all, for the reasons that some of them on these very days, as we hear, do not blush to go forth better dressed and are not afraid to mock the Christians who maintain the memory of the holy Passion [suffering of Jesus on the cross] by wearing signs of mourning.

This, however, we forbid most severely, that any one should presume at all to break forth in insult to the Redeemer [Jesus]. And since we ought not to ignore any insult to Him who blotted out our disgraceful deeds, we command that such impudent fellows be checked by the secular princes by imposing on them proper punishment so that they shall not at all

presume to blaspheme Him who was crucified for us.

3. That Jews Not Be Appointed to Public Offices

Since it would be altogether too absurd that a blasphemer of Christ should exercise authority over Christians, we, in this chapter, renew, because of the boldness of transgressors, what the Toledo Council has prudently decreed in this matter. We forbid that Jews be preferred for public offices since by pretext of some sort they manifest as much hostility to Christians as possible.

Moreover, if any one should thus turn over an office to them, after due warning he shall be checked by a severe punishment, as is fit by the provincial council which we command to meet every year. Indeed, the association of Christians with such a Jewish official in commercial and other matters shall not be allowed until whatever he has gotten from Christians through the office is transferred to the use of poor Christians, as the diocesan [local] bishop shall carefully direct. And he shall be dismissed in disgrace from the office which he has impiously assumed. We extend the application of this law also to pagans . . .

—From Jacob R. Marcus,
The Jew in the Medieval World,
pp. 137–139.

An Accusation of Jewish Desecration of the Host at Passau, Bavaria, 1477–1478

[The incident began] fourteen hundred and seventy-seven years after Christ's birth. At that time the Right Reverend Prince and Lord, Lord Ulrich of Passau, born von Nussdorf [d. 1480], was reigning.

It happened that a wanton and desperate fellow, usually known as Christoff Eysegreisshamer, unmindful of his soul's salvation and lusting for temporal goods, made an agreement, Judas-like, with the

Jews after inquiring whether if he brought them the Sacred Host, the body of our Lord Jesus Christ, they would buy it.

The Jews—those enemies and blasphemers of the crucified true, living God and of Mary his mother—lived at this time here in Passau on the Ilz [River] behind St. Georgenberg. They had often employed him and made use of him to go on errands and had dispatched him near and far. The Jews, these avaricious dogs, answered [Christoff], out of the great hatred which they had toward the Lord Jesus our Savior, that he should go ahead and bring the Host and they would pay him for it.

After the deal had been made, the seller and callous sinner, in his wickedness, laid a snare for the Holy Sacrament. In the already mentioned seventy-seventh year, on the Friday before St. Michael's day [September 26, 1477], he broke open the receptacle in which the Host is reserved in St. Mary's church in Freyung-in-the-Abbey [near Passau] and stole eight pieces of the Holy Sacrament, seized hold of them with his sinful hands, and wrapped them in a kerchief. He carried them on his person from that Friday till Sunday morning [September 28, 1477], and then in his faithlessness turned them over to the Jews to whom he sold them for a Rheinish Gulden, each Host thus amounting to thirty *pfennig* [pennies]. This was an insult to the holy Christian Church [reminding one that Judas sold Jesus for thirty pieces of silver].

The Jews—blasphemers of God—kept the Hosts and skeptically brought them to their synagogue, seized hold of the body of Christ with their sinful hands in order to crucify Him with savage eagerness and thus test the Christian faith. [If blood flowed from the wafer, then it was supposed to be the *real* body of Christ.] A Jew took a sharp knife and, when he had stabbed the Host on the altar in the syna-

gogue, blood flowed out of it and the face of a child appeared. The Jews, very much frightened, took counsel and sent two sacraments to Prague, two to [Wiener-] Neustadt, and two to Salzburg. And when they threw [the remaining] two wafers into a glowing baker's oven, they saw two angels and two doves fly out of it.

Later the evil-doer [Christoff] was seized in the year 'seventy-seven, before Lent [more correctly, 1478, before February 4], while breaking into a church at Germannsberg. He was then led prisoner to the episcopal palace at Passau, where he voluntarily confessed this great crime and told even more about the Jews. Thereupon the above-mentioned devout Right Reverend Bishop of Passau, Ulrich, who, as a Christian prince, was quite properly very much grieved by this crime, decided to exact adequate punishment. He commanded the noble and gracious knight, Lord Sebastian von der Alben—at that time his Grace's marshal—to seize all the Jews of Passau and to question them about the truth. [Ten men were seized.] They all with one accord confessed and showed the knife, the stone [altar], the place, and the oven where they had committed and perpetrated such a deed with the Holy Sacrament.

Four of them converted to the Christian faith and were brought to justice on Tuesday after Judica in Lent of the 'seventy-seventh year [more correctly, March 10, 1478]. The new Christians [the four converts] were executed by the sword; the Jews, by fire; and two of them were torn with pincers [and then burnt alive]. A few weeks after the others, the seller [Christoff] was executed, as the law demands . . .

—From Jacob R. Marcus,
The Jew in the Medieval World,
pp. 156–157.

The Excommunication of Uriel Da Costa, 1618

. . . I [Uriel Acosta] already discovered that the customs and institutions of the Jews were not at all in accordance with the prescriptions of Moses. If the Law, however, must be observed as scrupulously as it demands itself, then it was wrong of the so-called sages to invent so many things which deviate entirely from the Law. I could not be silent; I even believed that I was doing something pleasing in the eyes of God if I freely and openly defended the Law.

The Jewish sages of today have retained their customs as well as their vicious character; they fight stubbornly for the sect and the institutions of the abominable Pharisees, not without any eye to their own advantage, as has been said of them justifiedly by others: to take the place of honor in the synagogue, to be greeted with respect on the market place. They would not permit me to deviate even in the minutest detail from their rules; I was to follow scrupulously in their foot-steps in everything. Otherwise they threatened me with the ban [*cherem*] and complete excommunication in religious and secular matters.

However, since it would have hardly behooved a man who had given up his country and all exterior advantages for the sake of liberty to be intimidated by such threats, and since under such circumstances it would have been neither right nor just nor manly to submit to men who did not even have any legal authority, I decided rather to take everything upon myself, but to adhere to my opinion. So I was excommunicated, and even my brothers who had formerly been my pupils passed me on the street and did not dare to greet me out of fear of those men.

I decided to write a book to vindicate my cause and to prove from the Law itself the invalidity of the Pharisaic tradition and

MEDIEVAL JEWISH DRESS. Different areas of Europe required various types of garb. (Marie José Seaton)

observance, and the incompatibility of their traditions and institutions with the Law of Moses. While working on the book it happened (I must tell the whole story simply and faithfully) that after long deliberation I agreed firmly with the opinion of those who hold that the reward and punishment mentioned in the old Law are to be understood as happening in this world, who do not assume a life to come and the immortality of the soul. Aside from other reasons, I supported my argument by the fact that the Mosaic Law is completely silent about these matters and promises only this-worldly reward or punishment to those who observe or transgress the commandments.

My enemies were jubilant when they heard that I had arrived at this opinion; for they thought that they would now find sufficient support with the Christians, because their faith is based on the New Testament in which express mention is made of eternal salvation and eternal punishment, and they therefore believe in and recognize the immortality of the soul.

To prevent me from publishing my work and to turn Christian opinion against me, they published, before my book was printed, a pamphlet under the title *On the Immortality of the Soul* written by a physician. . . . They said that whoever denies the immortality of the soul has not far to go to deny the existence of God himself. Their children, incited by the rabbis and

29

their parents, gathered on the street and shouted curses after me and annoyed me with vilifications of all kinds, calling me heretic and apostate. Sometimes they gathered in front of my door, threw stones, and did everything to disturb me so that I would not even have peace in my own house.

When that pamphlet appeared I immediately wrote a pamphlet in my defense, in which I attacked the concept of immortality very strongly and in passing pointed out many things in which the Pharisees deviate from Moses. When the pamphlet was published the Jewish elders and deputies denounced me to the city authorities. They declared that I had written a book in which I denied the immortality of the soul and in which I not only had attacked them but had undermined the Christian religion [as well].

Upon their denunciation I was arrested but released after eight to ten days against bail. The judge imposed a penalty on me. I was sentenced to a fine of 300 florins beside the loss of the books. . . .

—From Carl Gebhardt,
Uriel Acosta,
An Example of a Human Life,
translation by Helen Lederer,
pp. 3–6.

OTHER THINGS TO READ

Abrahams, Israel, *Jewish Life in the Middle Ages:* Chap. 2, "Life in the Synagogue"; Chap. 3, "Communal Organization"; Chap. 4, "Institution of the Ghetto"; Chap. 5, "Social Morality"; Chap. 16, "The Jewish Badge"; Chaps. 17 and 18, "Private and Communal Charities."

Bamberger, Bernard J., *The Story of Judaism:* Part 5, "Within Ghetto Walls."

Caplan, Samuel, and Harold U. Ribalow, *The Great Jewish Books:* pp. 215–232 (Karo and the *Shulchan Aruch*).

Cohen, A., *Everyman's Talmud:* Chap. 11, "The Hereafter."

Feuer, Leon I., and Azriel Eisenberg, *Jewish Literature since the Bible,* II: pp. 107–120 (the ghetto); 125–128, 131–132 (Jewish education); 133–142 (matchmaking); 143–146 (restrictions on residence).

Freimann, A., and F. Kracauer, *History of the Jews in Frankfort:* Chap. 3, "Wenzel's Deposition to the Establishment of the Ghetto"; Chap. 4, "Pfefferkorn and the Dispute Concerning Jewish Books"; Chap. 6, "The Fettmilch Insurrection."

Gittelsohn, Roland B., *Modern Jewish Problems:* pp. 189–190, 193–194 (Jewish education in former times).

Jewish Encyclopedia: "Uriel Acosta," Vol. 1, pp. 167–168; "Church Councils," Vol. 4, pp. 77–78; "Frankfort-on-the-Main," Vol. 5, pp. 484–489; "Ghetto," Vol. 5, pp. 652–655; "Menasseh ben Israel," Vol. 8, pp. 282–284; "Rome," Vol. 10, pp. 444–467; "Spinoza," Vol. 11, pp. 511–520; "Venice," Vol. 12, pp. 408–416.

Marcus, Jacob R., *The Jew in the Medieval World:* pp. 24–32 (expulsion of the Jews from France); 34–40 (laws against Jews); 43–47 (the Black Death); 75–79, 86–87 (conditions for Jewish residence); 89–91 (business restrictions); 121–130, 137–141 (ritual murder charges); 151–158 (protection of the Jews); 200–204 (*Shulchan Aruch*); 212–221 (Jewish community); 378–380 (Jewish education).

Roth, Cecil, *A Bird's-Eye View of Jewish History:* Chap. 25, "Life in the Ghetto."

Sachar, Abram L., *A History of the Jews:* Chap. 19, "The Jew in the Medieval World."

Schwartzman, Sylvan D., *Reform Judaism in the Making:* Chap. 2, "The Jew of Medieval Europe."

Standard Jewish Encyclopedia: "Uriel Acosta," pp. 23–24; "Joseph Karo," p. 408; "Church Councils," pp. 442–443; "Frankfort-on-the-Main," pp. 699–700; "Ghetto," pp. 751–753; "Rome," pp. 1608–1610; "Spinoza," pp. 1748–1749; "Venice," p. 1874.

Universal Jewish Encyclopedia: "Uriel Acosta," Vol. 1, pp. 72–74; "Church Councils," Vol. 3, p. 202; "Frankfort-on-the-Main," Vol. 4, pp. 400–402; "Ghetto," Vol. 4, pp. 597–603; "Menasseh ben Israel," Vol. 7, pp. 312–313; "Rome," Vol. 9, pp. 187–192; "Spinoza," Vol. 10, pp. 5–8; "Venice," Vol. 10, pp. 401–404.

SUGGESTED ACTIVITIES

1. Arrange an interview with someone who escaped from Nazi Germany and prepare a detailed account about the circumstances of the Jews there. Here are some questions you will want to consider: How did Jewish life under the Nazis compare with that of the Middle Ages? What connection do you find between the two? And how do you explain the rise of nazism in the twentieth century?

2. Prepare a detailed chart of the organization of Jewish community life in the Frankfort ghetto. Then compare this with the organization of your own Jewish community. How are they similar? What are the major differences, and how do you account for them?

3. Imagine you are living during the ghetto period: prepare a modern newsmagazine article on Jewish life of the times.

SUBJECTS FOR RESEARCH

1. Read William Shakespeare's *The Merchant of Venice.* In what respects does the portrayal of Shylock reflect the circumstances of Jewish life in the ghetto? What attitudes toward Jews do some of the leading non-Jewish characters reveal? To what extent are some of these attitudes still in existence today? How do you explain this?

2. Look into the subject of Jewish mysticism. How and why did Kabalah originate, and what were some of its chief teachings? What influence has Jewish mysticism had upon the beliefs and practices of Judaism? How do you account for the renewed interest in Jewish mysticism today?

3. Check the word "Jews" or "Pharisees" in a *Concordance to the New Testament* and read some of the passages it cites. What conclusions do you come to about the attitudes of those who wrote the New Testament? What connection do you find there with some of the acts the Church once adopted against the Jews?

4. In recent years efforts have been made among the Jews to rescind the excommunication of Baruch (Benedict) Spinoza. Make a study of his life and determine why he insisted on approaching the study of the Bible as he did. Do you agree or disagree with his assumption? Why? Why, then, did the Jewish community of Amsterdam find it necessary to excommunicate him? How do you explain the current change in attitude toward him?

5. Secure a copy of the English translation of the abbreviated *Shulchan Aruch* and check the table of contents. With what areas of Jewish life does it deal? Select one of these and see what an adherance to the *Shulchan Aruch* would demand of you. In what ways would your present life as a Jew be different?

FILMSTRIPS TO SEE

Jews in Italy (UAHC), focusing on Jewish life in various ghettos, with scenes of old synagogues and ceremonial objects.

Passover Art of the Middle Ages (UAHC), offering vivid illustrations from three famous illuminated medieval *Haggadot.*

Menasseh ben Israel (UAHC), describing Jewish life in the seventeenth century and the success of this descendant of Marranos in securing the readmission of the Jews into England 350 years after their expulsion.

Torah in Jewish Life (Jewish Education Committee of New York), portraying the values and ideals of the Torah and its influence in Jewish life.

The Middle Ages (*Life*), describing the art and general pattern of social life during this long period in Europe.

Feudalism (Society for Visual Education), picturing the organization of European society in the Middle Ages from which the Jews were largely excluded.

A LIVE ISSUE

This chapter raises the question of whether the modern Jew will not finally disappear as he absorbs more and more of the culture of the Western world. Indeed, many today look upon this problem as especially acute because the younger generation's exposure to Jewish knowledge and experience has become so minimal, while the influence of the general environment and modern secular thought has grown enormously.

As a result, various proposals are currently being made in order to sustain the Jews. Some, as we have seen, call for considerable isolation from society. Others demand more intensive Jewish education and culture, the strengthening of Jewish community life generally, or numerous reforms in the beliefs and practices of Judaism.

The Basic Problem: It is plain that the Jew of today is confronted by essentially the same question that troubled those who lived nearly two hundred years ago: How, in the face of the inroads of Western culture, can Jews protect themselves from total assimilation?

Some Important Questions: (1) To what extent can the modern Jew isolate himself from the effects of Western culture? (2) In view of the forces operating upon him, how can the American Jew intensify his Jewish life? (3) What important changes are needed in Jewish education? (4) Would newer forms of Judaism be helpful in preventing assimilation? What, for instance? (5) Short of isolation, what other measures seem necessary to preserve the modern Jew?

What Do You Think? As you read about the situation facing the Jews in the late eighteenth century, consider the various answers they developed. Which, if any, are pertinent today? To what extent does the predicament of present-day Jewry call for different solutions? What do you recommend?

3.

A CHANGING AGE AND
THE JEWISH RESPONSE

A Growing Change in Attitude

Were you living in mid-eighteenth-century Europe, you would certainly have sensed the beginning of a change in attitude toward the Jews. Not that the ghetto walls were about to come down or every Jew was soon to be welcomed into society.

Far from it! There was still widespread prejudice against the Jews, and myths about them were still rampant among the common people. In fact, "blood libel" cases appear as late as the twentieth century. Most governments were not inclined to treat Jews as equals. And among the more enlightened minds of Europe prejudice against the Jews still appeared. From time to time even today anti-Semitism will crop up in various places.

Yet in the mid-1700's there was growing evidence that the situation was starting to improve, as the following newspaper clippings, presented in modern form but based upon actual happenings, indicate.

BRITISH NATURALIZATION GRANTED JEWISH MERCHANT OF NEW YORK

First Jew in American Colony to Secure Rights under Recent Act

NEW YORK, 1741—Moses Lopez, a New York merchant, who arrived here about ten years ago from Portugal, has been made a naturalized British subject. He is the first Jew to benefit by the Act of Parliament passed last year.

While the law does not grant full equality to Jews, it does provide them with the right to settle and engage in business and frees them from the requirement of taking an oath as a Christian. To be eligible, Jews must first reside seven years in the colony. . . .

NUMEROUS COUNTRIES PROTEST EXPULSION OF BOHEMIAN JEWS

Austrian Empress Urged to Rescind Banishment Order

VIENNA, 1745—Despite their defense of Austria against the invading armies of France, Empress Maria Theresa has ordered the expulsion of all 60,000 Bohemian Jews from the country and their payment of a fine of 160,000 gulden.

Word of this action promptly evoked official protests from the governments of England, Holland, Venice, and Hamburg, but to date these have been rejected by the empress and the Jews will be compelled to leave as announced. . . .

PRUSSIAN FINANCE MINISTER PROPOSES RELIEF FOR JEWS

Frederick II Urged to Reduce Restrictions, Taxes on Jews

BERLIN, 1745—Finance Minister Manitius of Prussia has appealed to Emperor Frederick II to relieve the Jews of many of the present measures directed against them.

Not only has he condemned religious hatred of the Jews, but he has also taken special pains to expose the falsehood of most of the charges leveled against them.

Reminding the emperor of their economic importance to Prussia, particularly in time of war, he has called for a sharp reduction in their taxes and much greater freedom. . . .

NOTED POLITICAL PHILOSOPHER CONDEMNS TREATMENT OF JEWS

PARIS, 1748—Baron Charles Montesquieu, former president of the Bordeaux Parliament, and a leading French political philosopher, has just published what critics have already termed "one of the most influential works of our times."

Entitled *The Spirit of the Laws,* the two volumes deal with all phases of modern life and are highly critical of religious intolerance, especially toward the Jews.

"Christian treatment of them," the author maintains, "condemns the nations of Europe as barbarians."

CHARLES MONTESQUIEU. A leading liberal French philosopher whose writings supported freedom for the Jews. (Photoworld)

There was further cause for Jewish optimism in the years that followed. The noted German poet and playwright Gotthold Lessing scored a huge success with his drama, *Nathan the Wise,* which maintained that the teachings of Christianity required justice for the Jews. In a work entitled *On the Civil Amelioration of the Jews,* published in 1781, Christian Wilhelm Dohm, a Prussian official, appealed for the gradual removal of all restrictions against them. And the very next year saw Emperor Joseph II's "Edict of Toleration" for Austrian Jewry that eliminated the Jewish badge, certain special taxes, and all restrictions against their appearing in public during Christian holidays. Opening up many new occupations to Jews, it also granted them the right to enroll in colleges and universities.

All this suggested that European Jewry was about to enter upon a new age.

The Effects of Scientific Discovery

Actually, the Jews were merely beginning to reap the benefit of powerful forces that were undermining the foundations of medieval life. From the sixteenth century on, the discoveries of science paved the way for the coming of an "Age of Reason" whose views were quite different from those of the Middle Ages.

The process started with astronomers like Nicholas Copernicus, Tycho Brahe, and Johannes Kepler, who in the 1500's succeeded in overturning the notion that the earth was the center of the universe, with the sun and planets moving about it in perfect circles. They proved instead that the sun was the center of the solar system and that the earth was simply one of the planets that rotated in ellipses around it.

More important than the discoveries themselves, however, was their method of arriving at them; namely, through scientific reasoning based upon their observation of natural phenomena and precise experimentation. No longer, therefore, was what the ancients or even the Church itself taught looked upon as undisputably true. Thus, in 1610, Galileo, a professor of mathematics, using his newly-invented telescope, forever put an end to the claim of the Greek philosopher Aristotle that the heavens operated under different physical laws. And the findings of Isaac Newton of England confirmed the fact that the universe functioned according to predictable mathematical laws of gravity and motion.

Since this was so, argued philosophers like Francis Bacon and René Descartes, should not man look upon the laws of nature as those basic principles of the universe formulated by God himself? The discovery of these laws through scientific methods, they said, not only established what was true but, in the process, was bound to bring man into harmony with the very essence of divine law. So the eighteenth-century English poet Alexander Pope summed it up when he wrote:

> . . . **All discord, harmony not understood,**
> **All partial evil, universal good,**
> **And spite of pride, erring reason's spite,**
> *One truth is clear, whatever is is right.*

Indeed, many concluded that if God's natural law, which governed the workings of the universe, were also applied to human life and society it would surely benefit all of mankind.

These ideas had a profound effect upon European thought and began to encourage a more reasonable approach toward all people. Before long, even the Jews came to be viewed in a different light. If only they were treated properly, so the argument ran, it would be "natural" for them to respond accordingly, which in turn would contribute to the welfare of society as a whole.

So the effects of the new scientific revolution went beyond the discoveries of the physical universe. They affected social life as well.

The Wider Effects of the Age of Reason

The Jews were affected in still other ways by the thinking of the Age of Reason. A series of futile wars between the Protestants and Catholics compelled Europe to adopt the principle of "toleration," or respect for the rights of those who followed different faiths, no matter what the ruler's religion. In view of this it seemed self-evident that the Jews also qualified for toleration. Indeed, said men like John Locke of England and Charles Montesquieu of France, since it was now clear that no religion possessed the whole truth, freedom of belief for all people was the only "reasonable" approach.

So, too, they insisted, was political freedom. Here Locke and Jean Jacques Rousseau of France argued that on the basis of natural law every government was subject to a mutual agreement or "contract" between the ruler and his subjects. Originally, these men pointed out, people had been free but, as they came to recognize their need for government, they agreed to accept a king. But, when this form of government no longer satisfied them, they had every right under the terms of the "contract" to change it. Hence, utterly unfounded was the medieval doctrine of the "Divine Right of Kings," which held that rulers were chosen by God and therefore not responsible to the people.

Note how the American Declaration of Independence, a product of the Age of Reason, incorporates these very ideas:

> When, in the course of human events, it becomes necessary for one people to dissolve the political bands which have connected them with another and to assume, among the powers of the earth, the separate and equal station to which the Laws of Nature and of Nature's God entitle them . . . they should declare the causes which impel them to the separation.

> We hold these truths to be self-evident, that all men are created equal, that they are endowed by their Creator with certain unalienable rights, that among these are life, liberty, and the pursuit of happiness.
>
> That to secure these rights, governments are instituted among men, deriving their just powers from the consent of the governed, that, whenever any form of government becomes destructive of these ends, it is the right of the people to alter or abolish it . . .

Freedom was also indispensable to economic life, held Adam Smith of England and others. Government, they insisted, should put an end to all restraints on trade so that natural laws might function freely for the benefit of all. A feudal system with its many restrictions merely retarded the growth of industry and commerce. Therefore, "laissez-faire," "hands off," and the economy would surely prosper.

The Age of Reason, then, held out the promise of increasing freedom for all, which a number of leading minds already contended must include the Jews.

Some Rays of Hope

Yet, improvement in their situation was slow in coming. In 1750, for instance, King Frederick the Great of Prussia issued a new Jewish charter that maintained almost all the old disabilities, including the ghetto and special taxes, causing a liberal French philosopher of the times to call it "A law worthy of a cannibal." Even as late as 1775, Pope Pius VI renewed all of the longstanding restrictions against the Jews of Rome, including confinement within the ghetto, wearing of the yellow badge, censorship of Jewish books, and compulsory attendance at services designed to convert them.

Indeed, old prejudices persisted even

36

FRANÇOIS VOLTAIRE. A noted French philosopher, dramatist, and essayist whose writings strongly influenced the course of the French Revolution. (Photoworld)

bankers, merchants, and manufacturers—enjoyed special privileges that enabled them to mingle freely with upper-class Christians with whom they shared common interests in music, philosophy, and literature. This convinced them that the liberal spirit of the Age of Reason was making inroads. They were likewise encouraged by the support of a growing number of liberal Christian philosophers and theologians, men like Johann Gottfried von Herder who in a work begun in 1784 predicted:

> A time will come when people in Europe will no longer ask who is a Jew or Christian, for the Jew will also live according to European standards and will contribute to the welfare of the state from which he has been shut out only by a barbaric constitution.

However, more than anything else, it was the efforts of Moses Mendelssohn, the leading Jew of the eighteenth century, that led them to believe that freedom was well on the way.

The Work of Moses Mendelssohn

Mendelssohn, the son of a poor Torah scribe, was born in 1729 in Dessau, Germany. As a young boy he received a thorough Jewish education in the course of which he was introduced to the thinking of Maimonides. In later years Mendelssohn blamed his hunchback and poor health upon his intense study of the philosopher's works, but, he added, "I love him nonetheless."

At fourteen, Mendelssohn followed his teacher to Berlin where he studied mathematics, Latin, French, English and German philosophy, and literature. There he also met the dramatist Gotthold Lessing, who subsequently patterned the hero of his *Nathan the Wise* after him.

Keenly aware of Mendelssohn's brilliance,

among the so-called "enlightened" minds of Europe. The same Voltaire who devoted his life to fighting against social and political evils, including what he regarded as the intolerance and superstition of the Church, attacked the Jews as "a greedy and selfish race." One of the greatest poets of Germany, Johann Wolfgang Goethe, considered them an "inferior and degraded race" and even applauded legislation directed against the Jewish community of Frankfort in 1807. And the brilliant German philosopher Johann Gottlieb Fichte asserted that the only way to protect the country against the unfortunate influence of Jewish ideas was to conquer Palestine and send all the Jews there.

Nevertheless, in Germany and elsewhere, some Jews—notably the wealthier class of

Lessing encouraged him to pursue his philosophical writing and even had one of his works published without his knowledge. Later an essay of his was awarded a prize by the Berlin Academy of Science over one submitted by the great Immanuel Kant, and gradually his genius as a philosopher gained him a reputation as the "German Socrates."

All the while, Mendelssohn remained an observant Jew, loyal to his people and faithful to the practices of his religion. His conception of Judaism emphasized its reasonableness, incorporating the very principles of the Age of Reason that, he said, God had revealed to the Jews through their long experience. He did admit, however, that over the years some superstitions, such as those connected with Kabalah, and certain undesirable practices had crept in which needed to be eliminated.

About this time, a Swiss clergyman named Johann Lavater challenged him in a book to refute his arguments in favor of Christianity or else convert. Mendelssohn responded by not only reaffirming the worthwhileness of his religion but emphasizing the need for Christians to live up to the ideals of their own faith through respect for Jews. Though his reply brought a prompt apology from Lavater, the incident roused Mendelssohn to the defense of his people wherever they came under attack. In addition to enlisting the support of his well-known non-Jewish friends, he began publishing several volumes in behalf of the Jews, including *Jerusalem,* in which he called for freedom of conscience for all people.

At the same time, he devoted himself to preparing the Jews for eventual participation in European life by organizing a movement that came to be known as *Haskalah* (הַשְׂכָּלָה, understanding), or "Enlightenment," designed to expose them to Western culture. A further step, he believed, was to get his people to abandon their Judeo-German dialect; and to accomplish this he began preparing a translation of the Bible into German, but reproduced in the familiar Hebrew characters.

His Five Books of Moses was an instant success, and translations of the Psalms and Song of Songs soon followed. Once able to read German, many gradually became acquainted with the thought and literature of the times.

Progress—and Protest

By the time of Mendelssohn's death in 1786, the movement in behalf of Jewish Enlightenment was well-advanced. One of his successors, David Friedlander, a prominent silk manufacturer, pioneered in the development of the popular "Jewish Free School"—"free" in the sense of "liberal"—where youngsters in the primary grades could carry on secular as well as Jewish studies. In Königsberg, a group of Mendelssohn's admirers organized a Society of the Friends of Hebrew Literature that issued a magazine in both Hebrew and German called *Ha-M'assef* (הַמְאַסֵּף, The Collector). Containing articles on history, philosophy, science, and literature, it not only introduced Western culture to the Jews of Poland but finally led the Jews of Eastern Europe to develop a *Haskalah* movement of their own.

Yet there were some who resisted Mendelssohn and his program of Enlightenment. Had there been a modern news-magazine published in 1783, this is the kind of account that would probably have appeared there:

ON THE RELIGIOUS SCENE

Jews

The first German Jewish translation of the Bible has been widely acclaimed by the Jews of Germany. But it has also run into trouble with a number of rabbis.

Trouble in Poland. Last year, when word of Moses Mendelssohn's proposed translation reached Poland, some of its leading Jewish scholars immediately expressed disapproval. "There is no need for Jews to read the Bible in German," they declared. "The only proper language for it is Hebrew."

Added Rabbi Ezekiel Landau of Prague, "Some of the notions people may get through such a translation could prove dangerous to Judaism."

When the German translation finally appeared earlier this year, its opponents in Wilno publicly burned it. "Unclean . . ." "Not fit to be put in Jewish hands," read the statement they issued. "We forbid Jews everywhere to own a copy or read it."

Mendelssohn Suspect. While Mendelssohn's reputation as an observant Jew is well-known, some are suspicious of his motives and question his emphasis upon Enlightenment.

"Adjustment to the ways of Europe means surrendering the Jewish faith," one of the Wilno rabbis asserts. "Mendelssohn himself proves this. Hasn't he already criticized Judaism by pointing to certain abuses that he intends to correct? And didn't he violate Jewish law by agreeing with the Duke of Mecklenburg-Schwerin that funerals

MOSES MENDELSSOHN. A widely-known, distinguished Jewish philosopher who devoted himself to the achievement of Jewish rights and the protection of Jews. He was particularly concerned with Jewish "enlightenment." (HUC, American Jewish Archives)

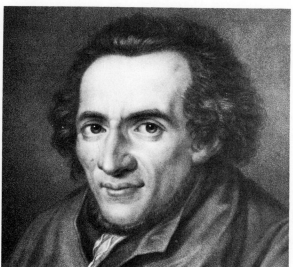

should be delayed a day or two lest someone be buried alive?"

Attack from Frankfort. This week renewed opposition broke out in Germany itself with an attack on the Bible translation by Phineas Levi Horowitz, rabbi of Frankfort-on-the-Main and a foremost talmudic authority.

In an impassioned address given in the synagogue, he warned the community against Mendelssohn's work. "It is a mockery of the teachings of our great rabbis of the Talmud," he declared, "a work of unprecedented wickedness in Israel that will surely undermine the Jewish religion!"

Forty-Seven Defiant. Despite his ban, Rabbi Horowitz received no support from forty-seven members of the Frankfort Jewish community who have announced that they intend to purchase copies.

"We agree that Jews must prepare themselves for emancipation," said one of their spokesmen, "and learning the German language is a very important move in that direction."

Trouble from Other Quarters

The hostility against Mendelssohn's work and the movement for Enlightenment in general was scarcely surprising. Certainly, those who opposed him realized that the spread of Western culture among Jews was bound to produce changes in ghetto life and, with them, modifications of religious belief and practice. But they also feared it would bring about wholesale assimilation, and here they cited with alarm the example of certain Jews who had already found the new culture so attractive that they were prepared to abandon their faith for acceptance into German society.

One such individual was David Friedlander himself, the disciple of Mendelssohn. Thoroughly frustrated by the refusal of Europe to cease its medieval treatment of the Jews, he considered the possibility of gaining freedom through the mere formality of a conversion. He therefore inquired of the Protestant Church whether it would be willing to accept Jews who agreed to be baptized without requiring them to believe in the divinity of Jesus, a

Reform Judaism—Then and Now

Major Developments during

Major Historical Events	Key Events among Jews	Important Men in Science and Culture
		1473—Birth of Nicholas Copernicus, who established the theory of the earth revolving around the sun (d. 1543).
1517—Protestant Reformation begins. **1541**—DeSoto discovers the Mississippi River. **1545**—Council of Trent introduces reforms in the Catholic Church (to 1563). **1558**—Queen Elizabeth I begins her reign in England.	**1516**—Ghetto introduced in Venice. **1534**—Birth of Isaac Luria, noted Kabalist (d. 1572). **1561**—Jews expelled from Prague.	**1561**—Birth of Francis Bacon, English philosopher of science (d. 1626).
	1567—*Shulchan Aruch* published.	**1564**—Birth of Galileo Galilei, who discovered the law of gravity (d. 1642). Birth of William Shakespeare (d. 1616). **1578**—Birth of William Harvey, who discovered the circulation of blood (d. 1657).
1588—Destruction of the Spanish Armada. **1607**—Virginia Colony permanently settled. **1618**—Start of the Thirty Years' War between Protestants and Catholics.	**1593**—Jews expelled from the papal states.	**1596**—Birth of René Descartes, French mathematician and philosopher of science (d. 1650).
		1627—Birth of Robert Boyle, founder of modern chemistry (d. 1691). **1632**—Birth of John Locke, English political philosopher (d. 1704).
1653—Cromwell rules England (to 1658).	**1654**—Jews settle in New Amsterdam.	

the Age of Reason, 1473–1779

Major Historical Events	Key Events among Jews	Important Men in Science and Culture
1664—New Amsterdam captured by the British, renamed New York. **1682**—Louisiana territory claimed by the French.	**1655**—Jews readmitted to England. **1665**—Sabbatai Zevi proclaims himself the Messiah.	
		1684—Birth of Charles Montesquieu, French political philosopher (d. 1755). **1694**—Birth of François Voltaire, French political philosopher (d. 1778). **1713**—Birth of Denis Diderot, French political philosopher (d. 1784).
	About 1700—Birth of the Ba-al Shem Tov, founder of Chasidism (d. 1760).	**1723**—Birth of Adam Smith, English "laissez-faire" economist (d. 1790).
1740—Start of the reign of Frederick the Great of Prussia (to 1786).	**1729**—Birth of Moses Mendelssohn (d. 1786).	**1744**—Birth of Jean Baptiste de Lamarck, founder of modern biology (d. 1829). **1749**—Birth of Johann Wolfgang von Goethe, German dramatist and writer (d. 1832).
	1750—Birth of David Friedlander (d. 1834). Jewish charter issued by Frederick the Great.	**1752**—Benjamin Franklin (d. 1790) proves lightning to be electricity.
1754—Start of French and Indian War (to 1763). **1769**—Birth of Napoleon (d.1821).		**1769**—Birth of William Smith, founder of modern geology (d. 1839).
	1772—Start of Orthodox opposition to Chasidism.	**1773**—Birth of James Mill, founder of modern psychology (d. 1836).
1775—American Revolution begins (to 1782).		**1775**—Birth of George Grotefend, decipherer of ancient Assyrian and Babylonian script (d. 1853).
	1779—Publication of Lessing's *Nathan the Wise.*	

proposition that the Church officials immediately rejected.

There were others, however, who actually abandoned Judaism. For the most part these were the so-called "salon" Jews, upper-class individuals of the late 1700's whose salons, or drawing-rooms, became the fashionable meeting places for the leading German philosophers, writers, artists, and socialites. Some, including two of Moses Mendelssohn's own daughters, Dorothea and Henrietta, and Henrietta Herz, the wife of a well-known Jewish philosopher-physician, became so enamored of their new life that they actually converted to Christianity.

These were followed by a flood of Jewish conversions undertaken mainly to secure the practical benefits of citizenship. Among them were those of such noted writers as Heinrich Heine and Ludwig Borne and of the parents of two young boys destined to become famous—Benjamin Disraeli, the future prime minister of England, and Karl Marx, the writer of the classic texts of communism.

KARL MARX. A leading socialist thinker and economist. His works are basic to communism. (Photoworld)

Questions to Be Answered

Thus, even before emancipation, some serious questions had been raised. One was whether the practice of Judaism was to remain as it was in the ghetto. Another involved the wisdom of exposing Jews to Western culture, and a third pointed to the grave problem of assimilation once European society became open to them.

Sides were already being drawn, but, as long as the Jews were still confined to the ghetto, the questions remained largely theoretical. However, little did the Jews of the late eighteenth century imagine they would be called upon so soon to deal with each of them.

QUESTIONS FOR DISCUSSION

1. In what ways are our own times a product of the Age of Reason? How has this affected your life today?

2. Why do the findings of science inevitably concern religion? What changes did the early scientific discoveries of the Age of Reason make in the established beliefs of Christianity, and how did this affect the Church itself?

3. From present-day experience, how would you expect the following doctrines of the Age of Reason to affect the Jew: (a) religious tolerance, (b) political equality, (c) economic freedom?

4. Why were men like Moses Mendelssohn so concerned with promoting Enlightenment among the Jews? In what ways has this had an influence upon your own life today?

5. Why did various rabbinical leaders oppose Enlightenment? Were they right? Why? To what extent is the Orthodox position today still based upon their arguments?

6. How do you account for the fact that the "salon" Jews abandoned Judaism? What other possible courses of action were open to them? What are possible alternatives for Jews today who live in an "open society"?

SIGNIFICANT DOCUMENTS

John Locke on "Toleration," 1689

. . . No private person has any right, in any manner, to prejudice another person in his civil enjoyments [privileges] because he is of another Church or religion. All the rights and franchises that belong to him as a man, or as a denison [resident], are inviolably to be preserved to him. These are not the business of religion. No violence nor injury is to be offered him, whether he be Christian or pagan.

Nay, we must not content ourselves with the narrow measures of bare justice; charity, bounty and liberality must be added to it. This the Gospel enjoins, this reason directs, and this that natural fellowship we are born into requires of us.

If any man err from the right way, it is his own misfortune, no injury to you; nor therefore are you to punish him in the things of this life, because you suppose he will be miserable in that which is to come.

What I say concerning the mutual toleration of private persons differing from one another in religion, I understand also of particular Churches which stand as it were in the same relation to each other as private persons among themselves. Nor has any one of them any manner of jurisdiction over any other; no, not even when the civil magistrate [ruler], as it sometimes happens, comes to be of this or the other communion.

For the civil government can give no new right to the Church, nor the Church to the civil government. So that whether the magistrate join himself to any Church, or separate from it, the Church remains always as it was before, a free and voluntary society. It neither acquires the power of the sword by the magistrate's coming to it, nor does it lose the right of instruction and excommunication by his going from it.

JOHN LOCKE. Noted British philosopher who argued in favor of universal freedom and toleration. (Photo-world)

This is the fundamental and immutable right of a spontaneous [natural] society, that it has power to remove any of its members who transgress the rules of its institution; but it cannot, by the accession of any new members, acquire any right of jurisdiction over those that are not joined with it. And therefore peace, equity, and friendship are always mutually to be observed by particular Churches, in the same manner as by private persons, without any pretence of superiority or jurisdiction over one another.

—From John Locke,
"First Letter on Toleration,"
in *Four Letters on Toleration,*
edited by A. Murray,
pp. 10–11.

From Lessing's *Nathan the Wise,* 1779

[It is the time of the Crusades. Nathan, a wealthy Jewish merchant, has just returned home to Jerusalem where he is informed that his adopted daughter was rescued from a fire by a young Christian knight, a member of the Templar's order.

Nathan meets the Templar, a penniless and lonely stranger, thanks him and offers him aid and friendship.

At first the Templar spurns Nathan because he is a Jew, but he finally allows him to replace the cloak he lost in the fire. Nathan weeps, and the Templar's disdain for the Jew suddenly turns to respect and friendship, as we see in this passage from Act II, Scene 5.]

Templar.

        But, Jew—your name is Nathan?
But, Nathan—you have spoken well,
   and sharply.
I know not what to answer. Surely—I—

Nathan.

Disguise yourself, dissemble as you will.
Here too I've found you out. You were
   too good.
Too honorable to be more polite.
A girl, all sentiment—her waiting
   woman,
All eagerness to serve—her father
   absent—
Fled that you might not conquer. Further
   cause
For thanks.

Templar.

I must confess you know the motives
That ought to be a Templar's.

Nathan.

        But a Templar's?
Ought only—and because his Order
   bids?
I know a good man's motives, and I
   know
Good men are everywhere.

Templar.

        With no distinction?

Nathan.

Distinguished by their color, form and
   dress.

Templar.

Not more or less in one place than
   another?

Nathan.

All such distinctions are of small
   account.
The great man everywhere needs ample
   space:
Too many, closely planted, dash themselves
Against each other. Average ones, like
   us,
Stand everywhere in crowds. But let not
   one
Cast slurs upon the others. Knots and
   gnarls
Must live on friendly terms. One little
   peak
Must not take airs, as 'twere the only
   one
Not sprung from earth.

Templar.

        Well said! But know you, Nathan,
What people practiced first this casting
   slurs—
What people were the first to call them-
   selves
The chosen people? How if I—not hate,
Indeed—but cannot help despising them
For all their pride, —a pride which has
   descended
To Mussulman [Moslem] and Christian,
   —that their God
Must be the one true God? You start to
   hear
Such words from me, a Christian and a
   Templar.
When, where, has this fanaticism of
   having

The better God, and forcing Him as best
   on all the world, e'er showed itself in
   colors
More black than here and now? Who
   here and now
Feels not his eyes unsealed? But be he
   blind
Who will!—Forget what I have said, and
   leave. [*Going.*]

Nathan.

You know not how much closer you
   have drawn me.
We must, we must be friends! Despise
   my people
With all your heart. We neither chose
   our people.
Are we our people? What does "people"
   mean?
Is Jew or Christian rather Jew or
   Christian
Than man? May I have found in you
   another
Who is content to be esteemed a man!

Templar.

You have, by heaven, you have! Your
   hand! I blush
That for a moment I should have
   misjudged you.

Nathan.

And I am proud; for 'tis the vulgar only
That rarely is misjudged.

Templar.

          And but the rare
That's not forgotten. Nathan, yes, we
   must,
We must indeed be friends.

        —From Gotthold Lessing,
          Nathan the Wise,
    in George A. Kohut (ed.),
      A Hebrew Anthology,
      Vol. II, pp. 1269–1271.

Mendelssohn's View of Judaism, 1783

I believe that Judaism knows nothing of a revealed religion, in the sense in which it is taken by Christians. The Israelites have a divine legislation: laws, judgments, statutes, rules of life, information of the will of God, and lessons how to conduct themselves in order to attain both temporal and spiritual happiness. Those laws, commandments, etc., were revealed to them through Moses in a miraculous and supernatural manner; but no dogmas, no saving truths, no general self-evident propositions. Those the Lord always reveals to us, the same as to the rest of mankind, by nature and by events, but never in words or written characters . . .

I, therefore, do not believe that the resources of human reason are inadequate to the persuading of mankind of the eternal truths requisite for their happiness; and that God has need to reveal them to them in a preter-natural [supernatural] manner. They who maintain this deny the omnipotence or the goodness of God . . .

He was, in their opinion, good enough to reveal to mankind the truths on which their happiness depends; but He was neither omnipotent nor good enough to grant to them the faculties of discovering them themselves. . . .

According to the notions of true Judaism, all the inhabitants of the earth are called to happiness; and the means thereof are as extensive as the human race itself, as liberally dispensed as the means of preventing hunger and other natural wants . . .

    —From Moses Mendelssohn, *Jerusalem,*
      Vol. II, pp. 89, 96, in Walter Jacobs,
        "Moses Mendelssohn and the
         Jewish-Christian Dialogue,"
   *Central Conference of American Rabbis
         Journal,* Vol. XIII, No. 3
      (October, 1965), pp. 48–49.

OTHER THINGS TO READ

Bamberger, Bernard J., *The Story of Judaism:* Chap. 36, ''Crossroads''; Chap. 37, ''Another Dawn.''

Browne, Lewis (ed.), *The Wisdom of Israel:* ''Convictions of Moses Mendelssohn,'' pp. 601–609.

Encyclopedia Britannica (latest edition): ''Nicholas Copernicus,'' ''Galileo Galilei,'' ''Isaac Newton,'' ''Frances Bacon,'' ''René Descartes,'' ''John Locke,'' ''Charles Montesquieu,'' ''Jean Jacques Rousseau,'' ''Gotthold Lessing,'' ''Moses Mendelssohn.''

Feuer, Leon I., and Azriel Eisenberg, *Jewish Literature since the Bible,* II: pp. 148–160 (Moses Mendelssohn); 164–170 (Nathan the Wise); 172–179 (plea for Jewish toleration); 212–218 (Heinrich Heine).

Graetz, Heinrich, *History of the Jews:* Vol. V, Chap. 10, ''The *Measfim* and the Judaeo-Christian Salon.''

Guttman, Julius, *Philosophies of Judaism:* pp. 291–303 (Moses Mendelssohn).

Jewish Encyclopedia: ''Haskalah,'' Vol. 6, pp. 256–258; ''Phineas Levi Horowitz,'' Vol. 6, pp. 468–469; ''Gotthold Ephraim Lessing,'' Vol. 8, p. 14; ''Dorothea Mendelssohn,'' Vol. 8, pp. 476–477; ''Henrietta Mendelssohn,'' Vol. 8, p. 478; ''Moses Mendelssohn,'' Vol. 8, pp. 479–485; ''Naftali Hirz Wessely,'' Vol. 12, pp. 506–507.

Jospe, Alfred, ''Moses Mendelssohn,'' Chap. 1 in Simon Noveck (ed.), *Great Jewish Personalities in Modern Times.*

Lowenthal, Marvin L., *The Jews of Germany:* Chap. 13, ''The Age of Reason''; Chap. 14, ''Romantics.''

Marcus, Jacob R., *The Jew in the Medieval World:* pp. 80–83 (Aaron Lopez's efforts to be naturalized); 84–87 (Frederick II's charter); 343–346 (Solomon Maimon in Poland).

Sachar, Abram L., *A History of the Jews:* pp. 267–272 (Moses Mendelssohn).

Schwartzman, Sylvan D., *Reform Judaism in the Making:* Chap. 3, ''The First Rays of Freedom.''

Standard Jewish Encyclopedia: ''David Friedlander,'' p. 710; ''Phineas Horowitz,'' p. 926; ''Gotthold Ephraim Lessing,'' p. 1189; ''Haskalah'' (Enlightenment), pp. 852–854; ''Moses Mendelssohn,'' pp. 1299–1301; ''Naphtali Herz Wessely,'' pp. 1906–1907.

Steinberg, Milton, *The Making of the Modern Jew.*

Universal Jewish Encyclopedia: ''Haskalah,'' Vol. 5, pp. 242–245; ''Phineas Horowitz,'' Vol. 5, p. 460; ''Gotthold Ephraim Lessing,'' Vol. 6, p. 613, ''Dorothea Mendelssohn,'' Vol. 7, p. 470; ''Henrietta Mendelssohn,'' Vol. 7, p. 471; ''Moses Mendelssohn,'' Vol. 7, pp. 471–474; ''Rachel Varhagen von Ense'' (Rachel Levin), Vol. 10, p. 396; ''Naphtali Herz Wessely,'' Vol. 10, p. 506.

SUGGESTED ACTIVITIES

1. Prepare the script for a documentary television program dealing with the developments of the Age of Reason and their effects upon European life.

2. Imagine you are living in the late eighteenth century, prepare a flyer for public distribution presenting arguments in favor of granting greater freedom for the Jews.

3. Present a role-play of the various positions taken during a meeting between Rabbi Phineas Horowitz, Moses Mendelssohn, and Henrietta Herz.

SUBJECTS FOR RESEARCH

1. What is the plot of Gotthold Lessing's play *Nathan the Wise,* and how did it serve to help the cause of the Jews during this period?

2. What was the reaction of the Roman Catholic Church to the discoveries of Galileo, and what personal consequences did it have for him?

3. What were some of the main effects of the Protestant Reformation upon European life? What immediate consequences did Martin Luther's position concerning the Jews have on the Lutheran faith?

4. What were the provisions of the Charter for the Jews issued in 1750 by King Frederick the Great of Prussia? How does this compare with the Edict of Toleration issued by Emperor Joseph II of Austria in 1781? How do you explain the difference?

5. Why did Mendelssohn see the need for moderate changes in certain accepted Jewish practices of the times? What were those he recommended?

FILMSTRIPS TO SEE

Moses Mendelssohn: Pioneer in Modern Judaism (UAHC), portraying the highlights of Mendelssohn's career and achievements in promoting Enlightenment.

Jews in Morocco (UAHC), illustrating many features of Jewish life of the Middle Ages still current among "Oriental" Jews.

The Story of Haym Salomon (UAHC), portraying the contributions of this Jewish patriot of the eighteenth century and some of the circumstances he had to overcome as a Jew.

France: Eighteenth Century (*Life*), describing the upheavals that took place after the Age of Reason.

Middle Ages (*Life*), picturing the art and social life of this lengthy period of European history.

Feudalism (Society for Visual Education), describing the organization of European society in the Middle Ages.

A LIVE ISSUE

Who is a Jew? This question currently being asked by the Jews themselves goes back to the very period described in this chapter. For, as we shall see, the issue arose only after the Jews became citizens of the countries in which they lived.

On the surface, the answer seems simple: A Jew, we might say, is anyone who believes in Judaism. Yet this would eliminate those who have no association whatsoever with religion. To identify Jews on the basis of their culture presents other difficulties. What about the non-Jew who speaks Hebrew or specializes in biblical or rabbinic scholarship?

Some consider the Jews a "nationality" because in most East European and Moslem countries they are recognized as an official "minority," operating under their own civil and religious law. Similarly, in the State of Israel, one might be looked upon as a Jew simply because he is a citizen of a predominantly "Jewish" nation. But this certainly wouldn't apply to Jews living in the Western world.

The Basic Problem: What, then, is it that makes a person Jewish?

Some Important Questions: (1) Is a Jew essentially anyone who claims to be Jewish? (2) Does belonging to Jewish organizations or contributing to Jewish causes make one a Jew? (3) Is being a Jew simply a matter of birth? What about the person who has only one Jewish parent? Or a non-Jew who converts to Judaism? (4) Does citizenship in the State of Israel automatically make one a Jew? How about the Arabs who live there? (5) Is synagogue affiliation the best way of determining whether one is Jewish?

What Do You Think? As you read this chapter, think about these questions. Is the answer given by the Jews of the early 1800's still satisfactory? If not, how would you define a Jew?

4. CITIZENSHIP AT LAST

Revolution Breaks Out

It was Monday morning, May 4, 1789. The place was the huge assembly hall in Versailles, just outside of Paris. There on the platform sat King Louis XVI of France, together with his queen, the prime minister, and other members of the government. They were awaiting the assembly of the Estates-General, made up of representatives of the nation's three "estates," or feudal classes.

The meeting had been arranged because of the country's desperate situation. France was virtually bankrupt because of continued wars, the extravagance of the royal court, and the failure of the upper classes to pay their proper share of taxes. But the nation also faced famine and civil war because of a series of poor harvests. To restore confidence in his regime and secure an increase in taxes, the king finally summoned an assembly representing all of France.

Entering the hall first were nearly three hundred members of the nobility, all dressed in "gold-worked, bright-dyed cloaks of velvet, rustling with laces, waving with plumes." They were followed by an equal number of the clergy in their white linen vestments and other churchly robes. Last came the six hundred representatives of the common people, mainly merchants and professionals, who wore slouched hats, black mantles, and plain white ties and carried notebooks with lists of their grievances against feudal abuses. Strongest objection was voiced against the oppressive taxation, forced labor on the roads, and imprisonment without trial.

The king was in no mood to listen to complaints. But the representatives declared that they would not approve an increase in taxes until their grievances were heard. Angrily, the king locked them out of the hall; they responded by forming a National Assembly that pledged itself not to disband until "the regeneration of the public order" was achieved.

King Louis now ordered his troops to disperse the delegates, but they refused; and, before other forces could be summoned, the people of nearby Paris rose to the assembly's defense. Mobs attacked soldiers and seized jails, among them the Bastille, a fortress and prison, whose inmates they promptly set free. Peasants from all over France began storming the castles of the nobles; eventually even the king and queen were taken prisoners.

The French Revolution had begun!

The End of Feudalism in France

The nobility's flight from the country encouraged the National Assembly to put an immediate end to the feudal system by adopting the Declaration of the Rights of Man and the Citizen. Modeled along the lines of the American Declaration of Independence of 1776, it likewise subscribed to the chief doctrines of the Age of Reason. Thus it opened with the statement that having long suffered from "contempt for human rights" the French people were determined to achieve their "inalienable rights" in terms of seventeen principles, beginning with:

Men are born, and always continue, free and equal in respect of their rights . . .

Others asserted the individual's "natural right" to personal liberty, representative government, just processes of arrest and trial, freedom of opinion, speech, and press, equitable taxation, and protection of private property.

Despite his opposition, King Louis XVI was compelled to sign the declaration. All that remained now was to produce a constitution restricting the king's powers and providing for representative government. After two years the task was completed, and on September 14, 1791, the constitution was approved.

This marked the end of feudalism in France, with its privileged guilds and masses of serfs, or peasants, dominated by the nobility and clergy. Eliminated, too, was the doctrine of the Divine Right of Kings under which France's monarchs had freed themselves of any accountability to the people.

Threatened by the situation in France, rulers of other European countries quickly formed an alliance to invade the country and restore the power of the king. When the efforts of the French nobility to free the king and queen failed, Prussia and Austria declared war against France and threatened to destroy Paris if the royal family were harmed in any way. Defiantly the French government put the king and queen on trial for treason and had them executed.

Enter: Napoleon Bonaparte

At first the war went well for France, but by 1795 a continuing struggle for power within the country and the increasing pressure of attacks by a coalition, or alliance, of armies that now included England brought the nation to the brink of disaster. A massive uprising in Paris, engineered by the royalists, led the government to call for help from one of its ablest officers, Napoleon Bonaparte.

A Corsican by birth, Napoleon was a captain in the artillery who had once put down a revolt at Toulon. Facing the rebels in Paris he moved quickly to prevent them from capturing the artillery and then turned it against them, killing about a hundred and putting an end to all resistance.

As a result of his success, Napoleon was appointed commander of the army of Italy, consisting at the time of thirty thousand ragged and starving men. Promising them glory and riches, he led them through a series of battles that succeeded in conquering most of Italy and forcing Austria to sue for peace on terms that ceded to France all of Belgium and various sections of Germany.

He then conducted a campaign against the British in Egypt. In three weeks he had conquered that country and was moving on to attack Syria. But Admiral Nelson's destruction of the French fleet ended any hope he had of ever bringing his army back to Europe.

Suddenly, a new crisis arose at home. Once again Austria, Russia, and Great Britain had declared war on France, and in Italy the French army was reeling from defeat. Momentarily facing invasion, the French people were on the verge of rebellion.

Hastily boarding a frigate, Napoleon slipped through the British blockade and returned home where he was hailed as the only person who could save France. He was immediately made one of the three consuls that governed the country and given still greater power when he won quick victories over the Austrians and the royalists at home.

Faced by new uprisings and the prospect of still another war in Europe in 1804, France declared itself an empire and made Napoleon emperor. Within a year he had put an end to civil strife and soundly defeated all of France's enemies.

Meanwhile, wherever Napoleon's troops marched, they introduced the principles of the French Revolution popularized by the slogan of "Liberty, Fraternity, Equality!" In Italy, Switzerland, Holland, Belgium, Poland, Spain, and many sections of Germany, kings and nobles were overthrown as the oppressed masses welcomed their liberators.

Although Napoleon was eventually defeated at the Battle of Waterloo in 1815, Western Europe never returned to feudalism. True, in most countries many of the former rulers and most of the nobility were restored to power. Even in France a brother of Louis XVI was made king. Nevertheless their powers were now somewhat more limited, and fear of those who continued to press for the restoration of all the former freedoms also served to restrain them.

What about the Jews?

When the revolution began, about fifty thousand Jews lived in France. However, nearly three-quarters of them were in Alsace-Lorraine, once part of Germany, where the people confined them to ghettos and subjected them to all sorts of humiliating restrictions.

The rest of French Jewry dwelt chiefly in the south. Most were descendants of former Spanish Jews who had been forced to emigrate in the late fifteenth century, and they were well-regarded by their fellow countrymen.

When the revolution broke out in 1789, the Jews were confident that they would soon receive their freedom. However, even as the mobs stormed the castles of the nobles, those in Alsace-Lorraine turned against the Jews. Blaming them for their suffering, the peasants destroyed the homes of numerous Jews and forced hundreds more to flee the country.

Gradually, the National Assembly restored order and put an end to the attacks on the Jews. Adoption of the Declaration of the Rights of Man also led many Jews to believe that the freedoms it promised would apply to them as well. Indeed, once universal religious freedom was approved, their representatives promptly submitted a petition for complete civil and political liberty.

However, this met with violent opposition, especially from the members of the National Assembly from Alsace-Lorraine, with the result that on January 27, 1790, only the Jews of southern France were granted full citizenship. Fear of riots, as well as the unyielding opposition of the delegates from Alsace-Lorraine, caused the assembly to postpone action on the rest of French Jewry.

The Jews Finally Gain Citizenship

Nevertheless, emancipation was bound to come. The National Assembly was well aware that failure to grant all Jews freedom was inconsistent with the principles of the revolution, and certain powerful delegates led the fight to end the discrimination against them.

One of these was Count Mirabeau, a prominent leader of the revolution and ardent admirer of Moses Mendelssohn, whom he saw as a prime example of Jewish talent that could benefit the Western world. "Do you want to make the Jews better men, useful citizens?" he asked his countrymen. "Then banish from society all humiliating distinctions against them . . ."

The liberal Catholic priest and noted revolutionary Abbé Grégoire was another of their champions. "If the Jew has faults it is Christian society that is responsible," he argued in a widely-circulated pamphlet entitled, *Proposals in Favor of the Jews.* "Therefore it is the Christian's duty to free him."

Many more joined with them. Count Clermont-Tonnerre demanded immediate citizenship for the Jews as atonement for all the past sins committed against them. The delegate Goddard even organized a public gathering at which the Jews of Paris appeared in their uniforms as national guardsmen, carrying good conduct statements signed by the leading citizens of the nation.

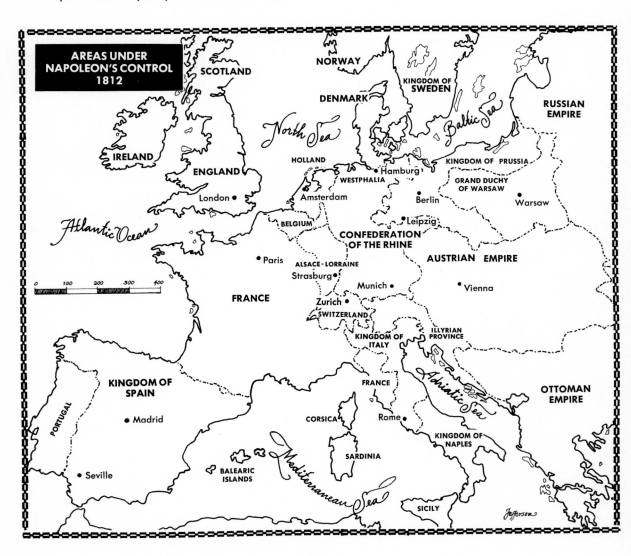

AREAS UNDER NAPOLEON'S CONTROL 1812

52

The National Assembly responded by relieving Jews of all special taxes in recognition of their important military and financial service to the revolution, but the majority of delegates still hesitated to take the final step. It was only after repeated calls for action that on September 27, 1791—more than two years after the start of the revolution—the assembly recognized all Jews of France as full citizens.

How they rejoiced over their new-found freedom! Lippman Cerf-Berr of Alsace-Lorraine, who had worked unceasingly to influence the assembly to take action, wept at the news, and in a letter to his fellow Jews at home he expressed his inner feelings:

> We have at last again obtained the rights of which we have been deprived for eighteen centuries. How deeply at this moment should we recognize the wonderful grace of the God of our forefathers! . . . This nation asks no thanks, except that we show ourselves worthy citizens . . .

French Jewry responded with wholehearted support for the country, which was then at war. Thousands joined the National Guard, and practically everyone contributed funds. Even synagogue valuables were sold to raise money for the cause.

Now, wherever the armies of France marched, they liberated the Jews. Often actually having to batter and burn down the ghetto walls, they freed the Jews of Holland, Belgium, Italy, and many sections of Germany. Fear of revolution also compelled rulers of other countries in Europe to extend better treatment to their Jews.

Napoleon and the Jews

Yet shortly after Napoleon became emperor of France, the Jews found their newly-won liberties threatened. Complaints against them, originating chiefly with the people of Alsace-Lorraine who had never become reconciled to Jewish emancipation, reached the emperor. They accused the Jews of lending money to the peasants at exorbitant rates of interest, claiming that this was the cause of continuing anti-Jewish outbreaks, and urged Napoleon to expel them. The royalists also attempted to exploit the situation and discredit the revolution that had granted the Jews citizenship by spreading the word that they were incapable of becoming good citizens and would always remain a dangerous foreign element in France.

Napoleon, who had his own prejudices about Jews and money-lenders, consulted with his Council of State. A few of the members, including the powerful Count Louis Molé, argued in favor of revoking their rights, but most defended them and urged the emperor to treat them fairly. In response, he issued two decrees. One postponed for a year the repayment of all debts owed Jews. The other called for their representatives from France, Germany, and Italy to meet at an assembly of Jewish Notables whose purpose, Napoleon stated, was "to revive sentiments of civic morality among those who have lived so long under degrading circumstances" and to consider whatever means necessary to have them abandon money-lending in order to become more useful citizens.

So, on July 29, 1806, a group of 112 rabbis, scholars, and businessmen gathered in Paris and formed the Assembly of Jewish Notables. They were hardly reassured to learn that the same Count Molé, who had been so hostile to Jews in the Council of State, was to address them in behalf of the emperor.

Questions to Be Answered

A modern newspaper would have reported the opening session somewhat as follows:

FRENCH JEWRY SHARPLY CRITICIZED; NOTABLES TO ANSWER 12 QUESTIONS

PARIS, July 29, 1806—Speaking for the emperor at the first session of the Assembly of Jewish Notables at City Hall today, Count Louis Molé, a leading member of the Council of State, expressed sharp criticism of the Jews.

"Jewish money-lenders," he asserted, "are impoverishing many Frenchmen, and this assembly is expected to correct the situation. It must prove that Jews are capable of becoming worthwhile citizens."

A Dozen Questions Raised

"Therefore," he continued, "the emperor calls upon this assembly," to provide acceptable answers to the following questions:

"(1) Are the Jews permitted to have more than one wife? (2) Do they consider a Jewish divorce legal without the approval of the French courts? (3) According to Jewish law, may they intermarry with Christians?

"(4) Do Jews regard all Frenchmen as their brothers? (5) What duties do they have toward their fellow citizens? (6) Do they look upon France as their country and feel obligated to obey its laws?

"(7) Who appoints the rabbis? (8) What civil authority have they? (9) Is it Jewish law or simply custom that determines how they are selected and what powers they have?

"(10) Are any occupations forbidden to Jews by their religion? (11) Does Jewish law prohibit them from lending money to fellow Jews at high rates of interest? (12) Does it permit them to do so with non-Jews?"

Delegates Stunned

For the most part, the delegates listened in stunned silence to what they felt was an attack on both their religion and their patriotism. At the conclusion of the count's remarks, the assembly's president tactfully assured him that the reply that would be given would convince everyone of the Jews' devotion to their country.

In less than a month the assembly came forward with its answers. Upon receiving them, Napoleon called them quite satisfactory and even sent word to the delegates that "His Majesty guarantees you free practice of Judaism and full enjoyment of political rights." Nevertheless, he added that he was not entirely convinced that the assembly's statement had the authority of Jewish law and asked that a special Sanhedrin, the highest court of talmudic times, ratify it.

The Work of the Great Sanhedrin

The delegates were deeply moved by the call for a Sanhedrin, which they viewed not only as evidence of Napoleon's sympathy for the Jews but an event of great historical importance. Accordingly, on February 9, 1807, seventy-one Jewish representatives, of whom two-thirds were rabbis, gathered in Paris to constitute a "Great Sanhedrin."

Step-by-step it proceeded to approve the actions of the Assembly of Jewish Notables. From the outset it agreed that Judaism had two main kinds of law. One was purely religious and remained permanently in force; the other was the civil and political law that had once regulated life in Palestine, but which, with the end of the Jewish state, was no longer operative. As French citizens, the Jews were now subject to the laws of the land, in this instance the French Code. Hence, those seeking to be married or divorced had first to obtain the state's permission before the appropriate religious rites could be performed. The Sanhedrin also pointed out that in Western countries polygamy had been banned by the rabbis for nearly 800 years.

Again following the Assembly of Jewish Notables, it insisted that Jews looked upon France as their country and all Frenchmen as their brothers. They loved their country and would gladly defend it militarily.

The appointment of rabbis, the Sanhedrin declared, was made by the local community under procedures that varied from place to place, and they possessed no judicial authority or police power. Their function was purely religious.

As for money-lending, the Sanhedrin pointed out, Mosaic law forbids taking any interest whatsoever. Jews had been forced into lending money because they were barred from so many other ways of making a living. However, now that they were free, they would certainly select more suitable occupations, such as farming and manufacturing.

The question of recognizing an intermarriage was the only one that caused serious controversy. Rabbinic Judaism had long frowned upon it because it served to weaken Jewish loyalties. (For many centuries the Church had also forbidden it.) Finally, the Sanhedrin responded. It maintained the prohibition against a rabbi performing an intermarriage, thus denying it the sanction of Judaism. But it nevertheless recognized such a marriage entered into under civil law as legal and therefore valid.

Napoleon's Reaction

Publicly, Napoleon expressed his complete satisfaction with the response of the Great Sanhedrin. Still, in a memorandum that he wrote even before it convened, he showed that his real intention was to control the Jews in order to redirect them to new occupations,

THE GREAT SANHEDRIN. An assemblage in 1807 in Paris of Jewish leaders from France, Germany, and Italy. (Hebrew Union College Museum)

conscript them for military service, and, if possible, encourage their assimilation.

Consequently, a year afterward, Napoleon enacted into law a series of decrees that he said were designed to provide a "training period" of ten years for French Jewry. Recognizing Judaism as one of the official religions of France, the law proceeded to organize the Jews, the rabbis, and synagogues into numerous districts, all under the control of a central body in Paris responsible to the government.

Among the Jews these new laws were known as the "Infamous Decree" because they singled them out for separate treatment. The most objectionable were those that attempted to regulate their occupations by shifting them away from money-lending to agriculture and to restrict their right of residence in order to reduce their number in Alsace-Lorraine. Interestingly, they also required Jews to adopt last names for purposes of better identification, because up until then they only had first names, followed by the name of their father. Thus, a male would simply be called "Isaac, the son of Abraham," and a female, "Rebecca, the daughter of Jacob."

Fortunately, French liberalism prevailed and most of the restrictions were short-lived. Within a few years the majority had been removed, and when the ten-year period ended none were renewed. Thereafter, French Jewry, for the most part, enjoyed complete freedom.

Religious Repercussions of Emancipation

If the climate of the Age of Reason had created such a strong desire for Enlightenment among the Jews, emancipation was bound to produce an even greater reaction.

Actually, it had already begun with the actions taken by the Assembly of Jewish Notables and the Great Sanhedrin. For they acknowledged that under the circumstances of emancipation the system of Jewish law that had prevailed in the ghetto had to give way to the civil institutions and processes of the countries in which Jews lived. Their decisions also indicated that a continuing sense of Jewish nationhood, fostered by centuries of oppression, was no longer appropriate. The emphasis instead was to be placed upon religion, with Jews now constituting a religious community rather than a political one.

Religious changes were also certain to follow. What impact, for instance, would Western culture have upon traditional Jewish belief? And what effect would the circumstances of emancipation have upon religious practice? For instance, once Jews adopted the use of the vernacular—the language of the country—would worship only in Hebrew continue to satisfy them? And how could the Sabbath be observed when Jewish stores would have to be open on Saturday?

These were a few of the questions that were beginning to arise. They made it plain to some that a new approach to Judaism would soon become a necessity.

QUESTIONS FOR DISCUSSION

1. In what ways did the existence of the feudal system contribute to the outbreak of the French Revolution? How might the course of Jewish history have been different if King Louis XVI had cooperated with the National Assembly instead of opposing it?

2. How do you account for the fact that the French were willing to emancipate the Jews of southern France, but not those of Alsace-Lorraine? Why do you suppose the Jews of southern France were willing to accept freedom under these conditions?

3. What arguments based upon the principles of the Age of Reason did the supporters of Jewish

emancipation advance? Why were these effective? How has your own life benefited from them?

4. What reasons did Napoleon give publicly for convening the Assembly of Jewish Notables and Great Sanhedrin? How do these compare with his real reasons? What conclusions do you come to about Napoleon as a friend of the Jews?

5. What answers would you personally give to the twelve questions that Napoleon put before the Assembly of Jewish Notables and Great Sanhedrin? How do your answers compare with those that they gave? How do you explain any similarities or differences?

6. How did the answers of the Assembly of Jewish Notables and Great Sanhedrin change the prevailing conception of the Jews? How do you account for their response? In what ways have their decisions affected your own Jewish life?

SIGNIFICANT DOCUMENTS

The French Declaration of the Rights of Men and of Citizens, 1789

The representatives of the people of France, formed into a National Assembly, considering that ignorance, neglect, or contempt of human rights are the sole causes of public misfortunes and corruptions of Government, have resolved to set forth, in a solemn declaration, these natural, imprescriptible and inalienable rights: that this declaration being constantly present to the minds of the members of the body social [society], they may be ever kept attentive to their rights and their duties; that the acts of the legislative and executive powers of Government, being capable of being every moment compared with the end of political institutions, may be more respected; and also, that the future claims of the citizens, being directed by simple and incontestable principles, may always tend to the maintenance of the Constitution and the general happiness.

For these reasons the National Assembly does recognize and declare, in the presence of the Supreme Being, and with the hope of His blessing and favor, the following *sacred* rights of men and citizens:

I. Men are born, and always continue, free and equal in respect of their rights. Civil distinctions, therefore, can be founded only on public utility.

II. The end of all political associations is the preservation of the natural and imprescriptible rights of man; and these rights are Liberty, Property, Security and Resistance of Oppression.

III. The Nation is essentially the source of all sovereignty; nor can any individual, or any body of men, be entitled to any authority which is not expressly derived from it.

IV. Political Liberty consists in the power of doing whatever does not injure another. The exercise of the natural rights of every man has no other limits than those which are necessary to secure to every other man the free exercise of the same rights, and these limits are determinable only by the law.

V. The law ought to prohibit only actions hurtful to society. What is not prohibited by the law should not be hindered; nor should any one be compelled to do that which the law does not require.

VI. The law is an expression of the will of the community. All citizens have a right to concur, either personally or by their representatives, in its formation. It should be the same to all, whether it protects or punishes; and all being equal in its sight are equally eligible to all honors, places, and employments, according to their different abilities, without any other distinction than that created by their virtues and talents.

VII. No man should be accused, arrested, or held in confinement, except in cases determined by the law, and according to the forms which it has prescribed. All who promote, solicit, execute, or cause to be executed, arbitrary orders ought to be punished, and every citizen called upon, or apprehended by virtue of the law, ought immediately to obey, and renders himself culpable by resistance.

VIII. The law ought to impose no other penalties but such as are absolutely and evidently necessary; and no one ought to be punished but in virtue of a law promulgated before the offense, and legally applied.

IX. Every man being presumed innocent till he has been convicted; whenever his detention becomes indispensable, all rigor [force applied] to him, more than is necessary to secure his person, ought to be provided against by the law.

X. No man ought to be molested on account of his opinions, not even on account of his religious opinions, provided his avowal of them does not disturb the public order established by the law.

XI. The unrestrained communication of thoughts and opinions being one of the most precious rights of man, every citizen may speak, write, and publish freely, provided he is responsible for the abuse of this liberty, in cases determined by the law.

XII. A public force being necessary to give security to the rights of men and of citizens, that force is instituted for the benefit of the community and not for the particular benefit of the persons with whom it is intrusted.

XIII. A common contribution being necessary for the support of the public force, and for defraying the other expenses of Government, it ought to be divided equally among the members of the community, according to their abilities.

XIV. Every citizen has a right, either by himself or his representative, to a free voice in determining the necessity of public contributions, the appropriation of them, and their amount, mode of assessment, and duration.

XV. Every community has a right to demand of all its agents an account of their conduct.

XVI. Every community in which a separation of powers and a security of rights is not provided for wants a constitution.

XVII. The right to property being inviolable and sacred, no one ought be deprived of it, except in cases of evident public necessity, legally ascertained, and on condition of a previous just indemnity.

—From R. W. Postgate,
Revolution from 1789—1906,
pp. 30–31.

Declaration of the Great Sanhedrin about the Nature of Judaism, 1808

We declare that the divine law, the precious heritage of our ancestors, contains religious as well as civil demands;

That by their nature religious demands are absolute and independent of circumstance and time;

That this is not the same with civil commands, that is to say, with those which touch upon government and which were designed to govern the people of Israel in Palestine when it had its kings, its priests, and its magistrates;

That these civil commands ceased to be applicable when Israel ceased to be a nation;

That in hallowing this distinction, which has already been established by tradition, the Great Sanhedrin declares it to be an incontestable fact;

That an assembly of men learned in the law, united in a Great Sanhedrin, can alone determine the consequences of such development; and

That, if the ancient Sanhedrins have not done so, it was only because political circumstances did not permit [it] and because, since the entire dispersion of Israel, no Sanhedrin has assembled until now.

Therefore, engaged in this pious enterprise, we invoke divine inspiration from which all good derives and consider ourselves obligated to advance, as far as it depends on us, the achievement of the moral regeneration of Israel; and

Therefore, in virtue of the right conferred upon us by our customs and our sacred laws, which determine that there resides in an assemblage of the learned men of the time the essential capacity to determine, in accordance with the needs of the case, that which is required by the above-mentioned laws, be they written or oral, we now proceed to declare that obeisance to the law of the state in matters civil and political is religiously required.

—From W. Gunther Plaut,
The Rise of Reform Judaism,
pp. 72–73.

From Napoleon's Ordinance Establishing Jewish "Consistories" [Councils], 1810

Article 1: There shall be established a synagogue and Israelite consistory in every department [district] containing two thousand people who profess the religion of Moses.

Article 2: In the case where there are not to be found two thousand Israelites in a single department, the consistory will include as many contiguous departments as are necessary for the inclusion of that number. The seat of the synagogue will always be in the city which has the largest Jewish population.

Article 3: In any case, there cannot be more than one consistory in a department.

Article 4: No special synagogue shall be established unless it is proposed by the consistory with the proper authority. Each individual synagogue shall be administered by a rabbi and two notables [lay leaders], all of whom shall be designated by the proper authority.

Article 5: There shall be one grand [chief] rabbi for each consistory.

Article 6: The consistories shall be composed of one grand rabbi, of another rabbi or as many as are necessary, and of three other Israelites, of whom two shall be chosen from among the inhabitants of the city which is the seat of the consistory.

Article 7: The consistory will be presided over by the oldest of its members who will assume the title of Elder of the consistory.

Article 8: There shall be designated by the proper authority in each consistorial circumscription [district] twenty-five notables chosen from among those who contribute the most.

Article 9: These notables shall proceed to elect the members of the consistory who must be acceptable to the proper authority.

Article 10: No one may be a member of the consistory (1) if he is not thirty years old; (2) if he has gone through bankruptcy and has not honorably reestablished himself; (3) if he is known to have practiced usury.

Article 11: Any Israelite who wishes to take up residence in France or in the Kingdom of Italy must give notice within three months of his arrival to the consistory closest to the place where he will establish his residence.

Article 12: The functions of the consistory will be: (1) to see to it that the rabbis are not able to give, whether in public or private, any instruction or explanation of the law which is not in conformity with the responsa of the Assembly of Notables, converted into doctrinal decisions by the Great Sanhedrin; (2) to maintain order within the synagogues, to supervise the administration of each synagogue, to regulate the collection and the use of those funds destined for the expenses of the Mosaic religion, and to see to it that, for the sake or the pretext of religion, there not be formed without express authorization any prayer assembly; (3) to encourage the Israelites of the consistorial circumscription, by whatever means possible, to engage in the useful professions, and to make known to the authorities those who do not have any avowed means of existence; (4) to inform the authorities each year of the number of Israelite conscripts [candidates for military service] in the circumscription. . . .

Article 20: No rabbi is eligible for election: (1) if he is not a native or naturalized Frenchman or an Italian of the Kingdom of Italy; (2) if he cannot obtain evidence of qualification signed by three Italian grand rabbis if he is an Italian, or French grand rabbis if he is French; (3) effective in 1820, if he does not know the French language in France and the Italian language in the Kingdom of Italy. One who has some understanding of Greek and Latin, in addition to an understanding of Hebrew, shall be preferred, other things being equal.

Article 21: The functions of the rabbis shall be: (1) to teach religion; (2) to restrict themselves to the doctrine set forth in the decisions of the Great Sanhedrin; (3) to hark constantly upon obedience to the laws, notably and in particular to those laws relative to the defense of the homeland, and to emphasize it especially each year at conscription time, from the time of the first call from the authorities until the law is executed; (4) to endeavor to make the Israelites consider military service to be a sacred obligation and to declare to them that, during the period in which they consecrate themselves to this service, the law absolves them from any observ-

ances which they cannot reconcile with it; (5) to preach in the synagogues and to recite the prayers which shall be written both for the Empire and the imperial family; (6) to perform marriages and to declare divorces; except that in no case shall the rabbis be able to proceed in these matters without the applicants' having been duly authorized by the prior civil act of marriage or divorce . . .

—Simeon J. Maslin,
Selected Documents of Napoleonic Jewry,
pp. 26–32.

OTHER THINGS TO READ

Bamberger, Bernard J., *The Story of Judaism:* Chap. 36, "Crossroads"; Chap. 38, "Morning— With Clouds."

Encyclopedia Britannica (latest edition): "France" and "Napoleon Bonaparte."

Feuer, Leon I., and Azriel Eisenberg, *Jewish Literature since the Bible,* II: pp. 161–163 (Jewish response to Napoleon); 172–179 (arguments in favor of Jewish emancipation).

Graetz, Heinrich, *History of the Jews:* Vol. V, Chap. 11, "The French Revolution and the Emancipation of the Jews"; Chap. 12, "The Jewish French Synhedrion and the Jewish Consistories."

Jewish Encyclopedia: "France," Vol. 5, pp. 467–470; "Napoleon Bonaparte," Vol. 9, pp. 167–168; "French Sanhedrin," Vol. 11, pp. 46–48.

Sachar, Abram L., *A History of the Jews:* Chap. 21, "The Fall of the Medieval Citadel."

Sachar, Howard M., *The Course of Modern Jewish History:* Chap. 3, "Emancipation in the West."

Schwartzman, Sylvan D., *Reform Judaism in the Making:* Chap. 4, "The European Jew Becomes a Citizen."

Standard Jewish Encyclopedia: "Alsace," pp. 83–84; "Consistory," p. 480; "Napoleon," pp. 1385–1386; "Sanhedrin," p. 1656.

Steinberg, Milton, *The Making of the Modern Jew:* Chap. 8, "The Process of Emancipation."

Universal Jewish Encyclopedia: "France," Vol. 4, pp. 376–378; "Napoleon Bonaparte," Vol. 8, pp. 100–101; "Napoleonic Sanhedrin," Vol. 9, pp. 363–364.

SUGGESTED ACTIVITIES

1. Prepare a picture-chart comparing the situation of the French Jews before and after their emancipation.

2. Write a script for a radio newscast on the sessions of the Great Sanhedrin.

3. Conduct a role-play dealing with the members of Napoleon's Council of State as they discuss the future of the Jews under French control.

SUBJECTS FOR RESEARCH

1. Compare the principles that underlie the French Declaration of the Rights of Man with those of the American Declaration of Independence. What do they share in common? How do you explain their striking similarities?

2. What economic, political, and religious groups in France supported the revolution? Which were opposed? What in general were the attitudes of both groups toward the Jews? How do you account for this?

3. Study the lives of Count Mirabeau and the Abbé Grégoire. In view of their particular backgrounds, how do you explain their support of Jewish emancipation?

4. Why was there such heated debate over the question of intermarriage in the Assembly of Jewish Notables and Great Sanhedrin? What different points of view were expressed? To what extent do their conclusions agree with the position of American Jewry today?

5. Make a study of some of the anti-Semitic arguments used against the Jews of Germany during the Hitler period. How do these compare with the ones that were voiced in Napoleon's day? How do you explain the results of your comparison?

FILMSTRIPS TO SEE

The Story of Haym Salomon (UAHC), portraying through the life of this American patriot some of the conditions endured by Jews of the eighteenth century and the efforts made to secure their freedom in the New World.

The Jews Settle in New Amsterdam—1654 (UAHC), revealing the circumstances faced by Jewish pioneers in America because of the customary restrictions of the times.

France: Eighteenth Century (*Life*), picturing some of the upheavals that took place in French life as a result of the Age of Reason.

Causes of the French Revolution (Heritage), presenting the major reasons for the outbreak of the revolution in 1789.

Feudalism (Society for Visual Education), describing the organization of European society in the Middle Ages from which the Jews were largely excluded.

A LIVE ISSUE

In recent years, the Reform movement has had an enormous increase in the number of boys becoming *Bar Mitzvah,* as well as girls being *Bat Mitzvah.* Yet originally, as this chapter discloses, Reform Judaism eliminated *Bar Mitzvah* and replaced it with a new ceremony called "Confirmation" that was to commemorate the advance of the individual from childhood to maturity.

Since then, Confirmation has been carried on by every Reform congregation and has even been introduced by many Conservative and Orthodox synagogues. But with the revival of *Bar Mitzvah,* the Reform movement finds itself with two observances that, on the surface at least, seem to celebrate essentially the same thing.

The Basic Problem: In view of the growing number of young people becoming *Bar* and *Bat Mitzvah* in Reform temples today, is the ceremony of Confirmation still needed? Or does Confirmation serve a sufficiently different purpose to justify its observance?

Some Important Questions: (1) In what way do the two ceremonies mark the same stage of the individual's development? (2) In traditional terms, what does becoming *Bar Mitzvah* mean? (3) As early Reform Judaism conceived of it, what was the meaning of Confirmation? (4) Is the form of the two observances the principal distinction between them? (5) Or is there a fundamental difference in the meaning of both, and, if so, what?

What Do You Think? As you read about Reform's early development, bear these questions in mind. What is your solution to the basic problem? If it were your decision, would you eliminate either *Bar Mitzvah* or Confirmation? Or, if you decided to retain both, what distinction would you make between the two?

5.

THE BIRTH OF REFORM JUDAISM

Religious Change—an Important Issue

For almost half a century, many Jews of Western Europe had been preparing for emancipation. By now the program of Enlightenment promoted by Moses Mendelssohn and his associates had familiarized them with European thought and culture, so that, as the response of the Assembly of Jewish Notables and Great Sanhedrin clearly reveals, when freedom finally came, few were hesitant about accepting citizenship and living under the law of the land.

With emancipation also came new economic opportunities for the Jews because an expanding capitalism, built upon the principle of ''laissez-faire,'' or free enterprise, encouraged them to explore every avenue of manufacturing, business, and the professions. They even began to find greater social acceptance, especially among the intellectuals with whom they shared much in common, and, by Napoleon's time, many prominent Jewish businessmen and political figures were likewise enjoying close associations with leading non-Jews.

Only in the area of religious practice was there reluctance to change. Most Jews still insisted that the Judaism of the ghetto had to be maintained, even though emancipation had radically altered the situation.

But a few were already questioning whether this was possible any longer. Among them was Lazarus Bendavid, a well-known German Jewish mathematician and philosopher of the early nineteenth century, who asked:

> To be a Jew, must I persist in wearing the long *kaftan* [the black outer-garment or gown worn by observant Jews of the times], and unclipped beard and earlocks, that have distinguished the Jew from the Gentile? Do these constitute the essence of Judaism? If I retain them will I not be looked upon as a bizarre alien and thereby jeopardize the very civic and political privileges for which I have fought and won?
>
> But if I discard them all, am I not stripping Judaism of its distinctive features . . . Should a process of modernizing Judaism be confined to personal appearance and dress, or should it also include the customs and doctrines of the home and the synagogue? . . .

Here Bendavid was raising four basic questions to which Judaism would ultimately have to respond: (1) Was every practice carried on in the ghetto essential? (2) Could emancipated Jews continue to observe them all? (3) Were any subject to change? (4) And, if so, which?

The Judaism of the Times

The problems that troubled enlightened Jews like Bendavid grew out of the very nature of Judaism as it was then practiced.

In most respects it was not very different from that presently carried on by the ultra-Orthodox of Israel or those found in certain large cities like New York and Montreal. Here they live together in "ghettos," like the Hundred Gates (מֵאָה שְׁעָרִים) section of Jerusalem. The men wear full beards, with curly earlocks covering their cheeks, and dress in long black *kaftans* and broad black fur-trimmed hats. Even the young boys keep their earlocks long and wear the same kind of clothes. Wives, of course, cover their heads with the customary *sheitel,* or wig, required of all married women.

Religious practice among the ultra-Orthodox is virtually the same as it was in the seventeenth and early eighteenth centuries, adhering strictly to the traditional 613 religious duties that Moses is said to have commanded the people of Israel. Of these, 365 are called "negative" commandments because they involve acts forbidden to Jews. Among them are wearing clothes containing a mixture of linen and wool and turning on the lights on the Sabbath, as well as prohibitions against such unethical conduct as stealing, swearing false oaths, and coveting other people's possessions.

The remaining 248 commandments are the so-called "positive" religious duties that include such moral responsibilities as showing kindness to strangers, giving charity, and respecting one's parents, and such religious practices as maintaining the dietary laws,

TALIT. The traditional prayer shawl with appropriate fringes, particularly those at the four corners. (Frank J. Darmstaedter, Jewish Theological Seminary)

fasting on the Day of Atonement, and celebrating the three major festivals of Sukot, Passover, and Shavuot.

Some commandments apply largely to one sex or the other. Only males, for example, are obliged to wear *tzitzit* (צִיצָת, fringes, associated chiefly with the *talit,* טַלִּית, or prayer shawl) and the *tefilin* (תְּפִלִין, phylacteries or prayer boxes) at daily worship. On the other hand, mainly women are expected to purify themselves periodically in the *mikveh* (מִקְוֶה, a collection of water or ritual pool).

Jewish life centers about the synagogue, which the people never refer to as a "temple" out of respect for the ancient sanctuary in Jerusalem that was destroyed by the Romans in 70 C. E. Either they use one of the Hebrew terms, like *Bet ha-Knesset* (בֵּית הַכְּנֶסֶת, House of Assembly), *Bet ha-Tefilah* (בֵּית הַתְּפִלָּה, House of Prayer), or *Bet ha-Midrash* (בֵּית הַמִּדְרָשׁ, House of Study), or the Yiddish word *shul,* from the German for school or place of learning.

Both worship and study are important religious duties. Men come to the synagogue daily for three services, and there, from early morning until late at night, those of every age will study the Bible, the Talmud, and other major religious works.

A Sabbath Service

Were we to attend a Sabbath morning service in an ultra-Orthodox synagogue in this country, we would be likely to have much the same experience as that pictured in the following fictional account:

> It was about nine o'clock that morning when we entered the small, dimly-lit *shul.* I could hear the chanting of the service and I started to go directly inside, but my friend seized my arm.
>
> "Upstairs," she motioned. "Women are not permitted on the main floor."
>
> We climbed a flight of steps to the balcony, which was the women's section. Every man below was bearded and sat wrapped in his *talit,* with his head covered by a small skull cap, called *kipah* (כִּפָּה, a cover-

> ing resembling a dome) or *yarmulke.* Even the young boys in their *talit* had ringlets of hair coursing down their cheeks in fulfillment of the commandment in Leviticus, "You shall not round off the side-growth of your head" (19:27).
>
> Beneath the *talit* everyone wore the familiar long black outer-garment that hung down to his ankles, a form of dress once common in Eastern Europe that the Jews retained as a mark of piety.
>
> The service, which I was told had been going on since seven o'clock, was being chanted in Hebrew by the *chazan* (חַזָּן, cantor) from a raised platform or *bimah* (בִּימָה) in the center of the synagogue. From time to time, the men would join in the chanting, occasionally rising to recite prayers by themselves as they swayed back and forth.

ORTHODOX JEW WEARING TEFILIN. The prayer boxes are worn on the head and left arm. (FPG)

Reform Judaism—Then and Now

The prayer book was entirely in Hebrew, and here and there I recognized a familiar passage like the *Shema* (שְׁמַע , "Hear, O Israel . . . ") and the *Kadosh* (קָדוֹשׁ , "Holy, holy, holy . . . "). But the rapidity with which the prayers were chanted made it very difficult to follow the service.

After a while, several men made their way to the Ark, where they opened the richly embroidered velvet curtain, and took out one of the Torahs. They then carried it to the *bimah* in the center of the synagogue and undressed it. One by one, seven men came up in turn to witness the chanting

THE INTERIOR OF AN ORTHODOX SYNAGOGUE. Note the special pulpit in the center. (Hebrew Union College Museum)

of the weekly portion, and each touched the fringes of his *talit* to the Torah, kissed them, and sang the appropriate blessings.

Afterwards, the rabbi gave an explanation of the passage in Yiddish, in which he explained the laws for observing the coming Passover festival. To my surprise, this was the only time he officiated in the service.

Finally, after another half-hour of worship, everyone sang the *En Kelohenu* (אֵין כֵּאלֹהֵינוּ, "There Is None Like Our God"), followed by the *Adon Olam* (אֲדוֹן עוֹלָם, "The Eternal God"), and the service came to an end. My friend and I exchanged "Good Shabbat" greetings. The men, I was told, would now enjoy a *kiddush* (קִדּוּשׁ, sanctification) over wine or whiskey before returning home.

I looked at my watch; it was half past twelve. We had been there for three and a half hours.

Three Alternatives for the Jew

To people like Lazarus Bendavid, this type of Judaism seemed out-of-keeping even in the nineteenth century, especially with the new circumstances of Jewish life at that time. Nor was he satisfied with the answer that Judaism had to be this way and that all change should be resisted even to the point, if necessary, of rejecting emancipation itself. Actually, in 1795, some of Amsterdam's Jews had opposed Dutch citizenship on these very grounds and, even as late as 1844, a number of religious leaders in Hungary took a similar stand. The majority of the rabbis also strongly resisted secular education for Jews at "Free Schools" and universities, fearing that it might ultimately lead them to forsake their faith.

Thus, from an official or "traditionalist" point of view, the only possible response to

emancipation was to carry on Jewish life precisely as it had developed in the ghetto. This, in fact, was the way a prominent rabbi of the times expressed it in his ethical will:

> . . . Never say, "Times have changed!" We have an old Father—praised be His Name—who has never changed and never will change. The order of prayer and the synagogue shall remain forever as it has been up to now, and no one may presume to change anything of its structure . . .

To men like Bendavid, however, there had to be some better alternative. But what others were there?

One, unfortunately, was to abandon Judaism, which was the course followed by Moses Mendelssohn's own children and other salon Jews. Though some claimed that they were attracted to Christianity because it seemed superior to their own faith, for most conversion was not really a result of religious conviction. It was simply a formality undertaken to open the door to wider social and professional opportunities.

A great many more Jews, however, were attracted to deism. This was the fashionable, non-sectarian faith of the time that viewed God simply as the Great Creator, who, in accordance with natural law, called for fair and reasonable treatment of every human being. The followers of deism claimed that having rid themselves of all supernatural belief and sectarianism—something they termed "pure superstition"—theirs was the only "reasonable" religion. Nevertheless, as usually happens with most so-called "universalistic" faiths, deism eventually proved too shallow and emotionally unappealing.

A second alternative, adopted by the majority of Jews, was simply to pay lip service to their religion while ignoring it in practice. Rarely now did they attend the synagogue or carry on more than a minimum of observance. For the most part, their Judaism became

Reform Judaism—Then and Now

ISRAEL JACOBSON. Prominent Westphalian business-man who first introduced reforms in the Jewish Free Schools he established and thus commenced the Reform process. (Hebrew Union College Museum)

largely a matter of identification with the Jewish community, a condition that finally prompted an eighty-six-year-old traditionalist rabbi to come out in favor of the one remaining alternative, religious change:

> Thought cannot be checked. It progresses. Those who advocate the principle of progress in all other directions cannot possibly expect that in religious matters alone antiquated notions should rule.
>
> If we refuse to reform our faith in accordance with the culture of the time we will force an even greater number of the present generation—yes, I may say, the majority of them—either to become hypocrites or to find their faith uncongenial.

Appeals for modest reforms were already being voiced. Mendelssohn's close friend, David Friedlander, was seeking revisions of the prayer book, and various articles in *The Collector,* the Hebrew literary magazine pub-

lished by a number of Mendelssohn's disciples, were suggesting other modifications of Jewish practice. A congregation was even founded in Amsterdam in 1796 for the purpose of making numerous changes in the worship, but it succeeded only in introducing a weekly sermon in Dutch and eliminating a few minor prayers.

Of the three alternatives, the way of religious change seemed to offer the likeliest answer for the modern Jew, and inevitably it gave rise to Reform Judaism.

The First Real Reformer

Interestingly, the first Reformer was a layman, not a rabbi, and the first congregation involved was actually connected with a school.

Once a Jewish Free School in which secular subjects could be taught was established in Berlin by David Friedlander, the idea quickly spread throughout Germany. In 1801 one was formed in Seesen, a small town about seventy-five miles south of Hanover, by Israel Jacobson, a wealthy businessman-banker and agent to the Duke of Brunswick.

Born in 1768, Jacobson had received a good Jewish education but only a limited secular one. His father, a pious man of some wealth who carried on many charitable projects in the Jewish community, had wanted his son to become a rabbi. However, Jacobson was more interested in the study of Western culture, particularly the writings of Moses Mendelssohn, Gotthold Lessing, and the French liberal philosophers, and he eventually decided to enter the business world. His career was greatly aided by an early marriage to the daughter of a wealthy agent of the Duke of Brunswick, whom he ultimately succeeded in the post.

As Jacobson witnessed Jewish life in the course of his business trips, he saw the need for many improvements, and he soon began to devote himself to reforms in Jewish education and synagogue worship. Over the opposition of the townspeople, he established a Jewish Free School in Seesen, maintaining a personal interest in it for the rest of his life, even to the point of getting to know all the students personally and reading many of their compositions.

To stimulate the interest and participation of the students, Jacobson introduced certain changes in the school's Sabbath services. For example, he had a number of prayers and hymns translated into German and he would periodically invite guest preachers to deliver a sermon in German which soon became a regular feature of the worship.

This was a real departure from customary synagogue practice where the service was completely in Hebrew and where the rabbi would deliver only two or three sermons a year. One was given prior to Passover, one during the High Holy Days, and sometimes another on Yom Kippur eve, and these were chiefly devoted to explaining the laws of the holidays.

When some of Jacobson's friends learned of his services, they secured permission to attend. Here, in contrast to the worship in their own synagogues, which was often noisy and incomprehensible, they found decorum and dignity. They could understand the prayers because they were recited in a language they knew, and they gained inspiration as well from the weekly sermon. Soon, to Jacobson's satisfaction, a sizable number began attending regularly.

More of Israel Jacobson's Reforms

Meanwhile Jacobson also devoted himself to improving conditions for his fellow Jews. Largely through his efforts—and on several occasions he succeeded only by threatening to resign from the duke's service—humiliat-

ing toll-taxes were removed from the Jews of Brunswick and Baden. On another occasion, when new reactionary laws were about to be imposed upon the Jews of Frankfort, he wrote a furious letter to the ruler, calling the legislation a product of "the barbaric Dark Ages." "If the Prince wishes to improve his Jewry," he told him, "then reason demands that they be free!"

Aware of what was taking place in France, he began to look upon Napoleon as a "savior of the Jews" and the best hope for German Jewry. So, in 1807, when the Duchy of Brunswick was incorporated into the French kingdom of Westphalia, he offered his services to the new ruler, Jerome, Napoleon's brother. Within a few months the Jews of Westphalia were granted equal rights, and Jacobson was put in charge of Jewish affairs.

With feverish energy he now attempted to transform them into desirable citizens. He

NAPOLEON BONAPARTE. After serving the revolutionary cause, he was eventually made emperor of France. (Photoworld)

Reform Judaism—Then and Now

established a modern educational system that included the founding of a second Jewish Free School in Cassel in 1808 and a college for teachers and rabbis two years later. He also continued the effort to develop more acceptable forms of worship, and in 1810 at his own expense—estimated at more than a hundred thousand dollars, a huge sum in those days—he constructed a new synagogue at the Seesen school, complete with bell tower and clock. Services there featured a portable organ to accompany the well-trained school choir.

At the public dedication attended by all the leading citizens of Westphalia, Israel Jacob-son, garbed in the robe of a minister, delivered the main address in which he called for the creation of new forms of religious practice and offered to provide every assistance. For, as he told the Jews who were present:

> Who would dare deny that the Jewish service is sickly because of many useless things, that in part it has degenerated into a thoughtless recitation of prayers and formulas, that it kills devotion more than it encourages it, and that it limits our religious principles to the knowledge which for centuries has remained in our

70

treasure houses unchanged and unenriched.

On all sides, enlightenment opens up new areas for [religious] development. Why should we Jews alone be left behind?

Let us be honest, my brothers. Our ritual is still weighted down with religious customs that are offensive to reason. They desecrate the holiness of our religion; they dishonor the reasonable person. My office as head of Westphalian Jewry is prepared to help, is greatly concerned with the improvement of our synagogues and schools, and seeks to spread the proper principles [of Judaism] abroad . . .

In the very same year, at his other school in Cassel, Jacobson introduced the religious ceremony of Confirmation to replace *Bar Mitzvah*. He felt that calling upon thirteen-year-olds merely to read a passage from the Torah and comment upon it did not properly mark their advance from childhood to maturity. Rather, he argued, they needed to be instructed in the meaning of their religion and their responsibilities as Jews and citizens, so that properly prepared they would observe the occasion by promising conscientiously to fulfill them.

So, during a regular Sabbath service at the Cassel school, immediately following the reading of the Torah, one of the students arose and came to the pulpit. After stating the basic beliefs of Judaism, he pledged that he would remain forever faithful to his religion and loyal to his country. Then Rabbi Loeb Berlin, the chief-rabbi of Westphalia, pronounced a special blessing upon him.

Later Jacobson made provision for girls also to be confirmed, which shocked the traditionalists even more because of the long-standing prohibition against females on the pulpit.

Thus, with his emphasis on new forms of religious practice, Jacobson paved the way for Reform Judaism.

Reform Moves to Berlin

Within a few years, however, Jacobson found it necessary to leave Westphalia. The collapse of the kingdom in 1813, followed by the defeat of Napoleon and his exile, deprived him of his authority. His work in Westphalia now at an end, he decided to move to Berlin where the Jews had already been emancipated.

Soon he was again occupied with his educational and religious reforms. In his home, on Shavuot, 1815, he conducted the first Reform service in Berlin, which also featured the Confirmation of his son. From then on worship was held there every Sabbath, with Jacobson himself doing much of the preaching.

Word of the new services spread rapidly, and they met with immediate success. For a long time many Berlin Jews had wanted a form of worship they could understand, with decorum and stirring music. Soon so many were crowding into Jacobson's home that it became necessary to hold a second service at the house of a friend, Jacob Herz Beer, a wealthy Berlin banker. As in Seesen, the services featured the use of an organ, many prayers and hymns in German, and a regular weekly sermon by guest preachers. Even special prayer books were produced, and soon plans were under way to build a temple.

However, within six months the king of Prussia forbade the services to continue. "The synagogue," he declared, "and not a private home is the proper place for Jewish worship. If changes are needed in worship, let the people persuade their rabbis to make them." Here he appeared to be acting upon the protest of the religious leaders of the Berlin Jewish community who were bent on maintaining traditional Jewish practice. But to the king's way of thinking, the matter also involved his own interests. For after the experience with the French Revolution and the reign of Napoleon, most rulers looked with suspicion upon change of any sort, even in religion.

European Reform Developments—to 1815

Important Historical Events	Key Happenings in Jewish Life	Major Developments in European Reform
1776—Signing of the American Declaration of Independence.		1778—Jewish Free School established in Berlin by Friedlander.
	1779—Publication of Lessing's *Nathan the Wise.*	
	1781—Dohm issues plea for Jewish emancipation.	
	1782—"Act of Tolerance" issued in Austria.	1783—Completion of Mendelssohn's translation of the Five Books of Moses.
		1784—Publication of *The Collector* magazine.
1789—Outbreak of the French Revolution.	1789—Struggle for Jewish emancipation in France.	
	1791—Granting of citizenship to French Jewry.	
	1796—Granting of citizenship to the Jews of Holland.	1796—Introduction of minor reforms by an Amsterdam congregation.
1798—Establishment of the Roman and Swiss republics under French control.		1801—Founding of a Free School at Seesen by Jacobson.
1804—Napoleon crowned Emperor of France.		
1806—Beginning of Napoleon's control of Germany.	1806—Meeting of the Assembly of Jewish Notables.	
	1807—Meeting of the Great Sanhedrin.	
1808—Napoleon issues decree regulating the Jews of France.	1808—Granting of citizenship to the Jews of Westphalia.	1808—Establishment of a second school at Cassel by Jacobson.
	1812—Prussian Jewry emancipated.	1810—Building of the new synagogue at Seesen. First Confirmation held at Cassel.
1814—Napoleon defeated and exiled. Start of the Congress of Vienna.		
1815—Final defeat of Napoleon at Waterloo.		1815—Beginning of Reform services in Berlin.

Nevertheless, because the Berlin synagogue was then closed for extensive repairs, the services were permitted to go on. But when the synagogue finally reopened in 1823, the Prussian ruler demanded that they cease. "Henceforth," the decree stated, "Jewish services must not contain changes in language, ceremony, prayer, or song," and, with this, Reform worship came to an end in Berlin.

Hamburg Establishes a Reform Temple

Meanwhile in 1817 in Hamburg, long an important port and center of trade which attracted many Jews, a group of sixty-six had formed a Reform association, or "society." The purpose was to promote religious discussion and provide a more modern type of worship, and one of the founders was Edward Kley, the director of the Hamburg Jewish Free School. As a friend of Jacobson, he had previously preached for him at the Seesen synagogue and helped prepare the prayer book used at his Berlin services.

The society's ritual followed the pattern of Seesen and Berlin. Services featured some prayers and hymns in German, the use of a choir and organ, a weekly sermon in the vernacular, and Confirmation for boys and girls. In all other respects, however, the tone of the worship remained quite traditional.

A year later, the members built a temple and elected Gotthold Salomon to be their rabbi. They also prepared a new prayer book, whose changes were few but highly significant. Unlike the traditional *siddur* (סִדּוּר, order of worship or prayer book), it opened from the left instead of the right, with the Hebrew of the prayers reproduced in German characters for the benefit of those who could not read Hebrew. The prayers were also translated into German and contained certain changes to conform to the beliefs of the

members. For example, instead of following the traditional *siddur* and praying for the coming of a "Redeemer," referring to a personal Messiah to deliver the Jews, the new prayer book substituted the term "Redemption," meaning a Messianic Age for all mankind. And, where the liturgy originally called for the return of the Jews to Palestine and the renewal of sacrifices in the Temple, the new prayer book simply asked that God accept prayer instead.

These changes reflected early Reform thinking. Not only did they recognize the need for more suitable forms of worship, but they also sought to bring Jewish belief into harmony with the enlightened views of the nineteenth century. Did modern Jews, the early Reformers asked, honestly believe that they were still in "exile" or that any single individual, even the Messiah, a descendant of King David, could miraculously restore them to Palestine? Did they really look forward to such a return or regard the restoration of sacrifices as desirable? If the answer to such questions was no, then honesty, they said, compelled them to change the traditional prayers.

Here they were encouraged by the opinions of several liberal rabbis who maintained that even the Talmud permitted the modification of prayers where necessary, as well as the use of the organ and the vernacular in worship.

The Start of a Movement

The establishment of the Hamburg Temple marks the real beginning of the Reform movement.

Though the members largely adopted the reforms of Israel Jacobson, the Hamburg Temple nevertheless represented something new. Jacobson's program had chiefly been his own and would probably have come to an end with his death. But the formation of a permanent congregation provided the necessary organization to insure the continuity of Reform. Actually, the Hamburg Temple remained in existence for over a century, down to the very time of Hitler's destruction of German Jewry.

Moreover, beyond changes in the form of the worship, the members recognized a number of other important needs. One was rabbinical leadership. Another was the modification of certain religious beliefs, and a third was a better understanding of the nature of historic Judaism.

With Hamburg, then, Reform finally became a movement and, as such, a much greater threat to those who were determined to defend Judaism against change. Hence it is not surprising that they reacted strongly.

QUESTIONS FOR DISCUSSION

1. In what ways did freedom for the Jews stimulate changes in religious practice and belief? How do you account for the fact that reforms started in the Jewish Free Schools rather than in the synagogues of local communities?

2. Compare the Reform service in your temple with that of the ultra-Orthodox Jews described in this chapter. What are some of the significant differences, and how do you account for them?

3. Do Reform Jews today abide by all of the 613 commandments of traditional Judaism? Which do they accept? Which do they reject? How do you account for this?

4. What prompted the various changes that Israel Jacobson and some of the other early Reformers introduced? Which are still part of Reform practice today? Has Reform modified any of them since? How do you explain this?

5. Why did Napoleon encourage men like Jacobson to embark upon reforms in Jewish worship? Why, however, did most of the kings who replaced him object? What conclusions, therefore, do you reach about the political climate most favorable to Reform?

6. How have services in your congregation been influenced by the Hamburg Temple? What effect has its reforms of the liturgy had upon certain prayers in your own *Union Prayer Book?* Are other changes necessary today?

SIGNIFICANT DOCUMENTS

The Dedication of Jacobson's Temple at Seesen, 1810

The many hundreds of persons who had been invited came from Brunswick, Cassel . . . and all surrounding places. Most of them had arrived in Seesen on the previous day, the sixteenth day of July. Some of them lodged in the ample buildings of the President [Jacobson], and others, for whom there was not enough room, were put up in the inn, and all costs were borne by Mr. Jacobson. In the evening he entertained everyone for dinner.

On the day of the dedication itself, on the seventeenth of July, at 7:00 in the morning, lovely music resounded from the roof of the temple (which was flat like a platform) and announced to the city the approaching festivities. At 8:00, all who had come to participate in the festivities assembled in the school hall of the well-known educational institution which President Jacobson had founded in Seesen. One could see persons of distinguished rank, scholars, Jewish, Protestant, and Catholic clergymen, officials, businessmen of all kinds, all walking together in complete concord, and tolerance seemed to permeate all members of this numerous company. Here friends met, acquaintances and comrades from university days who had not seen each other for a long time and found each other unexpectedly here. The manifold and different groups in this large assembly were most interesting. Everyone found something to talk about.

At 9:00, the ringing of bells announced that the ceremonies would begin. Someone explained in a loud voice how the procession from the hall into the temple would take place and what the celebration itself would consist of. Thereafter, everyone began the solemn processional under the ringing of bells. The procession was led by two flags and by the students of the Jacobson Institute [Free School] and the teachers. Then followed President Jacobson, the prefect of the Department [District] of Oker, Mr. Hanneberg, and the clerics and lay members of the Israelite Consistory from Cassel. Then came all the rabbis present, walking in pairs, in their clerical robes, and the Christian clergymen similarly. The mayor of the town and the deputy mayor came in their robes, the count of Brabeck, public officials of the kingdom who were present, and all other invited persons appeared in their best clothes. Finally, there came many other people from all classes and all faiths, who had come from the entire surroundings to observe the festivities. In solemn silence the long procession went from the auditorium of the school into the halls, through the doors into the street, and again through the doors of another house, and through this house into the court to the temple. Special admission cards had been printed for this festival in order to preserve order, and they had been distributed amongst all the participants in the procession.

After the procession had entered the temple proper, there came from the organ loft lovely music by sixty to seventy musicians and singers, and this put all hearts into the most solemn mood. After everyone had taken his seat, a cantata composed especially for this celebration by Dr. Heinroth, one of the teachers in the Jacobson Institute, was sung splendidly to the accompaniment of the rousing sound of the instruments.

The Jewish ritual now began, with Mr. Jacobson himself being the chief officiant and the rabbis assisting him. At the end, President Jacobson gave an address . . . After the scrolls of the Torah which were elaborately ornamented had been taken from the Ark with great ceremony, they were carried around the temple seven times, preceded by boys with burning wax candles. Then several chapters of the Pentateuch were read, first in Hebrew and at once in German, publicly and with a loud voice. Mr. [Baruch] Schott, director of the educational institution, then mounted the rostrum and talked to the assembled multitude. Then came a chorale accompanied by organ and full orchestra, and this was sung first in Hebrew and then also in German. At the end of this song, in the singing of which the Christians and Israelites participated with deep emotion, Church Counselor Heinemann delivered an address befitting the occasion. After this address there were further songs by the choir.

. . . At the end of the service, President Jacobson elaborately entertained at a table of two hundred in the school auditorium . . . and in other rooms for an additional one hundred persons. The students of the institute ate in the open, in the courtyard.

—From W. Gunther Plaut,
The Rise of Reform Judaism,
pp. 27–29.

The Rendition of a Traditional Prayer in the Berlin Reform Service, 1817

1. From the Traditional Prayer Book

With abounding love hast Thou loved us, O Lord our God, and with great and exceeding pity hast Thou pitied us. O our Father, our King, for our fathers' sake, who trusted in Thee and whom Thou didst teach the statutes of life, be also gracious unto us and teach us. O our Father, merciful Father, ever compassionate, have mercy upon us; O put into our hearts to understand and to discern, to mark, learn and teach, to heed, to do and to fulfill in love, all the words of instruction in Thy Law. Enlighten our eyes in Thy Law, and let our hearts cleave to Thy commandments, and unite our hearts to love and fear Thy name, so that we be never put to shame. Because we have trusted in Thy holy, great and revered name, we shall rejoice and be glad in Thy salvation. O bring us in peace from the four corners of earth, and make us go upright to our land; for Thou art a God who worketh salvation. Thou hast chosen us from all peoples and tongues, and hast brought us near unto Thy great name forever in faithfulness that we might in love give thanks unto Thee and proclaim Thy unity. Blessed art Thou, O Lord, who has chosen Thy people Israel in love.

> —Translation from the Hebrew
> by S. Singer,
> *The Standard Prayer Book,*
> pp. 47–48.

2. From the Berlin Reform Prayer Book

Great love, O Lord our God, hast Thou shown us; great and abounding pity hast Thou bestowed upon us. Our Father, our King, for our fathers' sake who trusted in Thee and whom Thou didst teach the statutes of life, be gracious also unto us and teach us. All-merciful Father, have mercy upon us and put into our hearts to comprehend the contents of Thy Law, that we may perceive and understand it, study and teach it anew, that its essence may be performed and fulfilled with love. Enlighten our eyes in Thy Law and keep us true to Thy commandments. Unite our hearts with love and reverence for Thy name that we may never be put to shame. Yea, we trust in Thy holy and revered name; we rejoice in Thy help, for Thou art the one who workest holiness and hast always shown kindness to us over other peoples and nations, in that Thou hast brought us near in truth to Thy holy name, for which we give thanks unto Thee and in unity offer our love to Thee. Blessed art Thou, O God, who has chosen Thy people Israel in love.

> —Original translation from the
> German in Edward Kley
> and T. S. Gunzberg,
> *The German Synagogue,*
> Vol. 1, p. 12.

From the Constitution of the Hamburg Reform Society, 1817

Since public worship has for some time been neglected by so many because of the ever decreasing knowledge of the language in which alone it has until now been conducted, and also because of many other shortcomings which have crept in at the same time—the undersigned, convinced of the necessity to restore public worship to its deserving dignity and importance, have joined together to follow the example of several Israelitish congregations, especially the one in Berlin.

They plan to arrange in this city also, for themselves as well as others who think as they do, a dignified and well-ordered ritual according to which the worship service shall be conducted on Sabbath and holy days and on other solemn occasions, and which shall be observed in their own temple to be erected especially for this purpose. Specifically, there shall be introduced at such services a German sermon and choral singing to the accompaniment of an organ.

Incidentally, the above-mentioned ritual shall not be confined to services in the temple; rather it shall apply to all those religious customs and acts of daily life which are sanctified by the church [synagogue] or by their own nature. Outstanding amongst these are the entrance of the newly-born into the covenant of the fathers, weddings, and the like. Also, a religious ceremony shall be introduced in which the children of both sexes, after having received adequate schooling in the teachings of the faith, shall be accepted as confirmants of the Mosaic religion.

—From W. Gunther Plaut, *The Rise of Reform Judaism*, pp. 31–32.

OTHER THINGS TO READ

Bamberger, Bernard J., *The Story of Judaism:* Chap. 39, "The Beginnings of Reform."

Feuer, Leon I., and Azriel Eisenberg, *Jewish Literature since the Bible,* II: pp. 161–163 (Jewish response to liberation); 181–186 (early Reform).

Graetz, Heinrich, *History of the Jews:* Vol. V, Chap. 15, "Reform and Young Israel."

Jewish Encyclopedia: "Aaron Chorin," Vol. 4, pp. 43–44; "Israel Jacobson," Vol. 7, p. 47; "Israel (Edward) Kley," Vol. 7, p. 524.

Levinger, Lee J., *A History of the Jews in the United States:* p. 212 (early Reform).

Marcus, Jacob R., "Israel Jacobson, An Appraisal," *Central Conference of American Rabbis Yearbook,* Vol. 38 (1928), pp. 386–481.

Philipson, David, *The Reform Movement in Judaism:* pp. 11–18 (Israel Jacobson); 21–38 (early reforms and the Hamburg Temple).

Plaut, W. Gunther, *The Rise of Reform Judaism:* pp. 27–38 (Seesen and the Hamburg Temple).

Schwartzman, Sylvan D., *Reform Judaism in the Making:* Chap. 5, "The Beginnings of Reform."

Standard Jewish Encyclopedia: "Hamburg," pp. 831–832; "Israel Jacobson," p. 1012; "Edward Kley," p. 1140.

Steinberg, Milton, *The Making of the Modern Jew.*

Universal Jewish Encyclopedia: "Aaron Chorin," Vol. 3, pp. 163–164; "Israel Jacobson," Vol. 6, p. 22; "Israel Kley (Edward Kley)," Vol. 6, p. 418.

SUGGESTED ACTIVITIES

1. Write the script for a television documentary on the life and times of Israel Jacobson.

2. Role-play a scene in which several worshipers at the Berlin Reform services are asked to defend their activities before the king of Prussia.

3. Prepare a newsmagazine account of the building of the temple in Hamburg.

SUBJECTS FOR RESEARCH

1. In one of the larger Jewish encyclopedias, locate a list of all the 613 traditional Jewish commandments. Then classify them according to religious practices and ethical conduct. In which category does Reform Judaism still accept most of them?

2. Study the life of Israel Jacobson. From your investigation, what were the chief factors that prompted him to engage in religious reforms?

3. From what statements of the Talmud did the liberal rabbis who supported the reforms of the Hamburg Temple draw their conclusions? Do these really justify them?

4. Compare the translation of the "Eighteen Benedictions" of the Sabbath morning service in the Orthodox *Siddur* with that found in the *Union Prayer Book.* What are some of the principal differences, and how do you explain them?

5. How are Sabbath morning services presently conducted among the Orthodox Jews in your community? In what ways do they resemble the one described in this chapter? How are they different? How do you explain the difference?

FILMSTRIPS TO SEE

Grandfather's World (Jewish Education Committee of New York), describing Jewish life in Eastern Europe as it existed several generations ago.

France: Eighteenth Century (*Life*), picturing the upheaval in French life as a result of the Age of Reason.

A LIVE ISSUE

In recent years, due largely to the ultra-Orthodox who have had a much greater influence than their numbers warrant, Reform Judaism has been faced with increasing opposition. The movement has been publicly attacked in Great Britain, Australia, South Africa, South America, and particularly in the State of Israel where, as part of the government, the ultra-Orthodox have control over all Jewish religious matters.

In this respect, then, the position of the ultra-Orthodox today is very much like that taken by the traditionalists toward early Reform as described in this chapter.

The Basic Problem: The Reform Jew recognizes his kinship with them in all matters of common concern. At the same time, he insists upon his right to carry on Judaism in his own way. But the ultra-Orthodox look upon him as ''disloyal'' and ''faithless'' and refuse to participate with him in any way. Moreover, in instances where they are in control, as in the State of Israel, they refuse to recognize Reform as a legitimate form of Judaism and deny its rabbis equal rights, including that of performing marriages. How, then, should the Reform Jew respond to all of this?

Some Important Questions: (1) Why do the ultra-Orthodox consider it necessary to oppose Reform Judaism by these means? (2) What rights does the Reform Jew insist upon and in what ways do the ultra-Orthodox seek to deny these? (3) How can the Reform Jew justify the legitimacy of his interpretation of Judaism in the face of their attack? (4) What stand should the Reform Jew take toward the ultra-Orthodox in America in matters of joint cooperation? (5) How should he react toward the denial of equal religious rights in the State of Israel and elsewhere?

What Do You Think? In reading this chapter, you will see how the early Reformers dealt with many of these issues. Would you recommend the same kind of response today? Or can you suggest other ways of coping with the situation? What do you think?

6. REFORM MEETS STIFF OPPOSITION

The Attack on the Hamburg Temple

> . . . Go to the government and ask them to humble these wanton [Hamburg] people so that the development of a new sect which no state should suffer be nipped in the bud. We understand that you live under a mild and just government which has always protected morality and religion. Go to them, therefore, and ask your senate that they stay the arm of the evil-doers.

So a rabbi of neighboring Austria appealed to the traditional Jews of Hamburg shortly after the temple published its prayer book.

This was only one of the measures taken by the traditionalists to put an end to Reform. They openly condemned the new congregation and its prayer book and called the members "sinful" and "traitors to Judaism." They ridiculed the few liberal rabbis who sanctioned the temple's reforms as men of "mediocre learning," "lacking in character," and guilty of spreading "lies and deception." They issued a public warning to the Jews of Hamburg against associating with temple members or participating in any of their practices. And, as in Berlin, they did not hesitate to appeal to the authorities to stop their services.

Fortunately, the Senate of Hamburg took no action. Instead, all the furor simply helped spread the word about the new congregation and its activities. And to acquaint as many more as possible with Reform worship, the members now organized a branch temple at Leipzig where an annual fair attracted Jewish merchants from all over Europe.

All the while, attacks on the Hamburg Temple continued. To traditionalists the new prayer book confirmed the fact that Reform meant not only to modify the service but to tamper with Jewish beliefs as well. The result was a greater resistance everywhere even to minor changes and the ultimate creation of a movement called "Orthodoxy," which claimed to represent the only true form of Judaism. Once traditionalist opposition to Reform became organized, it grew still more intense.

Why the Orthodox Were Hostile

That the Orthodox should have been hostile is not surprising. Their conception of Judaism viewed change of any kind as intolerable. Far worse, it was an offense against God himself.

Reform Judaism—Then and Now

According to the Orthodox, Judaism had been transmitted intact from one generation to the next. Originally revealed to Moses in the form of the Torah, it was ultimately communicated through the process of interpretation to the rabbis of the Talmud. So, indeed, declares *Pirke Avot* (פִּרְקֵי אָבוֹת, "The Sayings of the Fathers"), a section of the Mishnah:

> Moses received the Torah at Mt. Sinai and he transmitted it to Joshua. The latter transmitted it to the elders, and the elders to the prophets who, in turn, transmitted it to the Men of the Great Assembly [the rabbinical scholars who were said to have produced the prayer book and the beginnings of rabbinic literature].
>
> (*Avot* 1 : 1)

"Torah," then, is not merely the Five Books of Moses, nor even the entire Bible. It is the whole of Jewish tradition, incorporating the Talmud and all other authentic rabbinical works. For the Bible, as tradition claims, is simply the "Written Torah," but there is also the "Oral Torah" consisting of the rabbinical interpretations, no less inspired by God himself, which were transmitted by word of mouth from the time of Moses. During the first century B.C.E., these began to be organized in a more systematic way until they were gradually set down in writing, first in the Mishnah, compiled around 200 C.E., and then in the Talmud, which included the Mishnah and was completed around 500 C.E.

In the centuries that followed, the Oral Law was expanded through continued interpretation by the rabbis, and eventually much of it was compiled by different scholars into separate collections, or "codes." One was the *Mishneh Torah* (מִשְׁנֶה תּוֹרָה, Review of the Torah), produced by Maimonides in 1180. Another was the *Shulchan Aruch,* "Prepared Table," written by Joseph Karo in 1567 for Jews of Spanish descent. When Moses

MOSES MAIMONIDES. One of Judaism's greatest philosophers whose writings in the twelfth century served to bridge the teachings of Judaism and those of Greek philosophy.

Isserles amended it shortly afterward to conform to the traditions of the Jews of Central and Eastern Europe, it quickly came to be accepted as authoritative in matters of Jewish practice.

From the Orthodox standpoint, the *Shulchan Aruch,* as part of the Oral Law, was as much God-given as the Five Books of Moses themselves. Hence, as indicated in the following public statement issued in 1846 by two of the leading Orthodox rabbis of Germany, changes in accepted practice simply could not be tolerated:

> Our cherished brethren of Israel, we give you herewith a brief résumé of the principles of Judaism as they are designated in the Talmud, and as our fathers have observed them:
>
> a. The divine Law is unchangeable and eternal like its Author; neither time nor conditions can change, much less abrogate it.

b. The Oral Law is truly the word of God, as is the Written Law.

c. All institutions and regulations which were introduced into Judaism with the purpose of protecting the Law are as unchangeable as the Law itself.

Indeed, from this point of view, for human beings to modify even the most minor provision of God's Law was an affront to Him, a repudiation of the divinity of the Torah, and a serious sin. It would inevitably lead to a denial of God, assimilation, and even conversion to Christianity!

Thus, the danger of any change in Jewish life from the way it had been carried on in the ghetto was magnified, and even certain customs that had never been legislated by tradition, such as the wearing of the *yarmulke* or the *kaftan,* came to be viewed as sacred. Now the slightest modifications in Jewish practice were bound to meet with determined resistance on the part of the Orthodox.

The Response of the Early Reformers

The early Reformers, on the other hand, warned against the consequences of *not* modifying Jewish practice, notably in connection with synagogue worship. They pointed to the increasing number of Jews who were converting to Christianity, men like Edward Gans, a leading authority on German law, Joel Jacob, a noted poet, Heinrich Heine, the greatest German writer of his age.

Though most had become Christians because of the benefits to their careers conversion seemed to offer, the Reformers were convinced that they were also influenced by the prevailing nature of Judaism that ignored the spirit of the age as well as the religious needs of the enlightened, emancipated Jew. For, as one of the leading Reformers expressed it:

We wish to be, we should be, children of our time and, as children of this age, we must strive to realize for our contemporaries the true standpoint of Judaism which has never been content to be a faith divorced from life or a practice at variance from belief.

To insist that change was impossible, said the Reformers, was bound to produce the very consequences that the Orthodox themselves feared—disinterest, hypocrisy, and irreligion—and would ultimately lead to assimilation. So, in fact, observed a prominent Jew of Frankfort who wrote:

The number of those who withdraw themselves completely from all participation in religious services grows considerably from year to year, not because they do not experience the need of true religious edification, but because the services in the synagogue, as conducted at present, are not such as to meet this need.

Actually, argued the Reformers, Jewish tradition was not at all opposed to reasonable change. In fact the Oral Law itself sanctioned most of the very reforms they were advocating as, for instance, praying in the vernacular. The Mishnah states:

The following prayers might be recited in any language: the *Shema*, the *Tefilah* תְּפִלָּה, the prayer, or the so-called "Eighteen Benedictions" that comprise the central portion of the liturgy], and the grace after meals.

Hence, reading portions of the service in German in no way violated the teachings of Judaism.

Furthermore, they pointed out, where circumstances demanded, the Orthodox themselves frequently abandoned provisions of the Written and Oral Law. A case in point was the legal device called the *perozbul* (פְּרוֹזְבּוּל, after

81

a Greek word meaning "for the court"). Introduced by Hillel in Roman times, it effectively repealed the biblical law of Deuteronomy 15 that cancelled all debts every "sabbatical" or seventh year. For increasingly farmers and merchants had been unable to obtain loans during the sixth year, with the prospect that the economy would come to a standstill and create great suffering for many. But by permitting a lender to assert in court that he intended to collect the debt at any time, Hillel insured that the sabbatical year would not cancel the loan.

Another instance of a change in the provisions of the Bible is seen in the ordinance issued by Rabbenu (רַבֵּנוּ, our teacher, a title of high honor) Gershom around 1000 C.E., which prohibited polygamy among the Ashkenazic Jews of Central and Western Europe, a practice still carried on by some Jews of the East. Though the Bible clearly permits a man to have more than one wife, and there are some instances in the Talmud where rabbis are reported to have had several wives, Rabbenu Gershom officially put an end to the practice among Western Jewry.

Referring to such precedents the Reformers questioned why, in view of the vastly different conditions of the nineteenth century, they were not equally justified in making changes in synagogue worship.

The Geiger-Tiktin Controversy, 1838–1844

To the strictly Orthodox, however, the matter was not a subject for debate and, as Reform spread to other German communities, they opposed it with increasing vigor, as we shall see through a series of events described here as a modern newspaper might report them.

Typical was the battle they waged in Breslau, an important city in eastern Germany, over the election of a Reformer as a rabbi of the community:

RABBI ABRAHAM GEIGER ELECTED TO SERVE BRESLAU CONGREGATION

Reformer Chosen to Be Associate of Rabbi Tiktin; Chief-Rabbi a Leading Supporter of Orthodoxy

BRESLAU, July 26, 1838—Dr. Abraham Geiger, well-known Reform rabbi of Germany, was elected today by the Breslau congregation to serve as associate to Rabbi Salomon A. Tiktin, Orthodox chief-rabbi of the community. Rabbi Geiger was chosen by a vote of 56–1.

For the past six years, Geiger has served as spiritual leader of the Wiesbaden community where he introduced a number of modest reforms, including weekly sermons, a choir, and the ceremony of Confirmation.

Twenty-eight years old, Geiger is a university graduate with a Doctor of Philosophy degree, something quite unusual in view of the universal objection of rabbinical seminaries to college training for rabbis.

Geiger strongly advocates the scientific study of Judaism in an effort to discover ways in which it may be modified to meet modern conditions and edits a special periodical devoted to this purpose. "If we understand the spirit of Judaism and how it developed," he declares, "we will then be able to cure the ills of our present-day faith."

Tiktin succeeded his father in the post of chief-rabbi in 1821. He has opposed any change from strict Orthodox practice and has frequently led protests against reforms of Jewish worship.

Prior to Geiger's selection, many members of the Breslau congregation had urged the appointment of an associate-rabbi who would introduce moderate reforms. He immediately won wide support when he stated in his trial sermon that he advocated the adjustment of Judaism to the needs of the times. He has insisted, however, that such changes be approved by a special rabbinical conference called for the purpose.

The new rabbi will preach a weekly sermon in German and be in charge of educating the young people.

GEIGER WINS 15-MONTH FIGHT; GAINS PRUSSIAN CITIZENSHIP

Orthodox Faction Led by Chief-Rabbi Loses Legal Battle; Geiger Wins Right to Serve Breslau Jewish Congregation

BRESLAU, Dec. 6, 1839—After fifteen months of legal battling, Dr. Abraham Geiger today won the fight for Prussian citizenship against his Orthodox opponents led by Chief-Rabbi Salomon A. Tiktin. Geiger's replies to their charges were declared satisfactory by Prussian officials who immediately issued his final papers entitling him to full rights of citizenship.

The Orthodox group which opposes all reforms of Judaism had sought to bar him from serving as rabbi of the Breslau congregation.

According to law, Geiger, who was born in Frankfort and therefore not a citizen of Prussia, was technically ineligible for the post. Hence he applied for citizenship.

Four members of the congregation representing the Orthodox faction promptly petitioned the Prussian officials to refuse the request. They attacked him for his radicalism, called him unfit because of his university degree, and claimed that he was compelled to leave his previous post at Wiesbaden because he violated the Sabbath.

They also contended that his election as rabbi of the Breslau congregation was invalid and that

he was ineligible for the position because his views and practices were unacceptable to the Orthodox members. Among other complaints, they cited the fact that he preaches in German and wears a robe in the pulpit "in the style of non-Jewish clergymen."

In overruling their objections, the government vindicated Geiger. Immediately following the decision, the Breslau Reform congregation announced that he would deliver his inaugural sermon on January 4.

GEIGER-TIKTIN STRUGGLE HALTED; REFORM GAINS NOTABLE VICTORY

Geiger Given Post of Chief-Rabbi after Tiktin's Death; Orthodox Forbidden by Government to Quit Congregation

BRESLAU, Oct. 26, 1844—The threat by Orthodox members to resign from the Breslau congregation should Dr. Abraham Geiger succeed the late Chief-Rabbi Salomon A. Tiktin was ended today as a result of a government order.

Prussian officials not only confirmed Dr. Geiger's election as chief-rabbi but warned his opponents not to withdraw from the congregation. They also proposed the selection of a second rabbi to serve with Geiger.

This latest action is expected to end the Geiger-Tiktin feud which has raged ever since Geiger was elected associate-rabbi six years ago.

During the original struggle, the Orthodox faction had succeeded in delaying Geiger's appointment more than fifteen months while contesting his right to Prussian citizenship.

However, even after he was installed, Tiktin refused to recognize him as a colleague. He said that his opposition was prompted by a desire to protect Judaism against unwarranted change. As an example, he cited Geiger's statement in his inaugural sermon that "Judaism is not a finished tale; there is much in its present form that must be changed or abolished." "On the contrary," said Tiktin, "the safety of Judaism is involved in any single change, since all of its laws and practices are sacred."

Nevertheless, Geiger carried on his congregational activities, preaching weekly sermons in German, conducting classes for the young, lecturing and writing in behalf of religious reform. But Tiktin continued the fight against him. "Judaism," he stated on numerous occasions, "permits no criticism of its sacred teachings. Anyone who disobeys a single commandment is no Jew!"

The officers of the congregation tried in vain to put an end to the controversy by offering a compromise plan similar to one followed in Vienna and Prague, which would have made Tiktin the rabbi and Geiger the preacher. This was unacceptable to Geiger who believed it would divide the congregation, as well as give Tiktin authority to stifle all reforms.

Tiktin's continued antagonism finally compelled the congregation to suspend him from office. He appealed for support from his Orthodox colleagues, and in June of 1842 they published their statements which agreed that the commandments of Judaism could be changed only by God and that those guilty of altering religious practice in any way could not be considered Jews.

In self-defense, the board of the congregation appealed to liberal rabbis for their opinions. The two volumes of replies, published in 1842 and 1843, confirmed the fact that Judaism could be modified, especially in view of the circumstances of the times.

The Reform group suffered a setback, however, when the government declared Tiktin's suspension illegal and ordered him restored to his post. Once again the Orthodox renewed the attack on Geiger and succeeded in cutting off funds for his educational program and restraining him from wearing a robe at services.

Tiktin's death in March of last year temporarily halted the conflict but, when Geiger's election as chief-rabbi seemed assured, the Orthodox, under the leadership of Gedaliah Tiktin, son of the late

chief-rabbi, decided to withdraw and form their own congregation.

The government's order thus represents an important victory for Geiger's supporters in a struggle that has attracted worldwide attention.

ORTHODOX FACTION GAINS NEW SUCCESS; GEDALIAH TIKTIN GIVEN DISTRICT POST

Breslau Rabbi Appointed by Prussian Government; to Have Religious Authority over Silesian Jewry

BRESLAU, Jan. 30, 1854—Rabbi Gedaliah Tiktin, son of the late chief-rabbi of Breslau, was appointed today to serve as chief-rabbi for the entire district of Silesia, which includes the city of Breslau. He will also continue to serve as rabbi of the Breslau congregation, presently headed by Abraham Geiger.

Staunchly Orthodox like his late father, the younger Tiktin has consistently opposed the stand of his colleague, and a bitter feud between the two has gone on ever since he was elected co-rabbi of the congregation eight years ago.

In being chosen for the new post, Tiktin had the personal support of the Prussian king who approved his opposition to religious liberalism. "For political reasons," said the king, "it is desirable to confer the title upon him." Tiktin's appointment also had the backing of the leading Catholic and Protestant clergymen of Silesia.

Previously the Prussian government, which considered him unqualified for the position, had declined to recommend him. However, today the Cabinet yielded to the king's desire.

As chief-rabbi, Tiktin will be in charge of Jewish religious affairs throughout Silesia. Thus he will have authority over his colleague Geiger, something the Reform group regards as a serious setback.

Renewed Conflict in Hamburg

The struggle between the Reformers led by Geiger and the forces of Orthodoxy under the younger Tiktin never really ceased, and it was typical of the kind of conflict that went on wherever changes in Judaism were involved.

It next erupted in Hamburg, where for almost a quarter of a century the Orthodox had tolerated the temple's existence. However, when the congregation published a new prayer book, the reaction was violent.

NEW TEMPLE PRAYER BOOK DENOUNCED; BANNED BY HAMBURG CHIEF-RABBINATE

Temple's Revised Prayer Book Arouses Orthodox Hostility; Chief-Rabbi Issues Stern Warning against New Liturgy

HAMBURG, Dec. 1, 1842—Formed twenty-six years ago, the Hamburg Temple has once again become the target of attack in the Jewish community. The cause of the latest trouble is the temple's newly revised prayer book published last year.

Until the current issue erupted, the Hamburg community enjoyed comparative peace. But a sizable increase in membership compelled the temple to enlarge its house of worship and publish a new prayer book.

Actually, the new edition scarcely differs from the old. The same prayers for the rebuilding of Zion

ABRAHAM GEIGER. The unquestioned leader of Reform Judaism in Europe who ultimately became the head of its seminary in Berlin. (HUC, American Jewish Archives)

have been retained, and those calling for the coming of the Messiah and the deliverance of the Jews from exile have again been omitted.

However, Rabbi Isaac Bernays, chief-rabbi of the Hamburg community and spokesman for the Orthodox group, has been quick to denounce the prayer book. He has also issued a public warning that "any Jew worshipping with it is not fulfilling his Jewish obligations."

Temple officials have taken issue with him, declaring that he has no authority over them and expressing regret that the chief-rabbi has seen fit to stir up friction among the Jews of Hamburg.

"We have avoided really radical reforms," asserted the chairman of the temple's prayer book committee, "in order not to create a split in the community. However, we dare not abandon progress in Judaism. We must preserve the spirit of our religion and not permit non-essential, outmoded details to petrify Judaism."

Though the Hamburg Senate compelled the chief-rabbi to withdraw his warning, he recently renewed his prohibition against the prayer book.

Meanwhile the directors of the temple have been soliciting opinions from various liberal rabbis of Europe. Twelve received to date condemn the narrow attitude of the chief-rabbi and his followers and regard the prayer book as completely acceptable for Jewish worship.

Though the conflict raged on for several more years, the Orthodox were unable to halt Reform in Hamburg. However, the controversy did serve to discourage the temple thereafter from undertaking any but the most modest reforms.

Reform Comes to England

The situation in England followed a similar pattern. Once Reform was finally able to gain a foothold in London, it faced constant assault from the Orthodox who had general control over Jewish affairs.

ORTHODOX RABBINATE RENEWS ATTACK AGAINST LONDON REFORM CONGREGATION

Religious Ban Proclaimed against Entire Temple Membership; Chief-Rabbi Refuses to Wed Orthodox Groom to Reform Bride

LONDON, March 3, 1846—The opposition of London's Orthodox Jews against Reform grows more bitter daily. The latest incident is the refusal of Chief-Rabbi Nathan M. Adler to perform the marriage of an Orthodox man to a young lady whose father is Reform unless she promises never again to set foot in the temple.

This latest incident climaxes a series of events that began six years ago when twenty-four members of the German and Portuguese synagogues formed the West London Synagogue of British Jews. Plans of the founders called for shortening the service, eliminating certain prayers, providing more convenient hours for worship, and introducing an English sermon into the service.

However, attempts at reform had begun as far back as 1824 when some of the members of the Portuguese synagogue objected to the noise and lack of decorum during worship. A dozen years later several members actually petitioned the board to adopt the service of the Hamburg Temple, but a counter-petition by the Orthodox opposing even the most minor reforms was overwhelmingly approved by the congregation.

Three years later a number of reform-minded members again called for shorter services to be held at a more convenient time, the introduction of a choir and weekly sermons, as well as the elimination of the extra days of the Jewish holidays.

When the request was denied, they then asked permission to establish a branch synagogue near their homes in the West End of London, but this, too, was refused. A counter-proposal by the Orthodox permitting them to have a branch synagogue which would remain strictly traditional was in turn rejected by the Reformers who then withdrew to form the West London Synagogue of British Jews.

"We are acting to preserve Judaism for our children," their spokesmen stated. "We want to prevent Jews from leaving Judaism."

The reforms of the new congregation have been modest: a choir, some prayers in English, the weekly sermon, Confirmation, and the elimination of the extra days of certain Jewish holidays. Beyond providing translations of the prayers, the prayer book contains few changes in content.

Nevertheless, five days before the dedication of the new temple, the Orthodox rabbinate of London issued a stern warning making the use of its prayer book a serious violation of Jewish law. They subsequently forbade Orthodox Jews to participate in Reform ceremonies and declared temple members ineligible to take part in any activities carried on by the Jewish community.

Thus, when the Reform congregation applied to the Board of Deputies of British Jews, which has authority over Jewish affairs in England, to empower its rabbi to perform marriages, the request was promptly denied. The right of a Reform rabbi to perform a marriage in England is still disputed.

The chief-rabbi's current refusal to officiate at the wedding of an Orthodox and Reform Jew has further widened the breach that divides the Jews of London.

As in Hamburg, Orthodox opposition had a lasting effect upon the West London Synagogue. The congregation, which is still in existence, eventually obtained Parliament's consent for its rabbi to officiate at weddings, but for more than fifty years it made no essential change in its form of worship. In fact, in order to encourage the development of a more progressive form of Reform Judaism in London, a new organization, the Jewish Religious Union for the Advancement of Liberal Judaism, eventually had to be created.

Difficulties within the Movement Itself

It was not simply the opposition of the Orthodox that hampered Reform in Europe, however. The movement, as we shall see, had certain problems of its own.

That is why in May of 1837, Abraham Geiger, then still the rabbi of Wiesbaden, addressed an open letter to his liberal colleagues inviting them to attend a "rabbinical assembly" which was necessary, as he put it, to "revive the well-nigh vanished spirit of Judaism." He expressed the hope that, in view of stiffening Orthodox resistance, they would be able to agree on common Reform practice, for, he added, "I confess that I cannot conceive how we can hold up our heads if we do not stand up courageously for our own innermost convictions."

As a result, thirteen Reform-minded rabbis of Germany joined Geiger in Wiesbaden three months later to struggle with a number of issues then facing the young movement.

Among them, interestingly, are some that still trouble Reform Jews today.

QUESTIONS FOR DISCUSSION

1. How do you account for the fact that most European Jews of the nineteenth century were hesitant to become Reform? To what extent was this due to the shortcomings of Reform itself? To their fear of the Orthodox? To other factors?

2. How do the current views of official Orthodoxy in the State of Israel toward Reform compare with those who opposed Reform in Breslau, Hamburg, and London? How do you explain this?

3. In what respect does your own temple accept the Written Law? The Oral Law? How does this differ from the Orthodox view? What effect has the Reform attitude toward tradition had upon the practices of your temple?

4. How does the religious situation of the American Jew today compare with that of the European Jew in the first half of the nineteenth century? What particular religious needs do American Jews today seem to have? In what way are they different from those of the early Reformers?

5. Using Abraham Geiger in Breslau as an example, how did the functions of Reform rabbis differ from those of the Orthodox? Is this still true in your community today? How do you account for this?

6. In what ways did Orthodox opposition in Hamburg and London hinder the development of Reform Judaism? How does the existence of one or more Orthodox congregations in your community affect your temple? Why is the situation so different?

SIGNIFICANT DOCUMENTS

The Hamburg Temple's Response to the Warning against the Use of Its New Prayer Book, 1841

Since Rabbi Isaac Bernays has deemed it proper to declare in the local synagogues that our prayer book violates the fundamental principles of the Jewish religion, the directors of our new temple, after due consultation with its preachers, consider it incumbent upon themselves to declare, both to the members of our association and to all who attend our services:

1. Rabbi Isaac Bernays has no authority, as far as our organization is concerned, to condemn us publicly as he has; hence this condemnation is to be spurned as unseemly.

2. A malicious, intentional disregard of the contents of the prayer book is apparent in the judgment given; the accusations moreover evince the densest ignorance of all religious and liturgical knowledge.

3. Therefore such a proceeding can affect in nowise the members of our congregation who recognize in it only the expression of powerless partisanship. They regret it because the seed of discord has been sown in the community in so wanton a manner and because the cloak of religion has been used to cover such a course.

—From David Philipson,
The Reform Movement in Judaism,
p. 81.

From Abraham Geiger's Letter to the Board of His Breslau Congregation, 1846

. . . In my work on behalf of Judaism I have always thought it not sufficient merely to attempt to correct flaws by sporadic patchwork or whitewashing. Instead, I have duly recognized that the present generation is the outgrowth of a long series of distorted forms of a Judaism that has evolved through many unhappy centuries. Hence this form which now exists stands outside the pale of Jewry; it is no longer the vital element of the religion of the Jews.

There are those, few in number, who still hold on to this form outwardly, without, however, being imbued by it within. To them it is simply a matter of habit and fear.

There are others who do not care for it at all and have discarded it with indifference. Such a state of disastrous confusion, of total deceit which must undermine all truth and morality, can only deeply sadden anyone who views religion as a vital power and who looks to its institutions for strength and edification . . .

I conceive it my mission to dedicate my energies to the endeavor to cure this ailment. However, there are only two ways in which this can be done: either the people must once again be trained to accept an ideology and religious rituals which they have long outgrown, or else Judaism must give up all outworn forms and, devoid of all its nationalist elements from the past, . . . come forth in its eternal truth, in its lofty teachings, and with its appeal to mankind to hallow all of life.

The first course is as impossible as it is unjustified for, that which the spirit of history, in which God also manifests Himself, has cleared away and buried, no human reason can reawaken or revive. What remains is the alternative, which is what I have attempted to accomplish from the very beginning of my endeavors. I have always persisted in pointing to the sore spot in our present religious affairs; I have never contented myself with those little items that may satisfy transient curiosity and that may offer fleeting attraction because of the illusion of revival that they create . . .

All too frequently, the task of nurturing the seedlings of earnest manly faith and conviction has been made bitter for me. When some members of the community avowed the belief that the dichotomy between life and religion must be removed and indicated their desire to submit recommendations accordingly to the Rabbinical Conference [to be summoned for the purpose], I viewed their declaration as a sign of good will and sincerity, without, however, committing myself on the actual practical feasibility of their proposals. My attitude was denounced as apostasy.

When I declared myself in favor of introducing some German prayers into the service, without, mind you, deeming it advisable to conduct the entire service in German, much complaint was heard. In fact, it was even considered necessary to keep my endeavors behind lock and key, as it were, by giving me a colleague (whom I honor and esteem) to serve as a sort of drag.

Thus my position here has become such that I can no longer pursue my goals with that zeal and unrestrained freedom which I consider necessary. With every step I take, I glance furtively about me, in fear not for myself but for the possibility of continuing my constructive endeavors. I detect a variety of attempts to undermine the trust which the congregation has placed in me, and I must say that the thought of such a future fills me with fear . . .

—From Max Wiener,
Abraham Geiger and Liberal Judaism,
pp. 116–118.

From the Sermon Dedicating the New Temple of the West London Synagogue, 1842

The first solemn act, constituting us a "congregation of Jacob," has this day been performed. We have consecrated our synagogue to the worship of the Lord God of our fathers, to be henceforward, we trust, a beacon of light and a secure haven to the sons of Israel; and we have invoked a blessing on our house of prayer and upon all those who, with devout and grateful hearts, approach these precincts to seek the divine protection.

With these sacred sounds still in our ears, it might be well for us to retire to our homes, there to meditate on the goodness of Him, who has been with us in all our labors, suffered us to triumph over many difficulties, and permitted us to witness this day the realization of our fondest hopes . . .

Not, then, to weaken, but to strengthen our faith; not to trespass against, but to consolidate the great principles of that law which our fathers tremblingly heard amidst the thunders of Sinai—this synagogue has been established. Our unerring guide has been, and will continue to be, the sacred volume of the Scriptures; by that *alone* have we endeavored to regulate our principles.

In matters relating to public worship, we desire to reject nothing that bears the stamp of antiquity when that stamp is genuine and in accordance with the revealed will of God; nor to condemn anything because it is new, provided the newness of the measure be consonant with the spirit of the religion given us by the Almighty through Moses; a religion so framed as to adapt itself to all our destinies, in all their various phases, whether politically glorious on the throne of David, or politically prostrate in the thraldom of dispersion . . .

The time appointed for divine service is such as to enable the entire congregation, men, women, and children, to assemble prior to the commencement of prayer. The prayers will be read aloud by the minister [rabbi] only; appropriate psalms and hymns will be chanted by the choir, and responses made by the congregation. The reading of the Law will not be interrupted by the *Aliyah* [עֲלִיָּה, going up, the procession of readers called up in sequence to the Torah], for, as that institution has long lost its primary aim, the necessity for it no longer exists. Freewill offerings, unaccompanied by personal compliments, will be permitted in the synagogue on the three festivals of Passover, Pentecost [*Shavuot*], and Tabernacles [*Sukot*], as well as on such other days as occasions may require, after the book of the Law shall have been returned to the Ark.

It will be incumbent upon children of both sexes connected with this synagogue to be publicly confirmed in their faith at the age of thirteen years (if duly qualified); the catechetical [religious educational] exercises joined with this important ceremony will embrace the whole of the principles of the Jewish faith. As prayer will be offered up in Hebrew only and, as it is indispensable that every Israelite should perfectly understand the supplications he addresses to the Supreme Being, I confidently hope that the sacred language will be generally cultivated by both sexes of this congregation. The holy festivals will be celebrated on only those days commanded by God through our legislator Moses. The days commemorative of the great events of Jewish history will be duly observed.

Let it not be supposed that this house is intended as a synagogue of ease or convenience; that it has been established as a formal place of meeting for those who set at naught the declared will of God. No, my friends, such men need not labor for improvement; they need no sacrifice of time, ease, and means, to effect ameliorations in our religious worship, since any system will please that affords them a formal connection with a nominally religious community.

But for those who cherish a sincere love for their religion, who consider their well-being in this life and their immortal hopes hereafter to be indissolubly bound up in a rigid practical observance of the Mosaic Law, this synagogue has been reared.

—From W. Gunther Plaut,
The Rise of Reform Judaism,
pp. 47–48.

OTHER THINGS TO READ

Bamberger, Bernard J., *The Story of Judaism:* Chap. 41, "The Progress of Reform."

Browne, Lewis (ed.), *The Wisdom of Israel:* "The Words of Heinrich Heine," pp. 610–620.

Feuer, Leon I., and Azriel Eisenberg, *Jewish Literature since the Bible,* II: pp. 183–186 (Abraham Geiger); 211–218 (Heinrich Heine).

Fleg, Edmond, *The Jewish Anthology:* pp. 267–269 (views of Zunz and Geiger).

Jewish Encyclopedia: "Isaac Bernays," Vol. 3, pp. 90–91; "Abraham Geiger," Vol. 5, pp. 584–587; "Heinrich Heine," Vol. 6, pp. 327–330.

Levinger, Lee J., *A History of the Jews in the United States:* pp. 210–216 (early American Orthodoxy and Reform).

Philipson, David, "Geiger the Reformer," *Central Conference of American Rabbis Yearbook,* Vol. 20 (1910), pp. 246–283.

Philipson, David, *The Reform Movement in Judaism:* Chap. 3, "The Geiger-Tiktin Affair"; Chap. 4, "The Hamburg Temple Prayer Book Controversy"; Chap. 5, "Reform in England."

Plaut, W. Gunther, *The Rise of Reform Judaism:* pp. 39–50 (early Reform in Hamburg, Vienna, London); Chap. 3, "The Great Controversy: Tiktin vs. Geiger."

Schwartzman, Sylvan D., *Reform Judaism in the Making:* Chap. 6, "Reform Meets Major Opposition."

Standard Jewish Encyclopedia: "Isaac Bernays," p. 287; "Abraham Geiger," pp. 730–731; "Heinrich Heine," pp. 883–884.

Steinberg, Milton, *The Making of the Modern Jew:* Chap. 9, "Dissolution of Balance"; Chap. 10, "Suicide"; Chap. 11, "Dusk Children."

Universal Jewish Encyclopedia: "Isaac Bernays," Vol. 2, p. 226; "Abraham Geiger," Vol. 4, pp. 521–522; "Heinrich Heine," Vol. 5, pp. 297–301.

Wiener, Max, *Abraham Geiger and Liberal Judaism.*

SUGGESTED ACTIVITIES

1. Prepare an outline map of Western and Central Europe listing all the *major* cities. Then put a red circle around those in which a Reform

group operated. Run a line from each to a box outside the map and summarize the developments that occurred there.

2. Conduct a role-play of a scene between representatives of Rabbi Salomon Tiktin and Rabbi Abraham Geiger during some phase of their ministry in Breslau.

3. Produce a pamphlet describing the early history of your own temple. Be sure to include material on some of the main problems it faced and on the various stages through which it passed in developing its own religious practices and gaining acceptance in the community. Then, in a chart, compare these experiences with those of the West London Synagogue of British Jews.

SUBJECTS FOR RESEARCH

1. What decision about Jewish rights did the Congress of Vienna make following the downfall of Napoleon? How did this enable most European countries to revive the former restrictions?

2. Why exactly did Heinrich Heine, the great German writer, convert to Christianity? How did he react to his experience in later years? Did he ever successfully resolve the problems that led him to convert?

3. Read a biography of Abraham Geiger and see why, after growing up in a strictly Orthodox environment, he was attracted to Reform.

4. How, in spite of the opposition of the Board of Deputies of British Jews, did the West London Synagogue finally secure the right to have its rabbi perform marriages?

5. How is the Jewish community of Great Britain organized today? Does this still hamper the development of Reform and Conservative Judaism there? In what ways has the situation improved since the middle of the nineteenth century?

FILMSTRIPS TO SEE

David Einhorn: Father of the Union Prayerbook (UAHC), portraying the experiences in Europe of this American Reform pioneer.

Grandfather's World (Jewish Education Committee of New York), decribing through Yiddish literature the Jewish life of Eastern Europe as it existed several generations ago.

Judah the Prince: Teacher of Law (UAHC), presenting highlights in the life of this third-century scholar who succeeded in preparing the Mishnah.

Rav and Samuel: Teachers of Talmud (UAHC), picturing the activities of these famous heads of two Babylonian academies which contributed to the development of the Talmud.

A LIVE ISSUE

One of the more important problems with which the early Reformers wrestled was the observance of the Sabbath, and it is something that continues to trouble the movement. In fact, in 1965 the American Reform rabbinate devoted most of its annual convention to this very matter.

For centuries, traditional Judaism had successfully kept the Sabbath distinct from the rest of the week by prohibiting many kinds of activities and prescribing others. But, with emancipation and the break-up of the ghetto, as this chapter shows, most modern Jews eventually found it impossible to divorce themselves from the routine of Western society on Saturday and maintain the Sabbath in the traditional manner.

The Basic Problem: Observance of the Sabbath remains a serious religious obligation for Jews. Yet the realities of life in the Western world have compelled them to disregard the traditional prohibitions. The chief question, then, is whether the Sabbath can be observed at all by the modern Jew, and, if so, how?

Some Important Questions: (1) In view of the situation today, is it possible for most American Jews to maintain the Sabbath in the traditional way? (2) Yet is this essential to its observance? (3) Should our view of the Sabbath as a day of complete "rest" be replaced by some other interpretation? What, for instance? How, then, would the day be observed? (4) Should the Sabbath be commemorated chiefly on Friday night, thus making it possible for many more Jews to observe it? (5) Or, might it be preferable perhaps to have the Sabbath transferred to Sunday when many businesses are closed?

What Do You Think? As you read this chapter, you will find that these are some of the very questions the early Reformers raised. What answers did they propose, and how satisfactory were they? Which would you regard as worthwhile for today? What others could you suggest? What, then, do you think is the way to maintain the Sabbath in today's world?

7. TROUBLESOME QUESTIONS FOR REFORM

Questions to Be Answered

As the fourteen liberal rabbis gathered in Wiesbaden in the summer of 1837, they were deeply troubled. They found the opposition of the Orthodox growing ever more intense and discouraging many who otherwise would have been inclined to support synagogue reforms. Few of them, moreover, were prepared for the storm of abuse that rained down upon them. "A stumbling block before the people," they were called; "neither Jews nor Christians, but people without faith." Even the *cherem*, excommunication, was directed against them, as in 1836 when one of Europe's best-known rabbis issued this public pronouncement:

> **Avoid the pernicious company of these evil-doers, the innovators [Reformers] who have removed themselves far from God and His Law! Do not reside in their vicinity, and have no association with them.**

But the Reformers were also disturbed over the fact that they had not as yet been able to reach any agreement on a number of fundamental issues, particularly the following five:

—*Does Judaism give Reform the right to make changes?* The Orthodox reply was "no," but the Reformers were nevertheless introducing reforms in synagogue practice and religious belief. In what ways did Judaism itself validate their right to make changes?

—*What is essential in Judaism and therefore permanent?* From the Orthodox point of view, the answer was "everything," but this was hardly acceptable to Reform. Obviously, certain practices were outmoded, but were they to be preserved simply because they were said to be essential? What really was essential in Judaism and therefore permanent, and what was subject to change? And how could the one be distinguished from the other?

—*Is there any limit to the changes Reform may make?* The movement had already introduced a number of reforms in synagogue worship including the use of the organ and the vernacular, but some were demanding more sweeping changes, such as the elimination of the dietary laws and even circumcision. How far might the movement go without endangering Judaism itself? Or was there no limit whatever?

—*What particular changes does Judaism require?* Were reforms being introduced, as the Orthodox contended, merely to suit personal convenience and make Judaism less demanding or, as the Reformers insisted, because they were genuinely needed to preserve the Jew and his faith? But if changes were indeed necessary, where were they needed most?

—*Can Reform Judaism agree upon common principles and practices?* Thus far every liberal congregation seemed to be adopting the reforms it preferred, thereby opening the way to irresponsible change and possibly even chaos. To produce a stable, organized movement, Reform clearly had to reach some common agreement on principles and practices. What were these, and how could a liberal movement come to determine them?

In view of all this, Abraham Geiger realized that the meeting in Wiesbaden could not hope, as he put it, "to formulate a new Judaism nor to assume binding authority on those who attend. Rather," he declared "it is to afford honest men the opportunity of discussing the best methods of conducting their [rabbinical] office." In other words, the conference was designed mainly to explore the five major questions then troubling the movement.

It is not surprising, therefore, that no definite decisions were reached at the Wiesbaden Rabbinical Conference. In fact, from the very outset differences of opinion among the rabbis themselves and their fear that any action might lead to a permanent split among the Jewish people made this unlikely. Still, the meeting did enable a number of like-minded rabbis to discuss the principal issues and

recognize their importance to the future of Reform.

Question 1: Does Judaism Give Reform the Right to Make Changes?

Uppermost in the minds of those at Wiesbaden was the question of their authority to institute change. Repeatedly, the Orthodox had challenged Reform's right to make even minor modifications of synagogue worship since they viewed all existing practice as part of the sacred, God-given Oral Law which no human being could modify. "Whoever considers the Oral Law as subject to change," asserted one of Geiger's opponents, "is not to be considered a Jew but belongs to the sect of Karaites who separated themselves from the Jewish religion."

Karaism was a movement originating in the eighth century C.E. that rejected the authority of the Talmud and other rabbinical works which comprised the Oral Law. The name is derived from the Hebrew verb *kara* (קָרָא, "to read" the Bible) because the Karaites insisted that only the Bible, or Written Law, was God-given. The leaders of traditional Judaism quickly recognized the danger of Karaism, not only because it challenged the authority of the Oral Law but because they knew that rabbinic interpretation was absolutely essential to keep Judaism in touch with the changing conditions of life. Hence they fought the attempt to "return to the Bible," and within a few centuries succeeded in putting an end to the influence of Karaism.

The problem for the Reformers was to refute the charge of Karaism by showing that Judaism itself justified their right to introduce changes and that therefore those who supported reforms were not heretics. Abraham Geiger himself recognized this in an article called "The Judaism of Our Time and Its Aims," published in his own theological journal, in which he said:

> We need men who will show that Judaism has become what it is gradually and who will not hesitate to demonstrate by valid proofs that much which is now believed and observed . . . is the product of a certain age and can therefore be removed by time.

A response to his appeal was soon forthcoming. Reform's claim that it had the right to make changes was vigorously upheld by Leopold Zunz, one of the nineteenth-century's greatest Jewish scholars.

Zunz had served as a preacher at the Berlin Reform services held in the home of Jacob Herz Beer. When the Prussian government ordered them discontinued in 1823 on the grounds that they introduced unwarranted changes in Judaism, he embarked upon a scientific study of Jewish history and literature to determine whether Judaism in the past had ever permitted similar practices.

His reply took the form of a book published in 1832, *The Historical Development of the Jewish Sermon,* which quickly became a classic. Here he demonstrated that preaching in whatever language the people understood had been carried on by the early rabbis themselves in many localities. Moreover, he discovered that new prayers were constantly introduced into the ancient synagogue and that "prayers in the vernacular were permitted by all the authorities; yes, even commanded in certain instances."

Zunz's conclusion, then, was that Reform's efforts to improve the service were validated by historic Jewish practice and that some of the very same measures had been introduced by the early rabbis themselves. Indeed, he said that since synagogue observance developed through a process of change the Orthodox had no justification whatever for calling the Reformers "sinful." On the contrary, he wrote, "resistance to reforms in this field is to be regarded as stemming from prejudice and ignorance rather than from true knowledge."

Once begun by Zunz, the process of *Wissenschaft des Judentums,* the scientific study of Judaism, has since conclusively proved that Jews have always responded to the needs of different ages by introducing religious change. In fact, at one time or another, Judaism adopted many of the very same practices that the Orthodox often condemn.

With an affirmative answer to the first question, "Does Judaism give Reform the right to make changes?" the Reformers were reassured that they were pursuing the course historically taken by Judaism itself.

Question 2:
What Is Essential in Judaism?

Those at Wiesbaden realized that by endorsing religious change—especially eliminating

LEOPOLD ZUNZ. A great scholar of Judaism, he succeeded in proving beyond any doubt that Jewish practice had undergone certain changes historically. (HUC, American Jewish Archives)

outmoded practices—Reform was asserting that not all traditional observances were essential or, despite the Orthodox, commanded by God. For, if Jewish authorities in the past had considered every practice God-given, Judaism could never have undergone the changes it did. Common sense also indicated that certain practices were of greater consequence than others. Was not affirming the unity of God by reciting the *Shema,* for instance, more important than observing *tashlich* (תַּשְׁלִיךְ, "casting off" one's sins on the second day of Rosh Hashanah by shaking his garments before a body of water) or the prohibition against wearing *sha-atnez* (שַׁעַטְנֵז, "a mixture" of linen and wool)?

Indeed, practices which were no longer of value had to be abandoned if what was essential was to be preserved, which, said Geiger, was "Faith in the one holy and living God . . . that imbues man with a sense of higher striving for perfection . . . by sanctifying himself and becoming more godly . . . toward all mankind." All else, agreed Samuel Holdheim, another noted Reform rabbi of the period, was subject to change. New circumstances demand the reexamination of the forms Judaism has adopted in each age to express its beliefs and the modification of them where necessary.

He declared:

> Had the rabbis [of the Talmud] lived in our age and had they been influenced by its tendencies, as they were by the circumstances of their own times, they too would have explained the Bible in a different manner . . .

Thus, concluded the Reformers, the unmistakable essence of Judaism was its fundamental teachings about God and man, the relationship between them, the role of the Jew as the spokesman of God's ethical and moral demands, and the quality of each individual's life and conduct.

Question 3:
What Limits Are There to Change?

One of the main obstacles to agreement at Wiesbaden was the wide difference of opinion about how far Reform might go in making changes. Some, especially among Reform laymen, were prepared to carry them to extremes, and the prime example was those in the city of Frankfort who were shortly to form a society that would advocate the most radical kind of change.

Were we living in 1842, we would likely have heard many conversations such as the following one going on within the Frankfort Jewish community:

> "I was wondering whether you wouldn't want to join our Reform society?" the first man begins.
>
> "Not me!" replies the other man. "Look, I can agree with some of your ideas, such as having portions of the service in German, but your society is out to destroy Judaism!"
>
> "No, save it, you mean! Jewish life isn't going to survive in Frankfort unless we introduce a great many reforms. But the local synagogue won't consider any at all."
>
> "Reforms, you call them?" the other man breaks in. "You and your Reform society would do away with every Jewish observance if you were given the chance. I hear you don't even want a rabbi to conduct your services because he wouldn't be radical enough for you!"

Indeed, even those who were sympathetic to synagogue change were disturbed by the extremes of the Frankfort Reform Society. For in its statement of principles, it declared:

> 1. Judaism is not unchangeable; rather it is capable of developing in the light of new conditions.

2. **Various ritual practices, as well as the dietary laws, Jewish forms of dress and appearance [the beard, for example] are no longer binding.**

3. **Circumcision, as a religious act or symbol, is no longer required.**

4. **The Talmud is not recognized any longer as a source of authority for Jewish religious life.**

5. **Modern Jews no longer look forward to the coming of a Messiah who will lead them out of exile and back to Palestine. Instead, they regard the countries in which they dwell as their permanent and only homeland.**

The statements dealing with circumcision and the Talmud were particularly objectionable to responsible leaders of Reform who immediately labeled them ''too extreme,'' ''negative,'' and ''a step backward.'' Rabbi David Einhorn, who was to become one of the pioneers of Reform in America, termed them ''a confession of disbelief.''

Though the society soon withdrew its statements about the Talmud and circumcision, other incidents arose to discredit it further. No doubt the most damaging involved the refusal of certain members to have their children circumcised after several babies had died because of improper circumcision and the Frankfort Board of Health had adopted the following law:

If Jewish citizens desire to have their children circumcized, they must employ only persons who have been officially appointed as qualified to perform the rite.

This was interpreted by some society members to mean that Jews were now free to decide whether or not they wanted the rite performed, and they therefore refused to have their children circumcised. Orthodox and Reform leaders alike roundly condemned them,

calling the members of the society ''heretics'' and ''destroyers of Judaism.''

Shortly thereafter, the group went out of existence, but the attitude of others in Germany who shared similar views made the Reform movement all the more conscious of the need to set limits to change in order to avoid undermining Judaism.

Question 4:
What Changes Are Necessary?

By 1837, the year of the Wiesbaden Conference, Reform societies and congregations were beginning to spring up all over Europe. In some cases, as in Vienna where Isaac Mannheimer, one of the preachers at the Jacobson-Beer Berlin services, was rabbi, the reforms were quite modest. In others, as in Hamburg, they were much more extensive. Which, then, truly represented Reform?

Certainly, common agreement appeared necessary within the following six main areas in which reforms were being considered: synagogue worship, traditional prayers, Sabbath and holiday observance, the religious status of women, Jewish marriage and divorce laws, and Jewish mourning customs.

Synagogue Worship

Since most Jews no longer understood Hebrew, all Reformers were advocating some use of the vernacular in worship. They also sought to eliminate the constant hubbub during services and the rapid, often unintelligible, chanting of the prayers and Torah portion. In fact, during the Torah service it had almost become universal for people to leave the synagogue and converse with one another outside.

Reform Judaism—Then and Now

Reformers agreed that an orderly service was essential—a service conducted with decorum and providing a regular weekly sermon, the reading of the prayers, and a translation of the Torah portion. Most Reformers also advocated the singing of modern hymns in the vernacular as well as the use of the organ and a mixed choir of men and women.

To all of this, the Orthodox raised strong objection. They held, for example, that the use of an organ was prohibited because of the mourning for the destruction of the ancient Temple in Jerusalem where instrumental music had been part of the worship. Furthermore, to have a Jew play the organ on the Sabbath constituted "work"; and traditional restrictions against women in the synagogue ruled out any possibility of having a mixed choir.

In other instances, such as the introduction of modern hymns and the weekly sermon, the Orthodox were opposed simply because these were practices commonly carried on by non-Jews. From their point of view, that was sufficient to prohibit them.

Traditional Prayers

Reform Jews were generally dissatisfied with prayers in the traditional prayer book that dwelled on sacrifices and burnt-offerings or contained expressions of hostility toward non-Jews as a result of past persecution. All these, they said, were out of keeping with the spirit of the age.

They also objected to the customary repetition of numerous prayers which, they felt, simply added to the length of the service. For, even in Sabbath worship today, Orthodox congregations repeat the central portion of the liturgy, known as the Eighteen Benedictions, and recite four varieties of the *Kaddish* (קַדִּישׁ, Sanctification).

But the Reformers were much more critical of some of the beliefs contained in the traditional prayer book. One in particular was the hope that the Messiah, a powerful descendant of King David, would soon come to deliver the Jewish people from exile and to restore them to their ancient homeland in Palestine. There, enjoying permanent peace and prosperity, they would proceed to rebuild the Temple in Jerusalem and to reintroduce the ancient sacrificial worship. Even the righteous dead would be restored to life and rejoin their people. Then, according to this belief, all mankind would come to worship the one true God and witness the establishment of His everlasting Kingdom of justice, righteousness, and peace on earth.

The Reformers rejected such beliefs on three counts. First, they objected to the notion that Jews who now enjoyed citizenship should look upon themselves as exiles yearning to return to Palestine. Second, they felt that Judaism had outgrown the kind of worship that demanded animal and other types of sacrifices. Third, they found it hard to believe that the dead could be restored to life or that any single individual, even the Messiah, could so transform the world.

They subscribed, rather, to the idea of a "Messianic Age" for all mankind that would come about when every human being became wholly righteous and learned to live in harmony with his fellow men. Only then, they felt, would the world come to enjoy lasting peace and justice.

Yet, to the Orthodox, these beliefs were the essential teachings of the Oral Law, and to reject them was to deny the divinity of Torah itself.

Sabbath and Holiday Observance

Orthodox law prohibits thirty-nine major categories of "work" on the Sabbath, with many others growing out of them. Forbidden, for instance, are such things as turning on lights, cooking, the use of money, carrying a handkerchief, and numerous other acts. Even riding to the synagogue is forbidden.

Having originated in a totally different kind of society, many of these restrictions had now become impossible to carry out. People in large cities, for example, often resided too far from the synagogue to walk to services, and businessmen generally found it necessary to keep their businesses open on Saturday.

Keenly aware of this, the Reformers proposed a number of changes. Many were prepared to permit essential activities on the Sabbath, including riding to the synagogue, and some even advocated an additional service on Sunday so that Jews who worked on Saturday would have an opportunity to worship.

Holiday observance involved two special problems. One was the numerous traditional minor holidays, chiefly fast days, whose reason for continued observance Reform seriously questioned. Among them were days of mourning observed on the seventeenth of *Tamuz* (תַּמּוּז, the fourth month of the Hebrew calendar), when the Babylonians are said to have breached the walls of Jerusalem, and the tenth of *Tevet* (טֵבֵת, the tenth month of the Hebrew calendar), when Nebuchadnezzar began his siege of Jerusalem.

The second and more consequential issue involved the so-called "extra days" that had been added to all the major holidays except Yom Kippur. The result was that instead of celebrating just seven days of Passover, for example, as called for by the Bible, tradition required the observance of eight, and two days of Shavuot instead of one.

The practice had originated in Roman times when the majority of Jews began living in the Diaspora, that is, in countries outside of Palestine. Unsettled conditions sometimes made it difficult to notify them that the new moon, marking the start of a Hebrew month, had

been officially observed in Jerusalem, and without this information there was danger of celebrating a holiday on the wrong day. To protect against this, the rabbis prescribed that Jews living in the Diaspora should observe all of the major holidays for an extra day.

Now that the Jewish calendar could be scientifically calculated far in advance, the Reformers saw no further reason to retain the extra days and advocated observing only the days called for by the Bible.

Religious Status of Women

Historically Judaism had always respected women as wives and mothers, but it did not confer equal religious rights and responsibilities upon them. Thus, where traditional Judaism is strictly observed, they may not sit with men at worship, serve as witnesses in matters connected with Jewish ritual, or be included in a *minyan* (מִנְיָן, number), the quorum of ten adults required for public worship. Nor may they take an active part in the service, such as leading the congregation in prayer or reading from the Torah. Furthermore, until the present century, most Orthodox women were compelled to sit in less desirable sections of the synagogue, generally the balcony, and few ever received a formal Jewish education.

The Reformers called for giving women full religious rights. Orthodox practice, they argued, had originated in the Orient where women were considered inferior, but, in keeping with the spirit of the Western world, Judaism should recognize the complete equality of the sexes.

Jewish Marriage and Divorce Laws

Traditional marriage and divorce laws also put Jewish women at a great disadvantage. An example is the case of the *agunah* (עֲגוּנָה,

"tied" to a missing husband), the wife whose husband has disappeared and is presumed dead. If unable to produce any witnesses to his death, she can never remarry. As a result, many Jewish women whose husbands were killed in battle or who left home and were never heard from again have had to suffer in loneliness and misery.

Jewish women are also penalized by the traditional regulations that require a religious divorce in addition to a decree granted by the state. According to Jewish law, however, only the man can grant a divorce, or *get* (גֵּט, legal document), and it must be received in writing before the woman can remarry. Hence husbands often demand money or property before consenting to give their wives a *get*.

The institution of levirate marriage, which requires the brother of a husband who has died without children to marry the widow, creates further difficulties. Should her brother-in-law refuse, she must engage in the ceremony of *chalitzah* (חֲלִיצָה, "removing" a shoe) in which she removes his shoe, spits at him, and says, "Thus shall be done to the man who will not build [perpetuate] his brother's house." Failure to locate the brother-in-law or his refusal to participate in the ceremony means that the widow can never remarry.

The Reformers realized how unjust these practices were to women, and they also objected to certain features of the traditional wedding ceremony. One was the minor role assigned the bride in the wedding itself, since during the Orthodox ceremony only the man is permitted to speak or present a ring. But far greater dissatisfaction was voiced over the requirement of a marriage contract, called a *ketubah* (כְּתוּבָה, a "written" document), specifying the sum of money the groom must provide for his wife in the event she is widowed or divorced. Though originally introduced by Judaism as a reform designed to protect the woman, the *ketubah* was now looked upon as an unnecessary piece of commercialism in the wedding because married

women's rights were increasingly being protected by the courts under civil law.

The Reformers urged that only the most essential Jewish marriage and divorce regulations be retained, leaving all legal considerations, such as certifying the death of a missing husband, to the courts. They also called for an end to such practices as *chalitzah* that imposed disabilities on women, suggested certain modification of the *ketubah,* and recommended greater participation by the bride in the wedding ceremony.

Jewish Mourning Customs

Were you to visit an Orthodox family in mourning, you would find them observing the following customs throughout a seven-day period:

—They do not rise in greeting those who call on them.

—They sit on the floor or on low stools.

—They do not bathe, shave, or cut their hair.

—They wear no shoes or leather footwear of any kind.

—Their clothing has a small cut or tear.

—They do not leave the house to attend to business or personal affairs.

All this is part of "sitting *shivah*" (שִׁבְעָה), or observing "the seven" days of intense mourning for the dead.

The Reformers questioned most of these practices, asking in what way they actually contributed to a genuine spirit of mourning. Many also recommended a shorter mourning period in view of the financial hardship the seven days of *shivah* often caused a family.

MARRIAGE CONTRACT (*KETUBAH*). This particular *ketubah* comes from Florence, Italy, and dates from 1823. (Darmstaedter)

Why Reform Sought Changes

	The Situation in Orthodoxy	Why Reform Desired Changes
Synagogue Worship	Ritual entirely in Hebrew. Long, repetitive service with all prayers chanted. Organ and mixed choir barred. Lack of decorum.	All-Hebrew service difficult to follow. Service lengthy because of repetition. Rapid chanting made worship unintelligible. Reformers sought inspiring synagogue music, a shorter service, and decorum.
Traditional Prayers	Prayed for the coming of a personal Messiah to deliver the Jews from "exile" and restore them to Palestine. Prayed for the rebuilding of the Temple and restoration of sacrifices. Dead to be restored to life and return to Palestine.	As citizens, Jews no longer considered themselves in "exile" or desired to return to Palestine. Judaism had outgrown worship involving sacrifices and burnt-offerings, or belief in a personal Messiah and resurrection of the dead. Many preferred to believe that the Messianic Age would come only through the activities of all men in behalf of a righteous society.
Sabbath and Holiday Observance	No riding to the synagogue permitted on the Sabbath. Sabbath "rest" prohibited many types of activities. Extra days added to the major Jewish holidays. Observance of a great number of minor holidays, chiefly fast days.	Some Jews lived too far to walk to the synagogue on the Sabbath. Modern conditions required many to work on the Sabbath, thus preventing them from attending worship. Since the calendar could now be determined long in advance, there was no reason for retaining the extra days of the holidays. Most minor holidays seemed no longer necessary.

Question 5: How to Achieve a Common Reform Program?

By 1844, some twenty-five liberal rabbis were officiating in Germany. Some served Reform congregations, a few operated with Reform societies located in such prominent cities as Berlin and Breslau. Most of them, however, functioned within traditional synagogues, which, under their influence, had already begun to liberalize their practice.

Programs of religious change differed from place to place. Some offered only minor modifications; others, like that of the Frankfort Reform Society, went to extremes. Meanwhile, some liberal rabbis were busy revising the prayer book according to their own views, and every Reform temple and society proceeded to adopt the practices it preferred.

It was becoming apparent that without

in Jewish Practice

	The Situation in Orthodoxy	Why Reform Desired Changes
The Religious Status of Women	Women compelled to sit by themselves in a special synagogue section. Women barred from conducting the service. Women not counted toward a *minyan* or permitted to testify as witnesses in ritual matters. Formal religious education not generally provided for girls.	Reform maintained that the traditional position of women had originated in the East. Jews should now adopt the more modern Western standard of granting religious equality to women in worship and education.
Jewish Marriage and Divorce Laws	Many Jewish laws regulating marriage and divorce. Women disadvantaged by certain Jewish wedding practices. Special problems involving the *agunah* and *chalitzah*.	Now that Jews were citizens and subject to civil law, some of the Jewish marriage and divorce laws made for confusion. Jewish laws and practices that worked special hardships on women were not in keeping with the times.
Jewish Mourning Customs	Mourners required to make a small cut in one of their garments, sit on the ground, and refrain from shaving, bathing, and wearing shoes. Mourners expected to observe a seven-day intense mourning period.	Traditional mourning customs were not suitable expressions of grief for modern Jews. A seven-day mourning period frequently caused serious hardship to the family.

some agreement on principles and practices, the Reform movement faced an uncertain future. Geiger was aware of the problem when he wrote to a colleague:

> **Whatever we [Reformers] have achieved in the past, we owe to the courageous pioneering of individuals. The trouble is only that in such decisions, separately made, an agreement reached by most participants is absolutely required.**

But how could this be achieved? The only answer, some insisted, was to call another conference of rabbis. Perhaps now, seven years after Wiesbaden, it was possible to reach common agreement on a number of matters.

On to Brunswick!

The call for such a meeting was eventually sounded in the form of the following editorial by Ludwig Philippson, a liberal rabbi of

Magdeburg (a sizable community in central Germany) and editor of the most widely read Jewish weekly of the times, the *General News of Judaism:*

THE TIME IS NOW!

Let us speak plainly. The issue is no longer the permissibility or non-permissibility of this or that change in synagogue practice or Jewish regulation. The issue before us concerns the entire content of our religion in order to rescue it from deadening rigidity on the one hand and from complete non-belief on the other.

Every day Jewish laymen keep asking us [the liberal rabbis], "What are you doing about the situation?" Our answer must be forthcoming soon. The time is now! We must convene a conference of rabbis without delay to deal with the religious issues of our day!

The objects of such a conference should be, first, to bring the rabbis together to become better acquainted with one another's opinions; second, to agree upon the role rabbis must play in the present situation; third, to decide to create necessary Jewish institutions, such as a modern rabbinical seminary; and, fourth, to discuss the religious needs of the day, looking to agreement on a common program.

The time is now!

The editorial met with enthusiastic response from practically all the liberal rabbis of Germany and neighboring countries, and Philippson was encouraged to write the Jewish community of Brunswick for permission to hold the conference there. Official approval was soon forthcoming and the date of the meeting announced.

As the time for the conference approached, the rabbis were optimistic. Most were convinced that at Brunswick they would finally succeed in settling many of Judaism's most pressing problems.

QUESTIONS FOR DISCUSSION

1. Why was the *cherem,* or ban of excommunication, effective with the Jews of the Middle

LUDWIG PHILIPPSON. Widely-known editor of a Jewish periodical at whose call the Brunswick Conference was held.

Ages? How successful was its use against the Reformers? To what extent would the *cherem* be effective today? Why?

2. How do Orthodox and Reform Jews differ in their views of the way in which Jewish beliefs and practices developed? How does the interpretation of the Reform Jew justify the various changes he has made in worship?

3. What do you consider the most important beliefs of Judaism? Why can these never change? Are there any observances that are also essential? Which? Why do you consider these permanent?

4. Why did most of the Reformers look upon the members of the Frankfort Reform Society as radicals? Do *you* regard their principles as extreme? Why? In the light of your answer, how do you explain the reaction of the Reform rabbis of their day?

5. What were the early Reformers' objections to traditional synagogue practice and Sabbath and holiday observance? Judging from the services in your own temple, how has Reform overcome them?

6. In what ways are the attitudes of the early Reformers toward the religious status of women reflected in the present practices of your own temple? Why is the Reform attitude toward women even more important today?

SIGNIFICANT DOCUMENTS

A Traditional Prayer Eliminated by the Hamburg Prayer Book, 1841

From the "Additional Service for the Festivals"

On account of our sins we have been exiled from our land [Palestine] and removed far from our country and we are unable to go up [there] in order to appear and prostrate ourselves before Thee and fulfill our obligations in Thy chosen house, that great and holy Temple . . .

May it be Thy will, O Lord our God and God of our fathers, merciful King, that Thou mayest again in Thine abundant mercy have pity upon us and upon Thy sanctuary and mayest speedily rebuild it and magnify its glory.

Our Father, our King, speedily reveal the glory of Thy kingdom. Be glorified and exalted over us in the sight of all the living. Bring together our scattered people from among the nations and wondrously gather our dispersed ones from the ends of the earth. Bring us in joy to Zion, Thy city, to Jerusalem, the site of Thy sanctuary, with everlasting rejoicing.

There let us offer up before Thee our required burnt-offerings and our daily sacrifices in proper order. There in love we shall perform the additional sacrifice for Thee according to Thy commandment, as Thou hast written it for our sake in Thy Torah by means of Moses, Thy servant, out of Thy glorious mouth: "On the Sabbath, [you shall offer up] two perfect year-old lambs, and two measures of meal mixed with oil, and its appropriate libation. This is both the Sabbath and daily burnt-offering that shall be offered up regularly with their proper libation . . . "

—Adapted from the translation by S. Singer, *The Standard Prayer Book,* p. 339.

From the "Declaration of Principles" of the Frankfort Reform Society, 1842

In our day the difference between the inner truth of Judaism and its external form has become especially acute. Nurtured by the intellectual culture of the age, many of those who are accounted members of the Mosaic religious community have arrived at the conviction that most of the practical commands, the observance of which constitutes the bulk of present-day Judaism, rest on human and temporary premises. They claim rightfully that this external form is for the most part without significance—yes, even unworthy of pure religion—and they draw the inner content of divine truth, which an earlier generation found in the Law, from those treasures of wisdom alone which have won over to the truth so many great spirits of all nations. Thus thousands have renounced allegiance to talmudic rabbinical Judaism and are connected outwardly with the Mosaic religious community only by habit or by the control of the state or by family ties.

This condition of affairs is destructive and immoral; for as long as a man lives in a community, he should not pass as something altogether different externally from what he is in thought and inner conviction. The Jew who has grown indifferent to his religion on this account must decide whether he will continue to be known merely as a Jew by birth, thus sacrificing free will to habit and being deprived of all outward religious association that is expressive of his inner conviction, or whether, longing for some tangible form, he will join some other religious association. . . . But those who cannot content themselves with either of these alternatives will pin their faith to the belief in the capacity of Judaism for development and, instead of continuing in a state of indolent lethargy, will aim to harmonize their spiritual convictions with their professions. . . .

Moved by these considerations, a number of German Israelites have determined to give expression to their opinions of the present conditions in Judaism through a public declaration and to renounce formally their allegiance to all objectionable commands and to all antiquated customs, which to all intents and purposes they have rejected long ago.

Least of all is it our desire to hurt the susceptibilities of the strict adherents of rabbinical Judaism. Let us hope that success will crown this, our honest endeavor, not only to give our religion a worthier form but also to expound the pure content of Judaism and to remove from it everything which has degraded and dishonored it in the eyes of thinking men.

Every participant in this movement feels already great inner satisfaction in that he has chosen his standpoint in reference to the highest spiritual interests and has paid allegiance to the truth. Let us begin bravely, then, a task not only necessary from the civic standpoint and intellectually justified but also highly moral and, in all truth, pleasing to God.

—From David Philipson,
The Reform Movement in Judaism,
pp. 121–122.

A Modern Liberal Rabbi's Reaction to the Traditional Requirements for a Jewish Divorce, 1967

. . . Rigidity in the matter of the *get* borders on the inhuman. To condemn Jews who resort to civil divorce, without suggesting that the *halachah* [traditional Jewish law] on the subject of the *get* be modified, is bad enough. But it is sheer inhumanity and unforgivable, a genuine sin, to brand children born of Jewish women who remarry after a civil divorce as *mamzerim* [מַמְזֵרִים], bastards.

Our sages, I am confident, who were compassionate, would be the last to hold the *get* as sacrosanct . . . if they were living, as we do today, in a radically different environment and in an age when the minutiae of legal distinctions have lost their validity and when they appear inconsequential to the masses of our people. I am confident that the Almighty, who is merciful, regards children of such a union, despite the *halachah,* as perfectly legitimate, as much so as those who were born to people who remarry after having obtained a twelve-line Aramaic document.

For a *get* is nothing more than twelve lines written by a scribe in Aramaic, which the husband alone can authorize, and which he alone can give his wife when he chooses to divorce her. The exclusive right of divorce is vested in him. When he refuses to issue the document, there is practically nothing in Jewish law which can compel him to do so. The wife may find him revolting, but she cannot divorce him, or ever regain her freedom. This *per se* is fiercely unjust, a survival of primitive times. The injustice is compounded, however, when the husband demands an extortionate sum for the *get,* which is quite a common phenomenon of our day. In the face of such a situation, can anyone blame or condemn Jewish women for going to civil courts when they are obliged to end an unhappy marriage?

It is precisely such rigidity, such absolute refusal upon the part of our [traditional] rabbinical authorities to face reality which has made the *halachah* in our day not only irrelevant but unfortunately often even inhuman. No legislation can remain sacred, respected, and honored, when it ceases to serve the needs of the people. What Hillel did with the *prozbul* which allows a debt to remain in force after the seventh year, and what rabbinic authorities have done with interest charges which the Torah prohibits, should have been done long ago with the *get,* which, in the case of the *agunah,* deserted wife, has been the cause of indescribable human misery. . . .

Why not apply in these trying situations, where human happiness and the status of children are at stake, the rabbinic principle, *Dina de Malkhuta Dina* [Aramaic] (דִּינָא דְמַלְכוּתָא דִּינָא, "the law of the land is binding and valid")? In view of this principle, is it not unjust to dismiss a civil divorce as of no account and to deem the woman who remarried after obtaining it as still being affianced to the spouse from whom the civil courts divorced her? Is it not infinitely more moral and more humane to hold that a civil divorce is valid, even though objectionable from a Jewish point of view, and that children born to such a woman are legitimate, instead of stigmatizing them as *mamzerim,* bastards?

Is it not about time to grant the woman the right to sue and to obtain a divorce, a right which the husband now enjoys exclusively? Is it not about time to confess that the *halachah* surrounding the *get* is antiquated and unjust to the woman?

—From Rabbi Theodore N. Lewis, "Journal of a Rabbi" (book review), *The Reconstructionist,* Vol. 33, No. 13 (November 3, 1967), pp. 29, 30.

A Letter from the Brunswick Jewish Community Requesting Permission to Hold a Rabbinical Conference, and the Reply, 1844

1. The Request

To the honorable city council of the city of Brunswick. From the directors of the local Jewish community concerning a projected rabbinical assembly.

We have the honor to transmit to the honorable city council a letter which has been addressed to us by Rabbi Dr. Philippson of Magdeburg (of March 26). This letter expresses the desire to hold a projected meeting of several rabbis and Jewish clergymen in June of this year and asks us, in case we would be willing, to take the necessary steps and procure the permission of the respective official body.

As far as we are concerned, we declare that we are not only agreed that the meeting take place here but at the same time we are very willing indeed to do everything in order to make the visit of these gentlemen here most pleasant and to justify the flattering confidence they have put in us. We greatly value in every respect the noble and self-sacrificing striving of these honored clergymen and we hope that much good will come to our coreligionists from such an assembly, especially in respect to the possible resolution of different points of view through friendly discussion. This will also bring about that the reforms of our ritual, which in almost all congregations have either already taken place or are in the process of being introduced, would take a common direction as a result of progressive education.

Our gracious national government, together with our honored city council, has in the past constantly encouraged and protected all that which we have permitted ourselves to suggest for the welfare of our community and has done so with such truly fatherly concern that we confidently expect the granting of today's respectful request, namely:

That the city council be kindly pleased to intercede with the Ducal Ministry of State and obtain for us the permission for an assembly in June, in the city of Brunswick, of the projected assembly of several rabbis and Jewish clergymen.

Since time is very short to make the necessary preparations and to obtain a suitable locale for the assembly, and since a part of the rabbis and clergymen who live far away would each one in his own realm of activity have to make a number of preparations for such a journey, we add the most respectful request for the early disposal of this matter and remain your obedient servants of the honorable city council.

DIRECTORS OF THE JEWISH COMMUNITY

Brunswick, April 1, 1844

2. The Reply

We transmit to you herewith a copy of the letter of the Ducal Ministry of State of the twelfth of this month, from which you will see that there is no objection to the gathering of various rabbis in our city.

THE BRUNSWICK CITY COUNCIL
Brunswick, April 16, 1844

—From W. Gunther Plaut,
The Rise of Reform Judaism,
pp. 75–76.

OTHER THINGS TO READ

Bamberger, Bernard J., *The Story of Judaism:* Chap. 40, "The Science of Judaism"; Chap. 41, "The Progress of Reform"; Chap. 42, "Philosophies of Judaism."

Feuer, Leon I., and Azriel Eisenberg, *Jewish Literature since the Bible,* II: pp. 183–186 (Geiger's views on Reform).

Fleg, Edmund, *The Jewish Anthology:* "The Need of a Jewish Reform," pp. 304–317.

Freehof, Solomon B., *Reform Jewish Practice,* Vol. I: "Public Worship," "Marriage and Divorce," "Burial and Mourning."

Jewish Encyclopedia: "Agunah," Vol. 1, pp. 275–276; "Divorce," Vol. 4, pp. 624–628; "Levirate Marriage," Vol. 8, pp. 45–46; "Marriage," Vol. 8, pp. 347–349; "Mourning," Vol. 9, pp. 101–103; "Sabbath," Vol. 10, pp. 591–602; "Leopold Zunz," Vol. 12, pp. 699–704.

Philipson, David, *The Reform Movement in Judaism:* Chap. 6, "The Frankfort Society of the Friends of Reform."

Plaut, W. Gunther, *The Rise of Reform Judaism:* pp. 74–76 (the call for the Brunswick Conference); 107–111 (the science of Judaism); 142–145 (Messiah); Chap. 7, "Worship Reform"; Chap. 8, "Sabbath and Holiday Observance"; pp. 206–211 (circumcision); 215–219 (marriage regulations); 223–225 (mourning practices); 252–255 (religious status of women).

Schwartzman, Sylvan D., *Reform Judaism in the Making:* Chap. 7, "The Need for Reform Direction."

Standard Jewish Encyclopedia: "Divorce," pp. 567–568; "Covering of the Head," pp. 504–505; "Levirate Marriage," p. 1197; "Marriage," pp. 1272–1273; "Messiah," pp. 1308–1309; "Mourning," pp. 1369–1370; "Music," pp. 1375–1377; "Leopold Zunz," p. 1976.

Universal Jewish Encyclopedia: "Agunah," Vol. 1, pp. 132–133; "Divorce," Vol. 3, pp. 577–580; "Covering of Head," Vol. 5, pp. 262–263; "Levirate Marriage," Vol. 6, p. 638; "Marriage," Vol. 7, pp. 370–376; "Messiah," Vol. 7, pp. 499–503; "Mourning," Vol. 8, pp. 28–31; "Musical Instruments," Vol. 8, pp. 55–56; "Sabbath," Vol. 9, pp. 295–299; "Leopold Zunz," Vol. 10, pp. 677–679.

Wiener, Max, *Abraham Geiger and Liberal Judaism:* pp. 107–110, 265–269 (science of Judaism).

SUGGESTED ACTIVITIES

1. Attend a Sabbath service in an ultra-Orthodox synagogue and compare its practices with those of your own temple. In what ways are they similar? How do they differ? Transfer your findings to a series of slides or transparencies that you can show the class.

2. Compare the English translation of the Orthodox Sabbath morning service with that of the *Union Prayer Book?* Then, in chart form, indicate some of the major similarities and differences.

3. Attend an Orthodox wedding or other life-cycle observance, such as a *Berit, Bar Mitzvah,* or

funeral, and compare it with the corresponding Reform ceremony. Then briefly prepare a magazine article on that practice, explaining the differences and the Reform principles that seem to be involved.

SUBJECTS FOR RESEARCH

1. What were some of the differences in point of view expressed by various liberal rabbis in Wiesbaden, and why did these make it so difficult for the Reform movement to achieve a common program?

2. Why and how was Abraham Kohn, a Reform rabbi of Lemberg, poisoned by Orthodox fanatics?

3. What in general was the Reform point of view of Samuel Holdheim, who ultimately became the rabbi of the extremely liberal Berlin Reform congregation?

4. In view of Abraham Geiger's own attitude toward circumcision, why did he react against the refusal of several members of the Frankfort Reform Society to have their children circumcized?

5. What was the background and position of Ludwig Philippson, and why was his appeal for a rabbinical conference so well received?

FILMSTRIPS TO SEE

David Einhorn: Father of the Union Prayerbook (UAHC), describing some of the situations that this early American Reform leader faced in Europe.

Isaac Mayer Wise: Master Builder of American Judaism (UAHC), picturing some of the circumstances in Europe that prompted this American Reform pioneer to emigrate to the United States.

The Jewish Wedding in Art (UAHC), showing many features of the traditional Jewish marriage rites.

The Sabbath in Art (UAHC), describing many aspects of traditional Sabbath observance.

The Jewish Home (Jewish Education Committee of New York), portraying the customs practiced in observant Orthodox Jewish homes.

Torah in Jewish Life (Jewish Education Committee of New York), depicting the role of the Torah in the history of the Jewish people.

A LIVE ISSUE

A wide difference of opinion exists among Reform Jews today over the extent to which changes are needed in their faith's beliefs and practices. Some support only the most modest reforms, while others insist that quite radical changes are essential to meet present conditions.

This situation is by no means new. In fact, as we shall see in this chapter, the early leaders of the movement were just as sharply divided into two factions over how far change should go.

The Basic Problem: Now, just as then, one group is made up of those we will call "moderates," who stress the importance of religious continuity. Hence they rely on a slower, evolutionary process in which change is kept to a minimum. The so-called "radicals," on the other hand, generally advocate drastic changes on the grounds that new circumstances demand vastly different means of religious expression. They find unsatisfactory the minor changes introduced by the moderates.

Hence the movement finds itself divided between these two points of view.

Some Important Questions: (1) What justification do you find for the more moderate Reform point of view, and what are some of its shortcomings? (2) What are the arguments in favor of the more extreme or "radical" position, and what are some of its weaknesses? (3) Should Reform Judaism consistently follow one or the other, or is some compromise between the two preferable? What? (4) Specifically, then, what position would you have the movement take today regarding changes, for instance, in the *Union Prayer Book?*

What Do You Think? In this chapter, you will be confronted by both points of view among the more important leaders of nineteenth-century Reform in Europe. Consider the arguments carefully. Which position do you find more satisfactory in dealing with religious change, and which would you have the movement adopt today?

8.

SOME LEADING EUROPEAN REFORMERS

Aaron Chorin Is Unable to Attend

As the Brunswick Rabbinical Conference opened on June 12, 1844, almost every Reform leader was on hand. Missing, however, were some of the former ones, like Israel Jacobson, who were no longer alive and others too old to attend. One of these was Aaron Chorin, a seventy-eight-year-old liberal Hungarian rabbi who was seriously ill but sent a message of support to the meeting.

Chorin was well-known to those at Brunswick. For over forty years he had been a champion of Reform, often under the most difficult circumstances. As early as 1803, he had written a book declaring it possible to introduce changes into Judaism and, when he refused to retract his statements, his traditional colleagues had him stoned in the courtyard of the synagogue.

Though temporarily forced to give in, he soon renewed his call for changes in worship. Not only did he advocate prayers in the vernacular and the use of an organ—reforms he had already introduced into his own Hungarian congregation—but he also upheld the Jew's right to travel on the Sabbath when it was essential and urged modifications of Jewish mourning practices.

When the newly-formed Hamburg Temple was under attack, Chorin was among its staunchest defenders. He encouraged the members and justified their reforms by citing passages from the traditional sources themselves, for which the Orthodox roundly condemned him in such public statements as:

> . . .We know this Rabbi Aaron Chorin. He is a man of only mediocre knowledge in Talmud and commentaries, and far be it from us to lean on his pronouncements. Indeed, we know this man and his character! Who can rely on this kind of a person? . . .

Nevertheless, for the rest of his life he persisted in expressing his convictions about the need for religious change, with considerable effect upon liberally inclined Jews in Hungary, Austria, and Germany. Characteristic was the following message he sent to a conference of Hungarian rabbis just eleven days before his death:

> . . .The permanent elements of religion must be expressed in terms that appeal to the people and are consonant with the needs of life . . .
>
> I need not tell you that of all the external institutions the public [worship] service demands our immediate and undivided attention. He who is faithful to his God and is earnestly concerned for the welfare of his religion must exert himself to rescue our service from the ruin into which it has fallen and to give it once again that inspiring form which is worthy of a pious and devout worship of the one true God . . .

Abraham Kohn, Martyr to Reform

Another noted Reformer who was missing was Abraham Kohn, who had attended the earlier meeting in Wiesbaden. Having just accepted a new position in Lemberg, an important Jewish community of Eastern Europe, he found it impossible to be present.

Kohn, who was born in 1806 in Bohemia, was already a brilliant talmudist by the age of twelve. But he was also determined to obtain a good secular education as well, and he pursued secular studies secretly at night, rarely getting more than four hours sleep. Later on, while trying to support himself as a student at the University of Prague, he almost died of starvation.

Eventually, he was called to serve a small congregation in Austria where he interested himself in the question of reform. Soon he was writing articles for Geiger's *Scientific Journal for Jewish Theology,* urging, for instance, the elimination of certain mourning customs that had no basis in either the Bible or Talmud. At the Wiesbaden gathering, he insisted that traditional Judaism never intended to separate religion from life and that "only good" would "follow from . . . [Reform's] endeavor to rejuvenate the reli-gious forms and to reestablish the necessary harmony between life and faith."

At the time Kohn accepted the pulpit in Lemberg, he had also been invited by two prominent German congregations, but he recognized the greater challenge of Eastern Europe where religious liberalism had made little headway. But no sooner did he arrive there than persecution by the Orthodox began. He was insulted in public and forced to appear in court to answer a series of false accusations. At one point, his supporters had to press charges of malicious slander against one of his adversaries.

In 1848, after Kohn had spent four years in Lemberg, his opponents finally resorted to poisoning the family's dinner. Though the others recovered, the rabbi and his youngest child died, thus becoming martyrs to the Reform cause.

Gabriel Riesser, Reform's Most Distinguished Layman

Another Reformer absent at Brunswick was Gabriel Riesser, but only because he was not a rabbi. He was unquestionably one of the outstanding leaders in the fight for universal freedom and Reform's most distinguished spokesman.

Ironically, Riesser was the grandson of the chief-rabbi of Hamburg who had banned the reading of Mendelssohn's translation of the Bible. After completing law school in Germany, he was not admitted to the bar because he was a Jew, and this moved him to devote his life to the struggle for political and social freedom for everyone. Equality for the Jews, as he saw it, was merely part of the wider issue of freedom for all people, and he called upon his fellow Jews to "strive with word and deed for universal civil emancipation."

Nonetheless, he was particularly sensitive to the matter of Jewish rights and quick to take up the battle in his books, speeches, and in the periodical he published that he deliberately named *The Jew*. He objected above all to the claim that Germany was a "Christian country" and that Jews belonged to a different nationality. "To what other state do we German Jews owe our loyalty?" Riesser challenged his opponents. "Either we are Germans or we are men without a country!"

He fought for equality for Jews in each of the independent states then comprising Germany. Thus, in the early 1830's, he protested against the actions of one of the legislatures for failing to remove restrictions against them and presented a petition to the Senate of Hamburg demanding their citizenship. In 1842 he exposed the plan of the Prussian government to segregate Jews by grouping them in separate "corporations."

Following the revolution in 1848, in which at great personal risk Riesser took an active role, he was elected vice president of the German National Assembly and succeeded in removing the last restrictions against the Jews. But the new regime was short-lived and within two years he and many of his fellow liberals had to flee the country. Ultimately, however, his services to the cause of freedom were recognized and he became the first Jew to be appointed a judge in Germany.

Meanwhile, Riesser had foreseen that emancipation would require a more modern form of Judaism that at the same time had to remain thoroughly Jewish. Hence he ardently supported the reforms of the Hamburg Temple but opposed the radicalism of the Frankfort Reform Society. He also disapproved of unyielding Orthodoxy and, in defending Abraham Geiger against his opponents in Breslau, warned Tiktin's followers:

. . . **Those who battle for traditional opinions should recognize that personal persecution, intrigue, and slander have as their own result the dishonoring and shaming of the cause they seek to serve** . . .

Probably more than in any other way, however, Riesser advanced the Reform cause in nineteenth-century Europe by serving as the model of a political and religious liberal for large numbers of his fellow Jews.

Ludwig Philippson
Present at Brunswick

Who then were among those present at the Brunswick Conference? Naturally, Ludwig Philippson, who had arranged the meeting, was there.

He was the son of a publisher who at one time had taught at the Jewish Free School of Dessau. Even in his youth, Philippson gave promise of becoming a fine scholar when, at the age of fifteen, he produced a translation of several of the prophets. At twenty-two he was made rabbi of Magdeburg, where he began publishing his *General News of Judaism*, a weekly that he edited until his death in 1889. Its two purposes, as he stated in one of the early issues, were:

1. **To aid us [the Jews] in obtaining equal civil status and complete civil rights that will afford us the opportunity to amalgamate ourselves with the general population.**

2. **To expand our religion, to transplant the institutions of antiquity into the new age, and to have the requirements of the new age make their voice heard as they concern the institutions of antiquity.**

Like Riesser whom he greatly admired, he took an active part in German political life and was elected to the city council of Magdeburg. Also prominent in Reform circles, he pressed as early as 1837 for the establishment of a Jewish seminary to train liberal rabbis and teachers, something that was not achieved for nearly a half-century.

In general, Philippson took a middle-of-the-road position between those who advocated radical reforms and those who accepted only the most minor changes. Typical of his views was this statement he made about the use of German in the service:

> **All extremes must be avoided . . . Nobody wants to eliminate Hebrew altogether and no one opposes the introduction of German . . . Therefore Hebrew and German elements must both be contained in the service . . .**

Not surprisingly, his position was quite different from some of the others at Brunswick, who ran from one extreme to the other.

At the Extremes: Leopold Schott and Samuel Holdheim

Perhaps the most conservative of all the delegates was Leopold Schott, rabbi of a tiny community near the Swiss border. The most radical was unquestionably Samuel Holdheim, then of Mecklenburg-Schwerin, in northern Germany.

From the outset, Schott reacted to practically every change suggested at Brunswick as though it grew out of a sense of hostility toward Judaism itself. "Shall we always see Reform as negating, doing away with this Jewish practice or that?" he said in protest against proposals for reforms. "We must take a more positive stand in support of those [existing] rites that unite Jewry."

On the opposite side stood Holdheim, chief spokesman for the so-called radical Reform. "Anything which upon unbiased, careful scientific study contradicts the religious consciousness of the present age," he asserted at Brunswick, "has no authority for us," and during his lifetime he advocated some of the most extreme measures, including abolishing circumcision and transferring the Sabbath to Sunday.

Born in 1806 in Germany to extremely Orthodox parents, Holdheim was famous even as a youth for his mastery of Jewish learning. Attracted as well to secular knowledge, he later attended universities in Prague and Berlin, after which he accepted an appointment as the rabbi of a traditional congregation. It was not long, however, before he revealed his preference for a more modern form of Judaism, and in an essay in Geiger's *Scientific Journal for Jewish Theology* he wrote:

> **. . . The validity [of the religious ceremonies] can consist only in the fact that they are of living significance. This can be the case only if they answer local conditions and are suited to the contemporary state of culture. As soon as they no longer possess the power to fill such purpose and are retained nevertheless, . . . they have lost all value . . .**

In 1840, Holdheim moved to Mecklenburg-Schwerin where, in response to the Hamburg prayer book controversy, he stated his view that a modern rabbi could no longer unconditionally accept the Talmud:

> **The Talmud speaks with the ideology of its own time, and for that time it was right. I speak from the higher ideology of my time, and for this age I am right.**

He became still more radical when, seven years later, he accepted the pulpit of a newly-formed Reform congregation in Berlin and started to translate some of his principles into practice. The prayer book he produced appeared mainly in German, hats were eliminated, Sabbath services were conducted on Sunday, and all extra days of the Jewish holidays, except Rosh Hashanah, were abolished.

All this grew out of his conviction that what was fundamental in Judaism was its ethics and religious ideals, which existed for the benefit of humanity as a whole. He argued that the rest of Jewish law and ritual had been originally designed to emphasize this and had now come to be carried on largely for its own sake. Hence, Holdheim declared:

> We must strive earnestly for inner spirituality, and not outer formalism, and only those practices have religious values that are effective for awakening the loftiest Jewish thoughts and sentiments so that the Jew may fulfill his mission.

Here he based himself squarely upon the teachings of Second Isaiah, the great prophet of the Babylonian Exile, who had summoned his people to become the faithful "servant of the Lord" and "a light unto the nations" (Isaiah 42) in order that they might lead the whole world to acknowledge the true God and His righteous demands. Holdheim added:

> . . . [This mission] means the preservation in all its purity of the Jewish God-idea and the body of moral doctrine [as expressed in the Jewish tradition] which is based on justice and universal brotherly love. It means conveying this among mankind by the moral force of [the Jew's] example so that, in accordance with the prophetic messianic idea, justice and brotherhood may become dominant in all the earth.

So determined was Holdheim to eliminate every practice that did not conform to his universal ideal of Judaism that a noted Jewish historian of the period actually compared him to the apostle Paul who had eventually broken with Judaism. And after Holdheim died in 1860, his extremism led some people, including a prominent Berlin Orthodox rabbi, to object to his burial in the section of the cemetery reserved for rabbis.

Abraham Geiger, the Guiding Force of Reform

Few at Brunswick were prepared to follow either Holdheim or Schott. Rather, it was to Abraham Geiger that most turned for leadership, and even the Orthodox who opposed him looked upon him as the guiding force of Reform.

Born in 1810 in Frankfort, Abraham Geiger was the son of the rabbi of the community and was noted for his intelligence even as a child. By the age of three he could already read Hebrew and German fluently; by nine he had mastered the Bible and much of the Talmud. Secretly, he had also begun to read books on general history and was already questioning some of the teachings of traditional Judaism.

As a result of his university experience and the influence of a close friend, he determined to devote himself as a rabbi to modernizing Judaism. At his very first congregation, in Wiesbaden, he embarked upon preaching every Sabbath and introducing other improvements in the service.

Here he also began publishing his *Scientific Journal for Jewish Theology* for the discussion of current religious issues, among them Jewish mourning customs, instrumental music in the synagogue, and holiday observance. Geiger himself produced a number of the articles, including one on "The Role of Women in the Synagogue," and another entitled "Concerning the Establishment of a Jewish Theological Faculty," in which he called for the creation of a seminary where the scientific study of Judaism could be freely pursued. He was convinced that only a more thorough understanding of Judaism's historical development could equip Reform to make appropriate changes in Jewish belief and practice.

In Wiesbaden, his devotion to Reform provoked some opposition, but, as we have seen, it was only after he accepted the pulpit in

Breslau that the Orthodox seemed bent on destroying him. Nevertheless, he succeeded in introducing Confirmation into the congregation, as well as his own prayer book, which, while mainly in Hebrew, eliminated most of the repetitious prayers, all references to angels, resurrection of the dead, and restoration of the Jews to Palestine.

To Geiger, Judaism was intended to be a practical religion for everyday living, whose final goal was the establishment of a Messianic Age of universal justice through the pursuit of truth and righteousness. Though he agreed in theory with many of the proposals of his life-long friend Holdheim, his research convinced him that Judaism had developed chiefly through slow evolution in response to changing circumstances rather than by violent overthrow of the past. Hence he took a moderate position when it came to religious changes, arguing:

> **Revolution is not successful in religion which demands not only tearing away whatever is outmoded but strengthening that which exists and creating new things when necessity demands it.**

Above all, he wanted Reform to maintain strong, enduring ties with historic Judaism and the Jewish people and not end up as a separate sect of its own.

He was also anxious to develop greater unity within the movement itself and to bridge the gap between the many different points of view. Hence, as he moved on to serve congregations in Frankfort and Berlin, he persisted in promoting meetings of liberal rabbis, and even conferences (called ''synods'') between rabbis and laymen in order to achieve enough agreement on basic principles and practices to lead to the development of a common prayer book.

The founding of a Reform seminary to train rabbis and teachers in the scientific approach to Judaism was another of his life-long proj-

ects. At the age of sixty-three, he finally saw the establishment in Berlin of the *Hochschule für die Wissenschaft des Judentums,* the Advanced Academy for the Scientific Study of Judaism, where he himself served as professor of Jewish history and literature.

He lived only two more years. At his funeral on October 25, 1874, those who spoke paid tribute to him as the guiding force of the movement and ''the teacher of every liberal rabbi of the times.'' This was true not only in Europe, but even in far-away America where his disciples were the leaders of the Reform movement and his teachings dominated their thinking. To this very day, in fact, Geiger's influence remains strong within American Reform Judaism.

Hopes for the Brunswick Rabbinical Conference

Thus, in June of 1844, Philippson, Schott, Holdheim, Geiger, and twenty-two other liberal rabbis traveled to Brunswick for a historic conference. Each, however, carried with him different hopes for the outcome:

—Ludwig Philippson, who had arranged for the meeting, was confident that the rabbis would adopt a common Reform program and even establish a liberal rabbinical seminary.

—Leopold Schott, who adhered to most of traditional Judaism, merely wanted some minor changes in Jewish practice.

—Samuel Holdheim felt the time was ripe at last for the movement to strike out for the most sweeping reforms.

—Abraham Geiger, unable to be present at the start, urged his colleagues to avoid discussing religious principles but to concentrate instead on the practical needs of the day.

Despite the general optimism of those who gathered together at Brunswick, it was plain from the start that few of their hopes would be realized. The question that remained, then, was whether anything at all could be achieved there, or, for that matter, at any other meeting of Reformers.

QUESTIONS FOR DISCUSSION

1. How do you account for the fact that rabbis like Chorin, Kohn, Geiger, Holdheim, and the others, though all originally trained within Orthodoxy, turned to Reform? Do the same reasons still influence Jews in today's world? Why?

2. What connection do you find between the activities of men like Gabriel Riesser in the political area and their affiliation with Reform Judaism? How does this help to explain Reform Judaism's great concern with democracy and social action today?

3. To what extent are your own Reform beliefs and practices the result of the thought and activities of the leading European Reformers? How does your congregation reflect the position of Samuel Holdheim? Of Abraham Geiger?

4. What important contributions did the leading European Reformers make to the development of Reform Judaism as you know it today? What were some of the shortcomings of their program? To your knowledge, what has American Reform done about these?

5. In what ways does the scientific study of the Jewish past support a Reform view of Judaism? How does the scientific approach differ from that of Orthodox? How, then, do Reform views differ from those of Orthodoxy in the way they look upon the Bible and the Talmud?

6. How do the various views of Reform today as reflected by different temples compare with the positions taken by those who attended the Brunswick Conference of 1844? What conclusions do you come to about the necessity, or even desirability, of having all Reform Jews subscribe to the same practices and principles?

SIGNIFICANT DOCUMENTS

A Defense of the Reforms of the Hamburg Temple, by Aaron Chorin, 1820

For a long time now I have noticed with regret the sad situation of my coreligionists. A portion of them have surrendered to superstition, another to unbelief. While that harmful conglomeration of pious simulators, the *Chasidim* [Orthodox], spreads more and more and daily wins new supporters, another group eschews all religious obligations and declares as true only that to which the senses can witness. More on this on another occasion; presently only this "Word in Its Time." [The name of Chorin's book in which this defense appeared was *A Word in Its Time*.]

During the past year a circular letter from a greatly honored congregation in Germany [the Hamburg Temple] informed me that about three hundred of the most highly respected heads of families had resolved to arrange their worship service in such a manner that it would comply with a sense of dignity, with the spirit of the age, and at the same time with the principles of Judaism, strictly interpreted in accordance with the Holy Scriptures and the Talmud. At the same time I was asked to state whether the teachings of the Talmud permit:

1. To cleanse our liturgy from later additions (Heaven only knows when and by whom they were added!) and to restore it to its pristine simplicity.

2. To say one's prayers in the understandable language of one's country, so that the heart of the worshiper may know what the lips speak.

3. To hold a service to the accompaniment of an organ, so that harmony and order, which are now lacking in our synagogues, might be reintroduced.

4. Or whether such changes are prohibited because of the rule, "The customs

of Israel have the force of Torah," which, therefore, may not be altered.

Frankly, I could not at first muster much courage to make a public statement about this. The unpleasant treatment I had received when, with the best of intentions, I published my *Rosh Amanah* [רֹאשׁ אֲמָנָה, Principles of Faith], made me hesitant. I knew well the urge which some zealots have for persecuting others, which does not rest until it has done harm, which is deaf to all reason, insensitive to all progress, and resistant to all ennoblement.

But after mature thought my reason returned. What, I thought, shall truth remain repressed because weak people dislike it? Shall the sun hide its light because the night owl cannot bear it? No, I thought, I will publicly testify to the truth and not shrink back from the hatred which would likely descend on me.

And so I issued my treatise *Kineat ha-Emet* [קִנְאַת הָאֱמֶת, Zeal for Truth, published in Dessau, 1818], in which I hoped to deal with the above-mentioned questions in simple unambiguous terms. I stated that it was not only permissible but obligatory to free the worship ritual from its adhesions, to hold the service in a language understandable to the worshiper, and to accompany it with organ and song.

—From W. Gunther Plaut,
The Rise of Reform Judaism,
pp. 33–34.

Samuel Holdheim's Reply to the Reform Society of Arad, Hungary, 1848

1. Regarding the transfer of Saturday to Sunday, I answer thus: Since we cannot assume that God pronounced one particular day holy once and for all, and since we consider the biblical account of the exclusive sanctification of a special day merely as the mythical expression for the sanctification of man on a special day, naturally no religious reason prevents the transfer of the historical Sabbath to any other day of the week, especially if the matter is urgently demanded by the conditions of civic life; yes, even in the interest of the preservation of the concept of the Sabbath itself and its influence on the religious life of the congregation; hence in the interest of religion itself.

2. As I have demonstrated scientifically elsewhere, the dietary laws belong to the biblical laws of cleanliness, which have long since lost all significance. Inasmuch as the dietary laws were given to the Israelites alone, they are part and parcel of the conception of a special theocratic [priestly] sanctity of the Jewish people and therefore have lost all significance. Whatever, however, may have once been the reason for the dietary laws, this much is certain that this reason no longer exists for us and has no religious efficacy; every irrational practice, every belief in talismanic power is opposed to the spirit of religion. Therefore the abrogation of the dietary laws is highly desirable since, in addition to being a disturbing feature in the civic and social life of the Jews, these laws are particularly prone to continue the differences between them and the other inhabitants.

3. The abolition of the second days of the holidays, as well as the abrogation of all fast days except יוֹם כִּפּוּר [Yom Kippur, the Day of Atonement], has been recommended by the [Breslau] German rabbinical conference. To my mind not only is there no objection to such abolition but it is highly desirable in the interests of the religion.

4. The abbreviation of the service, the excision of all prayers unsuited to our

age as, for example, the sacrificial and messianic prayers of a Jewish national character, as well as the use of the vernacular in the public service, have also been recommended by the second [Frankfort] rabbinical conference. The removal of all disturbing ceremonials has taken place in very many Jewish congregations in Germany, and not even from the Orthodox standpoint can any objection be raised to praying with uncovered head.

5. Circumcision is the sign of the covenant concluded between God and Abraham, and his descendants . . . and its seal on the body of every Israelite. As long as such a covenant had significance for the religious consciousness of the Jews, as long as the idea of a close covenant of love excluding other nations was deeply rooted in the people's thought, . . . circumcision was the characteristic symbol of this covenant, and was therefore clung to with particular zeal in Israel. But after this idea of the particular covenant which underlies circumcision has ceased to be a religious truth and an object of faith, protest must be lodged against circumcision as the expression of an outlived idea.

—From David Philipson,
The Reform Movement in Judaism,
pp. 279–280.

From Abraham Geiger's Letter to the Board of the Berlin Congregation, 1869

I feel impelled to express to the esteemed board of directors the sense of elation with which I received the call to the rabbinate of the community there. . . . I have high regard for the duties of a preacher from the pulpit; I take delight in proclaiming the sacred message from a holy place, and am confident that its effect will be edifying, encouraging, and on occasion even inspiring and stirring. . . . However, I have at least the same high regard for the opportunity to give oral instruction on a scholarly level and to provide scholarly insights into Jewish theology.

In former times this was, in fact, the rabbi's most important function; it is only in more recent times that it has been forced to yield first place to the almost universally accepted practice of the sermon. Thus far it has not been revived to keep pace with the advances made in scholarly standards and insights. It is, however, precisely the nurturing of a living root of a healthy Judaism, properly interpreted, that forms the basis of my concept of the essential task of my position and office. . . .

The attention I have attracted both generally and from you in particular was paid, I am sure, at least as much to the scholarly aspects of my work as to my pulpit oratory. Let me admit it to you quite frankly: the one deciding factor which could move me to make a change in my position would be the opportunity to exercise my functions fruitfully by guiding the disciples of scholarship and by paving the way for such insights as will advance the welfare of both Israel and the rest of mankind.

In this connection, I must not attempt to conceal the fact that "the institutions now existing in the community (of Berlin)," as far as I have knowledge of them, could not satisfy me; I would feel content only if a theological college with a comprehensive program of studies were to be founded there, in which I could assume an active role. . . .

I would have been very happy to find in the wording of your offer some statement expressing the hope that such an institution might indeed be founded there and that I would be expected to contribute toward this end by willingly engaging my effort in this direction. . . .

As a matter of fact, I happen to know that preliminary steps have been initiated in Berlin toward the realization of an undertaking of this sort; that a committee has been formed for this purpose; and that, in fact, a curriculum has already been planned, circulars have been sent out, and pledges of contributions accepted. . . . All this I have learned quite by accident.

. . . The matter is of too great importance to me that I should sit back and wait. Therefore, instead of waiting for them to approach me first, I have acted contrary to my usual habits and addressed a frank inquiry directly to Professor [Moritz] Lazarus who, I understand, is chairman of the committee. I am now waiting for his reply which will have significant bearing on my decision. . . .

—From Max Wiener,
Abraham Geiger and Liberal Judaism,
pp. 131–133.

OTHER THINGS TO READ

Bamberger, Bernard J., *The Story of Judaism:* Chap. 40, ''The Science of Judaism''; Chap. 41, ''The Progress of Reform''; Chap. 42, ''Philosophies of Judaism''; Chap. 43, ''German Judaism Comes to Equilibrium.''

Feuer, Leon I., and Azriel Eisenberg, *Jewish Literature since the Bible,* II: pp. 183–186 (Abraham Geiger).

Fleg, Edmond, *The Jewish Anthology:* pp. 267–268 (scientific study of Judaism); 268–269 (Abraham Geiger).

Graetz, Heinrich, *History of the Jews:* Vol. V, Chap. 15, ''Reform and Young Israel''; Chap. 16, ''Awakening of Independence and the Science of Judaism''; Chap. 18, ''Events Preceding the Revolutions of February and March, 1848, and the Subsequent Social Advance of the Jews.''

Jewish Encyclopedia: ''Aaron Chorin,'' Vol. 4, pp. 43–44; ''Abraham Geiger,'' Vol. 5, pp. 584–587; ''Samuel Holdheim,'' Vol. 6, pp. 437–439; ''Abraham Kohn,'' Vol. 7, pp. 533–534; ''Lehrenstalt für die Wissenschaft des Judentums'' (Berlin Rabbinical Seminary), Vol. 7, p. 668; ''Ludwig Philippson,'' Vol. 9, p. 684; ''Gabriel Riesser,'' Vol. 10, pp. 410–411.

Philipson, David, *Centenary Papers and Others:* ''Samuel Holdheim,'' pp. 63–97; ''Abraham Geiger,'' pp. 99–147.

Philipson, David, *The Reform Movement in Judaism:* Chap. 2, ''The Second Generation of Reformers''; Chap. 3, ''The Geiger-Tiktin Affair''; Chap. 6, ''The Frankfort Society of the Friends of Reform''; Chap. 7, ''The Rabbinical Conferences, 1844–46''; Chap. 8, ''The Reform Congregation of Berlin''; pp. 277–281; Chap. 11, ''The Leipzig and Augsburg Synods.''

Plaut, W. Gunther, *The Growth of Reform Judaism:* pp. 44–46 (Breslau Seminary); 46–47 (Berlin Seminary).

Plaut, W. Gunther, *The Rise of Reform Judaism:* pp. 32–33, 35–36, 39–40, 152–154, 252–253, 256 (Aaron Chorin); pp. 18–19 and Chap. 3, ''The Great Controversy, Tiktin vs. Geiger''; pp. 111–112, 125–127, 156–158, 209, 231–232, 238–244, 248–249, 253 (Abraham Geiger); pp. 122–124, 138–139, 190–195, 228–230 (Samuel Holdheim); pp. 65–67, 115–117, 134–135, 258 (Abraham Kohn); pp. 19–21, 74–76, 133–134, 141–142, 199–200, 203–204, 232–233 (Ludwig Philippson); pp. 103–104 (Gabriel Riesser).

Schwartzman, Sylvan D., *Reform Judaism in the Making:* Chap. 6, ''Reform Meets Major Opposition''; Chap. 7, ''The Need for Reform Direction''; Chap. 8, ''Three Decades of Conferences, 1844–1871.''

Standard Jewish Encyclopedia: ''Breslau Rabbinical Seminary,'' p. 355; ''Abraham Geiger,'' pp. 730–731; ''Hochschule,'' p. 917; ''Samuel Holdheim,'' p. 917; ''Abraham Kohn,'' p. 1144; ''Ludwig Philippson,'' p. 1500; ''Gabriel Riesser,'' p. 1604.

Universal Jewish Encyclopedia: ''Aaron Chorin,'' Vol. 3, pp. 163–164; ''Abraham Geiger,'' Vol.

4, pp. 521–522; *"Hochschule,"* Vol. 5, p. 405; *"Samuel Holdheim,"* Vol. 5, p. 409; *"Abraham Kohn,"* Vol. 6, p. 432; *"Ludwig Philippson,"* Vol. 8, p. 487; *"Gabriel Riesser,"* Vol. 9, p. 163.

Wiener, Max, *Abraham Geiger and Liberal Judaism.*

SUGGESTED ACTIVITIES

1. Prepare a *Who's Who* for each of the leading Reform rabbis who attended the Brunswick Rabbinical Conference of 1844. Then keep it up to date with sketches of other European and American Reform leaders who will appear in later chapters of this book.

2. Create a series of Reform platforms based upon the different points of view of men like Schott, Philippson, Geiger, and Holdheim.

3. Conduct a debate on the subject: *"Resolved, that Samuel Holdheim's views on transferring the Jewish Sabbath to Sunday should be adopted by the Reform movement today."*

SUBJECTS FOR RESEARCH

1. What was the point of view of some of the other rabbis who attended the Brunswick Rabbinical Conference, such as Samuel Adler, Levi Bodenheimer, Solomon Formstecher, Salomon Herzheimer, and Gotthold Salomon?

2. Check the latest official statements by American Reform Judaism on the subject of the Mission of Israel and the Messianic Age. How do these compare with the views of Samuel Holdheim?

3. Before the Berlin Reform Seminary was founded, what other attempts did Abraham Geiger make to establish a rabbinical school? Why did these fail? (You will be particularly interested in the circumstances that caused the Breslau Seminary twenty years earlier to become Conservative rather than Reform.)

4. What actual contributions did Reform leaders like Gabriel Riesser make toward securing freedom for the Jews of Germany? For the German people as a whole?

5. Compare the views of Abraham Geiger and Samuel Holdheim in relation to: (a) the prayer book, (b) the religious status of Jewish women, (c) Confirmation, (d) circumcision, (e) the observance of the Sabbath, (f) holiday observance, (g) the use of Hebrew in worship, (h) Jewish marriage and divorce regulations, and (i) Jewish mourning customs. To what extent were their positions so very different?

FILMSTRIPS TO SEE

David Einhorn: Father of the Union Prayerbook (UAHC), describing the life and activities in Europe of this noted American Reform pioneer.

Dr. Leo Baeck: Man of Faith (UAHC), presenting the highlights in the life and work of this last head of the Berlin Reform Seminary.

Torah in Jewish Life (Jewish Education Committee of New York), depicting the role of the Torah in historic Jewish life, with special emphasis upon traditional belief and practice.

A LIVE ISSUE

With the gradual disappearance of most social differences that once divided Reform and Conservative Jews, various people have come forward with proposals to merge the movements. In the process, they stress some of the facts brought out in this chapter, particularly the early connection between the two movements and their common recognition of the need for religious change. A merger, they insist, would greatly strengthen liberal Judaism everywhere and enable it to carry on a much more effective program.

Those who are opposed, however, contend that, if nothing else, the widely different beliefs and practices of the two movements make such a merger extremely difficult if not impossible.

Yet this is a subject that is bound to be discussed again and again in the years ahead.

The Basic Problem: Obviously, such a merger offers many advantages and the idea is very appealing. But are the two movements sufficiently similar to make it possible, or is the difference too great?

Some Important Questions: (1) What attitude does Conservative Judaism take toward Jewish tradition? (2) How do its provisions for religious change compare with those of Reform? (3) What effect have these had upon the development of both movements? (4) How, then, do the beliefs and practices of present-day Reform and Conservatism differ? (5) What changes would one or the other have to make in order to achieve a satisfactory merger? (6) To what extent is "compromise" in religious matters possible or desirable? (7) What are some of the possible advantages of separatism?

What Do You Think? As you read about the decisions of the various Reform conferences and the rise of Conservative Judaism, bear these questions in mind. What conclusions do you reach about the desirability of a merger between the two movements? To what extent do you consider it likely? Would you personally support such a proposal? What changes in Reform would you be willing to accept in order to effect a merger?

9.

REFORM CONDUCTS SOME IMPORTANT MEETINGS

The Results of the Brunswick Rabbinical Conference

We have come here to deal with the practical needs of our people today, and we must remember that our purpose is, insofar as possible, to solve the many vexing problems faced by Jews and Judaism in the modern world.

That is why this Rabbinical Conference has been called—that the delegates may take counsel with one another in order to preserve and develop the Jewish faith and promote a greater religious consciousness on the part of all Jews.

So began Rabbi Joseph Maier of Stuttgart who was selected to preside over the meeting in Brunswick and, in his opening remarks, he advised his liberal colleagues:

We can achieve our sacred purpose, however, only if we bear three things in mind. First, we must have confidence in one another, though there be different points of view among us. Second, we must confine ourselves to the main problems of the day and not be side-tracked in our discussions. Finally, we know how involved many of the issues are and how time-consuming will be our discussions if all views are considered. Therefore we should look upon this conference as but the first session of a permanent liberal rabbinical body which shall continue to meet every year, seeking to overcome the many problems that we face as religious Jews.

The results proved him to be correct. Beyond affirming its right to make religious changes and agreeing to hold another meeting at Frankfort the following year, the Brunswick Rabbinical Conference went only so far as to appoint committees to recommend improvements in synagogue worship and needed reforms in Sabbath observance, marriage regulations, and beliefs concerning the Messiah. Nevertheless, Rabbi Maier was far from discouraged. In fact, in summing up the results for the delegates, he declared:

As we look back over the progress of our discussions during this first and certainly most difficult and important assembly, we have every reason to be satisfied. Even though the results are not of great import, at least so far, what has taken place gives us assurance that greater things will happen in the future . . .

To be sure, those who would like to make sweeping reforms will not be satisfied . . . and those of rigid and formal belief will condemn us . . . Still neither will deter us. Nevertheless, we shall pursue our task with zeal but also with that thoughtfulness which takes time and circumstance into careful consideration. . . .

The Succeeding Rabbinical Conference—Frankfort, 1845

Reform hopes for action, however, were more greatly realized the following year when the rabbis reassembled in Frankfort for their next conference. For, as a modern newspaper might report it, this is what they achieved:

CONFERENCE APPROVES LITURGY REFORMS; ADOPTS MANY OTHER CHANGES IN WORSHIP

Shortened Service, Use of Organ in Worship Sanctioned, Committees to Consider Mourning Customs, Women's Rights

FRANKFORT, July 28, 1845—A two-week meeting of thirty liberal rabbis in this city adjourned today after reaching a number of key decisions relating to synagogue reforms.

The conference, which began on July 15, spent most of its sessions debating the report of the Committee on Liturgy, appointed a year ago at Brunswick.

Among the actions the rabbis took was to approve the use of the organ and the vernacular in worship. However, the reading of the Torah and major portions of the liturgy, such as the *Shema,* will be retained in Hebrew. The conference also agreed to eliminate repetitious prayers as well as those calling for the coming of a personal Messiah to deliver the Jews out of "exile." Belief in a Messianic Age of peace and justice for all mankind will be substituted.

A motion by Ludwig Philippson, editor of the *General News of Judaism,* calling for the establishment of a liberal rabbinical seminary, was enthusiastically endorsed.

Previously appointed committees to consider changes in Sabbath observance and Jewish marriage regulations, as well as new committees to deal with mourning customs and the religious rights of women, have been asked to report at next year's conference, scheduled for Breslau.

Reform reaction was enthusiastic. The participants, said Abraham Geiger, had practical problems to deal with and sought honestly to solve them according to the needs of the times. "A new era of active participation in Judaism all over Europe will stem from this . . . Rabbinical Conference," added the presiding officer.

The anticipated attack of the Orthodox, who saw themselves as doing "battle in a holy cause in which victory is assured," was not long in coming. Much more serious, however, was the fact that Zacharias Frankel, a well-known rabbi of Dresden and founder of the liberal *Journal of Jewish Religious Interest,* had withdrawn from the conference after the third day. Indeed, as many feared, his action was bound to have grave consequences for the progress of the Reform movement. In fact, it led to the creation of a Conservative movement in Judaism.

124

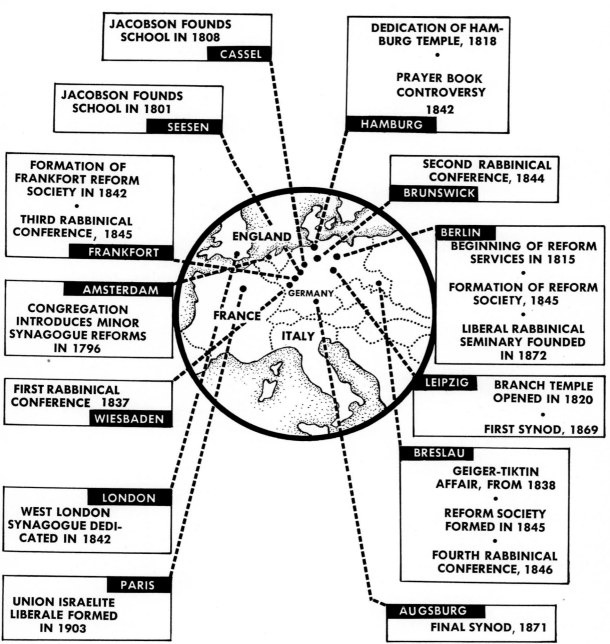

MAP OF REFORM DEVELOPMENTS IN EUROPE

JACOBSON FOUNDS
SCHOOL IN 1808
CASSEL

JACOBSON FOUNDS
SCHOOL IN 1801
SEESEN

FORMATION OF
FRANKFORT REFORM
SOCIETY IN 1842
•
THIRD RABBINICAL
CONFERENCE, 1845
FRANKFORT

AMSTERDAM
CONGREGATION
INTRODUCES MINOR
SYNAGOGUE REFORMS
IN 1796

FIRST RABBINICAL
CONFERENCE 1837
WIESBADEN

DEDICATION OF HAM-
BURG TEMPLE, 1818
•
PRAYER BOOK
CONTROVERSY
1842
HAMBURG

SECOND RABBINICAL
CONFERENCE, 1844
BRUNSWICK

BERLIN
BEGINNING OF REFORM
SERVICES IN 1815
•
FORMATION OF REFORM
SOCIETY, 1845
•
LIBERAL RABBINICAL
SEMINARY FOUNDED
IN 1872

LEIPZIG
BRANCH TEMPLE
OPENED IN 1820
•
FIRST SYNOD, 1869

BRESLAU
GEIGER-TIKTIN
AFFAIR, FROM 1838
•
REFORM SOCIETY
FORMED IN 1845
•
FOURTH RABBINICAL
CONFERENCE, 1846

LONDON
WEST LONDON
SYNAGOGUE DEDI-
CATED IN 1842

PARIS
UNION ISRAELITE
LIBERALE FORMED
IN 1903

AUGSBURG
FINAL SYNOD, 1871

ENGLAND

GERMANY

FRANCE

ITALY

The Birth of Conservative Judaism

Frankel was one of the most highly respected scholars at Frankfort. He had not been present at Brunswick and, as it turned out, was quite critical of its actions, particularly the appointment of committees to consider the use of Hebrew in the service and reforms of the marriage laws. For, as he saw it, the participants seemed far more intent on making religious changes than trying to preserve what had proven to be valuable in the past.

Frankel considered it a mistake to insist that Judaism conform to the "spirit of the times." To him the emphasis upon reason that marked the culture of Western Europe seemed to lack both the emotional warmth and permanence of Judaism, and he felt that the chief effort of Reform should be directed toward encouraging Jews to maintain those practices that had sustained them over the centuries. As a result, many Reformers felt that Frankel was much too traditional.

But he departed from strict Orthodoxy by acknowledging the need for some religious change. In each instance, however, he insisted that careful scientific study of the past show that it in no way affected the fundamental teachings of Judaism and that it had the full approval of "the will of the Jewish people."

Frankel called his approach "positive historical Judaism," in which he conceded that Jewish tradition had not actually been handed down by God but was the product of the Jews' historical experience and therefore capable of undergoing change when necessary. Yet the principal task of the modern Jew as he saw it was to preserve as much of the tradition as possible by maintaining Judaism largely as it had come down from the past.

Hence, when the rabbis at Frankfort decided that the use of Hebrew in worship was *desirable* but not actually *essential,* Frankel looked upon this as a repudiation of "positive

ZACHARIAS FRANKEL. A rabbi with liberal leanings who withdrew from the Reform Frankfort Rabbinical Conference over the issue of the use of Hebrew in worship. He ultimately headed the Conservative movement in Europe. (HUC, American Jewish Archives)

historical Judaism'' and withdrew from the conference, stating:

> . . . I disagree with such a decision, not only because I have a different point of view, but because I disagree with a tendency of the decision. . . . In my opinion this is not in the spirit of preserving but of destroying positive historical Judaism . . .

The delegates expressed "great astonishment" at Frankel's resignation. They pointed out in their reply that he had voted in favor of the resolution that the use of Hebrew was not essential. And that he had also admitted that the historic tradition of Judaism permitted the entire service to be recited in whatever language was necessary.

None of this succeeded in persuading Frankel to return. Yes, he said, he agreed in theory with the position of the conference, but he still regarded the use of Hebrew in worship as indispensable to the preservation of Judaism and the Jewish people.

Frankel's interpretation of "positive historical Judaism" promptly won him the support of those who favored a much more moderate approach to religious change. He now became the recognized leader of the movement which eventually in America (but not in Europe) took the name of Conservative Judaism, and in 1854 he was selected head of its newly-established seminary in Breslau. By the end of the century, the movement had also taken root in the United States where many looked upon Conservatism as a compromise between Reform and Orthodoxy.

With the rise of Conservative Judaism, Reform in Europe found itself with a new set of problems. Now not only did it face the competition of a new movement with considerable appeal to modern Jews, but it was also caught in a dilemma of its own. To embark upon sweeping changes could well lose it the support of the moderates within its own ranks; yet, reluctance to proceed with needed reforms was simply to follow the approach of the Conservatives. Inevitably, as the leaders wavered between the two courses, the movement lost much of its momentum.

The Final Rabbinical Conference— Breslau, 1846

What turned out to be the last of the Reform rabbinical conferences was held the following year in Breslau, a stronghold of Orthodoxy in eastern Germany. Conspicuous by their absence were the various Conservatives, led by Zacharias Frankel, who were attempting to arrange a conference of their own.

Nevertheless, as the Reformers assembled together in the summer of 1846, they were hopeful of good results. In his opening address as president, Abraham Geiger congratulated the rabbis for attending the conference in the face of attack and misinterpretation. But he also admitted:

> **The conditions are difficult and confusion in [Jewish] religious matters is on the increase. Despite this, you who are at this conference are again making the courageous attempt to clothe the essentials of Judaism into a form more suitable to the present and thus to breathe new life into our religion.**

That the Breslau Rabbinical Conference was extremely productive is evident from the following account as a modern newspaper might report it:

RABBIS ADOPT SWEEPING SABBATH REFORMS; ALSO ACCEPT HOLIDAY, MOURNING CHANGES

Conference Rejects Proposal for Transfer of Sabbath to Sunday; Decision Delayed on Reforms of Marriage Laws, Women's Rights

BRESLAU, July 24, 1846—During their twelve-day meeting here, the twenty-six delegates to the Reform rabbinical conference adopted sweeping changes in religious practice involving the Sabbath, Jewish holidays, and mourning customs. These actions were taken upon the recommendations of committees appointed at previous conferences.

"Any act designed to foster the religious spirit of the Sabbath," the conference asserted, "such as riding to the synagogue, or playing the organ, is not to be regarded as 'work.' Consciousness of the holiness of the Sabbath requires the kind of service that will inspire, regardless of the acts involved.''

Work was also permitted on the Sabbath if essential to one's livelihood or needed to perform some public service. However, a proposal to overcome some of the more serious problems with Sabbath observance by transferring the day to Sunday was rejected.

The conference agreed to eliminate all extra days of the Jewish holidays except for Rosh Hashanah, which is observed for two days even in Palestine.

Important reforms in mourning practices were also adopted. The mourning period has been shortened to three days, with the closing of one's business confined simply to the day of the funeral. Mourners are now permitted to shave, bathe, wear shoes, and sit on chairs.

The conference adjourned before action could be taken on committee reports recommending equal religious rights for women and various changes in traditional marriage regulations. However, the delegates plan to discuss these matters at next year's meeting scheduled for Mannheim.

In spite of its achievements, the Breslau Conference was sharply criticized by the more radical Reformers who had been in favor of transferring the Jewish Sabbath to Sunday. Among them was Samuel Holdheim who called the delegates lacking in courage for failing to adopt "the only possible solution" to the problem.

In reply, Abraham Geiger argued:

> An institution of Judaism that has existed for thousands of years and is one of its most fundamental cannot be legislated out of existence by a tiny rabbinical gathering. Certainly there is no objection to holding an additional "week-day" service on Sunday, and this matter can be taken up at next year's rabbinical conference.

But, as it turned out, political upheavals all over Europe made it impossible to hold another meeting for more than two decades.

A Synod, at Last

Meanwhile, the dissatisfaction with the Breslau Conference prompted a number of Reform societies and congregations, led by those in Breslau itself and Berlin, to call for the convening of a synod, a meeting composed of both rabbis and laymen, instead of another rabbinical conference. However, before it could be arranged, the revolutions of 1848 broke out.

The starting place again was France where a series of grievances against the monarchy, accompanied by a major business crash, led to riots in Paris, and in two days the king was forced to flee. Immediately, revolutions in support of democracy were set off in Italy, Austria, Hungary, Germany, and other parts of Europe. Many Jews, anxious to gain their own freedom, took part in the struggle, and among the leaders were prominent Reformers like Gabriel Riesser.

Despite initial successes, the revolutions in most countries ended in dismal failure. Newly-won constitutions were quickly withdrawn as royal armies regained control, and once again the Jews found their liberties denied and a number of the old restrictions restored. Many of the liberal Jews of Germany fled the country to take up a new life in America, and those that remained behind were now compelled to spend their energy struggling to regain political rights.

It was not until 1869 that conditions permitted the Reformers to convene a synod. By then, much of Western and Central Europe had restored certain rights to the Jews, though they did not as yet enjoy full equality. In Germany, for example, Jews were still denied the opportunity to hold public office or become full professors at universities.

Meanwhile, Reform was also being challenged by both Conservative Judaism, which now possessed its own seminary, and a more modern type of Orthodoxy, called Neo-Orthodoxy, promoted by Samson Raphael Hirsch, the rabbi of Frankfort. Hirsch, a university graduate who nevertheless retained his Orthodoxy, had undertaken to improve the decorum in the synagogue as well as the quality of Jewish education. In a series of popular books, he also sought to provide traditional Jews with a more modern interpretation of Judaism. Throughout he held firm to basic Orthodox belief and practice, claiming that what was needed was a reform of the Jewish spirit, not of Judaism, and he urged his followers in cities where Reformers or Conservatives were dominant, as in Frankfort and Berlin, to secede from the Jewish community.

All the more, then, did the Reformers feel the need for a meeting, and a synod of leading rabbis and laymen was announced for June 29, 1869, at Leipzig, a city in the very center of Germany.

The Leipzig Synod of 1869

In contrast to most of the rabbinical conferences, the Leipzig Synod was extremely well-attended. Represented were practically all the Reform movements then in existence, including those in England and the United States.

An air of optimism prevailed as the rabbi of the host congregation welcomed the delegates and called attention to the rapidly improving political status of the Jews which, he said, compelled them to renew the drive for religious reforms.

He was followed by the chairman of the committee that called the synod who pointed to the unwholesome conditions among the Jews. He stressed the widespread indifference to Judaism, particularly among the so-called traditional Jews who easily reconciled religion and life by ignoring their religious responsibilities.

Yet, as we note from the following account, as a modern newspaper might report it, the synod accomplished comparatively little.

SYNOD AT LEIPZIG FAILS TO ADOPT NEW REFORMS; MODERATE VIEWS DOMINATE LAY-RABBINICAL BODY

83 Delegates Representing 11 Countries Attend Gathering; Reaffirm Former Decisions on Jewish Practices and Beliefs

LEIPZIG, July 4, 1869—The first major Reform gathering in twenty-three years adjourned today after a full week of deliberation. The meeting took the form of a synod, a lay-rabbinical body, at which forty-nine laymen and thirty-four rabbis, representing sixty congregations of Germany, Austria, Belgium, Bohemia, Hungary, England, Galicia, Rumania, Switzerland, the United States, and the West Indies were present.

The synod spent most of its time simply reaffirming the decisions of earlier rabbinical conferences in approving the use of the vernacular and organ in worship and substituting belief in a Messianic Age for the traditional doctrine of a personal Messiah. The delegates also voiced their approval of a mixed choir at services, an inspiring memorial service for Yom Kippur, and a more effective program of religious education to supplement the secular studies of Jewish youth.

Many Reform leaders have expressed keen disappointment with the results. "The delegates spent most of the time talking about minor changes," one spokesman declared.

However, Moritz Lazarus, professor of philosophy at Berne University who served as the synod's president, pointed out that since numerous committees have been appointed to report at the next meeting, "this synod merely forms the foundation for future synods."

129

"Plans are under way for another meeting during the coming year," he stated, "at which time the more pressing issues will certainly be dealt with."

Outbreak of war between Prussia and France caused the synod to be postponed but, with the defeat of the French early in 1871, plans were immediately made to meet in mid-July in Augsburg, a city in southern Germany.

And, from the very start, it was clear that the results of this synod would be different.

The Final Synod—Augsburg, 1871

There are three reasons why the delegates were so much more successful at Augsburg. One was the establishment during the previous year of the *Hochschule,* the Advanced Academy for the Scientific Study of Judaism, Reform's first seminary. The fact that the movement would now be able to train its own rabbis was encouraging news indeed.

Secondly, the attendance was much smaller this time, with most of the moderates who had been a restraining influence at Leipzig absent. Hence the synod was composed largely of liberals who for a long time had wanted many more changes in beliefs and practices, with the result that a greater number of far-reaching decisions were now possible.

Finally, those who attended were sensitive to the criticism of the previous synod. In fact, it was this that prompted Professor Lazarus, who again served as president, to open the sessions with the statement that the Augsburg Synod was expected to be a "working" body rather than a "deliberating" one. The delegates, he asserted, should now be determined to adopt measures that would cope with the mounting problems in modern Jewish life.

The following account in the style of a modern newspaper indicates that the synod lived up to expectations:

AUGSBURG SYNOD STUDIES AND REVISES MANY JEWISH LAWS; PROVIDES GREATER RIGHTS FOR WOMEN

AUGSBURG, July 17, 1871—In the course of a week-long meeting here that closed today, a synod of fifty-two delegates from thirty liberal congregations of Germany, Austria, Hungary, Galicia, and Switzerland adopted numerous reforms of Jewish marriage laws.

In addition to encouraging greater participation of the bride in the marriage rites, the synod approved the double-ring ceremony, the elimination of many days when weddings are forbidden, and the acceptance of a civil death certificate in the case of a missing husband, thus enabling an *agunah* to remarry.

Other changes giving women greater religious equality were likewise approved. The synod declared them now eligible to be witnesses in Jewish ritual matters, and it abandoned the ceremony of *chalitzah* by absolving the brother-in-law of a childless widow from marrying her. Widows with children were also given permission to remarry after one year instead of the customary two.

The delegates sanctioned the use of the organ by a Jew at Sabbath services, as well as riding on the Sabbath where necessary for religious, charitable, or educational purposes. They likewise adopted resolutions calling for greater celebration of Chanukah, more effective training of cantors, and the appointment of committees to propose suitable reforms of the Jewish divorce laws.

While Reform leaders are highly pleased with the synod's accomplishments, its modification of traditional marriage regulations has called forth a storm of protest from 133 Orthodox rabbis.

Marriages performed on this basis, they declare, will not be regarded as Jewish. The Orthodox also demand the dismissal of all Reform rabbis and, where this is impossible, they urge traditional Jews to resign from the congregation and to form a new one.

After Augsburg, hopes were high that the following year's synod would finally put an

Accomplishments of the European Conferences and Synods

Problems	Brunswick Conference	Frankfort Conference	Breslau Conference	Leipzig Synod	Augsburg Synod
Mode of Worship	Committees appointed to recommend improvements in worship, including the use of the organ and the vernacular.	Use of the vernacular and organ in worship approved. Some Hebrew to be retained.		Use of the vernacular, the organ, and mixed choir approved. *Haftarah* portion to be read in translation.	Better training for cantors recommended.
Traditional Prayers	Committees appointed to consider the problem of repetition in the service and prayers involving the Jews' messianic beliefs.	Repetitious prayers eliminated. Substitution of belief in the coming of a Messianic Age for the doctrine of a personal Messiah.		Substitution of belief in the coming of a Messianic Age for the doctrine of a personal Messiah.	
Sabbath Observance	Committee appointed to consider the question.	Committee to report at next conference.	Riding to the synagogue permitted. Essential work and playing of organ on the Sabbath approved.		Playing of the organ and riding on the Sabbath for religious, charitable, and educational purposes approved.
Religious Status of Women		Committee appointed to consider the question.	Equal rights for women recommended by the committee.	Committee appointed to consider the question.	Women declared eligible to serve as witnesses in ritual matters.
Holiday Observance		Committee appointed to consider the question.	All extra days of the holidays, except for Rosh Hashanah, eliminated.	Inspiring memorial service for Yom Kippur proposed.	Wider celebration of Chanukah proposed.
Marriage Regulations	Committee appointed to consider the question.	Committee to report at next conference.		Committee appointed to consider the question.	Bride to participate more actively in wedding. Double-ring ceremony permitted. Most forbidden days abolished. Remarriage of *agunah* permitted with legal death certificate. *Chalitzah* abolished. Widows with children permitted to remarry sooner.
Divorce Laws				Committee on marriage regulations to consider the question.	Committee appointed to consider the question.
Mourning Customs		Committee appointed to consider the question.	Many traditional mourning practices eliminated. Three-day mourning period set.		

end to the problems with Jewish divorce laws. But no other synod was ever convened, mainly because the German Jew found himself preoccupied with new threats to his security.

The Rise of Modern Anti-Semitism

The end of the Franco-Prussian War saw the establishment of a single, unified German nation with a constitution that abolished "all restrictions in civil and political rights based on religious difference." Nevertheless, discrimination against the Jews increased sharply with the appearance of a new form of anti-Semitism based upon "racial" theories.

These theories, supposedly scientific but disclaimed by responsible authorities, maintained that the Germans belonged to a "superior Aryan race," descended from the ancient blue-eyed and blond-haired Teutons. The Jews, on the other hand, were said to come from an entirely different race, Asian in origin, which made it impossible for them ever to become part of the German people. It was claimed, too, that through their cunning, particularly their financial cleverness, they now dominated the real Germans and, unless the situation were remedied, the German nation would never realize its true destiny.

The notion of Aryan superiority appealed to many Germans; it also provided them with a supposedly "scientific" basis for their historic dislike of the Jews. The very year of the Augsburg Synod, a prominent professor of theology published a widely-circulated pamphlet in support of the new anti-Semitism, and each succeeding year witnessed a growing, ever more violent campaign among the German masses to "save the country from the alien Jews."

In the period following Augsburg, modern anti-Semitism succeeded in undermining Jewish confidence in emancipation and discouraging further efforts toward religious reform. However, this was only one of the many factors that sent European Reform into a decline from which it never really recovered.

QUESTIONS FOR DISCUSSION

1. Judging from the actions taken by the various rabbinical conferences and synods, which Jewish practices and beliefs seemed most in need of change? How do you explain this? To what extent were the European Reformers successful in adopting adequate reforms? How do you account for the fact that they failed in some cases?

2. How has your temple resolved most of the problems with which European Reform grappled? How do the solutions compare with theirs? As a result, what conclusions do you come to about the differences between American and European Reform?

3. In your judgment, was Rabbi Zacharias Frankel justified in withdrawing from the Frankfort Rabbinical Conference? Had the rabbinical conferences and synods adopted his position, what effect would it have had upon European Reform? How, too, might your own temple be different today?

4. In what ways does the existence of Conservative Judaism in the community affect your congregation? How do you suppose it affected the Reform movement in Europe? Why?

5. What differences among the Reformers themselves prevented the rabbinical conferences and synods from making greater progress? How do you explain these? How do they compare with the different points of view reflected today by various Reform congregations in your community or in other cities?

6. How do political conditions seem to affect Reform Judaism? Orthodox Judaism? Why? In what way do they explain what happened to Reform following the revolutions of 1848 and the Franco-Prussian War? How do they also account for the much larger number of Reform Jews in the United States today?

SIGNIFICANT DOCUMENTS

Frankel's Letter of Resignation from the Frankfort Rabbinical Conference and the Reply of the Delegates, 1845

1. Frankel's Letter

To the honorable officers of the Second Rabbinical Conference in Frankfort:

The maintenance of Judaism is the basic aim of my life and the goal of all my efforts for which I in my turn am prepared to bring every sacrifice. Hence, I find myself in irreconcilable opposition to contrary tendencies.

Already at the second session of the [Frankfort] Conference (May 17), I brought up the question of principle, so that we could understand each other and be entirely clear about the spirit of the conference. However, this point was not treated any further.

Yesterday's session had a result of which I can think only with sorrow. Only with deep pain do I recall that in a rabbinical assembly a question could come up for voting and could fail of agreement, concerning a subject which is an absolutely integral part of the religious interest of Judaism, a subject which should have been expected to enjoy the protection of the religious leaders of the people. The question was whether there is a legal—and if not a legal, an objective—necessity for the maintenance of the Hebrew language in prayer and whether this necessity is founded on religious considerations.

When this question was discussed in its practical implications, it was declared that the question at issue was whether rabbis should attempt to safeguard the remaining portion of Hebrew in our prayers. This, mind you, happened after a discussion in which all sides agreed that German prayers, too, ought to be accepted and made a part of the worship service.

The alternative question was whether the maintenance of Hebrew was only *advisable,* that is, a concession conditioned by circumstances of the present, but that a real effort should be to make its advisability superfluous and to eliminate Hebrew entirely from the worship service. It was in vain to show how the Hebrew language, the antiquity of which has been sanctified by millennia, gives sanctity and exaltation to prayer. It was in vain to point out that the Hebrew language must be safeguarded like a precious gem, for the sacred documents are written in it, and the understanding of these documents must not be lost as once it was amongst the Hellenistic Jews.

In vain it was stressed that, once Hebrew disappears from prayer, it will be lost altogether, for it will then be banished from the schools and thus another religious element will have disappeared from their already sparse curriculum. In vain was religious sentiment appealed to, for this should be significant in prayer which is heightened by the sacred sound of Hebrew. In vain it was emphasized that Hebrew prayer especially is a characteristic mark of the religious community of the Jew, for through it the Jew, wherever he meets another Jew, would recognize him as his coreligionist, would recognize his temple as his own house of worship, and find his prayer to be his own. In vain was the contention disproved that the youth would study Hebrew only with antagonism. For it can simply be said that if the parents do not nourish this antagonism, and if the school strongly supports Hebrew education, this obstacle will disappear by itself, as can be proven from examples.

In vain it was explained how, even for the female youth, the understanding of Hebrew prayers (of which there would not be a large number in any case) could be facilitated. In vain, finally, were the devotion, the religious force, and sanctity of Hebrew prayer and its edifying powers stressed. In vain—the majority of the Rabbinical Conference decided that Hebrew prayer was only *advisable* and that it would be the task of the rabbis to eliminate it gradually altogether.

I disagree with such a decision, not only because I have a different point of view but also because I disagree with the tendency of the decision. For this spirit leaves unheeded so many important elements and eliminates the historical element which has weight and power in every religion. In my opinion this is not the spirit of preserving but of destroying positive historical Judaism, which I declared distinctly before the assembly [conference] was my point of view. This spirit of the assembly deprives all its further decisions of any validity in the eyes of those who adhere to the positive historical position. As I explained to the assembly, not only voting is important but also motivation. Only those who have already made up their mind and merely want a formal approval for their position can find a superficial satisfaction in general voting procedures.

For these reasons I find myself moved to protest, not only against the above-mentioned decision but at the same time to declare that my point of view is entirely different from that of the assembly, and that, therefore, I can neither sit nor vote in its midst. But I must also express my regret that the assembly has not kept in view its stated high aim, "to obtain general confidence and thereby bring about compromise." Rather, it has again removed any opportunity for such compromise and has repelled the many thousands who will be deeply hurt by its decisions.

How much I had the above-mentioned aim before my eyes is emphasized by my presence in the assembly and by my desire to

do my share in bringing about a compromise. I wanted to work jointly with others and make this young institution one of reconciliation, one which would mature into a body which would represent general religious needs. Therefore, I overlooked many misunderstandings which my participation would elicit and many other things which were in opposition to my personal interest.

It is this same high and holy consideration which now moves me to separate myself from this conference. For when God, to whom our whole life belongs, admonishes and when an inner conviction calls, one must follow without respect to misunderstanding or misinterpretation of motives. The honest man values his conviction above all; he must primarily ask himself, his inner judge. If he is justified before him and finds his judgment validated, then he goes firmly on his way, and all other considerations yield before those of religion and truth.

I trust that as soon as possible the honorable officers will inform the distinguished assembly of the contents of this letter and that it will be made a part of the minutes. I have the honor, etc.

2. The Reply

The Second Rabbinical Assembly has received with great astonishment a letter from Chief Rabbi Dr. Frankel, of July eighteenth, which states that he resigned because of the debates of the seventeenth concerning the objective necessity of Hebrew in our prayers.

In the *General News of Judaism* of last year, No. 26, Dr. Frankel declared that he would appear in this year's Rabbinical Conference if the moderate views were represented by a number of men. He did appear. The result of the vote on the seventeenth was that thirteen members declared themselves for the objective necessity of Hebrew in prayer, three abstained, while fifteen declared themselves for the non-existence of such a necessity. The vote showed that in this respect Dr. Frankel did not at all stand alone and, therefore, if he wanted to follow his published declaration, he had the obligation to remain further in the assembly.

On the other hand, the conference vehemently denies that, through the vote of the majority, it has forsaken the view of a positive historical Judaism, which it had made its own on the sixteenth, by acclamation, together with Dr. Frankel. Yet Dr. Frankel in his letter suggests that the assembly had done the opposite. But the majority did not fail to recognize the high significance of the Hebrew language for the Israelites and the necessity of learning it in the schools; only it did not hold that it was unconditionally necessary for the worship service.

On the other hand, the minority which held the latter view did not in any wise claim that its opponents had left the positive historical point of view. Different points of view were involved here, not different tendencies.

The positive historical point of view desires progress out of that which exists. It does not desire haphazard creation without limits and without foundation. Therefore, our prayers shall be built on existing prayers and as much as possible develop in form and content out of tradition. The assembly cannot admit that the foundation of historic tradition is denied if one prays in a non-Hebraic tongue. Similarly Dr. Frankel would have to deny that the talmudists tampered with positive historical Judaism when they prayed the holiest of our prayers in Aramaic, indeed, when they permitted the entire service, with few exceptions, to be held in the non-Hebraic tongue. Even Dr. Frankel admitted this in

his vote concerning the non-existence of a legal necessity of Hebrew prayer. The assembly, therefore, believes that Dr. Frankel made this question forcibly into one of tendential import [importance from a partisan point of view] and, when he left the assembly, he left also his point of view and its consequences.

—From W. Gunther Plaut,
The Rise of Reform Judaism,
pp. 87–90.

The People's Demands of the Ruler of the German Province of Hesse, 1848

By your Royal Highness's proclamation of March 7, the wishes of the people are not fulfilled and their requests are incompletely granted. The people mistrusts your Royal Highness personally and sees in the failure to grant its requests a lack of straightforwardness. The people sees in this failure to grant its requests a proof of the necessity to band themselves still more closely together and to assume an attitude of stronger opposition to your Royal Highness.

The people of which we speak is no longer the mere idea of former times: no, it means Everybody, Everybody! Yes, your Royal Highness, Everybody! Even the army has declared itself unanimous!

The people demands its rights. It states its will that its future shall be better than its past, and this will is irresistible. The people has chosen a commission, which now demands for it and in its name:

1. The filling of all ministries, so far as this has not recently been done, by men who enjoy the confidence of the people.

2. The dissolution of the Diet [national assembly], which has been called together again, and its immediate resummoning as an electoral [elected] body.

3. Granting of complete freedom of the press on the lines laid down in section 95 of the administrative decree.

4. Complete amnesty for all political crimes committed since 1830.

5. Complete freedom of religious thought and practice and of conscience.

6. The exercise of influence on the German Confederation to establish a German popular house [of representatives]. The revocation of all ordinances restricting the enjoyment of constitutional rights, especially those affecting the right of petition, of union [forming groups], and of meeting.

7. A definite assurance that the legislative proposals promised in the proclamation of March 7, and now made even more imperative by the expression of these demands, shall be laid before the next assembly of representatives.

8. A decision on these points from your Royal Highness within 3 days, after which lapse of time, without a reply, you will be assumed to have given a refusal.

Now is the time for your Royal Highness to show your intentions to the people. Do not delay an instant in granting these demands in full! Cool-headed men assure your Royal Highness that this agitation has assumed a terrible aspect.

Armed help from the neighboring cities is already at hand; already we are familiar with the thought of a possible breach, and we know the power of the accomplished fact.

Your Royal Highness, yield! May God guide your heart!

—From R. W. Postgate,
Revolution—From 1789 to 1906,
pp. 250–251.

Invitation to the Leipzig Synod, 1869

At the close of the past century, the European Jews began to participate in the general activity of the world, owing to the gradual removal of the barriers which had excluded them from industrial life, social amenities, general and scientific culture, and public service. Under the influence of these completely changed conditions new and fresh life awoke in our midst in the province of religion, with the result that different views and many conflicts arose in the religious field.

In spite of the indestructible fealty of the Jews which is as ready today as at any time in the past to bring all sacrifices in act and suffering, there yet arose a growing confusion and an almost indescribable diversity among individuals and in congregations. Every individual was a law to himself as far as religious practices went, and the same was the case with congregations in their religious institutions. From these conflicts parties issued which called into being inner divisions, and in many places violent conflicts took place whereby the condition of Judaism became ever more confused and precarious. A religion of the minority, a religion of scattered small divisions, can be exposed to no greater danger than to become internally divided, conflicting, hesitating, and agitated by violent party strife.

It is readily comprehensible that such a condition can be cured only by organization and united action. Real improvement and betterment of the conditions can be accomplished only by the union of many, and such a union alone can obtain a true and sufficient authority.

With this in mind, twenty-four rabbis from all parts of Germany and Switzerland met at Cassel on August 11, 12, and 13 of last year. These rabbis recognized that the most effective remedy for the present conditions in Judaism lies in the creation of a union of the best-intentioned and ablest elements, but that such a union was not to be found in the assembling and the resolutions of a smaller or greater number of rabbis, but must be formed by the joining with the rabbis of the ripe scholars of Judaism and especially of the representatives of the congregations themselves. The conference of Cassel therefore resolved unanimously: (1) to convene a synodal assembly of rabbis, Jewish scholars, and representatives of the congregations; (2) to choose committees who are to formulate propositions for the synod.

It is apparent that nothing further could be done by the rabbinical conference than to determine of what class of men the synod shall be composed while all more explicit measures concerning the future composition of the synod, the order of business, the manner of voting, etc., had to be left to the first synodal gathering.

The committees on the cult [religious practice], the schools, the marriage laws, and other ritual matters promised to publish their reports sufficiently long before the meetings of the synod to enable all who expect to participate in the meeting to become thoroughly acquainted with and to examine them. Furthermore, it is scarcely necessary to state that by their participation in this first synod the congregations assume no responsibility for its resolutions and results. The object, above all else, is to lay the foundation for a large and more intimate, but altogether free union, devoid of all outer coercion—yes, for a visible and more effective organization and cooperation.

We therefore approach the Jewish congregations in general, and the governing boards in particular, with the request to participate through one or more representatives in the synodal-assembly that is to be convened during the summer of 1869. We do this with the consciousness that the honorable board is fully able to appreciate the real significance, the beneficial bearing [intent], of the proposed assembly.

We do not doubt that you have no wish to dissociate yourselves from the community of Israel and that you will contribute with pleasure toward ensuring its well-being and providing for its future. We see no other means whereby, in the spirit of our religion whose loftiest principle is brotherhood, as well as in the spirit of faith and freedom of conscience, we can effectually prevent further ruin.

We can think of no cogent reason for refusing to participate in this gathering. Every view, every tendency, will have the right to express itself. Verily, only the peace is upright, only that union real which results in mutual understanding and agreement, even though these involve much contention and struggle.

All these things we submit to you for consideration and beg you to let any one of the . . . committee know within four weeks whether you will participate in the synod.

May we all, mindful of what we owe to the glorious heritage of our fathers, the religion of four thousand years, soon see the work of union take shape before our eyes under the providence of God!

—From David Philipson,
The Reform Movement in Judaism,
pp. 289–291.

OTHER THINGS TO READ

Bamberger, Bernard J., *The Story of Judaism:* Chap. 43, "German Judaism Comes to Equilibrium"; Chap. 47, "Emancipation and Anti-Semitism."

Central Conference of American Rabbis Yearbook: Vol. 1 (1890), pp. 85–117 (the results of the various European conferences and synods).

Reform Judaism—Then and Now

Fleg, Edmond, *The Jewish Anthology:* Chap. 3, "The Three Aspects of Modern Judaism."

Jelenko, Edward W., "Samson Raphael Hirsch," Chap. 3 in Simon Noveck (ed.), *Great Jewish Personalities in Modern Times.*

Jewish Encyclopedia: "Rabbinical Conferences," Vol. 4, pp. 211–214; "Zacharias Frankel," Vol. 5, pp. 482–484; "Samson Raphael Hirsch," Vol. 6, p. 417; "Moritz Lazarus," Vol. 7, pp. 652–654; "Ludwig Philippson," Vol. 9, p. 684.

Lowenthal, Marvin, *The Jews of Germany:* Chap. 15, "Liberators"; Chap. 16, "Victory"; Chap. 17, "The Fruits of Freedom."

Philipson, David, *The Reform Movement in Judaism:* Chap. 7, "The Rabbinical Conferences, 1844–46"; Chap. 11, "The Leipzig and Augsburg Synods."

Plaut, W. Gunther, *The Growth of Reform Judaism:* pp. 44–46 (Zacharias Frankel); 46–47 (Berlin Seminary).

Plaut, W. Gunther, *The Rise of Reform Judaism:* pp. 74–94 (rabbinical conferences and synods); 133–145 (return to Palestine, mission, and Messiah); Chap. 7, "Worship Reform"; Chap. 8, "Sabbath and Holiday Observance"; pp. 215–225 (marriage and mourning practices); 244–255 (Jewish education and status of women).

Schwartzman, Sylvan D., *Reform Judaism in the Making:* Chap. 8, "Three Decades of Conferences, 1844–1871."

Standard Jewish Encyclopedia: "Conservative Judaism," pp. 479–480; "Zacharias Frankel," pp. 698–699; "Abraham Geiger," pp. 730–731; "Samson Raphael Hirsch," p. 910; "Moritz Lazarus," pp. 1479–1480;" Ludwig Philippson," p. 1500.

Universal Jewish Encyclopedia: "Rabbinical Conferences," Vol. 3, pp. 327–328; "Zacharias Frankel," Vol. 4, pp. 399–400; "Samson Raphael Hirsch," Vol. 5, pp. 378–379; "Conservative Judaism," Vol. 6, pp. 243–245; "Moritz Lazarus," Vol. 6, pp. 570–572; "Ludwig Philippson," Vol. 8, p. 487.

SUGGESTED ACTIVITIES

1. With the class comprising a Reform synod, take up one of the problems with which European Reform dealt. Are your class's decisions the same or different? Why?

2. Prepare a chart comparing the final decisions of the rabbinical conferences and synods with the practices currently carried on by your own congregation.

3. Attend a service at a local Conservative congregation. How does it compare with your own? In what respect does it differ from that of a modern Orthodox congregation? To what extent does Conservative Judaism still reflect the position of Zacharias Frankel?

   Prepare a list indicating the similarities and differences existing in an Orthodox, a Conservative, and a Reform service.

SUBJECTS FOR RESEARCH

1. Investigate the life and activities of Zacharias Frankel. How did they ultimately affect the Reform movement in Europe? What were his major contributions to Conservative Judaism? What influence has he had on the beliefs and practices of the Conservative congregations in your community?

2. What are the practices and beliefs of the present-day American Conservative Jew? How do they compare with those adopted by the rabbinical conferences and synods in Europe?

3. What contributions did Jews make to the initial success of the various revolutions of 1848? Why did these revolutions ultimately turn out to be failures? What happened to some of the Jews who participated in them?

4. What were some of Samson Raphael Hirsch's chief contributions to Orthodoxy? How did they affect the Reform cause in Europe?

5. What position did the Reform Societies of Berlin and Breslau take toward changes in Jewish belief and practice? How did this differ from the stand of Abraham Geiger?

FILMSTRIPS TO SEE

David Einhorn: Father of the Union Prayerbook (UAHC), presenting highlights in the life of this pioneer American Reformer who also attended several of the European rabbinical conferences.

Dr. Leo Baeck: Man of Faith (UAHC), describing the life and contributions of this outstanding European Reform leader who was the last head of the Berlin Reform Seminary and was actively identified with the World Union for Progressive Judaism.

The Jewish Wedding in Art (UAHC), portraying various aspects of traditional Jewish marriage rites.

The Anatomy of Nazism (Anti-Defamation League of B'nai B'rith), offering a documentary on the sources and tragic consequences of this German anti-Semitic movement of the twentieth century.

The Sabbath in Art (UAHC), picturing many traditional Jewish Sabbath observances.

A LIVE ISSUE

One of the factors that contributed to Reform Judaism's decline in Europe, as we shall see in this chapter, was the interference of the government in religious affairs. Therefore, in the interests of freedom for everyone, Reform Jews have consistently fought to maintain the principle of "separation of Church and State" and avoid any possible connection between government and religion.

For many years virtually all American Jews agreed with this position. Recently, however, some among the Orthodox who favor Jewish all-day schools have come out seeking government funds, with the result that American Jewry is now sharply divided over the issue of federal support for religious education.

The Basic Problem: The central question here is whether the contribution of government funds to the support of schools under religious auspices is a violation of the principle of separation of Church and State.

Those who object maintain that it is; those in favor claim it is not.

Some Important Questions: (1) Why has Reform Judaism insisted on complete separation of Church and State? (2) Why do most Reform Jews look upon government aid to schools under religious auspices as a violation of this principle? (3) In the interest of American Jewish unity, should Reform now abandon its position in favor of complete separation of Church and State? (4) Should it merely modify its stand by not objecting to government aid to all-day religious schools? (5) Or should it continue to maintain its original position?

What Do You Think? The outcome of this issue could have important consequences for American Jewry. Do you see why? What stand, then, should Reform take? As you read this chapter, try to arrive at your own conclusions.

10. WHY REFORM DECLINED IN EUROPE

The Achievements of European Reform

In the years following the Augsburg Synod it became clear that Reform in Europe had spent itself, and Moritz Lazarus, who had presided over the sessions, admitted as much in an address in 1886 when he stated:

> The decay of a religion, as well as of every religious society, must occur if a very large portion of its people no longer observe many hundreds of demands but nevertheless permit them to stand as religious duties.
>
> Several attempts at reform were made at the rabbinical conferences and synods, but these remained without any successors. The real reason why we have not continued with constant work at reforms is simple laziness.
>
> Yet a religion whose teachers and leaders lack the courage to deal with the question, ''What in fact are the requirements of Judaism and what must they eventually be?''—such a faith faces the greatest of dangers, its abandonment.

To him, as to others, religious progress seemed to have come to an end.

Reform's achievements in Europe had been considerable. ''Rarely has any brief period in Jewish history seen such an outpouring of the spirit,'' observes a noted scholar. It ''shaped the course of the American congregations in their adoption of the principles of Reform,'' declares another. Indeed, when we consider Reform's present-day beliefs and practices, we realize how very much the movement in Europe contributed.

Some Principal Beliefs from Europe

American Reform can, in fact, trace the following five principal beliefs to Europe: Judaism is subject to change, Judaism reflects God's continuous revelation, the Jews have a mission to fulfill, the Messianic Age will establish God's Kingdom on earth, and religion is the vital force in Jewish existence.

Judaism Subject to Change

As a product of historical development, Judaism is subject to change. The conviction that the Jewish faith underwent repeated modification was supported by the "Science of Judaism" with its careful investigation of the past. Thus, on the basis of his own research, Abraham Geiger was able to declare:

> **Judaism did not operate within narrow limits and removed from the world of reality. On the contrary, its spiritual power has revealed itself at all times at the very moment of important cultural developments. It was, in fact, receptive to those influences growing out of the centers of culture. It never shut them out, nor was it absorbed by them. It succeeded rather in incorporating them in accordance with its own genius, thus giving proof of its independent vitality.**

If this was true in the past, then Judaism had every reason to undergo further change in a modern world that was becoming so strikingly different.

Progressive Revelation

Judaism reflects God's continuous revelation to the Jewish people. Reform holds that more than simply responding to historical circumstance Judaism has advanced under the influence of God's inspiration, serving to expand and refine men's knowledge of Him and the conduct He demands.

This is the doctrine known as Progressive Revelation, which insists that religious knowledge is never static, but constantly grows as man discovers more about himself and his universe. Here, said Geiger, the Jew enjoys special spiritual sensitivity:

> **Does not the Jewish people have a religious genius?**
>
> **Was it not also an original force that enlightened its eyes so it could look more deeply into the higher spheres of the spirit, that it could distinguish more clearly the close relationship between the spirit of man and the Universal Spirit, that it could grasp the higher challenge of human existence and perceive the profound ethical quality in man with greater clarity and intensity as its unique insight? If this is indeed so, then this intimate contact of the spirit of the individual with the Universal Spirit, so they could break through all limited barriers, is revelation as possessed by the [Jewish] people as a whole.**

Historically endowed by God, then, the Jews seem to have a unique spiritual capacity that has proved of benefit to the whole human race.

The Mission of the Jewish People

The Jewish people exists primarily to carry out its mission to mankind. Its sensitivity to God's continuing revelation confers upon the Jewish people the task of bringing to all mankind the true knowledge of Him and the moral, ethical way of life He requires.

In fact, as Samuel Holdheim described it, this is the central objective of Judaism itself:

> **It is the destiny of Judaism to pour the light of its thoughts, the fire of its beliefs, the fervor of its feelings upon all souls and hearts on earth. Then all of these peoples, each according to its land and historic characteristics, will, by accepting our teachings, kindle their own lights, which will then shine independently and warm their souls. Judaism shall be the seed-bed**

The Messianic Age

of the nations, filled with blessing and promise. . . . Indeed, it is the task of Israel to make the pure knowledge of God and the pure law of morality of Judaism the common possession and blessing of all the peoples of the earth.

The Messianic Age, achieved through the spiritual conversion of all mankind, will see the establishment on earth of God's Kingdom of everlasting righteousness, justice, and peace. The success of the Jews' mission will transform every human heart and mind and bring about a world that Leopold Stein, the presiding officer of the Frankfort Conference, pictured in the following way:

To this task, or mission, God has appointed the Jews and dispersed them throughout the world in order that the entire human race may prosper.

LIGHTING THE CHANUKAH MENORAH. The ceremony reminds us of the lights in the Temple in Maccabean times.

> The messianic era is one in which "God will be king over all the earth," when "He will be one and His Name will be one," in which all peoples will turn to the Lord and "become His people," in which mankind will unite itself under "one God into one brotherhood," in which the earth through "justice, truth, and peace" will become a garden of God and a promised land.

Religion, Force in Jewish Existence

Religion is the central, vital force in Jewish existence. The particular genius of the Jews and their mission as the "living servant of God" make religion the indispensable element in Jewish life. No other force is comparable. As Abraham Geiger said:

> Inasmuch as Israel [Jewry] is and should remain unique, it is a *spiritual* bond that unites Israel. It is a *spiritual* life all its own which embraces all its members and which will remain unchanged, even under the most diversified circumstances . . . Of Israel's spiritual life, we can say that it exists and that it shows itself as a basic force.

In contrast to those who would base Jewish existence upon its culture or national identity, Reform has consistently emphasized religion as the essential element in uniting and preserving the Jews and providing them with their purpose for existence.

Europe's Contributions to Reform Practice

Beyond establishing Reform's central beliefs, Europe also contributed much to the movement's fundamental practices in the following areas: synagogue practice, Sabbath and holiday worship, life-cycle observances, religious status of women, and religious education.

Synagogue Practice

Starting with its insistence upon decorum in the synagogue, European Reform pioneered many of the present-day temple practices. It seated men and women together at worship, shortened the service by eliminating repetitious prayers, and established the use of the vernacular in addition to Hebrew. It introduced the mixed choir and organ, the weekly sermon and modern hymns into the service, as well as worship without hats, a practice that was adopted in 1845 by the Berlin Reform Congregation.

Sabbath and Holiday Worship

Many have been the contributions of European Reform to Sabbath and holiday worship. Not only did it succeed in eliminating most of the minor fast days and extra days of the major holidays but it also introduced an inspiring memorial service on Yom Kippur, provided for the wider celebration of Chanukah, and reinterpreted the Sabbath as a time for spiritual renewal rather than a day of rest from the traditional categories of "work."

Life-Cycle Observances

The Confirmation ceremony, many improvements in wedding rites, including the double-ring ceremony, and important modifications of Jewish funeral and mourning practices were introduced by European Reform. The Breslau Conference also sanctioned the use of modern surgical instruments and techniques in circumcision, a practice that has since been adopted by many Conservative and Orthodox Jews as well.

Religious Status of Women

In their efforts to improve the religious status of women, the movement in Europe abolished both the institution of the *agunah* and the practice of *chalitzah.* It likewise enabled women to participate actively in the wedding ceremony and in congregational life generally.

Religious Education

Present-day Reform's insistence upon a religious education for both sexes is a direct outgrowth of the movement's pioneering efforts in Europe. So is its concern that Jewish education be both modern and religiously oriented. "It must be more than Hebrew language instruction," declared Abraham Geiger. "The stress must be upon religious understanding and practice." Thus, practically all Reform congregations today provide instruction on many levels designed to develop a religious outlook based upon a scientific understanding of Judaism.

It is not surprising, therefore, that a foremost Reform historian, Dr. David Philipson, has stressed the "direct connection between the practical expression of . . . [Reform] principles in the United States and their original enunciation in Germany."

Yet in spite of its remarkable contributions, European Reform eventually went into a decline from which it never really recovered. The reasons for the decline, however, are not hard to discover and can be grouped into the following six causes: setbacks in freedom as Europe became conservative, the growth of anti-Semitism, the effective opposition by Orthodox Judaism, the interference by reactionary governments, the effects of competing movements both religious and secular, and the shortcomings of the Reform movement.

Cause 1: Setbacks in Freedom

One of the principal causes of the decline in the European Reform movement was the unsettled political situation in Europe which, from time to time, denied Jews many of their rights. After Napoleon's defeat, for example, the Congress of Vienna agreed that Jews should be allowed the privileges each country had granted them. Yet most rulers on returning to power claimed that it was Napoleon, and not the nation, that had granted the Jews citizenship. Hence they felt free to reintroduce most of the former restrictions. So, in Frankfort, the Jews were promptly moved back into the ghetto, and in Rome they were once more compelled to listen to sermons designed to convert them. Even in France, the "Jewish oath" was restored so that those testifying at a trial had to go to the synagogue first and swear before the judge, the rabbi, and ten witnesses that they would tell the truth.

Naturally, every political setback worked to the disadvantage of Reform, whose program of religious change counted upon Jewish emancipation. Without freedom, there seemed no reason for any change from traditional Judaism, and the Orthodox were quick to point out Reform's mistake in having confidence in Europe's enlightenment.

Still, conditions for the Jews eventually improved and, with it, Reform renewed its progress by establishing many new societies and congregations and holding the various rabbinical conferences and synods.

The revolution in 1830 in France, for instance, dethroned the king and led to the restoration of most of the Jews' rights but, in Germany, Austria, and Hungary, the struggle was more prolonged. Though revolutions in 1848 forced the kings to grant democratic constitutions, these proved short-lived. Actually, it was not until 1867 that Austrian Jews finally received equality, and in Hungary Judaism was not recognized as a legitimate religion until 1896. Even then, though technically free, most Central European Jews never fully enjoyed the rights to which the law entitled them.

In northern Italy, the Jews were more fortunate because, as soon as the Austrians were driven from power in 1859, their citizenship was restored. But all the Jews of Italy were not freed until a dozen years later when the Catholic Church was forced to surrender Rome to Italian control.

Even in as liberal a country as England it was not until 1858 that Lionel Rothschild was permitted to become the first Jewish member of the House of Commons and 1871 before Jews could receive degrees from Oxford and Cambridge universities.

However, in spite of the improving situation, most European Jews never felt quite secure. Always in mind was their people's plight in Russia where the democratic influences of the French Revolution had never penetrated. Even in the 1870's and 1880's the regime there continued to operate under the old feudal system that retained all the intolerable conditions of pre-revolutionary Europe.

What was worse, the authorities deliberately went out of their way to oppress the Jews and make them scapegoats for the intolerable conditions inside Russia. For by blaming the Jews for the widespread suffering, especially among the peasants, the Czars were able to divert hostility from their own corrupt regimes and stave off long overdue political reforms. Meanwhile, the greatest victims were the Jews who, as we shall see, had to endure the hostility of the Russian people as well as the barbaric treatment of the government.

Thus, the difficulties encountered by European Jews in securing and maintaining freedom seriously hampered the development of a liberal form of Judaism that counted upon their acceptance by the modern world.

Cause 2:
The Growth of Anti-Semitism

Also contributing to the insecurity of the European Jew was the growth of anti-Semitism, which frequently prevented him from enjoying the very rights he had been granted.

Building upon long-standing fear and dislike of the Jews, modern anti-Semitism fed upon the belief that they were dangerous to the nation. Even as far back as 1815, a German university professor had developed the thesis in his book, *The Menace of the Jews to the Welfare and Character of the Germans,* that they ''comprised a separate and inferior nation within the German nation.'' Expulsion of the Jews, selling their children into slavery, or sterilizing every Jewish male were among the solutions he and other writers proposed.

As Jews gained greater rights, the campaign against them intensified. Soon the view that they were an inferior people and responsible for most of the economic and social ills of the times became widely accepted. Even well-known intellectuals subscribed to this notion. For example, in 1855 as respected a scholar as Ernest Renan declared the Semites to be culturally inferior to other peoples and the noted composer Richard Wagner pictured the Jews as being ''the cause of German decay.''

By the end of the 1870's the argument that the Jews were a ''foreign race that did not belong in Europe and should be driven out'' was injected into political life. ''The Jews,'' warned Wilhelm Marr, son of a Jewish convert and founder of the Anti-Semitic League to Save the German Fatherland, ''are on the verge of triumphing over the Germans.'' His, however, was only one of a number of political groups that adopted anti-Semitism. Far more influential was the Christian Socialist Party, established by a court preacher named Adolf Stöcker, who openly campaigned against ''Jewish domination in business, the press, and politics" and who was elected to the German legislature in 1881.

The following year a convention of German and Austro-Hungarian anti-Semites met in Dresden and urged all European governments to exclude Jews from the army and prevent further Jewish immigration. Revived, too, were many of the old charges, including the accusation that Jews used Christian blood in the celebration of Passover, with the result that in 1882 fifteen Hungarian Jews were actually arrested on the charge of ritually murdering a Christian girl who had disappeared.

Even in as liberal a country as France anti-Semitism proved a powerful weapon in the hands of reactionaries in the celebrated Dreyfus Affair. On October 15, 1894, Captain Alfred Dreyfus, a Jewish officer on the French general staff, was falsely accused of selling military secrets to the Germans. Actually the guilty party was his fellow officer, Colonel Esterhazy, a non-Jew, whom the general staff was determined to protect, even to the extent of forging documents to incriminate Dreyfus. As a result, he was court-martialed, publicly branded a traitor, and sentenced to life-imprisonment on Devil's Island.

The enemies of democracy made much of the fact that Dreyfus was a Jew and cited his case as proof that Jews could not be trusted as citizens. Calling for the overthrow of all governments that accorded Jews equality, they attracted a wide following in France and elsewhere and, until 1906 when Dreyfus was finally cleared of the charges, they seriously threatened the future of democracy all over Europe.

Such incidents served to confirm the feeling of many European Jews that the rights they enjoyed were only temporary and could at any time be swept away by anti-Semitism. The result was a natural hesitancy to identify with any form of Judaism that counted upon Jewish emancipation.

Cause 3: Effective Orthodox Opposition

—They have forfeited all rights and privileges of membership in the Jewish community.

—The seats they have customarily held in the community synagogue are withdrawn.

—They are ineligible to hold any religious office in the community or to perform any religious act in the community synagogue.

—They may perform no charitable deed in behalf of the community, nor will their contributions of any sort be accepted.

—They shall not be permitted burial in the community cemetery nor be given a religious funeral.

So ran the main provisions of a *cherem*, or ban, enacted in 1842 by the Orthodox against the members of the West London Synagogue, and it was such measures that proved highly effective in discouraging many from associating with Reform.

Thus, contributing to European Reform's decline was the intense opposition of the Orthodox who not only attacked Reform Jews as "sinful" and "disloyal to Judaism" but, through domination of the organized Jewish community, succeeded in hampering the establishment of Reform temples. For going back to ghetto times, the law of most European countries required all Jews to belong to a *kehillah* (קְהִלָּה, collective group or community) that maintained their institutions, including the synagogue, and represented them before the civil authorities. As the overwhelming majority, the Orthodox generally controlled the community and were able to stifle religious change in existing synagogues and withhold financial support from newly-established Reform temples. Since the state collected taxes from every Jew for the maintenance of the Jewish community, the Reform Jew found himself having to help maintain the synagogues of the Orthodox while being denied any funds for the support of his own temple.

Even where this was not the case, the Orthodox were able to counter Reform in other ways. In Frankfort, for instance, Samson Raphael Hirsch, the rabbi of the community, had the government adopt a law permitting anyone who objected to change in synagogue worship to withdraw from the Jewish community and thereby deprive it of his financial support. In only three communities did the Orthodox ever carry out this threat, but the very existence of such a "Law of Withdrawal" served effectively to hold back Reform progress.

Cause 4:
Interference by the Government

Being in a position to speak for the Jews of the community, the Orthodox were frequently able to enlist the assistance of the civil authorities in suppressing Reform.

The rulers of Europe had long been accustomed to recognize the right of the Jews to manage their own affairs through their own community councils and, once disputes over Reform broke out, the Orthodox majority would generally turn to the government for support. So we will recall that, when Jacobson introduced Reform services in Berlin, the Prussian king issued a decree prohibiting any variation from traditional worship. Similarly, the Orthodox in England were able to prevent the rabbi of the West London Synagogue from performing marriages for some fourteen years, until Parliament finally granted him the right. Even today, there are countries—particularly the State of Israel—where liberal rabbis are still not permitted to officiate at weddings.

In most instances, the Orthodox found a strong ally in Europe's reactionary regimes, which feared changes of any sort and even looked upon liberal religion as suspect. Furthermore, as heads of so-called Christian countries, some rulers considered it their duty to promote the cause of Christianity. By blocking attempts to modernize Judaism they believed they were encouraging the conversion of those Jews who were dissatisfied with their faith.

In effect, then, the support of the government provided considerable assistance to the Orthodox and seriously hindered Reform progress.

Cause 5:
The Effect of Competing Movements

Competition from a variety of other movements among the Jews also affected Reform. One of these was Conservative Judaism. Though essentially Orthodox in practice, it managed to introduce certain minor changes in observance which enabled it to claim that it was both traditional and modern, thereby satisfying many who might have been attracted to Reform.

Traditional Judaism also reacted by coming forward with Neo-Orthodoxy, a more appealing interpretation developed by Samson Raphael Hirsch. By adopting various improvements in synagogue worship along the lines of the Conservatives and offering more reasonable explanations for traditional practice and belief—stressing in particular their ethical content—the Neo-Orthodox were able to retain the loyalties of many among the younger generation.

But two secular movements also challenged Reform. The first was socialism, which spread throughout Germany in the 1850's and 1860's under the leadership of Ferdinand Lasalle, a Jew by birth who, however, rejected

ZIONIST CONGRESS AT BASEL, SWITZERLAND. The speaker is Chaim Weizmann who became the first president of the State of Israel. The portrait is that of Theodor Herzl, the founder of the modern Zionist movement. (FPG)

religion. After the unsuccessful revolutions of 1848, many European Jews were attracted to socialism. They saw in its program of economic and political reforms the promise of achieving Judaism's messianic hope of universal equality, justice, and peace.

Unfortunately, in the years that followed, they were sadly disappointed to discover that prejudice persisted even among the socialists. Ultimately, with the triumph of socialism in Russia, most Jews were disillusioned. For, despite its dedication to socialist ideals, the Soviet Union has continued to mistreat its Jews.

Jewish nationalism, the second movement, sprang up mainly in Eastern Europe, but in the 1860's it also began to take root among those in the West who were discouraged by both the political reaction that developed and the unfulfilled promises of socialism. Mean-

while, the movement found encouragement in the nationalistic struggle of the Italians and Germans to unify their countries, then made up of a number of rival kingdoms. "Why should we Jews be less worthy of nationhood than other peoples?" asked the Jewish nationalists. "The Jews are a nation, destined to be resurrected with all other civilized nations," declared Moses Hess, a former socialist who had fled Germany after the failure of the 1848 revolution. And, with each setback in the struggle for full equality, more and more Jews came to see the establishment of a state of their own as the only realistic answer.

Thus, Reform was not alone in its attempt to improve the situation of the modern Jew. It faced serious competition from other movements, secular as well as religious, that vigorously sought his support.

Cause 6:
The Shortcomings of the Movement

Finally, in certain ways, European Reform itself was responsible for its own decline. For it never really developed into a unified movement, nor were its supporters able to agree upon a common religious program. True, the rabbinical conferences and synods did reach important decisions on numerous religious issues, but these received all too little publicity and few congregations actually adopted them. Most of the leaders, in fact, seemed reluctant to carry out a thoroughgoing revision of traditional practices and beliefs but preferred to follow a more moderate program of change that left their synagogues very much like those of the Conservatives.

Actually, the European movement never did achieve a permanent organization embracing all congregations or rabbis. It was not until 1908 that those in Germany were able to form a Union for Liberal Judaism and 1929 before a number of German congregations began using a common prayer book.

All during these years, moreover, Reform suffered from a serious loss of leadership, due chiefly to unfavorable political conditions following the defeat of Napoleon and the unsuccessful revolutions of 1848. As a result, thousands of Jews made their way to the United States, among them most of the eventual leaders of American Reform.

What Happened to European Reform?

But Reform in Europe did not die out. Actually, in certain countries it experienced a considerable revival of interest and growth.

This was true in England. There, in 1902, a Jewish Religious Union had been formed by both the Orthodox and Reform under the leadership of Claude G. Montefiore to win back those who had become indifferent to Judaism. However, the Orthodox withdrew when the organization conducted Saturday afternoon services almost entirely in English, to the accompaniment of choir and organ, and permitted men and women to sit together.

Adopting a new name, the Religious Union for the Advancement of Liberal Judaism, the group proceeded to organize a new Reform congregation in London that was considerably more liberal than the original West London Synagogue. It soon adopted its own prayer book, introduced special services on Sunday, and permitted women to officiate at worship. Today it has become the largest congregation in all England.

Under the leadership of Montefiore and Miss Lily Montagu, who for many years was the foremost Reform Jewess in Britain, the Religious Union went on to form similar Liberal congregations in most of the major cities of England, in contrast to the older and more traditional-minded Reform synagogues. In recent years, however, both groups have made an effort to cooperate for the benefit of the movement as a whole, and in 1966 they joined together to further the work of a common Liberal rabbinical school in London, the Leo Baeck College, established ten years earlier.

Reform in France made considerably less headway. It was not until 1903 that the *Union Israélite Libérale,* the Union for Liberal Judaism, was established. After a number of years, it finally built a temple in Paris where, in addition to Sabbath services, it conducted worship on Sunday. Following the end of World War II, the movement became somewhat more active and, in 1955, it established its own seminary in Paris for the training of Liberal rabbis and teachers.

In the late 1920's, Reform experienced a revival in Germany. By then, the movement already possessed a seminary of its own, a permanent rabbinical organization, a union of congregations, and a common Reform prayer book. Under the leadership of Rabbi Leo

Baeck it began to attract a much wider following among the young people, but the nature of German Jewish life, with its restrictive *Kehillah* organization, continued to impede Reform progress. So much so that, after a visit in 1929 to a Berlin Reform synagogue, a leading American Reform rabbi wrote:

> **Judging by the American standard of Reform, the German Reform service was Conservative, if not Orthodox. The services were conducted almost entirely in Hebrew. The women were seated by themselves in the gallery, and the men worshiped with covered heads.**

The catastrophe that befell the Jews under the Nazis marked the tragic end of German Reform. However, recently, some of the relatively few Jews living in Germany have reestablished a small Reform movement.

Reform Moves Westward

The Augsburg Synod was the high-water mark of European Reform. After 1871, as the various causes for its decline began to take their toll, the movement came to a virtual standstill in most of Europe.

By 1871, too, it was beginning to be evident that Reform initiative was passing to the 250,000 Jews of the United States. Here some seventy-five congregations were already Reform or sympathetic to it, and by that year the third major Reform conference had been held. Indeed, there was even talk among the leaders about establishing a permanent organization of Reform congregations to support a rabbinical seminary.

QUESTIONS FOR DISCUSSION

1. Which of the major European Reform beliefs and practices are still maintained by your own congregation? On the basis of this, to what extent is present-day Reform Judaism the product of the movement in Europe?

2. Which of the six main causes for the decline of European Reform do you believe was most responsible? Why? What possible efforts might the movement have made to overcome this? How do you explain its failure to make them?

3. In comparison with the situation in Europe, why would Reform Judaism be more likely to progress in America? What factors responsible for its decline in Europe were missing here? How do you account for this?

4. In what way does the organization of the Jewish community in the United States today differ from that of nineteenth-century Europe? What effect has this had upon American Jewish life in general? Upon Reform Judaism?

5. What competition does Reform presently face in the United States? How does this compare with the situation in nineteenth-century Europe? In what ways does American Reform Judaism benefit or suffer from the existence of other Jewish religious movements? From various Jewish secular causes?

6. To what extent has American Reform overcome the internal weaknesses of the movement in Europe? How does the situation within your own congregation justify your answer? Does present-day Reform have other weaknesses that work to its disadvantage? What?

SIGNIFICANT DOCUMENTS

Samson Raphael Hirsch's Views on Reform, 1836

> **In Mendelssohn's days, when the new movement of the spirit had begun but the Jewish life was yet untouched, then it would have been possible to construct the science of Judaism and to bring to the strong formal life the light and warmth of the spirit, and our condition would be different now.**

European Reform Developments—from 1815

Important Historical Events	Key Happenings in Jewish Life	Major Developments in European Reform
1815—Defeat of Napoleon at Waterloo.	1815—Reintroduction of restrictions against Jews in many sections of Europe. Start of immigration to America.	1818—Dedication of the Hamburg Temple.
		1820—Opening of a branch temple at Leipzig.
		1823—Government halts Berlin Reform services.
1830—Successful revolution in France.		1832—Zunz's *The Jewish Sermon* published.
		1837—Wiesbaden Rabbinical Conference.
		1838—Start of the Geiger-Tiktin affair (to 1854).
		1841—Hamburg prayer book controversy.
		1842—Dedication of the West London Synagogue of British Jews. Organization of the Frankfort Reform Society (to 1845).
		1844—Brunswick Rabbinical Conference.
	1845—Beginnings of Conservative Judaism.	1845—Frankfort Rabbinical Conference.
	1846—Removal of the remaining restrictions against French Jewry.	1846—Breslau Rabbinical Conference.
1848—Unsuccessful revolutions in many parts of Europe.	1848—Renewed reaction against Jews with the rise of anti-Semitism. Increase of Jewish emigration.	
	1850—Beginnings of Jewish socialism.	
1853—Crimean War.	1859—Jews of northern Italy emancipated.	

Important Historical Events	Key Happenings in Jewish Life	Major Developments in European Reform
1861—Start of the American Civil War. **1870**—Franco-Prussian War. **1871**—Unification of Germany and of Italy.	**1860**—Beginnings of Jewish nationalism. **1867**—Emancipation of Austrian Jews. **1871**—Final emancipation of Italian Jews. Removal of last restrictions from English Jewry. **1879**—Beginning of anti-Semitic political parties. **1881**—Start of Russian pogroms resulting in mass emigration to the United States. **1894**—Beginning of the Dreyfus Affair (to 1906). **1896**—Judaism recognized as a legal religion in Hungary. **1897**—Formation of the World Zionist Organization.	**1869**—Leipzig Synod. **1870**—Founding of the Reform rabbinical seminary in Berlin. **1871**—Augsburg Synod. **1899**—Formation of the Union of Liberal Rabbis in Germany. **1903**—Founding of the *Union Israélite Libérale* in Paris. **1908**—Union for Liberal Judaism formed in Germany.
1914—Start of World War I. **1917**—Start of the Russian Revolution leading to establishment of the Soviet Union. **1933**—German government taken over by Hitler. **1939**—Start of World War II.	**1942**—"Final Solution"—Decision of the Nazis to exterminate the Jews. **1948**—Establishment of the State of Israel.	**1909**—Jewish Religious Union of England becomes Reform. Start of new Liberal temples in leading cities. **1922**—Start of Reform revival in Germany. **1955**—Founding of Reform seminary in Paris. **1956**—Establishment of the Leo Baeck College in London.

Today it is no longer possible. The [Reform] opinions, not derived from true Judaism, have become active and vigorous and labor with hostile energy to undermine that which they pretend to represent. They must be combatted directly in the midst of life, so that many who still observe may comprehend what they observe; that many who reject may hesitate and examine that which they reject; that many a hand now raised, perhaps, in honest zeal to tear down or to build up something new, be held back and its owner be induced to inquire carefully concerning that which he had purposed to tear down or to build in other form, and with new additions . . .

I recognize as our nearest and most fundamental evil the false opinions and notions which prevail concerning the extent as well as the contents and meaning of our *mitzvot* [מִצְוֹת, religious commandments]. In these isolated, uncomprehended tasks and duties, Israel's essence is misunderstood, attacked, annihilated. At this spot the greatest stream flows away, and here the first effort should be made to repair the breach. When the demonstration has been given as to the special contents of Judaism, then the gaze may be lifted higher and the question be answered as to the position which Judaism as a whole occupies in the series of other phenomena, what its relation to mankind, what the position of man in the world as comprehended from Judaism, what the relation of the world to God, of God to it . . .

—From Samson Raphael Hirsch,
The Nineteen Letters of Ben Uzziel,
translation by Bernard Drachman,
pp. 217–218, 220–221.

From the Appeal of an Early
Jewish Nationalist, 1862

Have you never read the words of the prophet Isaiah, ''Comfort, comfort my people, says your God. Speak comfortably to the heart of Jerusalem, and cry unto her that the appointed time has come, that her iniquity is pardoned; for she has received at the Lord's hand double for all her sins. The voice of one that cries in the wilderness: Prepare the way of the Lord, make straight in the desert a highway for our God. Every valley shall be exalted, and every mountain and hill shall be made low, and the crooked shall be made a straight place, and the rough places plain. And the glory of the Lord shall be revealed, and all flesh shall see it together: For the mouth of the Lord has spoken it'' [Isaiah 40:1–5].

Do you not believe that in these words, with which the second Isaiah opened his prophecies, as well as in the words with which the prophet Obadiah closed his, the conditions of our own time are graphically pictured? Was not help given to Zion in order to defend and establish the wild mountaineers there? Are not things being prepared there and roads levelled, and is not the road of civilization being built in the desert in the form of the Suez Canal and the railroad which will connect Asia and Europe?

They are not thinking at present of the restoration of our people. But you know the proverb: ''Man proposes, God disposes.'' Just as in the West they once searched for a road to India, and incidentally discovered a new world, so will our lost fatherland be rediscovered on the road to India and China that is now being built in the Orient.

Do you still doubt that France will help the Jews to found colonies which may extend from Suez to Jerusalem, and from the banks of the Jordan to the coast of the Mediterranean? Then read the work which appeared shortly after the massacres in Syria, by the famous writer Dentu, under the title of *The New Oriental Problem*. The author did not exactly write it at the request of the French government but acted in accord with the spirit of the French nation, when he urged our brethren, not on religious grounds, but from purely political and humanitarian motives, to restore their ancient state . . .

—From Moses Hess,
Rome and Jerusalem, Letter 11,
translation by Meyer Waxman,
pp. 148–150.

From the Prussian Law of Withdrawal, 1876

1. A Jew who because of religious scruples desires to withdraw from the Jewish religious community (*Cultusgemeinde*), to which he belongs by common law or by dint of an administrative order, is permitted to do so without thereby being considered as having withdrawn from the Jewish community as such (that is, from Judaism). A Jew who having made use of this permission changes his residence, and thereby enters into the jurisdiction of another synagogue community, does not become a member of this community, if before or at the time of his settlement he makes a declaration before the court to the effect that he does not wish to become a member of this community.

2. The withdrawal from the synagogue community (*Cultusgemeinde*) obtains legal validity when the withdrawing member declares his intention personally before a judge of his domicile, provided he declares that such withdrawal is caused by religious scruples.

3. The acceptance of his declaration of withdrawal must be preceded by a suitable application. The judge must at once inform the trustees of the community of such application. The acceptance of the declaration may not take place until four weeks have passed and . . . later than six weeks after the receipt of the application by the court.

4. The only costs to be levied upon the applicant are the cost of copying and cash expenditures. . . .

6. The declaration of withdrawal has the following consequences:
   a. The withdrawing member no longer has those privileges which appertain to membership in the synagogue community and these privileges cease on the day of his declaration.
   b. The withdrawing member is relieved of financial obligations which are occasioned by his personal membership in the community. His obligation ceases at the end of the calendar year which follows his declaration of withdrawal. However, the right regarding the use of the synagogue cemetery and the obligation to contribute to its maintenance are reserved to the withdrawing member as long as he has not obtained the right to use another cemetery. Rights which accrue to the member through the civil law are not affected by the withdrawal. The withdrawing member must however continue to share in the expenses of the congregation for the above-mentioned period in the same manner as if he had not made his declaration. He must contribute to the support of an extraordinary building program, the necessity for which has been ascertained prior to the calendar year in which he has withdrawn from the community. He must continue to share in it for two additional years. He also continues to share in those obligations which the community itself owes to other parties. Obligations which do not stem from personal membership in the community, especially all costs for Jewish *public* schools, but excepting the religious schools of the community, are not affected by the withdrawal.

8. If a number of withdrawing members unite in order to institute a special service of their own, they may receive, through royal edict, the privileges of a synagogue community of their own.

—From W. Gunther Plaut,
The Growth of Reform Judaism,
pp. 337–338.

OTHER THINGS TO READ

Bamberger, Bernard J., *The Story of Judaism:* Chap. 43, "German Judaism Comes to Equilibrium"; Chap. 44, "Under the Heel of the Tsars"; Chap. 46, "The Era of Pogroms"; Chap. 47, "Emancipation and Anti-Semitism"; Chap. 50, "European Judaism before World War I"; Chap. 52, "The Last Glories of European Jewry."

Elbogen, Ismar, *A Century of Jewish Life:* Book 1, Chap. 1, "Emancipation in Central and Western Europe"; Book 2, Chap. 1, "Anti-Semitism as a Political Movement"; Chap. 2, "Anti-Semitism in Western Europe"; Chap. 3, "The Jews of Russia under Alexander III"; Book 3, Chap. 2, "Theodor Herzl and Political Zionism."

Feuer, Leon I., and Azriel Eisenberg, *Jewish Literature since the Bible,* II: pp. 199–205 (Claude Montefiore and Liberal Judaism); 220–227 (early Jewish nationalism); 236–238 (Dreyfus Affair).

Fleg, Edmund, *The Jewish Anthology:* Chap. 3, "The Three Aspects of Modern Judaism."

Gumbiner, Joseph H., *Isaac Mayer Wise, Pioneer of American Judaism:* Chap. 1, "An American in Bohemia, 1846."

Heller, James G., *Isaac M. Wise, His Life, Work and Thought:* Part 1, "The Setting"; Part 2, Chap. 1, "Family Childhood and Early Education"; Chap. 2, "The Later Years of His Education"; Chap. 3, "His Education (continued)"; Chap. 4, "Rabbi of Radnitz"; Chap. 5, "Departure and Arrival."

Jelenko, Edward W., "Samson Raphael Hirsch," Chap. 3 in Simon Noveck (ed.), *Great Jewish Personalities in Modern Times.*

Jewish Encyclopedia: "Anti-Semitism," Vol. 1, pp. 641–649; "Dreyfus Case," Vol. 4, pp. 660–688; "Zacharias Frankel," Vol. 5, pp. 482–484; "Samson Raphael Hirsch," Vol. 6, p. 417; "Russia—History," Vol. 10, pp. 518–528.

Levinger, Lee J., *A History of the Jews in the United States:* pp. 212–213 (the Reform of the German immigrants to America); 357–360 (anti-Semitism).

Marcus, Jacob R., *The Rise and Destiny of the German Jew:* Chap. 3, "The Origin of Anti-Semitism."

Philipson, David, *The Reform Movement in Judaism:* Chap. 13, "The Latest Developments in Europe."

Plaut, W. Gunther, *The Growth of Reform Judaism:* pp. 46–49 (European Liberal seminaries); Chap. 5, "Realignment in Europe"; pp. 100–109 (failures of Reform in Europe).

Roth, Cecil, *A Bird's-Eye View of Jewish History:* Chap. 29, "Anti-Semitism and the New Diaspora"; Chap. 30, "A New World."

Sachar, Abram L., *A History of the Jews:* Chap. 24, "The Russian Jewish Nightmare"; Chap. 26, "The Revival of Anti-Semitism"; Chap. 27, "Zionism."

Schwartzman, Sylvan D., *Reform Judaism in the Making:* Chap. 9, "Why European Reform Failed."

Standard Jewish Encyclopedia: "Anti-Semitism," pp. 122–129; "Leo Baeck," p. 216, "Conservative Judaism," pp. 479–480; "Alfred Dreyfus," pp. 575–576; "Moses Hess," pp. 895–896; "Samson Raphael Hirsch," p. 909; "Ferdinand Lasalle," p. 1171; "Claude Montefiore," p. 1347; "Orthodoxy," pp. 1460–1461; "Russia," pp. 1624–1629.

Universal Jewish Encyclopedia: "Anti-Semitism," Vol. 1, pp. 341–409; "Leo Baeck," Vol. 2, pp. 26–27; "Conservative Judaism," Vol. 7, pp. 243–245; "Alfred Dreyfus," Vol. 3, pp.

596–599; ''Moses Hess,'' Vol. 5, pp. 344–345; ''Samson Raphael Hirsch,'' Vol. 5, pp. 378–379; ''Ferdinand Lasalle,'' Vol. 6, pp. 542–544; ''Lillian Montagu,'' Vol. 7, pp. 625–626; ''Claude Montefiore,'' Vol. 7, pp. 628–629; ''Orthodox Judaism,'' Vol. 6, pp. 238–240; ''Russia,'' Vol. 9, pp. 278–286.

SUGGESTED ACTIVITIES

1. Conduct a debate on the subject: ''*Resolved,* that every American Jewish community should be organized under a representative council that would govern its affairs.''

2. Prepare a map of Europe indicating the major developments that took place in Reform Judaism from 1815 until the present.

3. Conduct a panel discussion for a religious school assembly on the subject: ''Reform Judaism Today in the State of Israel.'' As background, be sure to include pertinent information about European Reform's experience with Orthodoxy in the nineteenth century.

SUBJECTS FOR RESEARCH

1. Compare the Reform concept of the ''Mission of Israel'' with that of Second Isaiah who lived during the Babylonian Exile.

2. To what extent did Nazi anti-Semitism grow out of the racist doctrines encountered by the German Jews in the latter part of the nineteenth century?

3. How did the Neo-Orthodox program of Samson Raphael Hirsch differ from the Orthodoxy of East European Jewry?

4. What are the principles of Conservative Judaism in America today? How do they differ from those of your own congregation? From those of an Orthodox congregation?

5. What types of activity did Jewish nationalism recommend in the period before Theodor Herzl? How did the European Reformers react to them? Why?

FILMSTRIPS TO SEE

The Anatomy of Nazism (Anti-Defamation League of B'nai B'rith), describing the terrible consequences of German anti-Semitism in the form of Hitlerism.

Dr. Leo Baeck: Man of Faith (UAHC), picturing the highlights in the life of this great European Reform leader.

David Einhorn: Father of the Union Prayerbook (UAHC), presenting some of the experiences in Europe of this early American Reform leader.

Isaac Mayer Wise: Master Builder of American Judaism (UAHC), portraying some of the experiences in Europe of this pioneer American Reformer.

Sir Moses Montefiore: A Century of Service (UAHC), describing the activities of this defender of Jewry against anti-Semitism in the nineteenth century.

A LIVE ISSUE

A principal reason for the establishment of societies and congregations during the early days of Reform, as we note in this chapter, was the desire to provide a more satisfactory form of religious education.

Over the years this has remained a major concern of the movement, and especially is this so today when the effectiveness of American Jewish education in general is being widely questioned. Not surprisingly, the Reform religious school has also come in for criticism.

The Basic Problem: One of the chief complaints involves the relevance of what is being taught. To what extent, ask the critics, does Reform's program of religious education relate to the students themselves? For here, they contend, lies the key to the effectiveness of the Reform religious school.

Some Important Questions: (1) What do we mean by "relevance"? (2) How does it contribute to better instruction? (3) To what degree is the particular subject-matter involved in educating a Reform Jew relevant? (4) Must the program of a religious school always be relevant? (5) In what way do some of the following also contribute to the problem: (a) the amount of time available to the school? (b) school standards? (c) student discipline? (d) the students' Jewish experience? (e) the religious interest of parents?

What Do You Think? Since a sound religious education is so important to Reform, what conclusions do you come to? What proposals would you make for improving the program? How would these succeed in accomplishing the purposes of Reform education?

11. REFORM JUDAISM IN AMERICA

The American Scene in 1871

Writing in the 1840's in Ludwig Philippson's *General News of Judaism,* a reporter at the docks of Hamburg noted:

> **Over two hundred German Jews took ship here last week to seek a new fatherland in America. Their departure throws a cruel light on the situation in Germany. Nothing remains to them but misery or flight.**

This, however, marked the beginning of a steady stream of Jews fleeing from Central Europe, chiefly Germany. By 1871, some 200,000 had entered the United States, and here they found conditions strikingly different from what they had encountered in Europe.

With the wounds of the Civil War beginning to heal, America was expanding on many fronts. Commerce was booming. The factory system was already well-established, and the country was beginning to produce increasing quantities of iron and steel. Numerous inventions, among them the mechanical reaper, sewing machine, and elevator, were changing the patterns of American life. So, too, was the growth of public education and the slowly increasing number of colleges that would accept women.

By now, the continent had been spanned by both the telegraph and the Union Pacific Railroad, and the frontier was beckoning. A well-known New York newspaper editor was urging young Americans to "go West"; masses of people were already on the move to Texas and the Western territories.

A renewed spirit of democracy coursed through the land, encouraged by the leading writers of the day. Americans were reading the poetry of Walt Whitman that extolled the free society and the rights of individual conscience, the novels of Harriet Beecher Stowe and Mark Twain, with their contempt for slavery and snobbery, and the essays of Ralph Waldo Emerson, Henry David Thoreau, and Oliver Wendell Holmes in support of liberal religion and the dignity of man.

Very few obstacles indeed stood in the way of the Jews. For in the free atmosphere of America they encountered relatively little discrimination, organized anti-Semitism, or political reaction, and no interference whatever from the government in their religious affairs.

The German Jew at Home in America

That it was indeed a congenial climate that the German Jew found in the United States is clear from the following letter an immigrant of the period might well have written to a friend back in Germany:

January 10, 1871

Dear Jakob,

It is hard to believe that I have now been in America for five whole years! My thoughts frequently go back to that day when I made up my mind to come to this country. Just two things I wanted: the right to live as a Jew and a citizen, and a chance to make a living.

I'll never forget the voyage over. The ship was terribly overcrowded with German immigrants, most of them non-Jews, and a cabin that normally accommodated two passengers held as many as a dozen. The food was also very bad. During the six-week trip our meals consisted mostly of a bowl of watery soup, some rice or potatoes, and a crust of bread; we had meat only once. Then, with many days still to go, we ran out of water.

What we feared most was an outbreak of disease, but our prayers were answered when we landed safely at immigration headquarters in New York harbor.

I was simply astonished at the size of New York! So many tall buildings and paved streets; so busy, too, with manufacturing and commerce. And people told me how much more business was pouring into the city because of the telegraph.

Some of my fellow immigrants decided to remain there and work in the garment factories, but I made up my mind to settle in the Midwest. You can imagine how exciting it was to ride the steam-train all the way to Cincinnati, the oldest Jewish community in the West, with some 5,000 Jews! Very soon I started working as a peddler, carrying a small supply of goods in a knapsack and selling them to farmers in the area.

It took time before I was able to speak English and learn American ways. But, after the first year, I began making a reasonably good living.

You can't imagine the security we enjoy in this blessed land. It often happens that I must spend nights away from home, but I am treated by most farmers as though I were a member of their own family.

What I welcome most of all is the freedom. Here Jews and Christians are looked upon as equals, and those of our people who settled here earlier are highly-regarded as citizens.

During the recent Civil War, I am told, more than 10,000 of our brethren fought in both armies. Many rose to high rank; some even became generals. Presently, a number of Jews are judges and government officials, all greatly respected, and some also serve in Congress and various state legislatures. I have even heard that two Jews helped nominate Abraham Lincoln for the presidency.

People say there are about a quarter of a million Jews in the United States. Most of them come from Germany and, though one finds them everywhere, they live mainly in the East. New York, with about 75,000, has the most, and Philadelphia is next. There are also several very old Jewish settlements in the South, like Charleston and Savannah.

Most Jewish communities have their own mutual aid and burial societies, a synagogue, a B'nai B'rith lodge, and various literary groups and charities. Thanks to the growing number of public schools, Jewish boys and girls are able to get a good education. Quite a few who plan to enter the medical, legal, and teaching professions are studying at various universities.

The largest Jewish industry is clothing-manufacturing, which developed dur-

A JEWISH SHOP IN RICHMOND, VIRGINIA, 1887. Such shops were typical of those who became Jewish merchants. (HUC, American Jewish Archives)

ing the Civil War due to the need for uniforms, and one of the best-known firms is the Hart Brothers [later to become Hart, Schaffner and Marx] of Chicago. The best-known Jewish bankers include Kuhn, Loeb and Company, Hallgarten and Company, the Speyer Company, the Seligman Brothers, and Henry Greenebaum. But Jews are prominent in many other businesses, too. Nelson Morris is fast becoming one of the leading American meat-packers. Lazarus Straus, formerly of Georgia, carries on a thriving pottery business in New York, and Brentano conducts a very important publishing house.

Here in Cincinnati some of our brethren have done very well with their stores. Some day I hope I, too, will be able to have a shop of my own. I have my eyes on a good location in one of the nearby small towns, and if I can only save up enough money. . . .

But enough for now. I hope all is well with you and your family. I send my warmest greetings to all of you.

Your friend, Nathan

The Beginnings of American Reform

If the German Jew found political and economic circumstances in America to his liking, he also discovered that there was little to stand in the way of his practice of Reform Judaism if he so preferred. And by 1871 the movement had taken firm root here. Except in the East, Orthodox opposition remained feeble and unorganized. Nor was Reform challenged by any of the other Jewish secular or religious movements that competed with it in Europe.

By then Reform in America had already been in existence for almost a half century. Its beginnings were in Charleston, South Carolina, where as far back as 1824 forty-seven members of the Beth Elohim (בֵּית אֱלֹהִים, House of God) Congregation—led by the well-known writer and teacher, Isaac Harby—petitioned the synagogue trustees to improve the worship. At the time, Sabbath morning services lasted for more than three hours and were marked by constant disorder.

Influenced by events in Hamburg, the members called for better decorum in the synagogue and asked that the more important prayers be read or repeated in English, an English sermon be delivered weekly, and the service be shortened. These improvements, they maintained, would make it possible for more of the congregation to understand and enjoy the service. Their aim, they said, was to "enlighten the rising generation on the subject of their Holy Religion."

When their petition was rejected, twelve members left the congregation and organized the Reform Society of Israelites. By July of 1826, their number had increased to more than fifty. The worship they conducted included prayers and hymns in English as well as Hebrew, instrumental music, a shorter ritual, and fewer traditional ceremonies. They removed all reference to the resurrection of the dead, introduced Confirmation, and even permitted the congregation to worship with uncovered heads. They finally produced their own prayer book in 1830.

However, suffering from lack of rabbinical leadership, and being under constant attack from the Orthodox, the congregation lasted less than nine years. Most of the members eventually rejoined their former congregation.

In 1836, Gustav Poznanski became the new rabbi of Beth Elohim, though he was only a *chazan* (חַזָּן, a layman who conducts the service but, since the liturgy is chanted in the traditional synagogue, it usually refers today to the cantor). Having received most of his education in Hamburg where he undoubtedly was influenced by the reforms of the temple, he insisted upon decorum in the synagogue and introduced some prayers in English. He also delivered an occasional sermon.

Two years after his arrival, a fire destroyed much of the city, including the synagogue. Encouraged by Poznanski, thirty-eight members submitted a petition for the inclusion of an organ in the new building. It was promptly rejected by the trustees but, after much furor, it finally received the approval of the congregation, with the result that some of the traditional members resigned to form a congregation of their own.

Other reforms followed, including the elimination of the extra days of the holidays, which led to a bitter fight in the courts and the resignation of more members. However, Poznanski and his supporters were upheld and Beth Elohim remained staunchly Reform.

American Reform Gains Momentum

For a short while, this was the only Reform congregation in the United States. Most other synagogues were conducted along Orthodox lines, with at times some slight modification. Soon, however, Reform societies began springing up in Baltimore, New York, Philadelphia, Chicago, and elsewhere, and most quickly blossomed into congregations. What the members sought in the main were two things—a more understandable and appealing service and a more effective program of religious education; ''inspiring . . . the children for Judaism,'' one congregation put it, ''and for everything that is good, just, and noble.''

The first congregation to be organized as Reform right from the start was Har Sinai (הַר סִינַי, Mt. Sinai) in Baltimore. It was established in April of 1842 and immediately adopted the use of the Hamburg Temple prayer book.

In 1845, the members of the New York Reform society founded the Emanu-El (עִמָּנוּ אֵל, God is with us) Congregation. In a short time, it had published its own prayer book, introduced the organ and Confirmation ceremony, and eliminated the *talit* and the extra days of the holidays. Several years later, the membership also agreed to worship with uncovered heads.

Albany, New York, established the next Reform temple in 1850 under the leadership of Rabbi Isaac M. Wise, one of the best-known leaders of American Reform. From there he went on to become rabbi of the B'nai Yeshurun (בְּנֵי יְשֻׁרוּן, the sons of Jeshurun, another name for Jacob) Congregation of Cincinnati that became Reform in 1854.

For some time, a Reform society in Philadelphia tried to establish a congregation, but without success. There the Jewish community was dominated by the Orthodox under the leadership of Isaac Leeser, rabbi of Mikveh Israel (מִקְוֵה יִשְׂרָאֵל, the gathering of Israel) Congregation and editor of *The Occident,* one of the most widely-read American Jewish periodicals. Finally in 1856, the first Reform synagogue in Philadelphia was established through a merger of the Reform Society with the Keneseth Israel (כְּנֶסֶת יִשְׂרָאֵל, assembly

of Israel) Congregation, which had already shown interest in changing its form of worship.

In Chicago, too, a society was responsible for the formation of a Reform congregation. Several members of the Orthodox Anshe Ma-ariv (אַנְשֵׁי מַעֲרִיב, men of the west) Synagogue had grown dissatisfied with its practices and organized a Reform society. At the first public session of the group, on April 17, 1858, it urged Orthodoxy to eliminate many of its practices and make the services more understandable to modern Jews.

Two years later, under the leadership of Rabbi Bernhard Felsenthal, the members founded the Sinai Reform Congregation. The preamble to its constitution called for a more understandable service featuring a regular sermon in English, the elimination of all outmoded Jewish laws, customs, and practices, the substitution of observances more in keeping with modern life, and the creation of more suitable Jewish education for the young.

Reform soon spread to many other parts of the United States. By 1871, Reform temples were operating in Cleveland, Louisville, Milwaukee, Richmond, St. Louis, Boston, Memphis, Nashville, Detroit, Pittsburgh, and a number of other cities.

And while the Reform movement as such was gaining momentum, among the Orthodox, too, many congregations were in the process of modifying their services and introducing various minor reforms.

A Reform Organization in the Making?

There was further reason for Reform optimism in the belief that the movement would soon produce certain very necessary organizations, something we observe from a second letter that might have been written by the same German Jewish immigrant:

June 16, 1871

Dear Jakob,

It was so good to hear from you and to know that you and the family are well.

Things are still about the same with me except that I have now become active again in Reform matters. Our rabbi, Isaac M. Wise, is one of the important leaders of the movement in this country, and he has been after us to help him create a union of American congregations. As a matter of fact, he proposed such an organization as far back as 1848, but nothing came of it. Now, however, he seems to have stirred up a great deal of interest in this part of the country for the formation of at least a Reform union.

One of the main purposes would be to found and maintain a seminary to train Reform rabbis, something that Rabbi Wise also unsuccessfully attempted in 1855. Thus far, the movement has had to import its rabbis from Europe, but it is becoming clear that we need American-trained men who are well-acquainted with the ideas and spirit of this country.

Rabbi Wise also speaks of establishing a permanent organization of rabbis to guide the development of Judaism here. Two major attempts in the past failed, but rabbinical meetings have continued to take place from time to time. One such conference was held two years ago in Philadelphia, where those who attended adopted a number of basic Reform principles. And, just last week, another group of rabbis meeting here in Cincinnati voiced their support for the formation of a "union of congregations."

I may be overly optimistic, but I believe that this time they will succeed. One day soon we will get our Reform seminary and perhaps even a permanent rabbinical organization. Who knows?

Meanwhile, I am very distressed to hear some of the things that the anti-Semites are saying in Germany. I hope most Germans do not swallow such lies but, knowing how prejudiced some of them are, I fear the worst. That is why I think you should seriously consider coming to America. If you would want to settle here in Cincinnati I can certainly help you.

Please let me know your plans. My warmest greetings to you and your family.

Your friend, Nathan

A Remarkable Achievement

Whether Reform in America was about to succeed with its plans for organization remained to be seen.

The movement was already well established in this country. Actually, with several dozen liberal rabbis and some forty to fifty congregations located mainly in the Midwest and South, the American Reform movement was then larger than that of Europe. And the fact that so many traditional congregations were showing some liberal tendencies was also very encouraging.

The free atmosphere of America, of course, was all to Reform's advantage, and the liberal spirit and optimism of the age nourished its hopes. So much so that one of the early leaders of the movement could boldly assert:

The future of Judaism in this country is identical with the cause of progress and reform . . . This is an age of inquiry, criticism, and philosophy. The time of unquestioning faith and emphasis upon symbols closes itself; few and far apart are their supporters among the American Jews . . .

Dogmatism and mysticism must yield to liberal religion. Such is the spirit of the age and the essence of Judaism . . . The triumph of Judaism depends on the success of reform and progress.

All this seemed to be borne out by the facts. For the immigration of so many Jews from Germany combined with the rational climate of the age and the American atmosphere of freedom to give the Reform movement an enormous advantage. So much so that by 1871 Reform Judaism had actually become the majority faith of the American Jew.

But along with this remarkable achievement came some new difficulties for the movement.

Three Challenges to Reform

Three main challenges faced the American Reform Jew. The first concerned the "unaffiliated," or those who refused to identify themselves with the synagogue. Among them were some of the younger generation of Jews who had rejected Orthodoxy and, with it, Judaism in general, something that prompted Isaac M. Wise to declare:

> **The young and intelligent desert the Orthodox; the enlightened portion of the community pity their narrow-mindedness and ridicule their antiquated notions. Synagogues are deserted and [Jewish] schools unattended. This has hurt Judaism greatly.**

Thus Reform confronted the extremely difficult task of winning these unaffiliated Jews back to Judaism, a task made all the more difficult because they associated Reform Judaism with their distaste for Orthodoxy.

But a far greater number of the unaffiliated was made up of those who lived in the larger centers of the East, such as New York and Philadelphia, where most of the newcomers tended to settle. There the Orthodox dominated Jewish life and, though the masses of Jews were often indifferent to the synagogue and to most Jewish observance as well, they nevertheless tended to look upon themselves as "traditional," to whom association with Reform was emotionally or culturally unac-

ceptable. Thus, as Wise himself complained from time to time, Reform lagged seriously behind in the large Jewish centers of the East, and he was fearful that this might ultimately have grave consequences for the movement.

A second challenge to Reform was the predominantly European outlook of its membership. It was a fact that, like other immigrants, the first generation of Reform Jews in America was reluctant to shed the German language and culture it had brought to America. Thus, the vernacular used in most Reform congregations was German; it was also the language of the sermon and instruction in the religious school. With few exceptions, Reform prayer books were modeled after those of the Reform congregations in Germany, and the program of religious change was essentially that introduced by the Hamburg Temple or recommended by the German rabbinical conferences and synods. Yet the rapid Americanization of the younger generation called for a Reform Judaism that was far more American

ISAAC MAYER WISE. A leading American Reformer who succeeded in forming the movement's major organizations.

in character and language. As Wise commented:

> **Seeing that American youth is ignorant of German, in a short while its use in the synagogue will be meaningless. A German prayer book is against every sound principle and impedes the course of Reform.**

Finally, Reform in the United States had by no means overcome some of the internal problems that had been responsible for its decline in Europe. Every rabbi and congregation operated independently and, in spite of all the promising talk about organization, the movement still lacked even a common liturgy that would help unify it. The need to develop unity, then, was its third and perhaps greatest challenge.

In fact, in 1871, the movement was close to disaster because of an intense and bitter rivalry that divided East from West. To understand how and why this had come to be it is necessary to follow the careers of the handful of American Reform pioneers who led the movement.

QUESTIONS FOR DISCUSSION

1. In what ways did American Jewish life in the early 1870's differ from that in Germany? How did this affect the development of Reform Judaism in the United States?

2. How did Reform Judaism start in the United States, and why? How do you account for the fact that Charleston, rather than New York or Philadelphia, was the first community to adopt Reform?

3. In what ways was the movement in America influenced by European Reform? How do you explain this? To what extent, however, was American Reform in the 1870's different?

4. How do the present practices and beliefs of your temple compare with those of American Reform in 1871? Which have remained the same? Which are considerably different? What reasons can you find for the differences?

5. Why do you suppose Rabbi Isaac M. Wise was so anxious to create a union of congregations, a rabbinical seminary, and a permanent rabbinical association? How might the existence of any one of these prior to 1871 have benefited the movement?

6. What were some of the major weaknesses of Reform in 1871? How do these compare with some of the problems you observe in the movement today? In what ways has Reform's situation improved or worsened?

SIGNIFICANT DOCUMENTS

A Petition to the Trustees for Reforms by Members of the Beth Elohim Congregation of Charleston, 1824

Your memorialists [petitioners] seek no other end than the future welfare and respectability of the nation [Jews]. As members of the great family of Israel, they cannot consent to place before their children examples which are only calculated to darken the mind and withhold from the rising generation the more rational means of worshiping the true God.

It is to this, therefore, your memorialists would, in the first place, invite the serious attention of your honorable body. By causing the *chazan,* or reader, to *repeat* in English such part of the Hebrew prayers as may be deemed necessary, it is confidently believed that the congregation generally would be more forcibly impressed with the necessity of divine worship and the moral obligations which they owe to themselves and their Creator, while such a course would lead to more decency and decorum during the time they are engaged in the performance of religious duties.

It is not everyone who has the means, and many have not the time, to acquire a knowledge of the Hebrew language and

166

consequently become enlightened in the principles of Judaism. What, then, is the course pursued in all religious societies for the purpose of disseminating the peculiar [unique] tenets of their faith among the poor and uninformed?

The principles of their religion are expounded to them from the pulpit in language that they understand; for instance, in the Catholic, the German and the French Protestant churches. By this means the ignorant part of mankind attend their places of worship with some profit to their morals, and even improvement to their minds. They return from them with hearts turned to piety and with feelings elevated by their sacred character. In this consists the beauty of religion—when men are invoked by its divine spirit to the practice of virtue and morality . . .

With regard to such parts of the service as it is desired should undergo this change, your memorialists would strenuously recommend that the most solemn portions be retained and everything superfluous excluded; and that the principal parts and, if possible, all that is read in *Hebrew* should also be read in *English* (that being the language of the country), so as to enable every member of the congregation fully to understand each part of the service.

In submitting this article of our memorial [petition] to your honorable body, your memorialists are well aware of the difficulties with which they must contend before they will be enabled to accomplish this desirable end. But while they would respectfully invite the attention of your honorable body to this part of their memorial, they desire to rest the propriety and expediency of such a measure solely upon the reason by which it may be maintained . . .

Your memorialists would next call the particular attention of your honorable body to the absolute necessity of *abridging* the service generally. They have reflected seriously upon its present length and are confident that this is one of the principal causes why so much of it is hastily and improperly hurried over . . .

According to the present method of reading the *Parashah* [פָּרָשָׁה, Torah portion], . . . it affords to the hearer neither instruction nor entertainment, unless he be competent to read as well as *comprehend* the Hebrew language. But if, like all other ministers, our reader would make a chapter or verse the subject of an English discourse once a week, at the expiration of the year the people would, at all events, know something of that religion which at present they so little regard.

—From David Philipson,
The Reform Movement in Judaism,
pp. 329–331.

Preamble to the Constitution of the Chicago Sinai Congregation, 1860

Whereas, there appears to exist among Israelites a large degree of indifference in religious matters, threatening to drag life more and more to materialism and degradation, and stifling all nobility of sentiments, all sympathy for higher pursuits, all appreciation of the more sacred boons of humanity, while, on the other hand, Jewish religious life, clinging to obsolete ideas and maintaining antiquated usages, has taken its course in a direction of which we cannot approve; and,

Whereas, we share the conviction that a truly religious life is the most powerful agent to create noble thoughts and good morals; and,

Whereas, especially the Jewish religion, having a past of four thousand years, most glorious and eventful, is evidently destined in the future too to act a most important part in the development of mankind and in its onward course to the lofty position of the messianic time coming:

167

Therefore, a number of Israelites have associated with the avowed intention of fostering the inestimable inheritance of our fathers, of restoring the original spirit of simplicity, purity, and sublimity in Judaism, and thus to perpetuate the same and secure its duration.

The means of attaining this sacred object are chiefly as follows:

1. A divine service which, without divesting the same of its specific Jewish character, shall be in consistence with the laws of reason and truth and which, in its form, shall be such as will meet the demands of our time, claiming public instruction from the pulpit as a part of the same.

2. A sound religious education for the rising generation, by maintaining a school in which at least a thorough instruction in religion, Hebrew, and the branches connected therewith, be imparted—a school inspiring the tender hearts of the children for Judaism and for everything that is good and just.

3. The removal of usages and ceremonies partly outlived and partly based upon erroneous conceptions, and the substitution of others more vital, more truthful, and more apt to produce blissful effects, and the formation of such agencies and institutions which tend directly or indirectly to promote and fulfill the objects of religion and to advance its professors to a higher stage of perfection.

—From David Philipson,
The Reform Movement in Judaism,
pp. 337–338.

From a Letter Inviting Kaufmann Kohler to Become the Rabbi of the Beth El Congregation of Detroit, 1869

Your letter of May 7 to Dr. [Max] Lilienthal in C.[incinnati] was submitted to the undersigned, with the practical advice to write to you directly, honored *Herr Doktor,* which we are doing herewith, both in a semiofficial manner as the committee of the Jewish congregation of Detroit and, also, with especial personal respect, in consideration of the recommendations of Drs. Lilienthal and [Bernhard] Felsenthal. This by way of introduction and of clarification of several frank explanations which we feel that we must make, the more so as we would want to assume the responsibility for calling such a well-recommended man across the wide ocean only if the effort has been made in advance to come to a mutual understanding of the details, as far as is feasible.

Our congregation "Beth El" (there are several other Jewish congregations here) has been in existence for approximately nineteen years. Like most of the older American Jewish congregations, it started with very small means, as a continuation of the Orthodox Jewish synagogal worship, as far as the members, who came from all parts of Germany (extending as far [east] as the Vistula), could agree on the "tradition." These conditions, as well as those individuals who are accustomed to making mutual concessions, gave the functioning rabbis the opportunity to introduce "Reform." As a result, our congregation, which is a Reform congregation, nevertheless includes among its individual members all shades of ritual opinions, ranging from Orthodoxy, on the one hand, to religious indifferentism, on the other, and still, as a *congregation,* it favors *Reform.*

The older members, who are Orthodox, are constantly getting fewer, or else they passively submit to the innovations, so that you would not find here "a *young,* aspiring congregation which would naturally come to an *easy* understanding with a young forceful person inspired by fresh earnestness," but you would nevertheless find here a field which, although not as yet entirely cultivated, would be capable of such cultivation for the exalted views which you, *Herr Doktor,* express.

As regards our religious services of nineteen years ago, we have made tremendous progress and we should like to give you the following information about the manner of their conduct which is usual with us at present:

We have introduced the so-called *Minhag America* of Dr. I[saac]. M. Wise. This *minhag* is a *compromise* between the Sulzbacher *Tefilah* [Orthodox daily prayer book, published at Sulzbach, Bavaria, in 1828] and the [liberal] requirements of the most recent past. The prayers are considerably shortened, many have been omitted entirely, but all are recited in Hebrew. The *Barchu* [בָּרְכוּ ," Praise the Lord to whom all praise is due"], the *Shema* [שְׁמַע, "Hear, O Israel . . ."], the *Mi Chamocha* [מִי כָמֹכָה, "Who is like unto Thee"], and the *Kedushah* [קְדוּשָׁה, "Holiness," referring to the passages beginning with "Holy, holy, holy is the Lord of Hosts"] are recited by the choir to organ accompaniment. The beginning and the conclusion of the religious service are introduced by a Jewish hymn, and the sermon is preceded and followed by a German or an English song, according as the language in which the sermon is given is German or English.

The *Haftarah* [prophetic portion] is always recited in German or in English. The reading of the Torah is in Hebrew, the three-year cycle being used. There is no calling up to the Torah, nor is any *Misheberach* [מִי שֶׁבֵּרַךְ, "'The One who has blessed' Abraham, Isaac, and Jacob," a benediction associated with contributions given to the synagogue] made. The president and the vice president stand at the rabbi's side.

For special occasions (the first visit paid to the temple by new mothers, by newly-weds, and at the New Moon, etc.) suitable German or English prayers are traditional, this matter being left up to the rabbi. For Rosh Hashanah and for Yom Kippur, the Heidenheim *Machzor* [מַחְזוֹר, cycle, or High Holy Day prayer book, referring in this instance to one published at Rodelheim, Prussia, in 1800, by Wolf Heidenheim] was always used up to now, with the omission of long *piyutim* [פִּיּוּטִים, liturgical poems].

There are still a few people in our congregation who "recite" [the daily liturgy] *Shacharit* [שַׁחֲרִית, dawn or morning worship], *Musaf* [מוּסָף, additional service], etc. The above-mentioned order of the prayers has reference to *yom tov* [יוֹם טוֹב, holiday] and the Sabbath. For *yom tov* only, some unimportant additions are inserted into the *Minhag American tefilah* and all Hebrew prayers are recited more in a declamatory tone than in the old singsong manner (*nigun* [נִגּוּן, chant]), *by the rabbi.* The hat is still worn, but not the *talit.* Men and women sit together.

Until about six months ago our congregation maintained a German-English-Hebrew elementary school which was conducted by the rabbi with the aid of assistant teachers, and in which religious instruction also was given. The congregation dropped the elementary school because no such results were achieved as those which the public schools secured. The *religious instruction* of the young is now entirely entrusted to the rabbi, who is expected to devote Saturday afternoons and Sunday mornings to this duty. The children, with very few exceptions, understand German, although many of them speak English exclusively in conversation. Should this be a burden to the religious teacher at the beginning, nonetheless, the fact that the children speak English would furnish him the opportunity to get used to the vernacular himself in a short time.

One thing you may depend on, and that is, that every member of the congregation, which consists of approximately seventy members, is very much interested in providing the young with a religious and moral education and that the majority of the congregation will gladly give their support for a free and humane development of Judaism, under the scholarly leadership of a man who will know how to furnish scientific and theological bases for still further progress in the field of the improvement of Jewish conditions. At any rate, the majority of those members who bear the *burdens* of the congregation are animated by such sentiments.

The *financial* situation of the congregation does not permit the payment to the rabbi of a salary in excess of two thousand dollars ($2,000). A three-year appointment as well as a moderate reimbursement of traveling expenses would be approved.

Detroit is a pretty city of about 80,000 inhabitants. Our temple is new, and is situated on one of the most beautiful streets. In every respect it is a worthy and dignified house of worship.

A *single* man can get room and board in the best Christian [non-kosher] hotels for about $45 per month. At any rate, it would not cost more, indeed, considerably less, with a decent Jewish family. Less than the above salary was sufficient to maintain our rabbi decently during the war years, when prices were high, although he had a rather large family. Besides, an able man could earn quite a lot of extra money by giving private instruction, and weddings yield decent honoraria, also.

We felt obliged, most honored *Herr Doktor,* to acquaint you with the above. If the conditions which have been laid down appeal to you, please let us know your views, or inform us of your consent, *as soon as possible.* In the case of an affirmative reply from you, a call to you to assume the rabbinical position in Detroit should follow. Since this is written more in your interests than in those of the congregation, and since the position will become vacant on September 1, and we should like very much to have a rabbi for the holidays, we request an early reply.

Martin Butzel, M. Cohen, Herman Trueman
[Committee]
—From ''A Call to Detroit—1869,''
translation by Abraham I. Shinedling,
The American Jewish Archives,
Vol. 19, No. 1 (April 1967), pp. 37–40.

OTHER THINGS TO READ

Bamberger, Bernard J., *The Story of Judaism:* Chap. 45, ''The Golden Land.''

Elbogen, Ismar, *A Century of Jewish Life:* Book I, Chap. 4, ''The Jews in the New World,'' pp. 114–131.

Gumbiner, Joseph H., *Isaac Mayer Wise, Pioneer of American Judaism.*

Heller, James G., *Isaac M. Wise, His Life, Work and Thought:* Chap. 15, ''Call to Cincinnati''; Chap. 17, *''The Israelite* and the College''; Chap. 18, ''The Cleveland Conference and *Minhag America''*; Chap. 25, ''The Task Resumed''; Chap. 26, ''Conferences and Progress toward Union.''

Jewish Encyclopedia: ''Rabbinical Conferences,'' Vol. 4, pp. 211–217; ''David Einhorn,'' Vol. 5, pp. 78–79; ''Isaac Harby,'' Vol. 6, pp. 232–233; ''Hazan,'' Vol. 6, pp. 284–287; ''Judaism in America,'' Vol. 1, pp. 513–514; ''Isaac Mayer Wise,'' Vol. 12, pp. 150–160.

Knox, Israel, ''Isaac Mayer Wise,'' Chap. 4 in Simon Noveck (ed.), *Great Jewish Personalities in Modern Times.*

Learsi, Rufus, *The Jews in America: A History:* Chap. 5, ''Across the Continent''; Chap. 6, ''Old World Sorrows''; Chap. 7, ''Civil War''; Chap. 8, ''Religious Divisions.''

Levinger, Lee J., *A History of the Jews in the United States:* pp. 8–16 (origins of American

Jews); 170–174 (Rebecca Gratz and Penina Moise); Chap. 12, "The Second Wave of Immigration: From Germany"; Chap. 14, "The Basis of Judaism in America"; Chap. 15, "The Growth of Reform Judaism"; Chap. 16, "How Jewish Lodges and Charities Were Formed."

Masserman, Paul, and Max Baker, *The Jews Come to America:* Chap. 8, "The German Jews"; Chap. 10, "The Reform Movement."

Philipson, David, *The Reform Movement in Judaism:* Chap. 12, "Reform in the United States."

Plaut, W. Gunther, *The Growth of Reform Judaism:* Chap. 1, "American Beginnings"; pp. 18–26 (Cleveland and other early conferences); 50–52 (Zion College).

Reznikoff, Charles, and Uriah Z. Engelman, *The Jews of Charleston:* pp. 113–150, 200–207 (development of Reform in Charleston).

Schwartzman, Sylvan D., *Reform Judaism in the Making:* Chap. 10, "Reform in the America of 1871."

Standard Jewish Encyclopedia: "David Einhorn," pp. 603–604; "Isaac H. Harby," pp. 842–843; "Hazan," p. 863; "Rabbinical Conferences," pp. 1568–1569; "Isaac Mayer Wise," pp. 1916–1917.

Universal Jewish Encyclopedia: "Cantor," Vol. 3, pp. 17–18; "Isaac Harby," Vol. 5, p. 213; "Rabbinical Conferences," Vol. 3, pp. 327–328; "David Einhorn," Vol. 4, pp. 27–28; "Judaism in America," Vol. 6, pp. 240–241; "I. M. Wise," Vol. 10, pp. 539–542.

SUGGESTED ACTIVITIES

1. On an outline map of the United States, indicate where Reform congregations existed in 1871. What conclusions do you reach about where the real strength of the movement lay?

2. As though you were a Reform leader in 1871, write an article for the Anglo-Jewish press appealing for the immediate establishment of a union of congregations, a rabbinical seminary, and a permanent rabbinical organization.

3. Prepare a brief history of the founding of your own congregation. If it was originally Reform, why did the founders consider it necessary that the congregation be Reform? If it was originally traditional, what circumstances moved the members to adopt Reform, and what consequences followed their decision?

SUBJECTS FOR RESEARCH

1. What was a Jewish "Sunday school" like in America during the middle of the nineteenth century? (You will find some interesting accounts in Jacob R. Marcus, *Memoirs of American Jews, 1775–1865,* Vol. I.)

2. What were some of the day-to-day experiences of mid-nineteenth-century Jews in Germany and Central Europe that prompted so many of them to immigrate to America?

3. Who was Isaac Harby of Charleston, and what role did he play in the development of Reform?

4. Prior to the 1840's, from what countries had most of the Jewish settlers in America come? What form of Judaism did they adopt? What was their general reaction to the German Jews and Reform? Why?

5. Why didn't Zion College, the rabbinical school founded by Isaac M. Wise in 1855, succeed? As a result, what measures did he consider essential before another seminary should be established?

FILMSTRIPS TO SEE

Isaac Mayer Wise: Master Builder of American Judaism (UAHC), describing the life and achievements of this great American Reform pioneer.

300 Years: Memorable Events in American Jewish History (UAHC), presenting the background of key developments in the American Jewish community from its earliest days.

American Jewry in the Civil War (Jewish Education Committee of New York), offering a picture of American Jewish life prior to and during the early 1860's.

A LIVE ISSUE

Many efforts have been made to establish a permanent organization to speak for the American Jew. Rabbi Isaac M. Wise himself, as this chapter indicates, tried without success, and other attempts in this century, such as the creation of the American Jewish Conference during the Hitler period, proved short-lived.

Within recent years, however, a "conference" composed of the presidents of various national organizations has been formed to strengthen American Jewish life and provide greater support for the Jews of Israel, the Soviet Union, and elsewhere. Though the Reform movement is well-represented, not all Reform Jews, as Wise discovered in his own· day, favor such an overall body.

The Basic Problem: Those opposed to any central organization of American Jewry are fearful that it may suppress important differences among Jews and stifle dissenting opinion. They warn of the intolerance of certain groups in Jewish life today and cite the distressing experiences of Reform at the hands of the closely-organized Jewish communities of Europe. Nor are they reassured by the safeguards that the advocates promise.

Some Important Questions: (1) Is a permanent organization designed to represent the whole of American Jewry actually desirable? (2) What would be some of the practical benefits? (3) What are some of the possible dangers? (4) How would you attempt to protect against these? (5) In your opinion, are the benefits worth the risks?

What Do You Think? Reading this chapter should stimulate your own thinking about the issue. What conclusions do you personally come to about the position the Reform movement should take on this problem? To what extent are you convinced of this?

12. TWO PIONEERS OF THE "WEST"

An Appeal by the Moderates

On June 5, 1871, twenty-seven liberal rabbis meeting in Cincinnati urgently called for the formation of a "Union of Israelite Congregations of America." Terms like "Israelite" and "Hebrew" were commonly used in those days instead of "Jew," which many regarded as kind of an epithet, and this is no less reflected in the resolution they adopted:

> The members of the conference take upon themselves the duty to bring prominently before their congregations, to advocate and support by their influence, the following project of cooperation of the American Hebrew Congregations:
>
> The congregations to unite themselves into a Hebrew Congregational Union with the object to preserve and advance the union of Israel [Jewry]; to take proper care of the development and promulgation of Judaism; to establish and support a scholastic institute and a library connected with it for the education of rabbis, preachers, and teachers of religion; to provide cheap editions of the English Bible and textbooks for the schools of religious instruction, and to provide such other institutions which elevate, preserve, and promulgate Judaism . . .

This appeal, however, came only from the moderates headed by Rabbi Isaac M. Wise because none of the radical Reformers, or "Easterners" as they were called, were present. Personally hostile to Wise, they had boycotted the meeting of the "Westerners." In fact, their leader, Rabbi David Einhorn, originally of Baltimore but then serving a congregation in New York, was quick to attack the proposal in the press as another of Wise's schemes to control the Reform movement.

But Wise was far from discouraged. As one of the pioneers of Reform in the United States, he was accustomed to opposition, and he insisted on going ahead with his plans.

Here he received the fullest support of his close friend, Max Lilienthal, the rabbi of the other Cincinnati Reform congregation.

America's First Reform Rabbi

At the time he came to America in 1844, Max Lilienthal was one of the very few ordained

DR. MAX LILIENTHAL. A close friend of Isaac Mayer Wise, he also ministered to Cincinnati Jewry. (HUC, American Jewish Archives)

rabbis in the country, and he certainly was the first Reform one.

Born in Germany in 1815 to a well-to-do family, he promised his dying mother he would become a rabbi, and he enrolled at one of the leading European rabbinical academies in Fürth, in southern Germany, from which he received ordination. However, to the consternation of his teachers who regarded a college education as sinful, he also took doctoral work at the University of Munich. His brilliant record there gained him the offer of a position in the German diplomatic corps, something unheard of for a Jew, and he was inclined to accept until he discovered that first he was expected to convert to Catholicism. He furiously rejected the proposition.

Lilienthal now began to seek a pulpit in Bavaria. But by then the government, alarmed by the Orthodox over the "radicalism" of liberal rabbis, had passed a law forbidding congregations to engage any that were not thoroughly traditional. Because of his college education, Lilienthal was of course suspect.

Meanwhile, he had been spending his time studying Hebrew manuscripts in the royal library in Munich and publishing a series of articles in Ludwig Philippson's *General News of Judaism.* This brought him to the attention of the Russian minister of education who had turned to Philippson for someone to direct a modern Jewish school soon to be established in Riga, an important seaport in eastern Russia. Philippson highly recommended Lilienthal, and the minister promptly engaged him.

Russia in the Nineteenth Century

Russia, Lilienthal quickly discovered, was not at all like Germany. For the most part, the country remained untouched by Western culture, and still operated with a feudal system under the absolute control of the Czar, the nobility, and the Russian Orthodox Church. The rest of society was made up of a great mass of hopelessly poor, ignorant peasants, or serfs, bound to the soil of their overlords.

Jewish life in Russia was as bad as it had ever been during the Middle Ages. Herded within their own segregated communities, Jews enjoyed no political rights whatever and lived under constant threat of attack or expulsion. Since 1791, they had been confined to a single section of the country known as the Pale of Jewish Settlement, which was limited to a few provinces largely outside of Russia proper. There they were subject to harsh and unreasonable taxes, barred from numerous occupations, and denied the right to own land, employ Christians, or erect synagogues near churches. Even their religious books were subject to censorship, with many frequently burned.

Worst of all, however, was the Conscription Law adopted in 1827. It provided for Jewish boys of twelve to be drafted for six years of preliminary military schooling, followed by twenty-five years of service in the Russian army, during which every effort was made to convert them to Christianity. Fiendishly, the government also held the Jewish community responsible for conscripting its youth.

The intention of the Czar and his government was clear. It was to compel the Jews to give up their religion and assimilate. However, all the inhuman treatment only served to strengthen their sense of identity and intensify their loyalty to Judaism, which was either staunchly traditional or chasidic, the mystical interpretation that had arisen in the eighteenth century under the Ba-al Shem Tov (בַּעַל שֵׁם טוֹב, Master of the Good Name, a title given to wonder-workers).

Now, and quite unknown to Lilienthal, the Russian authorities had hit upon the scheme of using modern schools to undermine Jewish life.

Max Lilienthal Discovers the Terrible Truth

As Lilienthal worked to establish his school in Riga, he found little response from the masses of religious Jews who suspected his relations with the government. He did, however, have the support of those associated with the *Haskalah* (Enlightenment) movement led by Isaac Baer Levinson, known as the "Russian Moses Mendelssohn."

Upon opening the school in the beginning of 1840, Lilienthal devoted all his energy to making it a success. At the same time, in his sermons at the local synagogue, he voiced deep concern for the Jews of Russia and transmitted the assurances of the government that by adopting more modern ways they would ultimately gain their emancipation.

Lilienthal's success in Riga encouraged the government to expand the program by having him organize similar schools in every major Russian Jewish community. But the masses of Jews continued to be suspicious. "If the government is sincere," they told him, "then let it show its good faith by granting us freedom now, or at least removing some of the unfair restrictions."

Lilienthal brought their complaints to the attention of the minister of education who assured him that the government was acting in good faith and repeated its promise of eventual emancipation. To convince him, he even had the government issue a public pledge not to interfere in any way with the practice of Judaism.

But as the new schools were established, the government's treachery soon became clear. Lilienthal discovered that instead of appointing Jewish supervisors it chose Christians who were hostile to instruction in Jewish subjects. Meanwhile, the Czar was also enacting new anti-Jewish laws that further reduced the area of the Pale of Jewish Settlement and forced thousands out of their homes.

Reluctantly, he realized the terrible truth that the Russians had no intention of liberating the Jews but were simply using the new schools to wean them away from their faith.

Lilienthal Comes to America

Thoroughly disillusioned and embittered, Lilienthal left Russia for Munich, where he married his fiancée of many years. Then, in 1844, they both set out for a new life in America.

The contrast between conditions in the United States and those existing in Russia slowly restored his confidence. In a letter to his good friend Ludwig Philippson, he wrote:

My brotherly and friendly greetings from New York, from the blessed land of freedom, the beautiful soil of civic equality! Old Europe with its restrictions lies behind me, like a dream. The memory of the repellent Jew-hatred of Russia is like a distant mirage . . .

175

> It is necessary that you breathe this free air of America in order that you may be able to understand the pride and joy of her children. You must have shaken off the centuries-long dust of the old Jewish oppression in order to appreciate to the full the feeling, "I am a man like every other . . ."

Rabbis were in great demand, and Lilienthal was immediately elected to the pulpits of three traditional New York congregations which he served for five years. Though he was still in sympathy with much of Orthodoxy, as he became familiar with American life, he realized the need for change. In his very first year he insisted on decorum in the synagogue and organized a choir. On Shavuot, 1846, he also conducted the first Confirmation in the United States.

These innovations brought him into conflict with the more traditional members, and in 1850 he resigned. For the next five years he successfully operated a private boarding school in New York, attended chiefly by Jewish boys from other cities.

Lilienthal Helps Isaac M. Wise

Soon after he came to the United States he met Isaac M. Wise, who had just emigrated from Europe. Wise was deeply depressed by his first few days in New York. "I had never before seen a city so bare of all art and of every trace of good taste," he recalled. "Likewise, I had never witnessed anywhere such rushing, hurrying, chasing, running . . . All of this shocked my esthetic sense."

Acquaintances had advised him to take up peddling or learn a trade, rather than continue in the rabbinate. His own observations also convinced him that Jewish life in America was chaotic. Most synagogue members seemed to him generally ill-behaved and lacking in real

Jewish knowledge, and even the *chazanim* (plural of חַזָּן, lay readers of services) who served as their spiritual leaders appeared ignorant of all but the customary Orthodox practices.

However, before finally making up his mind, he decided to visit Lilienthal, to whom he had a letter of introduction, and in his *Reminiscences* he describes what took place:

> I stopped at a small house and rang the bell very timidly. A man in a dressing-gown, with a black velvet cap on his head, opened the door.
>
> "I would like to speak to Dr. Lilienthal."
>
> "I am he; step in."
>
> "I come from Bohemia. Here is a letter from Dr. W., your school friend, and here are some of my papers."
>
> Dr. Lilienthal read the letter and the first of the twelve documents I had given him when he went to the door and called: "Wife, bring coffee and cigars. I have received a guest." Turning to me, he gave me a friendly and hearty שָׁלוֹם עֲלֵיכֶם [*Shalom Aleichem*, literally, Peace be unto you or Welcome!]. "Hold up your head! Courage!" cried he. "You are the man. We need you."
>
> In short, Dr. Lilienthal was the first one to encourage me and inspire me with hope, and at the time this was of prime importance and significance for me . . . Within ten minutes I felt at home, and the impression which I received in the Lilienthal home perhaps decided my career in America.

Wise and Lilienthal remained life-long friends. Lilienthal even helped him secure his first pulpit in Albany, New York. Then, early in 1854, Wise became rabbi of the B'nai Yeshurun Congregation of Cincinnati, and when he began publishing his American Jewish weekly, *The Israelite* (renamed in 1875 *The American Israelite*), he made Max

Lilienthal its New York correspondent. Shortly afterward, and with Wise's enthusiastic endorsement, a sister Cincinnati congregation, B'nai Israel (בְּנֵי יִשְׂרָאֵל, children of Israel), elected Lilienthal its rabbi. He held this post for twenty-seven years, until his death at the age of sixty-seven.

Lilienthal as Rabbi in Cincinnati

B'nai Israel was an Orthodox congregation when Lilienthal commenced his ministry there in 1855, and he immediately introduced several reforms. He eliminated the reading of a number of prayers he considered objectionable and the auctioning off of various privileges, such as holding the Torah and opening and closing the Ark. "Religion and life must be reconciled," he declared. "Let us remove abuses [in the service] by enlightened action." Gradually, he influenced his members to accept other changes until the congregation was fully Reform.

Another of his major concerns was maintaining the separation of Church and State. He asserted:

THE NEW YORK SCHOOL. Campus of the Hebrew Union College-Jewish Institute of Religion in Manhattan.

PLUM STREET TEMPLE. The interior of this Cincinnati Reform synagogue shows the inauguration of Dr. Nelson Glueck as sixth president of the Hebrew Union College-Jewish Institute of Religion. (Marchi Photo Studio)

> Only this will save the Union [United States] and restore the denominational peace we have heretofore enjoyed and which we hope will be continued forever more on the virgin soil of American happiness and liberty.

Fearlessly, he fought to keep religion out of the schools, even to the point, on one occasion, of roundly condemning the leading Christian clergymen of the city at the very meeting they had called to protest a decision by the Cincinnati School Board to eliminate Bible reading in class.

But preserving harmony among the Jews was perhaps his chief interest, and he worked constantly to bring the Orthodox and Reform together for the benefit of Jewish life as a whole in America. Here he joined with Wise in his repeated attempts to establish a common American Jewish rabbinical body, union of congregations, and seminary, and defended him against the attacks of both the more radical Eastern Reformers and the Orthodox. He was nonetheless devoted to the cause of Reform and took part in many important activities of the movement, including the Philadelphia Rabbinical Conference in 1869 that adopted the first set of American Reform principles.

Isaac M. Wise— from Europe to America

As must already be apparent, Isaac M. Wise was one of the foremost leaders of American Reform. Born on March 29, 1819, in the tiny village of Steingrub, Bohemia, he was the son of a poor Hebrew teacher and the oldest of thirteen children. Even as a child he showed great promise in his studies and, after obtaining a university degree, he was finally ordained a rabbi at twenty-three.

His first congregation was in Radnitz, Bo-

hemia, and there, through the writings of scholars like Zunz and Geiger, he became acquainted with scientific Jewish scholarship and Reform. Meanwhile, he was becoming increasingly dissatisfied with the restrictions imposed upon him by the Orthodox authorities in such matters as granting divorces and modifying the service. He was also outraged by Austria's treatment of the Jews, particularly the law that limited the annual number of Jewish marriages, which he denounced and secretly ignored.

From his reading, Wise had already developed a special fondness for the United States, which to him represented the very opposite of all that he despised in Europe. Even then, he reminisced in his later years, "I had the American fever." But when he applied for permission to leave Austria, he was turned down, and he, his wife, and little girl had to flee across the border at night. Eventually, the family reached the port of Bremen and, in late May, 1846, they sailed for the United States. The voyage took sixty-three days and, when he landed in New York, Wise had all of two dollars in his pocket.

To support his family, he tutored pupils. Meanwhile, thanks to Max Lilienthal, he was asked to preach in New Haven and Syracuse, and his effectiveness there gained him an invitation to speak in Albany, where he was immediately elected rabbi of the Beth El Congregation.

Crisis in Albany

Wise had only been in the community a short time when he commenced a program of reforms. In addition to putting an end to the sale of *mitzvot*, or privileges in the synagogue, he trained a choir to sing at the services and began preaching weekly sermons. He also eliminated a number of prayers, particularly those referring to the coming of the Messiah, the return of the Jews to Palestine, and the reestablishment of Temple sacrifices.

With all this, he met only minor opposition from his members, but he was roundly criticized by Isaac Leeser, the well-known Orthodox *chazan* of Philadelphia who had this to say about him in his widely-read monthly, *The Occident:*

> **We most emphatically object to any such form of prayer which, as proposed by Dr. Wise, should exclude the petitions for the rebuilding of the Temple and the reestablishment of the sacrifices. We believe, in common with all Orthodox Jews, in the literal fulfillment of Scripture.**

Meanwhile, at Lilienthal's suggestion, Wise started preparing a prayer book, to be known as the *Minhag America* (מִנְהַג , "custom," referring in this case to the "customary liturgy" or "prayer book"). Even as early as 1848, the fact that he found Jewish education in America so inadequate moved him to call for a union of all the congregations. "It behooves us," he wrote in *The Occident,* "to be united as one man. Otherwise the house of the Lord will become desolate, or nearly so, in less than ten years." However, nothing came of this appeal or his attempt the same year to convene a meeting of all the rabbis.

In 1850, Wise encountered his first serious trouble in Albany. The previous year his daughter had died during a cholera epidemic, and his own illness and grief left him greatly weakened. On the advice of his doctor, he decided to go South for a rest.

Arriving in Charleston, he learned that Rabbi Morris J. Raphall, a recent arrival from England, had been attacking Reform. Subsequently, he attended a public debate between Raphall and Gustav Poznanski, the rabbi of the Charleston temple, during which the former appealed to Wise for support by asking, "Don't you believe in the coming of a personal Messiah and in the resurrection of the dead?" Wise answered with a thunderous "No!"

Word of this filtered back to Albany and, when he returned, he found the president and other members of the congregation determined to oust him. Three days before Rosh Hashanah, at a highly irregular meeting of the congregation, and after Wise's supporters had gone home, they voted to discharge him. Wise's friends urged him to disregard this, but, when he entered the synagogue to conduct Rosh Hashanah services, he found his seat on the pulpit occupied by one of his opponents. To avoid trouble, he took another seat. Then, as he describes it in his *Reminiscences,* when it came time for the Torah service, trouble erupted:

> **I step before the Ark in order to take out the Scrolls of the Law as usual and to offer [a] prayer. Spanier [the president] steps in my way and, without saying a word, smites me with his fist so that my cap falls from my head.**
>
> **This was the terrible signal for an uproar, the like of which I have never experienced. The people acted like furies. It was as though the synagogue had suddenly burst forth into a flaming conflagration.**

The police had to be called to restore order, and to prevent further trouble they closed the synagogue. Wise himself was arrested as "the ringleader of a rebellious mob" and taken off to court. Later, however, the case was dismissed and the president was found guilty.

Wise's friends in Albany rallied behind him, and within a week they organized the new Anshe Emeth Congregation (אַנְשֵׁי אֱמֶת, men of truth), the fourth Reform congregation in America. In rented rooms on the upper floor of an ordinary building, Wise conducted the Yom Kippur services. Shortly afterward, the members purchased a former church, and the services now featured the use of the organ and family pews.

The congregation prospered. Nearly a half-century later, when old wounds had healed, a merger took place with the original Beth El Congregation, to which the combined name Beth Emeth (בֵּית אֱמֶת, house of truth) was given.

Wise as Rabbi in Cincinnati

At the age of thirty-six, Isaac M. Wise accepted an invitation to become rabbi of Cincinnati's B'nai Yeshurun Congregation. In 1864, Cincinnati was the oldest Jewish community west of the Allegheny Mountains, with a population of somewhat more than 3,000 Jews.

The congregation was the younger of the two in the community and had been formed in 1840 chiefly by German Jews whose numbers had been steadily increasing. The previous rabbi had been strictly Orthodox, and, though some reforms had been attempted, the synagogue was largely traditional.

Wise was soon occupied with training a choir to sing modern synagogue music composed by the great Viennese cantor, Solomon Sulzer, and the following year he also succeeded in having an organ installed. Meanwhile, his sermons made such an impact on the entire community that the older B'nai Israel Congregation invited him to become its rabbi as well. He declined the offer but consented to preach for the congregation every Saturday afternoon. After some six months, and upon his recommendation, the congregation invited his good friend Max Lilienthal of New York to become its rabbi.

Wise's congregation grew steadily until soon it was recognized as one of America's leading Reform temples. Together with many others in the South and West, it adopted the *Minhag America* prayer book which he published in 1857. Eight years later he introduced the late Friday evening service which was destined to become widely accepted not only by Reform congregations but by Conservative and Orthodox ones as well. Eventually, in 1871, the membership discontinued wearing hats.

Wise's activities went far beyond the confines of the congregation. Almost as soon as he was settled in Cincinnati, he began publishing his English weekly, *The Israelite.* The next year he also put out *Die Deborah,* a German periodical, for those who could not read English. In addition to news items, they both ran his unceasing appeals for the creation of a union of congregations, an American Jewish university with a rabbinical training school, and a permanent rabbinical organization. They also carried his own novels and plays, his refutations of atheism, his attacks on prejudice and anti-Semitism, and his strong objections to the view that the United States was a "Christian nation." In contrast to his rival, David Einhorn, who preferred the use of German in the service, Wise called for Reform's adoption of English. "Progress and liberalism," he insisted, "are dependent upon this."

Despite Leeser's prediction in *The Occident* that *The Israelite* would never survive, Wise succeeded in publishing it for nearly fifty years, and it is still being published today. But for a long time, Wise was hard-pressed to meet expenses, and he went deeply into debt to keep it alive. At one point, in order to pay the bills, he even gave up smoking cigars, something he greatly enjoyed. Fortunately, *The Israelite's* circulation expanded, mainly in the South and West, and it finally became self-supporting.

The Cleveland Rabbinical Conference of 1855

Though nothing had come from his first attempt to organize a union of congregations in 1848, Wise continued to work for his idea. Now, in August of 1855, joined by eight colleagues, he issued another call for a conference in an article in *The Israelite*. Under the heading, *Shalom Al Yisrael* (שָׁלוֹם עַל יִשְׂרָאֵל, "Peace Be Upon Israel"), he wrote:

> In the name of Israel's God and Israel's religion, the ministers and delegates of the Israelitish congregations are respectfully requested to assemble in a conference to take place the 17th day of October, 5616 [1855], in the city of Cleveland, to deliberate on the following points . . .

Five items were mentioned: (1) to create a permanent "Union of American Israel," (2) to organize a synod representing the congregations, (3) to create a common American Jewish prayer book, the *Minhag America,* (4) to produce a program of Jewish education for the young and the more advanced, and (5) to consider all other matters raised by the delegates.

The three-day meeting opened on October 17 with some eighty representatives from eight major communities, and Wise was chosen to preside. As the first order of business, the delegates voted to establish a permanent synod to represent American Jewry and to promote the necessary religious changes, institutions, and programs. Plans were also approved to create a common prayer book for American Jewry and a sound program of religious education.

The following four principles were then adopted:

> 1. **The Bible as delivered to us by our fathers and as now in our possession is of immediate divine origin and the standard of our religion.**
>
> 2. **The Talmud contains the traditional, legal, and logical exposition of the biblical laws which must be expounded and practiced according to the comments of the Talmud.**

> 3. **The resolutions of the synod in accordance with the above principles are legally valid.**
>
> 4. **Statutes and ordinances contrary to the laws of the land are invalid.**

In the interests of harmony with the Orthodox, Wise had accepted these principles, and he returned home enthusiastic over the results of the Cleveland Conference. In fact, writing in *The Israelite* ten days later, he said of it:

> None can predict or even imagine the influence which this body will exercise upon our institutions, our position in society, and the development of our religion on this American soil.

But a storm of criticism came down upon him from the East. He later wrote in his *Reminiscences:*

> [It] denuded my tree of hope of its blossoms. Protests against the resolutions of the [Cleveland] conference were published in Balitmore, Charleston, and New York . . . They fell like lightning from a clear sky. No one expected them, for they proceeded from the Reform camp whose active support we counted upon confidently.

Heading the attack was the Har Sinai Congregation of Baltimore, led by its rabbi, David Einhorn. In an open letter to *The Occident,* the temple condemned the statement supporting the authority of the Talmud by asserting:

> . . . The members of the German Rabbinical Conference, who counted among their number theologians of acknowledged reputation, took a decided stand in many of their propositions and resolutions against the whole Talmud-halachic exposition of Scripture. Can it hence be affirmed that these men have ceased to be Israelites?

The said [Cleveland] platform would condemn Judaism to a perpetual stagnation . . .

Further attacks went so far as to accuse Wise himself of wanting to become "the Jewish archbishop of American Israel."

In vain, he and his supporters tried to defend their actions at Cleveland, arguing that the Talmud *was* a vital part of Judaism, that, far from being rigid, it, too, had undergone change, and that the Cleveland declaration represented the only possible basis for unity between the Orthodox and Reform. But the Easterners would have none of it, and now the Orthodox also began to be critical. They expressed fear, for instance, that the *Minhag America* would eliminate certain traditional doctrines, such as belief in the coming of a Messiah and the return of the Jews to Palestine, which proved to be the case when Wise published it two years later.

Thus, before the year was over, it was clear that the Cleveland Conference had failed to achieve either of its two objectives: religious reform and American Jewish unity. Even worse, it sowed dissension not only between the Orthodox and Reform but among the Reformers themselves, with unfortunate consequences to the movement that lasted for more than a generation.

Zion College and Failure Again

The establishment of a Jewish university in America was another of Wise's great ambitions. Here he saw the possibility of training American Jewish leadership for succeeding generations, not only as rabbis and teachers

HISTORIC HAR SINAI CONGREGATION. This Baltimore congregation was the first originally Reform synagogue. (HUC, American Jewish Archives)

but as dedicated laymen who would pursue secular professions and occupations.

Thus, as early as September of 1854, shortly after he came to Cincinnati, Wise published a call, signed by himself and twenty-two others, for a general meeting that would seek to establish in Cincinnati:

> . . . A college on the pattern of German universities, connected with a theological seminary and a seminary for teachers, in order to promulgate science and the interests of Judaism among our fellow citizens.

The outcome was the formation of the Zion Collegiate Association which about 300 Cincinnatians joined. Evidently they had been moved by Wise's appeals in *The Israelite,* especially one published shortly after the conference that read, "Let us educate our ministers here in our own college, and we will soon have American ministers, American congregations."

Zion College opened in the fall of 1856 with fourteen students and five professors, two of whom were Wise and Lilienthal. But after only one year, the school was forced to close for lack of funds.

Disappointed but not discouraged, Wise continued to press for a Jewish university. However, the experience with Zion College made him more aware of the realities. He now realized how much more financial support was necessary, something that no single community alone, not even Cincinnati, could provide. Hence, it had to be a national undertaking, involving as many communities and congregations as possible. And he also came to the conclusion that the college had to limit itself to what was most essential, the training of rabbis and possibly teachers.

So, with the support of his close friend Max Lilienthal, Wise turned his primary efforts to the creation of a "union of congregations" which would be responsible for maintaining the seminary. He received fresh encourage-ment in 1871 when twenty-seven Reform rabbis who had come to Cincinnati for the purpose of revising the *Minhag America* unanimously adopted a resolution calling for a "Union of Israelite Congregations of America." Its principal objective, they stated, would be to establish a rabbinical school.

A Possible Ray of Hope?

In view of the controversy that had followed both the Cleveland Conference and the publication of the *Minhag America* without certain traditional beliefs, the participation of the Orthodox was now out of the question.

Could the Reformers, then, be persuaded to cooperate? Certainly the antagonism of the Eastern faction presented what seemed to be an insurmountable obstacle. In fact, even then, David Einhorn, in opposition to Wise, was attempting to establish his own rabbinical seminary in New York.

On the surface, the prospects for a Reform "union" seemed dim. Yet there was one ray of hope; that was the very fruitful meeting that had taken place two years before, in 1869, in Philadelphia. For, in spite of the fact that the Easterners had sponsored it, Wise had decided to attend, and out of it had come a set of Reform principles that seemed to satisfy both sides.

QUESTIONS FOR DISCUSSION

1. How do you account for the opposition Max Lilienthal met at the hands of Russian Jewry? Why did the Jewish masses reject Enlightenment as a means of improving their condition? How has current Soviet policy toward the Jews been affected by Russia's experience under the Czars?

2. What advantages did the early American Reformers have over those in Europe? What special difficulties did they face? To what extent

have these carried over into present-day American Jewish life?

3. In what ways was Wise's ministry in the United States different from that in Bohemia? What shortcomings did he discover in the American Jewish community of his day? How did he hope to overcome them?

4. What particular problems in American life gave Lilienthal and Wise the greatest concern? How do you explain their reaction? To what extent does the Reform movement still share their point of view?

5. How do you account for the rift in Reform ranks after the Cleveland Conference of 1855? What effect did this have upon the development of the movement? What traces of this conflict do we still find within Reform today?

6. Why are Lilienthal and Wise considered moderate Reformers? To what extent does the movement today agree with their views? Where does it differ? What influence, then, have the moderate Reformers had upon the movement?

SIGNIFICANT DOCUMENTS

An Early Experience of Max Lilienthal in Russia, 1839

Soon afterwards [following Lilienthal's arrival in Russia], another messenger, Mr. J. of my congregation in Riga, arrived, urging me to come as soon as possible to that city in order to enter upon my duties. As the [Russian] minister had not yet returned to the capital [St. Petersburg], I followed the advice of the Bavarian ambassador not to leave the city before having made his personal acquaintance, even if I had to stay some weeks longer, as I could expect no advancement in Russia if not favored by the highest authorities. I therefore resolved to await his return.

But now began some disagreeable occurrences. I was not aware of the law that no foreign Jew whatever, if not called by the government, had a right to enter the Rus-

sian empire and, as soon as discovered, had to leave again immediately. As I was not yet installed into my office and had no passport from the Department of Public Instruction, this law was also applicable to me.

One Saturday morning, therefore, I received a notice to appear immediately at the Bureau of Police for Strangers. I was brought before the Chief Secretary who, although a Russian himself, spoke all the modern languages with remarkable fluency. He asked me three times if I was a Jew for, wearing neither a beard nor the Polish *schubetze* [garments worn by traditional Jews] and being dressed like himself, he could and would not believe that I was a Jew. But when I answered in the affirmative, he read me the above-mentioned law and told me that I had to leave St. Petersburg immediately.

I explained to him all the circumstances of my case . . . But all was in vain until I told him that I should report the case to the Bavarian ambassador who would procure from the general of police the permission for me to stay till the minister would return.

After some reconsideration, during which a friend of mine handed him twenty-five rubles [Russian money], I got a card for eight days. This short time having elapsed, I was summoned again, and this time I did not get the cards for another fortnight before the secretary of the legation went with me to the general of police who reluctantly granted me the demanded permission.

But during this time, the passport of Mr. J. from Riga had expired. He had lived with me but I begged him to change his lodging as soon as he had informed me of this fatal circumstance, having experienced troubles enough for myself from the amiable [irony] Russian police. The Russian Jews have no right whatever to come into Russia proper; they live either in the provinces formerly forming the Polish kingdom, or in those which belonged to Turkey. Into Russia proper and the capitals they can only come if authorized by the governor of their provinces, this authority having been confirmed by the senate (the supreme court) of St. Petersburg or the local supreme authorities.

Mr. J., therefore, had to have his passport renewed by the general of police and, although having spent some money and time, he had to wait till Saturday midnight when the general, leaving the theatre, came again to his office in order to attend to his business. During this time he hid himself in several houses of his friends in order not to be arrested by the police. Nevertheless, the captain of the ward was in search of him and, thinking that he was still living with me, a soldier appeared in my room on Saturday afternoon ordering me to appear before the captain. I feared something was again amiss with me and I begged the soldier to go, telling him that I would appear immediately. But he insisted upon accompanying me through the streets, whereas I felt mortified. It is dangerous to temporize with the Russian police, and therefore I followed him . . .

There I was examined; I was asked if I know the whereabouts of Mr. J. and, answering in the negative, I was permitted to go home. Mr. J., frightened by this incident, thought himself safer nowhere than in the police department itself and he hurried thither, passing the whole evening before he got his passport signed again.

I had hurried to my lodgings and had hardly been there a few hours when the captain himself, with four soldiers, entered my room, demanding that I should state the abode of Mr. J., as he was sure that I knew it. I denied this in the most positive manner; but, being unable to explain myself in Russian and he being unacquainted with either German or French,

he became enraged and threatened to arrest me if I would not give him the information. Troubled and alarmed, I mentioned the house of a nobleman whose acquaintance I had made, where Mr. J. never had been but where, as I supposed, the captain would receive a rather unwelcome reception for his untimely intrusion at night. Satisfied with this information, he left, and I on my part felt sure he would return when he found out the deception.

And thus it came to pass. At the aristocrat's house he was rebuked for his visit; he then hurried back to arrest me but the bird had flown. He had to leave without attaining his purpose; but for three days I had to stay in bed, so much did the miserable affair affect me. When Mr. J. reported himself the next morning to the captain with his new passport, the officer told him how I had deceived him, but knowing that I was acquainted with the Bavarian minister he let the whole affair drop. Nevertheless, I had the satisfaction to hear one year afterwards that he was discharged from office for some misdemeanor as an officer.

No one believes how much the poor Jews are vexed and troubled with these passports, and how much money is extorted from them by the subaltern [junior] officers. Each and every one of them, even if the permission is already granted by the chief, asks and expects something for writing the passport, for presenting it for signature, for putting the seal to it, for recording it, etc., and, if the bribery is refused, the petitioner is surely brought into trouble which will cost him three times the amount. The emperor knows of the bribes; in the theatre such officers are represented in several plays, but all efforts at extirpating bribery in Russia proves totally abortive.

—From David Philipson,
Max Lilenthal, American Rabbi,
pp. 168–171.

David Einhorn's Protest Against the Cleveland Conference, 1855

According to a statement in the *Israelite* of October 26, it appears that a conference composed of several rabbis and private persons lately met at Cleveland, Ohio, and, on motion of the Rev. Dr. Isaac M. Wise of Cincinnati, adopted the following part of a platform:

> That the Talmud is acknowledged by all (Israelites) as the legal and obligatory comment on the Bible.

We, the undersigned [members of the congregation], having solely the interest of our holy religion at heart, respond to the solemn duty imposed on us of offering our most decided protest against the said platform, and on the following grounds:

It is an indisputable fact that a very large portion of Israelites who are admitted to possess a profound knowledge of Sacred Scripture, and whose attachment to Judaism cannot be questioned, do not consider the talmudic exegesis of the Bible, which so frequently clashes with the spirit and text of Scripture, as legal and obligatory. Even the most distinguished biblical scholars of antiquity, Ibn Ezra, Maimonides, Samuel ben Meir, Levi ben Gershom, and others are not seldom at variance with the talmudic interpretation of Holy Writ.

Is it, therefore, justifiable that the great majority of our fellow believers who carry out in practice such anti-talmudic interpretations—who, for instance, shave their beards with a razor—should be denied the name of Israelite? The members of the German Rabbinical Conference, who counted among their number theologians of acknowledged reputation, took a decided stand in many of their propositions and resolutions against the whole talmudo-halachic exposition of Scripture. Can it hence be affirmed that these men have ceased to be Israelites?

The said platform would condemn Judaism to a perpetual stagnation, consign its countless treasures, available for all times, to the narrow confines of an exclusive Jewish nationality, and expose to derision its entire historical development, as well as the incontestable results of a wholesome biblical research. The declared legitimacy of talmudic authority cannot heal but, on the contrary, will render permanent our unhealthy religious condition which consists not in the present conflict of parties but must be sought for in the demoralizing effects of an antagonism between theory and practice and in an opposition between prescriptive rules and the unyielding nature of religious and social wants.

We also appreciate peace in Israel as a precious boon; but a peace which necessarily degrades Judaism, our greatest boon, appears to us to be too dearly bought and is in the highest degree of a precarious tenure, when a few men in the name of collective Israel set up articles of faith which deny to dissenters a place in the communion of professing Israelites.

May the free American Israel keep a strict watch on hierarchical movements which would again forge its chains, though under the most charming lullabies of peace, now in the guise of dogmas, and ere long by a *Minhag America.* The plan of a consistory which was originally intended to be established is an omen of significant import. The great work of peace-making being once finished, and everything brought under one hood, it would be an easy matter to change this hood into a bishop's mitre—and nothing more reasonable but that the great united flock must needs have a chief pastor—and all is ready for the advent of Jewish popes.

Let us rather thank God for the blessings of religious liberty we enjoy in this country, equally secured to all denominations; and may we not put a yoke on our own shoulders which would interfere with the full expansion of the old and reformatory [Reform] Judaism and eventually reduce both to miserable caricatures.

—From W. Gunther Plaut,
The Growth of Reform Judaism,
pp. 23–24.

The Creation of the *Minhag America* Prayer Book, 1856–1857

The Principles Adopted by the Committee Appointed by the Cleveland Conference

1. No one man is authorized to make a prayer book for the congregations;

2. The ancient form of the service is to be preserved;

3. Individual congregations are to decide how much English or Hebrew they will use;

4. Whatever is against the concepts of biblical Judaism, American Israel, or the wants and demands of the time is to be omitted. The service is not to be beyond a reasonable length, and there is to be provision in it for the use of choir and organ.

The Prayer Book Committee's Objections to the Traditional Prayer Book, as Reported by Isaac Mayer Wise

It was out of the question to retain the old prayers unchanged because the belief in the coming of a personal Messiah descended from the house of David had disappeared from among the people. The return to Palestine, the restoration of the Davidic dynasty, of the sacrificial cult, and the accompanying priestly caste were neither articles of faith nor commandments of Judaism, while the lamentations over oppression, persecution, and the accompanying cry for vengeance were untrue and immoral so far as American Jews were concerned. The kabalistical [mystical] portions which had crept into the prayer book and the obstinate adherence to the doctrine of the bodily resurrection were regarded as unjustified. We also agreed that the Sabbath service including the sermon should not last longer than two hours. . . .

We resolved to publish an English and German, as well as a Hebrew, version of the prayers, and that it should be left to each congregation to decide what language it wished to use. . . .

From an Account by Wise of the Completion and Publication of the Minhag America

The commission [committee] met in my library and finished the work in thirty-eight sessions. They adhered anxiously to tradition; they had no desire to found a new religion nor institute a new cult. They wished to recast the old and traditional prayers reverently so they might be brought into accord with the religious consciousness of the time and the democratic principles of the new fatherland.

After the work had been finished, Bloch and Company had to defray the cost of publication. . . .

Before the last leaf had left the press, it had been derided and decried throughout the land, although only the first part (without services for New Year's Day and Day of Atonement) had appeared. The name, *Minhag America,* was popular but not the book, which was attacked savagely in both camps (Orthodox and Reform) in the East and rejected. My congregation was the first to adopt the book, but not without objections being raised. . . . The old prayer book was deeply rooted in home, school, and synagogue.

187

Reform Judaism—Then and Now

It was in the summer of 1857 that the *Minhag America* finally appeared. For eleven years I had cherished the idea, and now it was consummated, but it was attacked with all the weapons possible immediately upon its appearance, and yet it is the only monument of the first Cleveland Conference and is now [in 1875] used in at least one-third of all American Jewish congregations. . . .

—From James G. Heller,
Isaac M. Wise,
His Life, Work and Thought,
pp. 302–304.

OTHER THINGS TO READ

Bamberger, Bernard J., *The Story of Judaism:* Chap. 44, "Under the Heel of the Tsars"; Chap. 45, "The Golden Land."

Gumbiner, Joseph H., *Isaac Mayer Wise, Pioneer of American Judaism.*

Heller, James G., *Isaac M. Wise, His Life, Work and Thought:* Chap. 6, "First Weeks in America"; Chap. 18, "The Cleveland Conference and *Minhag America.*"

Jewish Encyclopedia: "David Einhorn," Vol. 5, pp. 78–79; "Haskalah," Vol. 6, pp. 256–258; "Hazan," Vol. 6, pp. 284–287; "Max Lilienthal," Vol. 8, pp. 86–87; "Russia—History," Vol. 10, pp. 518–528.

Knox, Israel, "Isaac Mayer Wise," Chap. 4 in Simon Noveck (ed.), *Great Jewish Personalities in Modern Times.*

Learsi, Rufus, *The Jews in America: A History:* Chap. 4, "In War and Peace"; Chap. 5, "Across the Continent"; Chap. 6, "Old World Sorrows"; Chap. 7, "Civil War"; Chap. 8, "Religious Divisions."

Levinger, Lee J., *A History of the Jews in the United States:* Chap. 12, "The Second Wave of Immigration: From Germany"; Chap. 13, "The Civil War: Jews in the North and South"; Chap.

14, "The Basis of Judaism in America"; Chap. 15, "The Growth of Reform Judaism"; Chap. 16, "How Jewish Lodges and Charities Were Formed."

Masserman, Paul, and Max Baker, *The Jews Come to America:* Chap. 9, "Judaism in the Fifties"; Chap. 10, "The Reform Movement."

May, Max B., *Isaac Mayer Wise.*

Philipson, David, *Centenary Papers and Others:* "Max Lilienthal," pp. 149–190; "Isaac Mayer Wise," pp. 11–62.

Philipson, David, *Max Lilienthal, American Rabbi.*

Philipson, David, *The Reform Movement in Judaism:* pp. 339–353 (early American Reform leaders).

Plaut, W. Gunther, *The Growth of Reform Judaism:* Chap. 1, "American Beginnings"; pp. 19–23 (Cleveland Conference).

Schwartzman, Sylvan D., *Reform Judaism in the Making:* Chap. 11, "The Creators of American Reform."

Standard Jewish Encyclopedia: "David Einhorn," pp. 603–604; "Haskalah," pp. 852–854; "Hazan," p. 863; "Max Lilienthal," p. 1210; "Russia," pp. 1624–1630; "Isaac M. Wise," pp. 1916–1917.

Universal Jewish Encyclopedia: "Cantor," Vol. 3, pp. 17–18; "David Einhorn," Vol. 4, pp. 27–28; "Haskalah," Vol. 5, pp. 242–245; "Max Lilienthal," Vol. 7, pp. 62–63; "Russia," Vol. 9, pp. 278–286; "I. M. Wise," Vol. 10, pp. 539–542.

Wise, Isaac M., *Reminiscences.*

SUGGESTED ACTIVITIES

1. Write the script for a television documentary on the life of Max Lilienthal or Isaac M. Wise.

2. Conduct a debate on the subject: "*Resolved,* that the position of Wise on the principles adopted by the Cleveland Conference of 1855 was in the best interests of Reform."

3. Prepare a newsmagazine article on the early development of Reform Judaism in the United States.

SUBJECTS FOR RESEARCH

1. What type of Orthodox Judaism did the United States have in the middle of the nineteenth century? How did it compare with that of Eastern Europe?

2. What role did Isaac Leeser play in the development of American Jewish life in the mid-1800's? What was his general attitude toward Reform Judaism? Toward Isaac M. Wise and David Einhorn?

3. Compare one of the services found in any edition of the *Minhag America* with that contained in the most recent edition of the *Union Prayer Book*. What do they have in common, and where do they differ? How do you account for the differences?

4. What was Max Lilienthal's position on the observance of *Tishah B'Av* (the ninth of *Av*)? How did his Cincinnati congregation react? Compare Lilienthal's stand with that of the Reform movement today.

5. What were Isaac M. Wise's views on the Bible? How did they differ from those of Reformers like David Einhorn? With which does present-day Reform agree, and why?

FILMSTRIPS TO SEE

Baal Shem Tov: The Teachings of the Hasidim (UAHC), picturing the teachings and spirit of this eighteenth-century East European Jewish religious movement.

David Einhorn: Father of the Union Prayerbook (UAHC), portraying the life and contributions of this great early American Reform leader.

Isaac Mayer Wise: Master Builder of American Judaism (UAHC), presenting highlights in the life of this outstanding Reform pioneer in the United States.

Jews in the Soviet Union, in two parts (UAHC), describing Jewish life in modern Russia through which the Jews' past experiences are reflected.

300 Years: Memorable Events in American Jewish History (UAHC), providing a view of important historic happenings in American Jewish life that underlie the development of Reform.

A LIVE ISSUE

During the past quarter of a century, most Reform congregations have reintroduced a number of traditional rituals that include the lighting of the Sabbath candles, the chanting of the *Kiddush,* and the *Bar Mitzvah* ceremony. Some have also adopted the wearing of the *talit* and skull-cap at services, as well as other traditional practices.

The Basic Problem: This, in turn, raises a fundamental question about Reform's attitude toward traditional ceremonies. Some claim that since most Reform congregations had abandoned many of them by the early part of the twentieth century the movement is fundamentally opposed to them. But, as many others insist, Reform sanctions the introduction of any religious practice—traditional or not—that is meaningful to modern Jews.

Is Reform, then, operating contrary to its principles by reintroducing more and more traditional practices?

Some Important Questions: (1) How does Reform differ from traditional Judaism in its view of religious practice? (2) Does the reintroduction of certain traditional observances mean that Reform is becoming ''Orthodox''? (3) To what kinds of traditional practices did the movement originally object, and why? (4) Would this bar the reintroduction of any that were meaningful to modern Jews? (5) To what extent, then, are the recent trends in Reform consistent with its principles?

What Do You Think? To help you decide, you should pay particular attention to the views of the early American Reformers as reported in this chapter. Do the objections to various traditional ceremonies on the part of the more radical Reformers mean that the movement's present trends are contrary to its teachings? Or are those who advocate more traditional practices in the temple acting within the proper spirit of Reform?

13. THE ACHIEVEMENT OF REFORM ORGANIZATION

Harmony at Philadelphia, 1869

Among those who opposed Wise's efforts to organize the movement were some of the ablest Reformers of the times. In addition to David Einhorn, there was Samuel Adler of New York, Samuel Hirsch of Philadelphia, and Bernhard Felsenthal who came from Chicago but nevertheless sided with the Easterners.

All were among the eleven who attended the Philadelphia Rabbinical Conference in 1869 that the radical Reformers had called largely in opposition to Wise and the moderates. The invitation in part read:

> . . . What is needed to strengthen this power [of Reform Judaism] and to extend its realm to ever wider circles is an understanding of like-minded rabbis concerning the principles—not the forms—of a new ritual and of the solution of various practical and religious questions, especially in the field of marriage law . . .

To their great surprise, Wise himself turned up. It was an attempt on his part to conciliate them.

The participants spent much of the time dealing with the problems of traditional marriage and divorce laws, and they passed resolutions permitting the double-ring ceremony, giving the bride a more active role in the wedding, eliminating the rite of *chalitzah,* and accepting civil divorce. Then they proceeded to adopt a set of Reform principles that contained the following seven provisions:

1. The messianic aim of Judaism is not the restoration of the ancient Jewish state in Palestine under the reign of a descendant of King David. Rather, it is to establish God's moral Kingdom on earth for all mankind.

2. Far from being punishment for their guilt, the dispersion of the Jews from ancient Palestine was designed to enable them to carry on their mission to all the peoples of the earth, bringing to them the true knowledge and worship of God.

3. The ancient priesthood and sacrifices represent only a historical stage in the

development of Judaism. These have since been replaced by the conception of the entire Jewish people serving as priests in their mission to mankind and requiring moral purification for that task.

4. All religious distinctions between a descendant of the ancient priesthood—the so-called *kohen* [כֹּהֵן, priest]—and the rest of Jewry is abandoned.

5. As a people of religion, the Jews have been chosen by God for their special mission to mankind, thus revealing His love for all His children on earth.

6. Judaism believes in immortality, the existence of the soul after death, but rejects all belief in the resurrection or restoration of the body after death.

7. Though knowledge of Hebrew is the sacred responsibility of every Jew, Jewish worship should be conducted in the language that the majority understands in order that prayer be intelligible.

As a moderate Reformer, Wise had a number of reservations about these principles. Nevertheless, he gave them his approval and expressed the hope that the group might develop into a permanent rabbinical body for the benefit of American Jewry as a whole. His cooperation, he believed, would help heal the breach between the two factions and gain him much-needed support for his congregational union and seminary.

Samuel Adler of New York

Among the Easterners present at the conference, four in particular were recognized as the leaders. One was Samuel Adler of New York, acknowledged to be the greatest scholar among the Reformers of his day.

Born in Germany in 1809, he was the son of a noted Orthodox rabbi who died when Samuel was only thirteen and left the family in poverty. Nevertheless, the boy managed to secure an excellent Jewish and secular education, achieving both rabbinical ordination and his Doctor of Philosophy degree.

Before coming to America in 1857, Adler served as rabbi of two German congregations for more than twenty years. He also participated in all of the major European rabbinical conferences and was a member of the committee dealing with Sabbath observance. To him the Sabbath was to be a day of self-consecration to religious ideals, and he therefore urged a more liberal interpretation of the traditional prohibitions against "work."

Adler was likewise an ardent champion of equal religious rights for women. It was he, in fact, who introduced the resolution at the Breslau Conference in 1846 declaring that women had the same right as men to receive a Jewish education and take part in public worship.

Upon arriving in America he became the rabbi of Temple Emanu-El of New York where he succeeded Rabbi Leo Merzbacher, another of the rabbis that Isaac M. Wise met when he first came to this country, and he served there for seventeen years until his retirement. Unlike his predecessor, he fully shared the radical views of David Einhorn. Indeed, characteristic was the answer he gave to the organizers of the Chicago Sinai Congregation when they asked him how they should proceed:

I would state that the first and most important step for the congregation to take is to free its service of shackling lies, to remove from it mention of things and wishes which we would not utter if it had to be done in an intelligible manner. Such are the lamentations about oppression and persecution, the petitions for the restoration of the sacrificial cult, for the return

American Reform Developments—to 1871

Major Events in European Reform	Key Reform Developments in America
1823—Reform services in Berlin ended by the government.	1824—Organization of the Charleston Reform Society.
1832—Publication of Zunz's *The Jewish Sermon.*	
1837—Wiesbaden Rabbinical Conference.	
1838—Beginning of the Geiger-Tiktin affair (to 1854).	
1841—Hamburg Temple prayer book controversy.	1841—Building of the Charleston temple with an organ.
1842—Dedication of the West London Synagogue of British Jews. Organization of the Frankfort Reform Society.	1842—Organization of the Har Sinai Reform Society in Baltimore.
1844—Brunswick Rabbinical Conference.	1844—Arrival of Max Lilienthal in the United States.
1845—Frankfort Rabbinical Conference.	1845—Formation of the Emanu-El Congregation in New York.
1846—Breslau Rabbinical Conference.	1846—First Confirmation conducted in the United States. Isaac M. Wise comes to America.
1848—Beginning of large-scale emigration from Germany as a result of the unsuccessful revolution.	1850—Formation of a Reform congregation in Albany.
	1854—Founding of *The Israelite* by Wise.
	1855—Reform adopted by two Cincinnati congregations. Holding of the Cleveland Rabbinical Conference. Opening of Zion College in Cincinnati. Arrival of David Einhorn in the United States.
	1856—Reform adopted by the Keneseth Israel Congregation of Philadelphia.
	1857—Publication of the *Minhag America* prayer book by Wise.
	1858—Formation of the Chicago Sinai Reform Society.
1869—Leipzig Synod.	1869—Philadelphia Rabbinical Conference.
1871—Augsburg Synod.	1871—Congregation "union" called for by a rabbinical meeting in Cincinnati.

of Israel to Palestine, the hope for a personal Messiah, and for the resurrection of the body.

In the second place, let us eliminate fiction and exaggeration; and, in the third place, make the service clear, intelligible, instructive, and inspiring . . .

Adler was a man of enormous Jewish knowledge, who wrote a great many scholarly articles. His interest in Jewish learning also led him to concentrate on improving Jewish education in his congregation and on developing what in his day was considered a model religious school.

His contributions to the Reform cause were widely recognized, so that, when a permanent rabbinical organization was finally established in 1889, Samuel Adler, then eighty, was immediately made its honorary president.

Samuel Raphael Hirsch of Philadelphia

Another of the leading Easterners was Samuel Raphael Hirsch, who also came from Germany. At the age of twenty-three he had become rabbi of Dessau, an important city in the central part of the country, and three years later published his *Religious Philosophy of Jewry,* a brilliant and highly-acclaimed work in which he succeeded in applying to Judaism the philosophy of George Wilhelm Friedrich Hegel, a noted nineteenth-century thinker. Hirsch's conclusion was that to follow the will of God, as the people of Israel conceives it, is to enjoy the greatest freedom and to perform the highest service for mankind.

When the congregation became dissatisfied with his Reform outlook, Hirsch resigned his post to become the chief-rabbi of Luxemburg, then under the control of the more liberal Dutch, where he remained for nearly a quarter of a century. In the meanwhile, he attended all the principal rabbinical conferences and published an important work, *Reform in Judaism,* that had a profound effect on the movement.

Finally, in 1866, he accepted the pulpit of Congregation Keneseth Israel of Philadelphia where he succeeded David Einhorn. It was at Hirsch's home three years later that the Philadelphia Conference met and adopted its principles.

Like his predecessor Einhorn, with whom he had much in common, Hirsch was a staunch advocate of radical Reform. Both, in fact, frequently joined in attacking the more moderate Wise, whom Hirsch personally disliked and whose organizational efforts he constantly opposed.

In 1889, after twenty-two years of service in Philadelphia, he retired to spend the last year of his life with his son Emil G. Hirsch, rabbi of the Chicago Sinai Congregation, and his son's wife, who was David Einhorn's daughter.

Bernhard Felsenthal of Chicago

Bernhard Felsenthal was the third leading member of the Eastern faction. Born in 1822 in a tiny east-German village, he had originally intended to enter government service, but found this impossible as a Jew. Instead, he became a teacher at a Jewish school where, as he continued his studies of the Jewish sources, he came to accept the Reform position.

Like so many others, he immigrated to the United States after the unsuccessful revolution of 1848. He first went to Louisville, then to Madison, Indiana, where he taught in the local Jewish religious school.

Almost from the start, he identified himself with American Reform. A speech before the Madison congregation in which he proposed changes in the Sabbath service created quite

BERNHARD FELSENTHAL. Although an Eastern Reformer, he was one of the early Reform champions of Zionism. (HUC, American Jewish Archives)

a stir; so did his articles on Reform in Wise's *The Israelite* and Einhorn's *Sinai.* He was especially sympathetic to the more radical Reform point of view and maintained close friendships with all the leading Eastern Reformers.

In April of 1858, at the urging of friends, he moved to Chicago to take a position as a clerk in the Jewish banking firm of Greenebaum Brothers. Knowing of his scholarly interests, the company provided him with a private study behind his office, and it was here that a small group from the then Orthodox Chicago K.A.M. Congregation organized a Reform society.

Felsenthal was elected secretary and promptly drew up a list of twenty-seven religious principles for adoption that formed the basis of a widely-circulated pamphlet, *Kol Kore Bamidbor* (קוֹל קוֹרֵא בַּמִּדְבָּר , A Voice Crying in the Wilderness). In it he pleaded for the improvement of Jewish religious life by eliminating antiquated beliefs and practices and concentrating on the more vital rites and doctrines.

The Reform Society soon developed into the Chicago Sinai Congregation and Felsenthal was elected its first rabbi. Both David Einhorn and Samuel Adler promptly conferred a rabbinical degree upon him, calling him well-qualified by reason of his Jewish learning and character. Three years later he gave up this post to organize the Chicago Zion Congregation, whose spiritual leader he remained for twenty-three years.

At the time of the Philadelphia Conference, Felsenthal vigorously opposed the reestablishment of the ancient Jewish state in Palestine. Later in life, however, he changed his mind and became an ardent champion of Zionism, even helping to form the first Zionist society in the United States in 1896.

The frightful conditions of East European Jews, particularly in Russia, appalled him, and he urged their immediate resettlement in Palestine. "Millions of oppressed Jewish brethren appeal: 'Help us! Assist us!' " he wrote. "We listen compassionately to this appeal, and it is our duty to help and assist." Nor did he see any contradiction between Zionism and the Jews' mission to mankind. "A small and well-organized nation [of Jews in Palestine]," he declared, "can work more efficaciously for good than many millions scattered and disorganized."

Felsenthal was likewise deeply concerned with promoting Jewish knowledge. It was he who first suggested the creation of the American Jewish Historical Society, which was finally founded in 1892. He also took great interest in the work of the Jewish Publication Society and served for twenty years on its Publication Committee until his death in 1908.

David Einhorn—His Years in Europe

The undisputed leader of the Eastern faction, of course, was David Einhorn, whose position on Reform was shaped by his early experiences in Europe. Even in America he never wavered from it.

Born in 1809 in a tiny German village, he was a brilliant student as a youth and was able to complete his rabbinical training at the Talmudic Academy of Fürth by the age of seventeen. During this period he was also mastering the classics and mathematics.

Following his ordination, he attended several universities where study of comparative religion strengthened his conviction that Judaism, like other faiths, had undergone numerous changes in the course of its history. His conclusions, as he eventually expressed them in Philippson's *General News of Judaism,* led him to adopt a Reform point of view:

> **In all its stages, Judaism shows its capacity for continuous development, both as to its form and its spirit. The latter, particularly, became ever clearer and purer in the human consciousness, and no Jew who knows his religion will deny it the power of constant self-improvement.**

DAVID EINHORN. He was the leader of the Eastern Reformers, the so-called "radical" faction. (HUC, American Jewish Archives)

Meanwhile, Einhorn's attendance at university turned his teachers at the Talmudic Academy against him, and they denounced him as an "unbeliever" and a "transgressor." For ten years they did everything possible to prevent him from being engaged by any synagogue. Thus, when the Wellhausen congregation invited him to serve, they persuaded the Bavarian authorities not to approve his appointment.

At last, in 1842, he obtained his first pulpit in Hoppstädten, a small east-German community, where he found a group of members eager for the introduction of prayers and sermons in German. During his ministry there, he also participated in the major Reform rabbinical conferences from 1844 to 1846. At the one in Frankfort, he urged the use of the vernacular in the service. "People need prayer as the expression of their innermost thoughts, convictions, and sentiments," he argued, "and this can only be attained through the mother tongue." He also called for the reading of the *Haftarah* in German and the abolition of all prayers for the return of the Jews from "exile."

At the Breslau Conference, where he was appointed chairman of the committee to review the Jewish dietary laws, he contended that they were never intended for the modern world. Similarly, in presenting the report of the committee on religious rights for women at Breslau, he ridiculed the notion that women were naturally inferior in matters of "holiness." "It is our sacred duty," he insisted, "to declare with all emphasis woman's complete religious equality with man."

In 1847, over the most violent protest of his former teachers, who called him an "insolent, wicked infidel," David Einhorn succeeded his life-long friend Samuel Holdheim as rabbi of the congregation in Mecklenburg-Schwerin. However, after several years, the opposition of the more traditional members compelled him to resign, and he accepted a position with the Budapest Reform Congregation, which had modeled its program after that of Berlin by conducting its main service on Sunday and worshiping without hats.

But he never took office there because the Orthodox were able to persuade the Austrian government to close the temple as a "radical" institution, and for four years the officials refused to listen to any of his appeals. Meanwhile, he used the time to good advantage by producing an important book, *The Principles of Mosaic Religion,* in which he described the main teachings of Judaism, contrasting them with its rites, which he considered nonessential. During this period, he also worked on a new prayer book that was destined to become one of his great contributions to American Reform.

Einhorn's Role in the United States

In 1855, at the age of forty-six, he decided to accept the pulpit of the Har Sinai Congregation of Baltimore, the first temple organized from the start as Reform. In his installation address he told the members:

> We have come to a turning point. Our entire religious and moral life is in peril. Mere outward forms which render the service more attractive are of no avail. They merely hide the inner decay. Judaism must be reformed from within. . .
>
> It is the Jewish faith that is the fountain of our strength. For ours is the belief in the One and Only God; ours is the belief in the innate goodness and purity of all things created by Him. Ours is the belief in the one human family . . . over whom God will eventually rule as King.

Quickly Einhorn became recognized as the leader of Reform in the East, and it was he who headed the opposition to the Cleveland Conference of 1855 with its declaration that the Talmud remained binding. He would have none of it; nor would he accept any of Wise's other compromises with the Orthodox. No matter what the cost, he insisted, Reform had to be honest and reject traditional teachings and practices that were clearly outmoded. These, he said, "had to change according to different stages of culture, national customs, industrial, social and civil conditions."

What then, Einhorn was asked, was permanent in Judaism? He replied:

> The inner or fundamental teachings of our religion. These are the Ten Commandments, belief in the One Eternal God, faith in the goodness that is in all men and in their right to equal happiness under equal laws, the belief that some day all mankind will find this happiness here on earth in a great Messianic Age. These are the Jewish teachings that cannot be altered or changed.

To publicize his views, he began publishing a German-language magazine, *Sinai,* through which many were persuaded to support the Eastern position. Others were also influenced by his prayer book, the *Olath Tamid* (עוֹלַת תָּמִיד, The Perpetual Offering), which he published in 1858. Einhorn's prayer book differed from Wise's *Minhag America* in two main respects. First, the prayers were rendered in German, not English. But, of far greater consequence, Einhorn's prayer book offered a thorough revision of the traditional liturgy, rather than simply a translation, so that it eventually became the basis for the movement's *Union Prayer Book.*

David Einhorn fought for his convictions on political issues as well. When the Civil War broke out in 1861, he spoke out boldly against both slavery and those who supported it. The people of Baltimore, who were very much pro-South in their sentiments, reacted violently; rumor soon had it that he would be lynched. He was finally persuaded to find safety in Philadelphia and, very late one night, he and his family, protected by a bodyguard of their friends, fled the city.

Later, the Baltimore congregation invited Einhorn to return, but the letter it sent infuriated him. "Meaning it for your own good," the officials had written, "it will be desirable . . . if in the future you will avoid any remarks, referring to the excitement of the day, from your pulpit." Einhorn immediately dispatched his resignation and, when a congregational committee called upon him to reconsider, he told them, "I left Europe only to have the right of free speech. I will never obey such orders!"

Einhorn then accepted a position with the Keneseth Israel Congregation of Philadelphia, moving on in 1866 to take a New York pulpit that, through a merger of synagogues, became the Beth-El Congregation. There he started publishing the *Jewish Times,* in which he repeatedly called for annual rabbinical conferences and, in opposition to Wise, urged the establishment of a seminary in New York. Three years later he helped prepare the first set of American Reform principles at the Philadelphia Conference.

He died in 1879, just a week before his seventieth birthday, but he had lived to see his daughters marry two of the most gifted of the younger Reform rabbis—Emil G. Hirsch, the brilliant spiritual leader of the Chicago Sinai Congregation, and Kaufmann Kohler, who was destined to become the fourth president of the Hebrew Union College.

The Founding of the Union and the College

Though Reform unity seemed dim in the year 1871, events two years later suddenly brightened the prospects for the achievement of some of Wise's goals. First came the offer of a $10,000 endowment for the proposed rabbinical college from Henry Adler of Lawrenceburg, Indiana, followed by a call issued by five Cincinnati synagogues to all congregations in

Israel Aaron
1859–1912

Henry Berkowitz
1857–1924

Joseph Krauskopf
1858–1923

David Philipson
1862–1949

EARLIEST GRADUATES. These four were members of the first graduating class of the Hebrew Union College, 1883. (HUC, American Jewish Archives)

the West and South to send delegates for the purpose of forming a congregational union.

The meeting was held in Cincinnati on July 8, 1873, and delegates from thirty-four congregations, representing twenty-eight cities and thirteen states, promptly voted to establish the "Union of American Hebrew Congregations" whose main objective would be to create and maintain a "Hebrew Theological College." Here again they showed their preference for such terms as "Hebrew" and "Israelite" to the word "Jew."

At its initial meeting in Cleveland the following year, the new union, which now consisted of fifty-five congregations, called for the opening of the "Hebrew Union College."

Responding to its mandate, Wise wrote in *The Israelite,* "This is a national affair of the greatest importance to the House of Israel on this continent."

Wise himself was elected to serve as president of the new school. Following the opening exercises which took place on October 3, 1875, the college began conducting classes for thirteen "noisy" students in the basement of Max Lilienthal's temple, with a faculty consisting of Wise, Lilienthal, and one paid instructor. Eight years later, the Hebrew Union College graduated its first class, composed of Israel Aaron, Henry Berkowitz, David Philipson and Joseph Krauskopf, all of whom eventually occupied important pulpits. By 1900, the year of Wise's death, its graduates numbered sixty-one.

The Creation of a Permanent Rabbinical Body

Within a decade, the effects of Reform organization were noticeable. Even some of the wounds between the East and West were beginning to heal. In his farewell sermon to the congregation in 1879, David Einhorn finally gave his personal blessing to the Union of American Hebrew Congregations. By then, too, another prominent Easterner, Bernhard Felsenthal, who served on the examination committee of the Hebrew Union College, had been invited to become one of its professors.

There were other promising signs as well. One was the formation in 1880 of a Rabbinical Literary Association that met annually to discuss questions of Jewish belief and practice. Another was the convening of a Reform rabbinical conference in Pittsburgh in 1885 that, as we shall see, adopted a new platform for the movement.

By now the movement was well aware of the need for a permanent rabbinical body. Therefore, at the 1889 convention of the

The Achievement of Reform Organization

Union of American Hebrew Congregations, and with Wise's hearty encouragement, the union's chairman took the occasion to invite the rabbis who were present to attend a special meeting for that purpose. They quickly adopted the following resolution:

> We, the rabbis here assembled, organize ourselves into a "Central Conference of American Rabbis" and appoint a committee of five to report a plan of organization.

The following day, they approved a report calling for the rabbinical body to hold meetings annually, publish a yearbook, and support colleagues in need. Then they unanimously elected Wise, now 71, as the organization's first president, a position that he held for the rest of his life. A year later ninety rabbis had already become members of the Central Conference.

The Death of Wise

During the ten remaining years of his life, Wise was universally hailed as the "architect of American Judaism." Still he persisted in his labors for Reform until he was stricken one Saturday afternoon late in March of 1900.

That morning he had preached a sermon on the power of prayer to his congregation in the Plum Street Temple, and at the conclusion of the service he greeted each person with a warm handclasp and a *Gut Shabbos* (A Good Sabbath). After lunch with his family, he went to the Hebrew Union College to teach "his boys." Shortly afterward he felt faint, but apparently recovered quickly. During the night, however, he suffered a stroke and went into a coma from which he never regained consciousness. He died at sundown on Monday, March 26, 1900, just three days prior to his eighty-first birthday.

In conveying the news to the members of the Central Conference of American Rabbis,

199

the acting president expressed his regard for Wise's achievements in these words:

> Dr. Wise was the pathfinder of American Israel and American Judaism. I do not ignore or belittle what other men have done for Judaism, but I verily believe that Dr. Wise was original, independent, and fearless in breaking the way through the intricate confusion caused by the conflict of a traditional religion with modern life.

And at the special service in his memory on the Saturday following his death, the memorial address took as its text this verse from II Samuel (3:38):

> "Do you not know that a prince and a great man has fallen this day in Israel?"

QUESTIONS FOR DISCUSSION

1. How do you account for the fact that though the early American Reform rabbis were trained in traditional seminaries they ultimately broke with Orthodoxy? To what extent does this also explain why some traditional Jews are currently joining Reform congregations?

2. Why were men like Samuel Adler and Samuel Hirsch so opposed to Wise's principles and program? How did their position differ from his? What would be Reform's reaction to their point of view today?

3. How do you explain Bernhard Felsenthal's change of mind about the return of Jews to Palestine? Why was his pro-Zionist position so unusual for a Reform rabbi of the nineteenth century? To what extent does the movement today share Felsenthal's position?

4. With which of the principles adopted by the Philadelphia Rabbinical Conference of 1869 do you agree? With which do you disagree? What would you substitute here?

5. Why is David Einhorn regarded as a "radical" Reformer? Where did his position differ from that of more moderate Reformers like Wise and Lilienthal? In what respect does your congregation reflect Einhorn's position?

6. What did Isaac M. Wise contribute to present-day Reform? To what extent has the movement adopted Wise's views on Reform?

SIGNIFICANT DOCUMENTS

From Bernhard Felsenthal's
A Voice Crying in the Wilderness, 1859

. . . The sources of universal religious truths are: Nature *about* us—the universe; Nature *within* us—the life of the spirit and the history of mankind. The sources of specifically Jewish principles are the history of Judaism and its confessors [believers] . . .

"The Bible is not the source of Judaism!"

"It is not? Well, that is heresy, indeed."

"Softly, my Orthodox friend. We say the Bible is not the *source* of Judaism, but we consider it a product of Judaism, and we concede, without reservation, its most splendid and holiest product. But Judaism is older than the Bible. Judaism originated at the moment when God breathed into the first man the breath of life. *For the kernel* of Judaism is natural religion in the soul of man . . ."

The only dogma which we consider binding upon all our members is: *Absolute freedom of faith and of conscience for all* . . .

Every Israelite has the right and the duty himself to search the sources of religious truth with the aid of his God-given intellect. For truth is not inculcated in us by others; the human spirit is not penetrated from without, rather from within; outward shines the light of divine truth . . .

—From Emma Felsenthal,
Bernhard Felsenthal, Teacher in Israel,
pp. 243, 250.

Isaac M. Wise's View of Reform Judaism, 1859

Reform is distinguished from innovation in that the former has purpose and limits, the latter has none. . . . Reform must move within the sphere of Judaism. . . . To extinguish a system signifies not to reform it. This latter term can only mean to expose and abolish errors, misconceptions, or malpractices but always remaining in the main within the given limits of the system. . . .

Successful attempts may be made to reconcile religion and philosophy, as Maimonides did with Judaism and Greek philosophy; but then as to the reformer of philosophy, philosophy is the basis, so Judaism must be the basis to the reformer of Judaism. Therefore reform has its limits, of which the reformer must be conscious.

The reforms in Judaism, during this century, have a double tendency, a reform of doctrines and theories and a change of forms. Criticism, this mighty lever of modern learning, seized also upon national literature. Under this heading comes much of modern knowledge which is in direct contradiction of old concepts of Judaism. This is the first part of Reform, which we style theoretical reform. This . . . proved many an established conception and accepted doctrine as unfounded and untrue, purporting always to guard religion against the incursions of superficial skeptics, and remaining always within the limits of scriptural Judaism. . . .

Practical reform involves a change of forms, new forms for new conceptions. Many customs and practices, intended to keep Jews and Gentiles separate, laws about eating, drinking, dressing, etc., have become obsolete. What shall we do now with these laws, when we are citizens of almost all civilized countries, and by our own free will come in contact with all classes of people? Evidently they exist no more for us.

Next comes the problem of music, of the sermon, of decorum, of forms and ceremonies. . . . Therefore reform stepped in between the extremes, endeavored to draw a distinct line of demarcation between essence and form, idea and symbol, the eternal and the transient parts of Judaism, to stop the violation of essential laws, and reorganize the scattered fragments of conflicting opinions. Wherever reform has not this object in view, it is [mere] innovation.

Reform, therefore, has its limits, strictly marked by the Bible itself, beyond which the Jewish reformer can not and dare not go. He may explain the Bible, by the aid of ancient and modern researches and obtain results directly contrary to established views, but he cannot go beyond it. Thus Reform has purpose and limits, and innovation has not.

—From James G. Heller,
*Isaac M. Wise,
His Life, Work and Thought,*
pp. 559–560.

An appeal for a Union of Congregations by Moritz Loth, First President of the UAHC, 1872

The building of temples and worshiping therein is not sufficient to spread the beneficial light of our religion. We must have rabbis who possess the ability to preach and expound eloquently the true text of our belief. Such rabbis we can only have by educating them, and to educate them we must have a Jewish Theological Faculty, an institution which is as necessary for the future glory of our religion as air and water are essential to sustain animal life.

And, in order to take the initiatory steps

to establish such a college, I respectfully recommend to you to appoint a committee of twelve members, and request our sister congregations of this city to appoint committees of the same number, who shall meet and take into consideration the calling of a general conference of all the congregations of the West, South, and Northwest, with a view to form a union of congregations, the object of which should be:

First, to establish a Jewish Theological Faculty. Second, to publish proper books for our Sabbath schools. Third, to adopt a code of laws which are not to be invaded under the plausible phrase of reform; namely, that *milah* [מִילָה, circumcision] shall never be abolished, that the Sabbath shall be observed on Saturday and never be changed to any other day, that the *shechitah* [שְׁחִיטָה, ritual slaughtering] and the dietary laws shall not be disregarded, but commended as preserving health and prolonging life, as it has been statistically proved in such cities as London, Prague, Pressburg, and Budapest.

And it shall be a fixed rule that any rabbi who, by his preaching or acts, advises the abolishment of the *milah,* or to observe our Sabbath on Sunday, etc., has forfeited his right to preach before a Jewish congregation, and any congregation employing such a rabbi shall, for the time being, be deprived of the honor to be a member of the Union of Congregations.

I hope that you will act favorably on my recommendations, and that it will receive the support of our sister congregations, which would lead to a Union of Congregations at large, and the adoption by that body of some safeguard against the so-called reform, which, if not checked, may become disastrous to our cause.

—From W. Gunther Plaut, *The Growth of Reform Judaism,* p. 29.

OTHER THINGS TO READ

Bamberger, Bernard J., *The Story of Judaism:* Chap. 45, "The Golden Land."

Felsenthal, Emma, *Bernhard Felsenthal, Teacher in Israel.*

Feuer, Leon I., and Azriel Eisenberg, *Jewish Literature since the Bible,* II: pp. 190–198 (selections from Wise and Kohler).

Gumbiner, Joseph H., *Isaac Mayer Wise, Pioneer of American Judaism.*

Heller, James G., *Isaac M. Wise, His Life, Work and Thought.*

Jewish Encyclopedia: "Samuel Adler," Vol. 1, p. 199; "Conferences of American Rabbis," Vol. 4, pp. 215–217; "David Einhorn," Vol. 5, pp. 78–79; "Bernhard Felsenthal," Vol. 5, pp. 361–362; "Hebrew Union College," Vol. 6, p. 311; "Emil G. Hirsch," Vol. 6, pp. 417–418; "Kaufmann Kohler," Vol. 7, p. 533; "Union of American Hebrew Congregations," Vol. 12, pp. 344–345; "Isaac M. Wise," Vol. 12, pp. 541–542.

Knox, Israel, "Isaac Mayer Wise," Chap. 4 in Simon Noveck (ed.), *Great Jewish Personalities in Modern Times.*

Kohler, Kaufmann, "David Einhorn, the Uncompromising Champion of Reform Judaism," *Central Conference of American Rabbis Yearbook,* Vol. 19 (1909), pp. 215–270.

Lefkovitz, Maurice, "Samuel Hirsch," *Central Conference of American Rabbis Yearbook,* Vol. 25 (1915), pp. 174–190.

Levinger, Lee J., *A History of the Jews in the United States:* Chap. 12, "The Second Wave of Immigration: From Germany"; Chap. 14, "The Basis of Judaism in America"; Chap. 15, "The Growth of Reform Judaism"; Chap. 16, "How Jewish Lodges and Charities Were Formed."

Masserman, Paul, and Max Baker, *The Jews Come to America:* pp. 172–201 (Reform in America).

May, Max B., *Isaac Mayer Wise.*

Philipson, David, *Centenary Papers and Others:* "Isaac Mayer Wise," pp. 11–62.

Philipson, David, *The Reform Movement in Judaism:* pp. 339–353 (early American Reform leaders); 353–357 (Philadelphia and Pittsburgh Conferences).

Plaut, W. Gunther, *The Growth of Reform Judaism:* Chap. 1, "American Beginnings"; Chap. 2, "Congregational Union in America"; pp. 29–31 (Philadelphia Rabbinical Conference); 50–55 (Hebrew Union College); 145–147 (Zionism).

Schwartzman, Sylvan D., *Reform Judaism in the Making:* Chap. 11, "The Creators of American Reform."

Silverman, Joseph, "Samuel Adler," *Central Conference of American Rabbis Yearbook,* Vol. 19 (1909), pp. 415–423.

Standard Jewish Encyclopedia: "Central Conference of American Rabbis," p. 420; "David Einhorn," pp. 603–604; "Bernhard Felsenthal," p. 672; "Hebrew Union College-Jewish Institute of Religion," pp. 876–877; "Emil G. Hirsch," p. 908; "Samuel Hirsch," p. 908; "Kaufmann Kohler," pp. 1143–1144; "Union of American Hebrew Congregations," p. 1855; "Isaac Mayer Wise," pp. 1916–1917.

Universal Jewish Encyclopedia: "Samuel Adler," Vol. 1, p. 97; "Central Conference of American Rabbis," Vol. 3, pp. 88–92; "David Einhorn," Vol. 4, pp. 27–28; "Bernhard Felsenthal," Vol. 4, pp. 273–274; "Hebrew Union College," Vol. 5, pp. 282–283; "Emil G. Hirsch," Vol. 5, pp. 373–374; "Samuel Hirsch," Vol. 5, p. 379; "Kaufmann Kohler," Vol. 6, pp. 428–430; "Union of American Hebrew Congregations," Vol. 10, pp. 344–345; "Isaac M. Wise," Vol. 10, pp. 539–542.

Wise, Isaac M., *Reminiscences.*

SUGGESTED ACTIVITIES

1. Prepare a map of the United States indicating the places where important Reform happenings took place in the nineteenth century.

2. Present a role-play of a meeting between Isaac M. Wise and his followers and David Einhorn and his.

3. Write a newspaper article under the headline of either: "Reform Movement Establishes Union of Congregations" or "Reform Rabbis Organize Central Conference."

SUBJECTS FOR RESEARCH

1. What roles did Samuel Adler, Samuel Hirsch, and David Einhorn play in the German rabbinical conferences they attended?

2. What position did nineteenth-century Reform generally take toward Zionism, and why? What arguments did Bernhard Felsenthal raise? What other Reform rabbis agreed?

3. Why were David Einhorn and Samuel Hirsch anxious to establish a Reform seminary in New York? What efforts did they make toward this? In the light of Wise's achievement, why were they unsuccessful?

4. What was the original curriculum for the training of rabbis at the Hebrew Union College? At what age did students begin, and how long was the course of study? How does all this compare with the education of a Reform rabbi today?

5. What activities, other than supporting the Hebrew Union College, did the Union of American Hebrew Congregations carry on prior to the start of the twentieth century? How do these compare with its activities today?

FILMSTRIPS TO SEE

Isaac Mayer Wise: Master Builder of American Judaism (UAHC), portraying the activities and achievements of this great American Reformer.

David Einhorn: Father of the Union Prayerbook (UAHC), picturing the life and contributions of this American Reform pioneer.

Within the Family of Liberal Judaism (UAHC), describing the nature and activities of the major American Reform organizations.

300 Years: Memorable Events in American Jewish History (UAHC), providing highlights of the important happenings in American Jewish life as background for the development of Reform.

A LIVE ISSUE

Various problems mentioned in this chapter continue to trouble the movement but none more than the so-called conflict between science and religion, which, as we shall see, also gave considerable concern to nineteenth-century Reform.

Not only did the early Reformers have to deal with the accuracy of certain stories in the Bible—particularly those in the early chapters of Genesis—but they also had to reconcile the teachings of Judaism with those of science for their generation.

The problem, however, has become much more serious today as a result of the enormous expansion of scientific knowledge and the greater reliance of people upon its findings. Indeed, this has even led some to question the validity of Judaism itself in a scientific world.

The Basic Problem: The issue really focuses on whether the teachings of science have now replaced those of religion or whether Judaism still offers modern man much that is true and very necessary for his survival.

Some Important Questions: (1) In what particular areas is scientific knowledge of greatest value? (2) What, for instance, are its limitations in arriving at a knowledge of God, the hereafter, and other important religious beliefs? (3) To what extent is religion still important in terms of human conduct, personal morality, and social ethics? (4) Does the fact that the Bible and other pieces of Jewish literature contain some material that is unscientific mean they are no longer valuable or that religion is ''untrue''? (5) Does one really have to choose today between science and religion?

What Do You Think? The Reformers of the nineteenth century wrestled with many of these questions and found what to them seemed a satisfactory solution. As you read about it, what is your own reaction? Do their answers satisfy you? How do *you* resolve the issue between science and religion? How does this affect your understanding of the Bible and other sources of Judaism? What is its effect upon Judaism itself?

14. AMERICAN REFORM ESTABLISHES ITS PRINCIPLES

Kaufmann Kohler Responds to an Attack

The year was 1885. Kaufmann Kohler, rabbi of Temple Beth-El of New York, had just received a letter from the president of his congregation in which he asked permission to publish the rabbi's series of five sermons on "the aims and objects of Reform Judaism."

For six years Kohler had been the rabbi of Temple Beth-El, having succeeded his father-in-law, David Einhorn. He had come over from Germany in 1869 at the age of twenty-six to serve the Beth-El Congregation of Detroit, and from there went on to the Chicago Sinai Congregation. Ten years later he accepted the pulpit of the New York congregation.

Kohler was highly pleased with the president's request:

> I am encouraged that our congregation today realizes more than ever before the necessity of decided Reform measures for the sake of stemming the tide of appalling skepticism and of rousing anew the interest and active zeal of our young people for the sacred cause of Judaism.

Then he added:

> I need not say that, in taking up the gauntlet cast at Reform, I meant no offense to the representatives of Orthodoxy. I simply claim for our advanced views, for our no less sincere religious convictions, the same respect we are willing to accord to theirs.
>
> We cannot allow our cause to be represented as a matter of mere convenience and frivolity. Indeed, I felt that if I had kept silent at the unexpected and entirely uncalled for denunciation of Reform Judaism by "one who had just come to sojourn with us and will needs be a judge" I would not have been true to my trust as rabbi of Temple Beth-El, and still less so to the traditions of the pulpit once occupied by the matchless Reform champion, Dr. Einhorn, whose outspoken and unfaltering fealty to the Reform principles commanded for him the respect and admiration of friend and foe.

Published under the title *Backwards or Forwards,* Kohler's sermons further clarify why he was moved to deliver them:

> A rabbi of renown appearing in New York has boldly challenged Reform Judaism by the open declaration that he who disowns the statutes and ordinances of traditional Judaism on principle has forfeited the name of Jew!

The Challenge of Conservative Judaism

The rabbi to whom Kohler referred was Alexander Kohut, one of Europe's leading rabbinical scholars who had also been a member of the Hungarian parliament. Kohut had just come to New York to occupy the pulpit of Temple Ahavath Chesed (אַהֲבַת חֶסֶד, the love of mercy), a moderate Reform congregation, and his presence in America raised the hopes of the Conservatives who had as yet been unable to stem the Reform tide under men like Wise, Einhorn, and others.

It was not long before Kohut launched his attack on Reform. In a series of lectures on *The Ethics of the Fathers* that also appeared in print he roundly condemned the changes the Reformers had introduced:

TEMPLE BETH-EL. This congregation of New York City was where Kaufmann Kohler served as rabbi. (HUC, American Jewish Archives)

> A Reform which seeks to progress without the Mosaic-rabbinical tradition is a deformity. He who turns away in principle from the standpoint of the validity of Mosaic-rabbinical tradition, such a one has banished himself from the camp of Israel.

Though Kohut admitted that some changes were needed, he nonetheless insisted that all of the teachings stemming from Moses and the rabbis of the Talmud, which he termed "the Mosaic-rabbinical tradition," were God-given and therefore virtually unchangeable. At best, recognized rabbinical authorities might make certain "tactful" modifications, but nothing more. Here he was in complete agreement with the "positive-historical" stand of Zacharias Frankel and Conservative Judaism.

Accepting the challenge, Kohler immediately responded. The real issue, he said, is:

> Must we, or can we, observe the ordinances and statutes bequeathed to us by Mosaic-rabbinical Judaism? Must we, in order to be real Jews, keep all the rites and ceremonies prescribed by law and tradition? [Rather,] should we not replace them by forms more adequate to the age, more expressive of . . . the awe of holiness?

Kohut refused to be silenced. He promptly joined forces with Sabato Morais, who had succeeded Isaac Leeser as *chazan* of the Mikveh Israel Congregation in Philadelphia. Morais, who was staunchly traditional in his views, had successfully resisted every attempt by his members to introduce changes in the worship. Moreover, with the founding of the Hebrew Union College, he became all the more determined to establish a seminary of his own that would train American rabbis along traditional lines.

The situation was further aggravated in 1883 by the so-called *terefah* banquet (טְרֵיפָה, literally "torn," referring to an animal unfit to be eaten, but more widely used as a term for "non-Kosher food") that had taken place in Cincinnati during the annual meeting of the Union of American Hebrew Congregations. There some two hundred persons had been served a menu that included shrimp and other forms of shell-fish, together with meat and a dairy dessert.

The Jewish press promptly attacked Wise, the union, the college, and Reform Judaism as a whole. Wise himself admitted that it was all a caterer's mistake, but this did not satisfy his opponents. One in particular, Marcus Jastrow, the scholarly rabbi of Rodeph Shalom (רוֹדֵף שָׁלוֹם, one who pursues peace) Congregation of Philadelphia, even succeeded in having his members withdraw from the union.

The controversy also roused new interest in Morais' plan for a traditional rabbinical college, and early in 1886 he was able to establish the Jewish Theological Seminary in New York, with himself as its first president. Under his successor, Solomon Schechter, a distinguished British Jewish scholar who became widely known for his discovery of many ancient Hebrew manuscripts in a storeroom atop a Cairo synagogue, the seminary became formally identified with Conservative Judaism.

The Reformers responded in turn with calls for a rabbinical conference that would establish once and for all their position in the face of the mounting opposition from the more traditionally minded. Finally, on November 2, 1885, Rabbi Kaufmann Kohler addressed the following letter to his colleagues:

> Having consulted with several friends and colleagues, among whom I will mention as seniors, Rabbis Samuel Hirsch of Philadelphia and Isaac M. Wise of Cincinnati, and received encouraging responses, I herewith take the liberty of inviting all such American rabbis as advocate reform and progress and are in favor of united action in all matters pertaining to the wel-

fare of American Judaism, to meet in conference on November 16 and 17 at the Temple Rodef Shalom (Rabbi Lippman Mayer) of Pittsburgh, for the purpose of discussing the present state of American Judaism, its pending issues, and its requirements, and of uniting upon such plans and practical measures as are demanded by the hour.

Sincerely trusting that this call, simply suggested by me, will be favorably received and, even at some sacrifice, heartily responded to by all friends and supporters of the cause of Reform and Union in American Judaism, I am

Fraternally yours . . .

As Kohler himself subsequently explained to those who attended by ''practical measures as demanded by the hour'' he meant:

. . . To unite on a platform which . . . positively asserts the Jewish doctrine, a platform broad, comprehensive, enlightened, and liberal enough to impress and win all hearts, and also firm and positive enough to dispel suspicion and reproach of . . . discontinuing the historical thread of the past . . .

Another Reason for Reform Concern

But other matters also troubled the Reformers. One, certainly, was the great mass of Jewish immigrants who were fleeing from Eastern Europe because of new oppression by the Russian government.

In March of 1881, the more liberal Czar, Alexander II, had been assassinated by a Russian radical, and the government turned violently reactionary, making use of anti-Semitism to divert the attention of the masses from their real grievances. Attacks upon Jews, called *pogroms,* soon erupted throughout the Pale of Jewish Settlement while officials turned their backs lest, as one put it, ''he endanger the lives of his soldiers for the sake of the Jews.''

Also enacted were new and more severe regulations, called the ''May Laws'' because they were adopted in May of 1882, that were designed to complete the isolation of the Jews by restricting their right of movement, occupation, and ownership of property. Gradually, too, even the privilege of attending Russian high schools and universities was sharply curtailed through a quota system.

Realizing their peril, thousands began to flee, with most of them coming to the United States. Between the years 1881 and 1885 more than 38,000 entered the country, increasing the Jewish population by some 15 percent. By then, however, it was clear that this was just the beginning. The prospect was that hundreds of thousands more would soon be on the way.

Because of the conditions under which they had lived, most of the newcomers were largely unskilled and unfamiliar with the culture and social practices of the West. Similarly, the religious among them appeared to be fanatically Orthodox. Hence the Reformers tended to look upon them as a ''backward element,'' not only culturally and socially but religiously as well. ''Relics of the past,'' one of the rabbis described them, ''whose extravagances cannot flourish in the genial soil of America.''

Unquestionably, those who met in Pittsburgh were sensitive to the new situation posed by East European Orthodoxy, and they were determined to counter its effect at all costs.

The Renewed Challenge of Science

Two other forces at work in the American Jewish community of 1885 also gave Kohler and the others great concern. One was the renewed challenge of science, especially following the publication of Charles Darwin's *The Origin of Species* in 1859.

In the centuries after Isaac Newton's discovery of the laws of gravity and motion, science had greatly expanded its study of natural phenomena. The atomic theory was now well-established and, thanks to the work of Faraday, Ampère, Ohm, and others, the whole field of electricity was opened up. By now, too, most people were convinced that the earth and the entire solar system operated strictly according to natural law.

This, said Darwin, was no less true in the case of living things. The evidence he had accumulated during thirty years of research, including a five-year voyage as naturalist aboard the H.M.S. *Beagle,* confirmed the fact that existing plants and animals had evolved from lower forms through their struggle to survive. With the publication of his *The Descent of Man* in 1871, he extended his theory to include the human race as well. His theory soon came to be considered by some as a direct challenge to the biblical account of creation.

Meanwhile, the scientific approach to the Bible, generally referred to as ''Biblical Criticism,'' raised other questions. Baruch Spinoza, the great seventeenth-century philosopher, and Jean Astruc, a French Catholic physician who lived a century later, had shown that Moses alone could not have composed the first five books. Later studies not only confirmed this but proved that the Bible was produced over as much as fifteen hundred years and incorporated many changes in religious thought and practice. Thus, the Scriptures seemed far more the product of inspired human beings than the work of God.

Leading atheists seized upon all this to attack religion as false. Those who suffered most were the Christian fundamentalists who regarded the Bible as written by God himself and hence literally true in every detail. But even liberal faiths, such as Reform Judaism

which accepted the results of Biblical Criticism, found themselves in some difficulty.

Little wonder, then, that in his opening remarks at the Pittsburgh Conference, Kaufmann Kohler called upon his colleagues to make their position on the subject of science perfectly clear:

> . . . **We ought to unite on a platform . . . that recognizes every honest opinion and does not denounce modern research, whether in the field of science or in the field of comparative religion, ethnology, and Biblical Criticism, but at the same time positively asserts the Jewish doctrine.**

The Appeal of Ethical Culture

The other troublesome matter to those at Pittsburgh was the attraction of a number of Jews to Ethical Culture, a ''universal'' and ''nonsectarian'' movement founded by Felix Adler.

FELIX ADLER. Son of a Reform rabbi, he founded in 1876 the Society for Ethical Culture, a universal and nonsectarian movement which attracted some Reform members. (HUC, American Jewish Archives)

Reform Judaism—Then and Now

A son of the rabbi of Temple Emanu-El of New York, Adler had originally trained to become a rabbi, but doubts about the existence of God caused him to reject the rabbinate. He became a university professor instead. Then, in 1876, he organized the Society for Ethical Culture whose primary aim was ''to advance the science and art of right-living,'' but without religious or sectarian belief. Branch societies were ultimately established in other leading American cities, and in England and Germany. The members undertook a variety of social-service projects, such as providing free kindergartens and nursing care for the poor, and also created special Ethical Culture schools for the education of their own children.

Most of the new movement's members were Jews, which was particularly disturbing to those at Pittsburgh. The followers of Ethical Culture, they said, were failing to realize that their very ideals were rooted in Judaism and based upon the demands of a righteous God. So, indeed, declared Kaufmann Kohler in his address ''Source and Character of Jewish Ethics'' when he stated:

> The ultimate source of ethics . . . is God . . .
>
> **It is a grievous mistake to believe that the human mind, however powerful, can invent or create a God for others to follow and to trust in. Professor [Felix] Adler, speaking not long ago with profound admiration of the Jewish God of Righteousness and Holiness, felt called upon at the same time to state that he could not accept the God of the Hebrews as his, simply because he could not accept the idea of revelation. While believing in a moral government of the cosmos, he shrinks from believing in a God who lives and speaks and acts for man. Certain it is that without a divine revelation there could be no prophecy. It is the God seen who makes**

> **the seer; it is the God felt who makes the prophet. . . .**
>
> **Judaism in fact is the only religion that makes the moral uplifting of man, individually, socially, and historically, its aim and object . . . Modern ethics tends toward a return to the first principles of Jewish ethics, the construction of a society upon the foundations of justice, truth, and peace, a striving for character and manhood.**

Reform Adopts a Platform

In addition to Kohler, the nineteen Reform rabbis who gathered in Pittsburgh included Isaac M. Wise and Emil G. Hirsch, who was especially noted for his involvement in social issues.

Also among the group were Joseph Krauskopf, then of Kansas City, and David Philipson of Baltimore, both in their twenties and both members of the first graduating class of the Hebrew Union College. Krauskopf eventually served a Philadelphia congregation for over thirty-five years, during which he carried on Sunday worship with the use of his own prayer book, *The Service Manual.* Philipson, a disciple and close friend of Wise, later became the rabbi of B'nai Israel Congregation of Cincinnati where he remained for forty-three years. His many articles and books dealing with Reform's development earned him the title of ''historian of the movement.''

Wise, who was chosen to preside at Pittsburgh, immediately called upon Kaufmann Kohler to present his declaration of Reform principles based largely upon the statements of previous rabbinical conferences. It was quickly approved and turned over to a committee for final revision.

Meanwhile, the rabbis proceeded to debate the issue of Sunday services. The result was a compromise in which they urged the ob-

Leading Nineteenth-Century Reformers

Key Reform Events	European Reformers	American Reformers
	David Friedlander (1750–1834), radical religious Reformer who pioneered in developing Jewish Free Schools.	
	Lazarus Bendavid (1762–1832), philosopher and mathematician, who stressed Jewish moral values over practices.	
	Aaron Chorin (1766–1844), pioneer Reform rabbi in Hungary.	
	Israel Jacobson (1768–1828), earliest of the German Reformers who introduced Confirmation and many reforms in worship.	
1778—Establishment of the Jewish Free School in Berlin.		
1783—Completion of Mendelssohn's Torah translation.		
		Isaac Harby (1788–1828), noted American writer who organized an early Reform society in Charleston.
	Edward Kley (1789–1867), preacher at the Berlin Reform services and organizer of the Hamburg Temple.	
	Leopold Zunz (1794–1886), scholar and pioneer of the science of Judaism who defended Reform practice.	
		Leo Merzbacher (1800?–1856), early New York liberal rabbi.

Reform Judaism—Then and Now

Key Reform Events	European Reformers	American Reformers
1801—Founding of the Seesen school by Jacobson.		*Gustav Poznanski* (1805?–1879), Reform *chazan* of Charleston who converted the congregation to Reform.
	Samuel Holdheim (1806–1860), radical Reformer who advocated many extremes in Jewish practice.	
	Gabriel Riesser (1806–1863), noted Reform layman who fought for democratic rights.	
	Abraham Kohn (1807–1848), Reformer in Eastern Europe who was martyred.	
		David Einhorn (1809–1879), radical Reform leader of the Eastern faction.
		Samuel Adler (1809–1891), New York Reform rabbi and the movement's leading scholar; supporter of Einhorn.
1810—Dedication of the Seesen temple with organ. First Confirmation.	*Abraham Geiger* (1810–1874), leading philosopher and guiding spirit of European Reform.	
	Ludwig Philippson (1811–1889), Reform editor who convened the Brunswick Rabbinical Conference.	
1815—Start of Berlin Reform services.		*Max Lilienthal* (1815–1882), probably the earliest ordained rabbi in America; a close friend of Wise and rabbi in Cincinnati.
		Samuel Hirsch (1815–1889), brilliant Reformer at whose home the Philadelphia Rabbinical Conference was held.

Key Reform Events	European Reformers	American Reformers
1818—Dedication of the Hamburg Temple.		
		Isaac M. Wise (1819–1900), chief organizer of the Reform movement and Cincinnati rabbi.
1824—Organization of the Charleston Reform Society.	*Moritz Lazarus* (1824–1903), Reform philosopher who presided over the Leipzig and Augsburg synods.	*Bernhard Felsenthal* (1822–1908), Chicago Reformer and early Zionist leader.
1832—Publication of Zunz's *The Jewish Sermon.*		
1841—Hamburg Temple controversy. Building of the Charleston temple with an organ.		
		Kaufmann Kohler (1843–1926), convener of the Pittsburgh Conference; later, president of Hebrew Union College.
1844–1846—German Rabbinical Conferences. Arrival of Lilienthal (1844) and Wise (1846) in America.		
		Emil G. Hirsch (1852–1923), Chicago Reform rabbi and strong advocate of social justice.
1855—Cleveland Conference. Opening of Zion College.		*Joseph Krauskopf* (1858–1923), member of the first class of Hebrew Union College; Reform rabbi in Philadelphia.
1873—Founding of the Union of American Hebrew Congregations.		
1875—Founding of Hebrew Union College.		
1885—Pittsburgh Conference.		

servance of the Jewish Sabbath as an important "bond with our great past and a symbol of Jewish unity all over the world" but also approved of holding services on Sunday for the benefit of those having to work on Saturday.

By then the committee on Reform principles had completed its work. What the delegates heard and unanimously approved was soon universally called the Pittsburgh Platform.

The Pittsburgh Platform's Eight Planks

The Platform opened with this preface:

> In view of the wide divergence of opinion and of conflicting ideas in Judaism today, we, as representatives of Reform Judaism in America, in continuation of the work begun at Philadelphia in 1869, unite upon the following principles:

The First Plank
Judaism and God

> We recognize in every religion an attempt to grasp the Infinite One and, in every mode, source, or book of revelation held sacred in any religious system, the consciousness of the indwelling of God in man.
>
> We hold that Judaism presents the highest conception of the God-idea as taught by our Holy Scriptures and developed and spiritualized by the Jewish teachers in accordance with the moral and philosophical progress of their respective ages. We maintain that Judaism preserved and defended, amid continued struggles and trials and under enforced isolation, this God-idea as the central religious truth for the [entire] human race.

Here the Reform leaders were responding to several issues. One, of course, was the old question of Reform's right to modify Jewish practices and beliefs, something that the more traditional Jews still disputed. Another had to do with the uniqueness of Judaism at a time when greater familiarity with other faiths was leading some people to claim that all religions were really the same. "Why not, then, have one great universal religion of mankind?" these people argued.

As if in reply, the rabbis at Pittsburgh emphasized the superiority of their religion. Other faiths, to be sure, contained a measure of truth. But none, not even the so-called universal ones, possessed a God-concept as lofty and fully-developed as that of Judaism.

Here, too, was their response to Ethical Culture. Belief in God, they insisted, is indispensable, and any system of morals and ethics that does not flow from it is inadequate.

The Second Plank
The Bible and Science

> We recognize in the Bible the record of the consecration of the Jewish people to its mission as the priest [people] of the One God and value it as the most potent instrument of religious and moral instruction.
>
> We hold that the modern discoveries of scientific researches in the domains of nature and history are not antagonistic to the doctrines of Judaism, the Bible reflecting the primitive ideas of its own age, and at times clothing its conception of Divine Providence and justice, dealing with man, in miraculous narratives.

Here the rabbis were reacting not only to the challenge of science but to agnostics like Robert Ingersoll, a widely-known lecturer who scoffed at the Bible. With their own liberal views of the Bible's development, the Reformers freely admitted that it was the product of a pre-scientific age. Hence, where it contradicted the discoveries of science, it simply reflected the limited knowledge of those who wrote it and who often had to fall back upon "myth" to convey deeper religious insights.

Nevertheless, they insisted, the Bible offers important truths about man and his struggle against evil, and it has much to teach about the history of the Jews and the development of their faith. By no means, they said, has it lost its capacity for "religious and moral instruction," even in a scientific age.

The Third Plank
Jewish Ceremonies and Laws

We recognize in the Mosaic legislation a system of training the Jewish people for its mission during its national life in Palestine.

Today we accept as binding only the moral laws and maintain only such ceremonies as elevate and sanctify our lives but reject all such as are not adapted to the views and habits of modern civilization.

In line with their conviction that Judaism was the product of historical development, those at Pittsburgh reaffirmed the position taken by the French Assembly of Notables and Great Sanhedrin that certain areas of law that had once regulated Jewish life in Palestine had to be abandoned.

But here they were also replying to Kohut's insistence that every Jewish ceremonial law was sacred and unchangeable. Only valid, they argued, were those observances that were in harmony with modern life and served to emphasize the Jews' moral and ethical responsibilities. On this basis, they felt justified in doing away with such traditional rites as putting on *tefilin*, the two small leather boxes containing appropriate biblical passages

which are worn by traditional Jews on the head and arm during weekday morning prayers, and observing *tashlich*, or casting away one's sins into a body of water.

The Fourth Plank
Jewish Diet and Dress

We hold that all such Mosaic and rabbinical laws as regulate diet, priestly purity, and dress originated in ages and under the influence of ideas altogether foreign to our present mental and spiritual state. They fail to impress the modern Jew with a spirit of priestly holiness. Their observance in our days is apt rather to obstruct than to further modern spiritual elevation.

Among the practices those at Pittsburgh had in mind were the laws of *kashrut* (כַּשְׁרוּת, what is ritually fit, or the Jewish dietary regulations) that determine the foods Jews are permitted to eat, how animals are to be slaughtered, and the manner in which meat is to be prepared, taking special care to separate it from any contact with milk products. Reacting to such laws, Emil G. Hirsch once remarked, "Diet is not a religious affair."

Nor, as they saw it, was religion a matter of dress or ritual purity requiring Jewish women, for example, to bathe in a *mikveh*, the special kind of ritual bath, or to wear a *sheitel*, wig, to cover their hair. Similarly, they chose to ignore all distinctions between Jews based on "priestly" or "levitical" descent that entitled them to special privileges in the traditional synagogue, such as being called upon first to read from the Torah.

The Fifth Plank
The Messianic Age

We recognize in the modern era of universal culture of heart and intellect the ap-

MIKVEH. A Jewish ritual bath as shown in this engraving from Amsterdam, 1783. (Collection of Rabbi William A. Rosenthall)

proaching of the realization of Israel's great messianic hope for the establishment of the kingdom of truth, justice, and peace among all men.

We consider ourselves no longer a nation but a religious community and therefore expect neither a return to Palestine nor a sacrificial worship under the administration of the sons of Aaron nor the restoration of any of the laws concerning the Jewish state.

In presenting their views of the Messianic Age, those at Pittsburgh were simply reaffirming earlier Reform pronouncements. What was different here, however, was their confidence that the growing spirit of tolerance and understanding they experienced in America marked its rapid approach. In fact, as they expressed it in the following plank of their platform, they even saw those of other faiths helping to bring the Messianic Age into being.

**The Sixth Plank
A Developing Judaism and Its Mission**

We recognize in Judaism a progressive religion, ever striving to be in accord with the postulates of reason. We are convinced of the utmost necessity of preserving the historical identity with our great past.

Christianity and Islam, being daughter religions of Judaism, we appreciate their providential mission to aid in the spreading of monotheistic and moral truth. We acknowledge that the spirit of broad humanity of our age is our ally in the fulfillment of our mission, and therefore we extend the hand of fellowship to all who cooperate with us in the establishment of the reign of truth and righteousness among men.

While asserting the need for Jewish self-preservation, the Reformers recognized that since both Christianity and Islam had drawn heavily upon the teachings of Judaism their followers inevitably contributed to the achievement of its mission. Also, confident that the other religions could overcome their former prejudices and work for the good of all people, those at Pittsburgh were moved to forgive and forget centuries of Jewish mistreatment at their hands.

The Seventh Plank
Immortality of the Soul

We reassert the doctrine of Judaism that the soul of man is immortal, grounding this belief on the divine nature of the human spirit which forever finds bliss in righteousness and misery in wickedness.

We reject as ideas not rooted in Judaism the beliefs both in bodily resurrection and in Gehenna [Hell] and Eden [Paradise] as abodes for everlasting punishment and reward.

Here the Reformers rejected certain notions about the afterlife that probably found their way into Judaism during the Persian period. For according to the religion of Persia, each person who has died crosses a bridge that spans hell. If he has been wicked, the bridge becomes so narrow that he tumbles off, but, if righteous, a wide road leads him to the glorious "region of light." Eventually, in a final judgment, all persons receive their everlasting punishment or reward.

Despite objections by various rabbis of the Talmud, traditional Judaism insisted on adopting similar beliefs. It held, for instance, that depending upon one's previous conduct the dead either endure the tortures of a fiery *Gehinnom* or enjoy the blessings of a heavenly Garden of Eden, named after the original paradise of Adam and Eve.

Rejecting such beliefs, the Reformers saw the soul as coming from God, its source, and returning to Him after death in joy or sorrow, depending upon the kind of life the individual lived. The dead, they said, also find immortality in the lasting effects of their deeds upon those who live on after them—their family, friends, associates, the Jewish people, and mankind generally.

The Eighth Plank
Social Justice

In full accordance with the spirit of Mosaic legislation which strives to regulate the relation between the rich and poor, we deem it our duty to participate in the great task of modern times to solve on the basis of justice and righteousness the problems presented by the contrasts and evils of the present organization of society.

In keeping with the teachings of the prophets, the rabbis called upon their people to help overcome the suffering endured by most Americans in the 1880's.

In part, this was the result of the increasing immigration that saw more than half a million persons enter the United States annually between 1881 and 1884. Most arrived without funds and in immediate need of clothing, shelter, and employment. Others who came under special "work-contracts" that called for the cost of transportation to be taken out of their wages found themselves badly exploited.

But conditions were no better for the rest of the people. In many of the larger cities, such as New York and Chicago, living conditions were often frightful. Tenements without adequate heat or sanitary facilities teemed with large families living in single rooms, and many children were unable to attend school for lack of food and clothing. In such surroundings, disease, malnutrition, and infant mortality took an appalling toll. In fact, a quarter of all children born in New York died before their first birthday.

Working conditions were scandalous. Most people, including women and children, worked as much as twelve hours a day in overcrowded sweatshops. Families that carried on piecework in their rooms earned less than a dollar for a fifteen-hour day. Many were also out of work due to the introduction of machines and a series of "panics," severe depressions, that sent many firms into bankruptcy. Meanwhile, companies were resisting the growth of labor unions with lockouts and strike-breakers that frequently led to violence and bloodshed.

Small wonder, then, that those at Pittsburgh saw the participation of Jews in the solution of social ills as an essential part of Judaism.

Reaction to Pittsburgh

To no one's surprise, the Conservatives and Orthodox roundly condemned the Pittsburgh Platform and those responsible for it. The *American Hebrew,* a Conservative weekly published in New York, proposed that any Conservative congregation that belonged to the Union of American Hebrew Congregations should immediately withdraw since it was now identified with the "radical creed" of Pittsburgh. It also urged traditionalists to form a union of their own in opposition to the "radical closed corporation . . . dominated by one man or a clique of men."

The demand for a Conservative seminary became more insistent. "There can be no doubt of the need," said the *American Hebrew,* "due to the baleful influences which have perverted the Cincinnati institution [Hebrew Union College]," and the following year the Conservatives established their own Jewish Theological Seminary.

Though some Reform Jews reacted unhappily to the new platform, the great majority in both Europe and America hailed it. Even moderates like Isaac M. Wise described it as "opening a new chapter in the history of American Judaism," and the Conference of Rabbis of Southern Congregations, meeting in New Orleans, unanimously endorsed it as being "in harmony with the spirit of progressive Judaism and in keeping with the oldest conceptions of our faith."

The enthusiasm was understandable. The Pittsburgh Platform was a bold, optimistic pronouncement that spoke directly to the issues of the times. Moreover, as the work of men who represented both the East and West, it promised renewed harmony in Reform ranks.

So well, indeed, had those at Pittsburgh done their work that the platform they produced guided the movement for over half a century.

QUESTIONS FOR DISCUSSION

1. What is the position of Conservative Judaism regarding religious change? How does it differ from that of Reform as expressed by Kaufmann Kohler? Why are these differences important?

2. In what ways did large-scale East European Jewish immigration challenge the Reform Jews? What effects has that immigration had upon the membership of your congregation? Upon its practices and beliefs?

3. How has Reform Judaism attempted to reconcile the teachings of Judaism and science? To what extent does the Second Plank of the Pittsburgh Platform meet the problem? What

other possible areas of conflict between science and religion still need to be resolved?

4. How do you explain the attraction of some Jews to Ethical Culture? What objections did the Reform leaders of the 1880's raise against it? Why did they regard Judaism as superior?

5. In what ways was the Pittsburgh Platform an improvement over the principles adopted in Philadelphia in 1869? With what additional problems did it deal, and what answers did it offer?

6. What principles of the Pittsburgh Platform does your congregation currently follow? Which has it rejected?

SIGNIFICANT DOCUMENTS

The Russian May Laws, 1882

1. As a temporary measure and until a general revision is made of the legal status of the Jews, they are forbidden to settle anew outside of towns and townlets (boroughs), an exception being made only in the case of existing Jewish agricultural colonies.

2. Until further orders, the execution of deeds of sale and mortgages in the names of Jews is forbidden, as well as the registration of Jews as lessees of real estate situated outside of town and townlets, and also the issuing to Jews of powers of stewardship or attorney to manage and dispose of such real property.

3. Jews are forbidden to transact business on Sundays and on the principal Christian festivals, the existing regulations concerning the closing on such festival days of places of business belonging to Christians to apply in future to Jews as well.

—From Lucien Wolf,
*The Legal Sufferings of the
Jews in Russia,*
p. 84.

From Alexander Kohut's Sermon Series, "The Ethics of the Fathers," 1885

The chain of tradition continued unbroken from Moses through Joshua, the elders, the prophets and the men of the great synagogue, down to the latest times. On this tradition rests our faith, which Moses first received from God on Sinai. On this foundation rests Mosaic-rabbinical Judaism today; and on this foundation we take our stand . . .

But you may ask: Shall the fence around the garden, shall reverence be extended around everything that the past hedged in . . . ? "Remember the days of old," said Moses, *and have regard to the changes of each generation* (Deut. 32:7). The teaching of the ancients we must make our starting point, but we must not lose sight of what is needed in every generation . . .

Let us now revert to the question raised at the outset: Is Judaism definitely closed for all time, or is it capable of and in need of continuous development? I answer both Yes and No. I answer Yes, *because religion has been given to man,* as it is the duty of man to grow in perfection as long as he lives, he must modify the forms which yield him religious satisfaction in accordance with the spirit of the times. I answer No, insofar as it concerns the Word of God which cannot be imperfect. . . . You Israelite, imperfect as you are, strive to perfect yourself in the image of your perfect God. Hold in honor His unchangeable Law and let it be your earnest task to put new life into the outward form of our religion . . .

Our religious guide is the Torah, the Law of Moses, interpreted and applied in the light of tradition. But, inasmuch as individual opinion cannot be valid for the whole community, it behooves individuals and communities to appoint only recognized authorities as teachers; such men, that is to say, as acknowledge belief in authority and who, at the same time, with comprehension and tact, are willing to consider what may be permitted in view of the exigencies of the times and what may be discarded, without changing the nature and character of the foundations of the faith . . .

A reform which seeks to progress without the Mosaic-rabbinical tradition is a deformity—a skeleton without flesh and sinew, without spirit and heart. It is suicide; and suicide is not reform. We desire a Judaism full of life. We desire to worship the living God in forms full of life and beauty; Jewish, yet breathing the modern spirit. Only a Judaism true to itself and its past, yet receptive of the ideas of the present, accepting the good and the beautiful from whatever source it may come, can command respect and recognition . . .

I do not know whether it will be my good fortune to have your sympathy in my religious attitude—that of Mosaic-rabbinical Judaism, freshened with the spirit of progress, a Judaism of the healthy golden mean. I hope I shall . . .

—From Moshe Davis,
*The Emergence of
Conservative Judaism,*
pp. 222–224.

From Kaufmann Kohler's
First Sermon in the Series,
''Backwards or Forwards?'' 1885

. . . There is a novelty offered to our New York Jews in the appearance of a new rabbi of renown who, with laudable courage and independence, gives free utterance to his rigid conservatism, boldly challenging Reform Judaism by the open declaration that he who disowns the statutes and ordinances of Mosaic-rabbinical Judaism on principle has forfeited the name of Jew.

Of course, the novelty of the learned speaker's notions and attitude creates a stir and a welcome sensation throughout the Jewish circles of New York, and an opinion about the influence to be exercised by the new rabbi for whom I cherish the highest regard, both as an eminent scholar and as a most sincere and earnest advocate of Conservative Judaism, would be rather premature. Personally, I gladly and heartily wish him the greatest success, and I have little doubt that, being supported and encouraged by our *exclusively* conservative local press, he will exercise a wholesome influence upon the consolidation and the right coalition of the different elements of our congregations, which are at present too often brought together without unity of purpose and principle.

But the gauntlet thrown into our face must be taken up at once, and I today simply propose to ask the question; Are we progressing, or ought we to retrograde? . . .

Must we, after having dropped the obsolete observances of by-gone days, after having worked for thirty-five years in this country for emancipation from the yoke of Mosaic-talmudical Judaism, again bend our neck to wear it in order to be complete Jews in the sense of Orthodoxy, or may we persist in claiming, as we did thus far, to stand on a far higher ground, whilst discarding a great many of the ceremonial laws of the Bible and tradition, and placing ourselves on the standpoint of prophetical Judaism, with the messianic aim as its world-embracing goal?

Mosaic-rabbinical Judaism is retrospective. It has not the courage to stand on its feet. It subsists on the merits of our forefathers . . . Its very ritual, its whole mode of worship, it considers only as a feeble substitute for the temple sacrifice. It longs for the restoration of temple and state in Judea, hoping for the restitution of the entire Mosaic system of social, political, and religious life.

Reform Judaism, on the contrary, looks

forward with hope for a far brighter future, beholding in the Messiah the ideal of mankind to be realized by the Jewish people through all the factors and agencies of civilization and progress and in the temple on Zion's hills, the house of prayer to be opened on all spots of the globe for all nations to worship the Most High as the Father of all men. Its golden era lies not behind but before us.

Which of the two views then is more in congruity with the drift and spirit of our age and of all ages of human history? Which are we to espouse? The one that turns the dials of the time backward, or the one that proudly points to the forward move of history? The one that wails over the ruins of the past, over the decay of ritualistic religion, over the downfall of creeds and blind authority-worship, or the one that hails the rising faith in all that is divine in man, the building up of a religion which already our prophets of yore proclaimed to be as broad as man and as wide as the globe?

The question is, in fact, a threefold one: Can we, or must we, believe exactly what our fathers believed concerning revelation and the Law, resurrection and the messianic future? Must we, or can we, believe that the tablets of the covenant were expressly made, and the Ten Words engraved on them, by the very hand of God because the Bible says so? Can we, or must we, believe that all the laws and narratives given in the books of Moses have been dictated to the very letter by God?

Suppose we have, by tracing the origin of all the biblical narratives about the primeval ages, received the strong impression or gained the firm conviction that they are but traditions and legends transmitted by men of primitive culture. Or suppose we have, by closely examining all these laws attributed to God, found them to contain many traces of rude barbarism which our reverential love of God forbids us to ascribe to Him as author.

Ought we on this account no longer consider ourselves as standing within the pale of Judaism? No. I do not believe that the Mosaic statutes about the sacrifices, the incense, and the priestly apparel, or the sanitary and criminal laws, are unchangeable ordinances of God dictated from heaven. I distinguish in the Bible the kernel from the husk, the grain from the chaff, the spirit from the temporary form. Just as the infant requires a different kind of nourishment than the grown man, so the Bible, as the revelation offered to an uncouth and uncivilized age, contains another pabulum for the soul than what is demanded by a cultured age . . .

Must I, then, because I cannot accept the traditional beliefs—take, for instance, only the belief in the resurrection of the body, the only immortality belief Mosaic-talmudical Judaism owns and offers—renounce Judaism because one rabbi, or five hundred Orthodox rabbis, say so?

—From Kaufmann Kohler,
*Studies, Addresses and
Personal Papers,*
pp. 201–204.

OTHER THINGS TO READ

Bamberger, Bernard J., *The Story of Judaism:* Chap. 45, ''The Golden Land''; Chap. 46, ''The Era of Pogroms''; Chap. 49, ''American Judaism, 1880–1914.''

Bentwich, Norman, ''Solomon Schechter,'' Chap. 5 in Simon Noveck (ed.), *Great Jewish Personalities in Modern Times.*

Browne, Lewis (ed.), *The Wisdom of Israel:* ''The Philosophy of Felix Adler,'' pp. 668–671; ''Practices of Orthodox Judaism,'' 707–718.

Reform Judaism—Then and Now

Davis, Moshe, *The Emergence of Conservative Judaism:* Part II, ''New Alignments (1870–1886)''; pp. 231–241 (founding of Jewish Theological Seminary).

Elbogen, Ismar, *A Century of Jewish Life:* pp. 343–345 (Pittsburgh Conference).

Feuer, Leon I., and Azriel Eisenberg, *Jewish Literature since the Bible,* II: pp. 193–198 (selection from Kaufmann Kohler).

Gumbiner, Joseph H., *Isaac Mayer Wise, Pioneer of American Judaism.*

Heller, James G., *Isaac M. Wise, His Life, Work and Thought:* Chap. 30, ''Chiefly of the Pittsburgh Conference.''

Jewish Encyclopedia: ''Felix Adler,'' Vol. 1, p. 194; ''Rabbinical Conferences,'' Vol. 4, pp. 214–215; ''Dietary Laws,'' Vol. 4, pp. 596–600; ''Kaufmann Kohler,'' Vol. 7, p. 533; ''Alexander Kohut,'' Vol. 7, pp. 537–538; ''Sabato Morais,'' Vol. 8, pp. 679–681; ''Solomon Schechter,'' Vol. 11, pp. 93–94.

Knox, Israel, ''Isaac Mayer Wise,'' Chap. 4 in Simon Noveck (ed.), *Great Jewish Personalities in Modern Times.*

Kohler, Kaufmann, *Studies, Addresses and Personal Papers:* pp. 201–235, ''Backward or Forward?''

Levinger, Lee J., *A History of the Jews in the United States:* Chap. 15, ''The Growth of Reform Judaism''; Chap. 17, ''The Third Wave of Immigration: From Russia.''

Masserman, Paul, and Max Baker, *The Jews Come to America:* Chap. 12, ''The Russian Jew in America''; Chap. 13, ''The Jews in the Labor Movement.''

Philipson, David, ''The Pittsburgh Rabbinical Conference,'' *Central Conference of American Rabbis Yearbook,* Vol. 45 (1935), pp. 190–206.

Philipson, David, *The Reform Movement in Judaism:* pp. 353–357 (Philadelphia and Pittsburgh Conferences).

Plaut, W. Gunther, *The Growth of Reform Judaism:* pp. 29–41 (Philadelphia and Pittsburgh Conferences, Ethical Culture).

Schwartzman, Sylvan D., *Reform Judaism in the Making:* Chap. 12, ''Reform Produces the Pittsburgh Platform.''

Standard Jewish Encyclopedia: ''Felix Adler,'' p. 30; ''Dietary Laws,'' pp. 560–561; ''Jewish Theological Seminary,'' pp. 1048–1050; ''Kaufmann Kohler,'' pp. 1143–1144; ''Alexander Kohut,'' p. 1144; ''Sabato Morais,'' pp. 1350–1351; ''Rabbinical Conferences,'' pp. 1568–1569; ''Solomon Schechter,'' pp. 1666–1667.

Universal Jewish Encyclopedia: ''Felix Adler,'' Vol. 1, pp. 91–92; ''Rabbinical Conference,'' Vol. 3, pp. 327–328; ''Dietary Laws,'' Vol. 3, p. 564; ''Kaufmann Kohler,'' Vol. 6, pp. 428–430; ''Alexander Kohut,'' Vol. 6, pp. 436–437; ''Sabato Morais,'' Vol. 7, pp. 638–640; ''Solomon Schechter,'' Vol. 9, pp. 393–394.

Wise, Isaac M., *Reminiscences.*

SUGGESTED ACTIVITIES

1. Write a radio newscast dealing with the creation of the Pittsburgh Platform.

2. On the basis of your congregation's practices and your observation of Reform needs today, have the class prepare a platform for the modern Reform Jew. Then prepare a chart comparing this with the Pittsburgh Platform.

3. Conduct a debate on the subject: ''*Resolved, that the rabbis at Pittsburgh should have insisted on maintaining the dietary laws.*''

SUBJECTS FOR RESEARCH

1. In addition to his role at the Pittsburgh Conference, what other important Reform contributions did Kaufmann Kohler make?

2. How was the Conservative movement in the United States established? What are its basic principles today?

3. During what years did the greatest number of East European Jews come to America, and

why? In what ways did Reform Jews try to help them?

4. How and why was the Society for Ethical Culture founded? What are its present membership, program, and activities?

5. In carrying out the Jewish dietary laws, what are the principal regulations a traditional Jew must observe?

FILMSTRIPS TO SEE

Isaac Mayer Wise: Master Builder of American Judaism (UAHC), depicting the activities and contributions of this pioneer organizer of American Reform.

David Einhorn: Father of the Union Prayerbook (UAHC), portraying the experiences and contributions of this distinguished early American Reformer.

300 Years: Memorable Events in American Jewish History (UAHC), presenting the important happenings in the history of the American Jewish community as background for the development of Reform.

Jews in the Soviet Union, in two parts (UAHC), providing scenes of Jewish life in modern Russia through which the Jews' past experiences are reflected.

Call for the Question: The Synagogue in the Community (UAHC), describing the role of the Reform temple in the area of social action.

A LIVE ISSUE

During the early 1930's, as we shall see in this chapter, Reform Jews were sharply divided over Zionism's aim to create a national homeland in Palestine for the Jews. But the establishment of the State of Israel put an end to the debate, and today the movement enthusiastically supports it.

Yet controversy over certain aspects of Zionism continues, particularly its negative view of the Diaspora, or those Jewish communities that exist outside of Israel. For, from the very beginning, Zionism has insisted that anti-Semitism and assimilation threaten the survival of Jews in the Diaspora and that their only hope is to settle in Palestine. Hence, in its view, mass *aliyah* (עֲלִיָּה, "going up," or immigration to Israel) is essential.

The Basic Problem: Many Jews object. They challenge this outlook on the Diaspora, particularly in democratic countries like the United States. They also question the wisdom of wholesale immigration of Jews to Israel, even if it were practical.

But many Reform Jews also find a contradiction here with their own religious beliefs, particularly with their view that life in the Diaspora is vital to the Jews' mission.

Some Important Questions: (1) Historically, is Zionism's assessment of the Diaspora justified? (2) Does anti-Semitism or assimilation make Jewish survival possible only in Israel? (3) Would the immigration of all American Jews to Israel be desirable? (4) Would the immigration of some be helpful to Israel? Why? (5) Is there a contradiction between mass *aliyah* and Reform's concept of the Jews' mission? (6) Does support for the State of Israel require the Reform Jew to accept Zionism's view of the Diaspora?

What Do You Think? As you read about the rise of Zionism, what conclusions do you come to about its general attitude toward the Diaspora? To what extent do you find it justified? What position, then, should you as a Reform Jew adopt?

15. THE CALL FOR A NEW PLATFORM

Growing Discontent with the Pittsburgh Platform

As the year 1935 approached, Reform in America made plans to observe the fiftieth anniversary of the Pittsburgh Platform. It had successfully guided the movement for half a century and, as the work of leading Reform pioneers, it was cherished by many.

Yet, as indicated by the following comments, the Pittsburgh Platform no longer satisfied a growing number of the rabbis:

> A new statement, a new declaration of principles is imperative, a declaration that will recognize and reassert the spiritual and ethnic community of Israel and take sympathetic cognizance of the Palestine that is being rebuilt . . . Such a declaration, I urge, should be made forthwith.
>
> —Rabbi Abraham Feldman
> (Hartford), 1937.

> . . . From our vantage point, looking back at the past half century, we see that those who created the Pittsburgh Platform took too limited a view of "the hour." In their concern with the American scene, they

ignored the dark clouds on the horizon, not only in Eastern but also in Western Europe . . .

> —Rabbi Samuel Cohon
> (Cincinnati), 1935.

> The Pittsburgh Platform contains some fine old doctrines and pious wishes, but of course in revering it we recognize its limitations.
>
> —Rabbi Sidney Tedesche
> (Brooklyn), 1935.

> . . . That [Pittsburgh] Platform, conceived in sincerity when liberty was new and universalism seemed at hand, no longer sets the proper boundaries for our convictions nor gives proper bound to our vision . . .
>
> —Rabbi William Rosenblum
> (New York), 1936.

Furthermore, as some of the critics were quick to point out, the Pittsburgh Platform was not really an official pronouncement of the Reform rabbinate as such since it was adopted four

225

years before the Central Conference of American Rabbis had come into existence.

So, in response to the situation, the members of the Central Conference approved the following resolution at their annual meeting in 1934:

> **The year 1935 will mark the fiftieth anniversary of the "Pittsburgh Platform."**
>
> **In view of the many ideological and material changes in Jewish and general life which have taken place since then and which have had their inevitable repercussion on our Reform point of view, we recommend that the . . . Central Conference of American Rabbis plan to have presented at next year's sessions a symposium re-evaluating the platform with a view of formulating a [new] pronouncement touching the philosophy and program of present-day Reform Judaism.**

The critics of the Pittsburgh Platform cited five main reasons for their dissatisfaction: the end of the Reform revolution, changes within the American Jewish community, the growth of anti-Semitism, the rise of Zionism, and dissatisfaction within Reform.

Reason 1:
The End of the Reform Revolution

In the first place, the Pittsburgh Platform seemed mainly a product of Reform's revolutionary period which, in the critics' opinion, the movement had now outgrown. In its earlier days, Reform, to be sure, was in revolt against Orthodoxy, and like all revolutionary movements it sometimes went to extremes. In this respect, it was not unlike the French Revolution that sought to do away with such worthwhile institutions as religion and the calendar in the name of liberty and that even executed thousands of loyal Frenchmen who dared to differ.

Similarly, many among the early Reformers in America were hostile toward traditional Judaism. In the process, they concentrated much more on doing away with various practices than in developing new ones to replace them and, in opposition to the Orthodox, stressed matters of belief rather than observance. Reflecting this spirit was the Pittsburgh Platform because it was clearly as much an attack upon traditional belief and practice as it was an expression of Reform Judaism. But this was to be expected from men like Kaufmann Kohler and Emil G. Hirsch who were not only committed to the radical position of David Einhorn but had come to Pittsburgh to refute the rising group of Conservatives.

In the years following 1885, matters were carried to still greater extremes. Many in the movement took the Pittsburgh Platform to mean that Reform had broken completely with all of tradition. They looked upon the whole of rabbinical literature, including the Talmud, as worthless and considered distinctive Jewish practice objectionable largely because it was also carried on by the Orthodox. And to some, Reform simply became anything that suited their personal convenience.

Yet the pendulum was clearly beginning to swing back. Just as the excesses of the French Revolution finally gave way to orderly, stable government under Napoleon, so Reform was bound eventually to arrive at a more moderate position. By 1935, Reform in America was already a movement of nearly three hundred congregations, with four hundred rabbis and some 200,000 members. Long forgotten were its revolutionary days when it had to fight for its existence. As one of the critics of the Pittsburgh Platform put it, "Reform has passed the stage of tearing down and rooting up and is entering the period of constructive upbuilding." In the minds of a growing number of his colleagues, a change from the revolutionary doctrines of 1885 seemed long overdue.

226

Reason 2: Changes within the American Jewish Community

The composition of American Jewry in 1935 was also vastly different from what it had been a half-century earlier, and this became a second reason for seeking a new Reform platform.

At the time of the Pittsburgh Conference, American Jewry numbered only about 300,000, most of whom had come from Germany. Many of those who had been exposed to Reform in Europe soon identified with the movement in the United States, and even some of the more traditional Jews turned to Reform as they adjusted to American life. Thus, in the early 1880's, the majority of affiliated Jews belonged to temples, which prompted men like Isaac M. Wise and others to predict that within a few years all of American Jewry would be Reform.

However, in 1935 the situation was totally different. Now, of the nearly four and a half million Jews in the United States, at least three and a half million were of East European origin. As a result, the former German Jewish majority represented only a tiny minority of the American Jewish community.

Mass immigration of East European Jews, as we know, had already commenced as far back as the time of the Pittsburgh Conference. For, in Russia, the government was following a course designed, as a high official put it, to starve to death a third of its six million Jews, convert another third to Russian Orthodoxy, and drive the remaining third from the country. To escape the pogroms, poverty, and misery, as many as could fled, with the result that three-quarters of the Jewish immigrants to the United States in the half-century after Pittsburgh were from Russia.

The rest came mainly from Hungary and Rumania where conditions were almost as bad. In Hungary, anti-Semitism reached violent proportions, and in Galicia, then part of the Austro-Hungarian Empire, the Church joined with the peasants and merchants to boycott Jewish shops and bar Jews from most professions and crafts. Even the old ritual murder charge was revived.

Rumania was still worse. There Jews were looked upon only as foreigners, who in addition to being denied all civil and political rights were subject to expulsion at any time. Nor were they permitted to attend Rumanian schools, own property, or work even as peddlers.

Excluding those who were socialists and rejected religion in general, most of the Jews who came to the United States were strictly Orthodox. Never having encountered liberal Judaism before, they were shocked by Reform. Reform Jews, in turn, were repelled by their ways that seemed so out of keeping with American life, and relations were further strained by the wide social and economic gulf that separated them.

With the passing of time, the newcomers gradually adjusted to their surroundings. Eventually, some recognized the need for reasonable religious changes and, like the Reformers before them, started to improve the worship by insisting upon greater decorum in the synagogue and incorporating some English into the service. They also gradually abandoned other things, such as wearing the *sheitel* and going to the *mikveh.* But Reform as represented by the Pittsburgh Platform was much too extreme for most of these Jews from Eastern Europe, who preferred a more modern form of Orthodoxy or else found their way into Conservative Judaism.

As social and economic handicaps were overcome, a number of the older generation and many more of their children began to join Reform temples, bringing with them an appreciation for some of the traditional ceremonials. Slowly, more and more temples began to reintroduce such rituals as the blowing of the *shofar* (שׁוֹפָר, ram's horn) on the

Reform Judaism—Then and Now

High Holy Days, the chanting of the *Kiddush, Bar Mitzvah,* and others. The Reform service now took on greater warmth and emotional appeal, which succeeded in attracting still others from among the second generation of East European Jews.

To many Reform rabbis, most of whom were of East European origin themselves, this was sufficient evidence that the movement had outgrown the Pittsburgh Platform, with its great emphasis upon belief to the neglect of practice. Thus, in his lecture entitled

''Jewish Thinking'' given before the 1934 gathering of the Central Conference, Rabbi William Rosenau of Baltimore made this appeal for more ceremonialism in Reform:

> **It should be stated that the proper evaluation of ceremonies . . . should not be overlooked. Ceremonies are an important form of Jewish teachings. Their use was and is all too quickly abandoned in some Jewish circles. The relative influence of**

YEMENITE SHOFAR BLOWER. Deeply resonant sounds emerge from this extra long ram's horn. (State of Israel Government, Press Office)

> **the abstract and the concrete ought ever to be borne in mind. Every rabbi should make use of those ceremonies that are worthy of survival. On account of the tendency of rationalism to run riot, it is no more than proper that ceremonies be judged fairly and impartially in Judaism.**

Many agreed with him. In the light of the new circumstances of American Jewish life, they were convinced that the attitudes of the Pittsburgh Platform, especially toward ceremonialism and tradition, were far from adequate.

Reason 3:
The Growth of Anti-Semitism

Enormously encouraged by the freedom America offered in 1885, the rabbis at Pittsburgh were confident that democracy, "with liberty and justice for all," would some day sweep away all intolerance. Optimistically, they saw their age as:

> . . . **the approach of the realization of Israel's great messianic hope for the establishment of the kingdom of truth, justice, and peace among all men.**

But fifty years later, the Jews were far less confident about the future, particularly in view of the growth of anti-Semitism following World War I. A violently anti-Semitic National Socialist Party whose members were known as Nazis had come to power in Germany in 1933 under the leadership of Adolf Hitler. The Jews, said Hitler, were an inferior race that had corrupted the superior Aryan people, the true Germans, who must be protected from them at all costs.

Systematically, the Nazis now began to eliminate Jews from every phase of German life, boycotting their stores, barring them from government posts, the railroads, and every educational institution. Jews were no longer permitted to practice medicine or dentistry, work for a newspaper or radio station, or appear in the movies or on the stage. Imprisonment and mass murder in concentration camps soon followed.

Encouraged by Hitler's success, others elsewhere adopted anti-Semitism for their own political ends. In Austria, the violently anti-Semitic Christian Socialist Party also took over control in 1933. Fascist groups in Poland, with the active support of the Church, campaigned for the elimination of Jews from Polish life. The growing influence of the fascist Iron Guard encouraged Rumania to introduce new restrictions against the Jews, and Hungary quickly followed suit. In communist Russia as well, where officially anti-Semitism was considered a crime, the old hatred of the Jews was revived. Now, however, they were persecuted as "counter-revolutionaries," "capitalists," and "Zionists." Even in such liberal countries as England and France, fascist parties, subsidized by Nazi Germany, sprang up to poison the people's minds against the Jews.

Nor was America immune. The period after World War I saw the rise of the rabidly anti-Semitic Ku Klux Klan and other hate groups spreading prejudice and rousing public opinion against Jews. Even a leading automobile manufacturer of the time warned the nation of the growing Jewish menace and published the forged *Protocols of the Elders of Zion*, which told of an alleged conspiracy among Jewish leaders to control the world. Soon certain prominent universities were introducing quotas that limited the number of Jewish students, particularly in professional schools, and Congress itself, in an act directed chiefly against Jews, sharply restricted immigration from Eastern Europe.

With the Great Depression of 1929, anti-Semitism grew more intense. Now, several native fascist-type organizations, supported largely by Nazi Germany, held huge mass meetings in leading American cities and poured out a steady stream of Jew-hatred. The early 1930's saw greater use of quotas to restrict the entrance of Jewish college students and greater discrimination against the employment of Jews in some of the largest businesses and industries. Many hotels, summer resorts, and residential areas were also openly refusing to accept Jews.

Fortunately, with the lifting of the Depression, most Americans came to recognize that anti-Semitism was being used as a weapon against democracy. Nevertheless, American Jews were shaken by the experience. They now realized that anti-Semitism was far from dead, that the world still looked upon Jews with unreasonable suspicion and even with murderous hatred, and that the Messianic Age, confidently predicted by the Pittsburgh Platform, was an exceedingly long way off.

In the face of hostility, Reform Jews reacted as Jews always have, by turning inward toward their own faith and people for comfort and strength. However, they soon discovered to what extremes the Pittsburgh Platform had carried them. To many, Judaism had become simply a vague "religious persuasion," divorced not only from Jewish knowledge and religious practice but from any feeling of common Jewish peoplehood as well. Small wonder, then, that the preacher at the Central Conference convention of 1934 called for a renewed sense of "unity of people and faith." "Liberal Judaism," he declared, "must be reunited with the Jewish people."

Indeed, as far back as the end of World War I, Rabbi Stephen S. Wise, an eloquent spokesman for American Jewry and founder of the Free Synagogue of New York, had pointed to some of these very shortcomings. Reform, he said, had become too much of a "denomination," too divorced from the masses of Jewry, and in serious need of renewing its spiritual kinship with the whole Jewish peo-ple. To counteract this, he founded a new seminary, the Jewish Institute of Religion, in New York which would train rabbis not only for Reform congregations but for all other interpretations of Judaism. By 1935, more than fifty of its graduates were members of the Central Conference and among the most ardent advocates of change in the Pittsburgh Platform.

Reason 4: The Rise of Zionism

To most Reformers in 1885, the traditional Jewish belief that the Jews were in "exile" seemed inconsistent with emancipation. Hence, they reacted negatively to both the messianic hope for the reestablishment of the Jewish nation in Palestine and the more practical efforts of early Zionists in Eastern Europe. For, in reaction to the pogroms of 1881, a number of Russian Jews were calling for the restoration of Jewish nationhood as the only answer to persecution.

In a widely-circulated pamphlet entitled *Auto-Emancipation,* a Russian Jewish physician, Leon Pinsker, urged his people to seek their own territorial independence, which in turn prompted certain Russian Jewish students to form "Lovers of Zion" societies. Eventually, despite the opposition of the Turks who then controlled Palestine, tiny groups of these young men and women painfully made their way there to establish several colonies.

However, an organized Zionist movement as such did not come into being until a dozen years after the Pittsburgh Conference. It was only then that under the leadership of Theodor Herzl the first Zionist congress finally met in Basel, Switzerland, and declared itself in favor of establishing "a Jewish Homeland in Palestine."

Herzl, a Viennese newspaper correspondent, had been shocked by the anti-Jewish reaction to the trial of Captain Alfred Dreyfus which he had been covering. If as liberal a country as France could be engulfed by this hatred of the Jews, he reasoned, then their only hope was to have a state of their own. He became so consumed with the idea that he wrote a small book, *The Jewish State,* published in 1896, in which he described how this could be achieved. It met with such enthusiasm that the very next year the World Zionist Organization was created to carry out Herzl's plan.

Confidence in emancipation, however, led most Reformers in Europe and America to oppose the establishment of a Jewish state. Even as late as 1935, though deeply concerned over the peril of the Jews under the Nazis, many Reform rabbis were still against Zionism. In fact, sharp differences over the question compelled the Reform rabbinate that very year to adopt a so-called "neutrality resolution" which stated:

> **Whereas, We are persuaded that acceptance or rejection of the Zionist program should be left to the determination of the individual members of the conference themselves,**
>
> **Therefore, Be It Resolved, That the Central Conference of American Rabbis take no official stand on the subject of Zionism . . .**

Yet in America there had always been certain Reform rabbis who were sympathetic to Zionism, and some even played a prominent role in the development of the movement. One was Bernhard Felsenthal who helped form the first Zionist society in the United States. Two others were Stephen S. Wise and Gustav Gottheil, who in 1898, with his son Professor Richard Gottheil, organized the Federation of American Zionists that later became the Zionist Organization of America.

Among the leaders of the Zionist movement in 1935 were Reform rabbis like Stephen S. Wise and Abba Hillel Silver and a growing number of others who had become active in

the cause. In large measure, Reform support was the result of the deteriorating situation of European Jewry. With fascism spreading, hundreds of thousands were desperate and the only immediate solution seemed to be Palestine, to which about 130,000 had already gone.

Fortunately the country was now able to absorb them. In spite of the fact that Palestine had been badly neglected under many centuries of Arab and Turkish misrule, the Jews had achieved wonders in draining the swamps, ridding the country of its dread diseases, reclaiming much of the eroded soil, and developing irrigation and electric power. Even amidst growing Arab hostility during the period from 1922 on, when the League of Nations appointed Great Britain to govern Palestine, the Jews managed to establish hundreds of thriving farm colonies and several modern

THEODOR HERZL. A Viennese correspondent, he was stirred by the widespread anti-Jewish sentiment produced by the Dreyfus affair. He wrote *The Jewish State* and thereby became the founder of the modern Zionist movement. (HUC, American Jewish Archives)

cities, like Haifa, Jerusalem, and Tel Aviv. They had also succeeded in converting Hebrew into a living language that was now being taught by excellent schools at every level, going all the way up to the famed Hebrew University.

To this undertaking, American Jews of all shades of opinion, including Reform, had contributed generously. Now the desperate plight of European Jewry called for even greater American Jewish effort, involving huge sums for the rescue of a growing stream of refugees and the upbuilding of Palestine to accommodate them.

Thus, fifty years after Pittsburgh, the Reform movement faced a vastly different situation that moved Rabbi James G. Heller of Cincinnati, a leading Reform Zionist, to say to his colleagues:

> **I cannot see where there are any irreconcilable differences that are involved in the opposition, historic and contemporary, of Reform Judaism and Zionism that we could not at least make an attempt to compose.**

Reason 5:
Dissatisfaction within Reform

Finally, there were a number of rabbis who complained of certain shortcomings in American Reform itself.

The failure of the movement to grow, as indicated by the negligible increase in membership in the 1930's, disturbed many. In the ten years from 1920 to 1930, the Reform movement had expanded from 205 congregations representing 31,000 families to 254 congregations with 60,000 families. But in 1935 the number of Reform congregations had increased by just two and the total membership had actually declined by 7,000. "A shocking fact," declared a leading Reform

spokesman. Clearly, Reform was failing to attract American Jewry.

At the same time, the loyalties of Reform Jews themselves seemed to be growing weaker. Many now attended temple only on the High Holy Days. Others seemed to lack a sense of kinship with their fellow Jews and were reluctant to contribute to their relief and rescue. "Shallow" was a frequent criticism of Reform in the middle 1930's, causing Rabbi Abraham Feldman of Hartford to declare before the Central Conference:

> **The plague of de-Judaization is rampant in our life. I make bold to assert that we of the Liberal wing are responsible for much of it. We have sinned through omission. We have erred through dissociation [with fellow Jews] and aloofness. And it is time we recognize the error and set out to correct it while it is yet time.**

"A thoroughgoing and far-reaching program for the revival of religious loyalties" is needed, asserted Rabbi Samuel Goldenson of New York, then president of the Central Conference. Indeed, he went on:

> **. . . The time has come for the reassertion of the things that our fathers valued throughout the ages and for the reaffirmation of those truths and loyalties which may sustain us in our desire for continued existence as Jews . . . The primary obligation that rests upon us . . . is to keep the fires of Jewish learning and aspiration burning. Practical and thoroughgoing means should be devised and persistent efforts made to bring the knowledge of Jewish history and literature to our people and to imbue them with a love for Jewish values. . . .**

Others criticized Reform for its lack of religious warmth. "Our whole movement," said Rabbi Samuel Schulman of New York, "betrays a weakness insofar as there does not seem to be any mystic passion in it." Needed to counteract Reform's "over-rationality," some argued, was greater emphasis upon Hebrew, music, art, and other forms of Jewish expression.

Again, much of the discontent tended to center upon the Pittsburgh Platform that many felt failed to sustain the third and fourth generation Reform Jew. Nor, apparently, did it address itself to the needs of the movement in 1935.

Focus on the Pittsburgh Platform

Thus, as the Reform rabbis gathered together in Chicago for their 1935 annual convention, the program focused on the Pittsburgh Platform.

Its fiftieth anniversary was to be appropriately observed by having Rabbi David Philipson, the only living participant, present some of his reminiscences of the conference in Pittsburgh.

Following this, the rabbis were to conduct a searching discussion of the platform, with leading supporters and critics scheduled to review its principal doctrines.

Yet, though dissatisfaction over the Pittsburgh Platform had been mounting during the previous decade, two questions still had to be answered. First, was Reform really prepared to abandon it? And, if so, would the movement be able to agree upon a new platform?

QUESTIONS FOR DISCUSSION

1. In 1935, to what statements of the Pittsburgh Platform would each of the following have objected: (a) an Orthodox Jew? (b) a Conservative Jew? (c) a Zionist? (d) a Reform Jew from a more traditional background? (e) a Jew living in Germany? Why?

2. How do you account for the enormous increase in anti-Semitism between the end of World War I and the outbreak of World War II? How do you explain the failure of those who wrote the Pittsburgh Platform to anticipate this? How, then, would you rewrite their statement about the coming of the Messianic Age?

3. Why did Reform fail to attract the East European Jews who came to the United States? Why, then, did many of their children affiliate? How would this tend to change the character of the Reform Judaism that was based upon the Pittsburgh Platform?

4. Why, originally, did many Reform Jews object to the aims of Zionism? Why, in 1935, was there increasing support for the upbuilding of Palestine? What is the present attitude of the members of your congregation to the State of Israel? How do you explain this?

5. Judging from Reform's experience during the previous half-century, what were some of the shortcomings of the Pittsburgh Platform? Had you been living in 1935, what particular changes would you have recommended? Why?

6. Why, in 1935, were many Reform Jews in favor of retaining the Pittsburgh Platform? What are some of its features that you would want to incorporate in a Reform platform for today?

SIGNIFICANT DOCUMENTS

From Theodor Herzl's *The Jewish State,* 1896

The Jewish question still exists. It would be foolish to deny it. It is a remnant of the Middle Ages, which civilized nations do not even yet seem able to shake off, try as they will.

They certainly showed a generous desire to do so when they emancipated us. The Jewish question exists wherever Jews live in perceptible numbers. Where it does not exist, it is carried by Jews in the course of their migrations. We naturally move to those places where we are not persecuted, and there our presence produces persecution. This is the case in every country, and will remain so, even in those highly civilized—for instance, France—till the Jewish question finds a solution on a political basis. The unfortunate Jews are now carrying anti-Semitism into England; they have already introduced it into America.

I believe that I understand anti-Semitism, which is really a highly complex movement. I consider it from a Jewish standpoint, yet without fear or hatred. I believe that I can see what elements there are in it of vulgar sport, of common trade jealousy, of inherited prejudice, of religious intolerance, and also of pretended self-defense. I think the Jewish question is no more a social than a religious one, notwithstanding that it sometimes takes these and other forms. It is a national question, which can only be solved by making it a political world question to be discussed and settled by the civilized nations of the world in council.

We are a people—one people . . .

No human being is wealthy or powerful enough to transplant a nation from one habitation to another. An idea alone can compass that: and this idea of a state may have a requisite power to do so. The Jews have dreamt this kingly dream all through the long nights of their history. "Next year in Jerusalem" is our old phrase. It is now a question of showing that the dream can be converted into a living reality.

For this, many old, outgrown, confused and limited notions must first be entirely erased from the minds of men. Dull brains might, for instance, imagine that this exodus would be from civilized regions into the desert. That is not the case. It will be carried out in the midst of civilization. We shall not revert to a lower stage, we shall rise to a higher one. We shall not dwell in mud huts; we shall build new and more beautiful and modern houses, and possess them in safety. We shall not lose our acquired possessions; we shall realize them.

We shall surrender our well-earned rights only for better ones. We shall not sacrifice our beloved customs; we shall find them again. We shall not leave our old home before the new one is prepared for us.

Those only will depart who are sure thereby to improve their position; those who are now desperate will go first, after them the poor; next the prosperous, and, last of all, the wealthy. Those who go in advance will raise themselves to a higher grade, equal to that whose representatives will shortly follow. Thus the exodus will be at the same time an ascent of the class.

The departure of the Jews will involve no economic disturbances, no crises, no persecutions; in fact, the countries they abandon will revive to a new period of prosperity. There will be an inner migration of Christian citizens into the positions evacuated by Jews. The outgoing current will be gradual, without any disturbance, and its initial movement will put an end to anti-Semitism. The Jews will leave as honored friends and, if some of them return, they will receive the same favorable welcome and treatment at the hands of civilized nations as is accorded to all foreign visitors. Their exodus will have no resemblance to a flight, for it will be a well-regulated movement under control of public opinion. The movement will not only be inaugurated with absolute conformity to law but it cannot even be carried out without the friendly cooperation of interested governments who would derive considerable benefits from it.

Security for the integrity of the idea and the vigor of its execution will be found in the creation of a body corporate, or corporation. This corporation will be called "The Society of Jews." In addition to it there will be a Jewish company, an economically productive body.

An individual who attempted even to undertake this huge task alone would be either an impostor or a madman. The personal character of the members of the corporation will guarantee its integrity, and the adequate capital of the company will prove its stability . . .

—From Theodor Herzl,
The Jewish State,
pp. 19–20; 27–28.

The Nuremberg Laws Adopted by
Nazi Germany, 1935

*The Reich [German Nation]
Citizenship Law of September 15, 1935*

The Reichstag [German Legislature] has adopted unanimously the following law which is herewith promulgated:

ARTICLE I

A subject of the state is he who belongs to the protective union of the German Reich and who, therefore, has particular obligations toward the Reich.

ARTICLE II

A citizen of the Reich is only that subject who is of German or kindred blood and who, through his conduct, shows that he is both desirous and fit to serve faithfully the German people and the Reich. . . .

*First Supplementary Decree
of November 14, 1935*

ARTICLE III

Only citizens of the Reich, as bearers of full political rights, can exercise the right of voting in political affairs and can hold public office.

ARTICLE IV

A Jew cannot be a citizen of the Reich. He cannot exercise the right to vote; he cannot occupy public office.

ARTICLE V

1. A Jew is anyone who is descended from at least three grandparents who were racially full Jews. . . .
2. A Jew is also one who is descended from two full Jewish grandparents if:
   a. He belonged to the Jewish religious community at the time this law was issued or who joined the community later.
   b. At the time the law was issued he was married to a person who was a Jew or was subsequently married to a Jew.
   c. He is the offspring from a marriage with a Jew, in the sense of Sec. 1, which was contracted after the coming into effect of the Law for the Protection of German Blood and Honor of September 15, 1935.
   d. He is the offspring of an extramarital relationship with a Jew, according to Sec. 1, and will be born out of wedlock after July 31, 1936.

The Law for the Protection of German Blood and Honor, September 15, 1935

Imbued with the knowledge that the purity of the German blood is the necessary condition for the continued existence of the German people, and animated by the inflexible will to ensure the existence of the German nation for all future times, the Reichstag has unanimously adopted the following law. . . .

ARTICLE I

Marriage between Jews and subjects of the German or kindred blood are forbidden. Marriages concluded despite this law are invalid, even if they are concluded abroad in order to circumvent this law.

ARTICLE II

Extramarital relations between Jews and subjects of German or kindred blood are forbidden.

ARTICLE III

Jews may not employ in domestic service female subjects of German or kindred blood who are under the age of 45 years.

ARTICLE IV

1. Jews are forbidden to display the Reich and national flag or to show the national colors.

2. The display of the Jewish colors, however, is permitted for them. . . .

ARTICLE V

1. Whoever acts in violation of the prohibition of Article I will be punished with penal servitude.

2. The man who acts in violation of Article II will be punished with either imprisonment or penal servitude.

3. Whoever acts in violation of Articles III or IV will be punished with imprisonment up to one year and with a fine or with either of these penalties.

—From Nathan Zuckerman,
The Wine of Violence,
pp. 143–145.

The Neutrality Resolution on Zionism Adopted by the Central Conference of American Rabbis, 1935

Your Committee on Resolutions wishes to report on the resolutions that have been submitted for its consideration . . . The resolution as submitted will be read and there will follow . . . the recommendation of the Resolutions Committee, with a reformulation of the resolution where changes were deemed advisable.

In the past, despite the fact that for many years members of the Central Conference of American Rabbis have believed that there is no inherent incompatibility between Reform Judaism and Zionism, this conference has repeatedly adopted resolutions expressing its deep dissent from the principles and policies of the latter. We believe that the time has come for a change in the attitude these former actions implied.

When there is an honest difference of opinion in respect to the nature of Reform Judaism, anti-Zionists should not force their views down the throats of Zionists, nor in turn should Zionists now demand that the conference, at least in the present status of the problem, commit itself to the Zionist philosophy and program. A policy of neutrality and of mutual respect and tolerance should be fostered.

We cannot blot out the record of the past. But we can determine our present stand. Be it, therefore, resolved that the Central Conference of American Rabbis as a body harbors at present no opposition to Zionism and will permit to every constituent member the right to determine his own spiritual convictions and his own practical stand upon this important problem.

Rabbi Felix A. Levy (Chicago)
Rabbi James G. Heller (Cincinnati)
Rabbi Barnett R. Brickner (Cleveland)

Your committee offers a substitute resolution which it recommends for your adoption:

Whereas, At certain foregoing conventions of the Central Conference of American Rabbis, resolutions have been adopted in opposition to Zionism, and [Omitted from the final version: *Whereas, We believe that such an attitude no longer reflects the sentiment of a very substantial section of the conference membership, and*]

Whereas, We are persuaded that acceptance or rejection of the Zionist program should be left to the determination of the individual members of the conference themselves, therefore

Be It Resolved, That the Central Conference of American Rabbis takes no official stand on the subject of Zionism; and be it further

Resolved, That in keeping with its oft-announced intentions, the Central Conference of American Rabbis will continue to cooperate in the upbuilding of Palestine and in the economic, cultural, and particularly spiritual tasks confronting the growing and evolving Jewish community there.

DISCUSSION

Rabbi Newfield (Birmingham): I am in harmony with the spirit of the substitute resolution but I believe the second clause should be omitted. If we adopt a resolution to bring about a spirit of harmony, it is unnecessary to have this statement. We have never taken a vote on the incompatibility of Zionism and membership in the conference and we cannot know how many favor and how many do not favor a change of attitude. I therefore move the elimination of the second paragraph.

Rabbi Goldenson (New York): I regret exceedingly that this resolution was offered at this session of the conference. This convention has already accepted a recommendation that a commission shall be appointed to draft a platform stating the position of Reform Judaism on various subjects. I am sure it will include Zionism. Why not in all fairness wait for the action of the deliberate body to be appointed that shall deal with this very important controversial matter? I do not believe that the conference at this time should make a declaration, however timid and negative it is, which in intent will be tantamount to a declaration that we have reversed our attitude on Zionism.

Rabbi Foster (Newark): I think we should be clear. Zionism as we use the term today represents an entirely different idea than it did in the minds of those who drew up the Pittsburgh Platform.

Rabbi Heller (Cincinnati): I am opposed to any attempt to define the creed of Reform Judaism and to congeal it. We should meet issues as they arise, as this conference has done in the past. But the present resolution does not constitute a declaration of policy. It says in effect that the question is an open one from now on. The time is approaching when the majority of the members of this conference will no longer believe as their forebears did that there is a fundamental incompatibility between Reform Judaism and Zionism; and that Judaism even from a spiritual point of view is best furthered through denial of the reality of a Jewish nation and a Jewish people.

Rabbi Bernstein (Rochester): Although I am a Zionist I am opposed to this resolution because it is weak and timid. It requires the conference to be neutral on the subject of Zionism. The Jewish national hope is an integral and indispensable element in my liberal Judaism. I can no more be neutral about this question than about the existence of God or the need for social justice. I believe that the conference should take a positive stand endorsing Zionism. If it is not prepared to do so at the present time, let us not bind ourselves to purportless inaction but postpone a decision until we are ready for it.

A motion to table the resolution on Zionism was lost by a vote of 51 to 53.

A motion to omit paragraph 2 of the substitute [committee's] resolution was adopted.

A substitute motion that Zionism is not incompatible with Reform Judaism was lost. The amended resolution was adopted by a vote of 81 to 25.

—From the *Central Conference of American Rabbis Yearbook*, Vol. 45 (1935), pp. 102–103; 110–112.

Reform Judaism—Then and Now

From a Statement on Israel and
the Diaspora, by David Ben-Gurion,
First Prime Minister of Israel, 1965

. . . All Diaspora Jewish communities live in what I call a condition of exile, whether or not they are aware of it or recognize it as such.

What are these "facts of exile"?

First, outside Israel, wherever they live, Jews are a minority. They are thus to a greater or lesser extent dependent upon the will of the majority. The majority may grant or withhold from them equal rights. The minority is helpless to make its own decision in the matter. Whatever status is enjoyed or suffered by the Jewish minority rests upon the will and decision of others and not upon its own will.

Second, the economic and social structure of such communities is on the whole different from experiences and conditions of the majority people. Even religious Jewry cannot completely observe in the Diaspora all the laws of traditional Judaism. [Third], The Jewish religion, unlike all other religions, is rooted in the soil of the Land of Israel, and its survival is bound up with the land of its origin. Many of the Jewish religious precepts can be observed only in Israel. Indeed, according to the ancient sages, residence outside Israel, when this is not unavoidable, is a grave religious offense, and any Jew who lives abroad when he can come to Israel is considered by the Talmud as having forsaken God.

Fourth—and this follows from the third point—there can be no such thing in the Diaspora as life within an all-Jewish framework. The Jews are there subordinate to the sovereign framework of the general community . . .

. . . Jews in the Diaspora who wish to preserve their Jewishness find themselves caught between two contending spheres of influence. As a citizen, the Jew derives both his material and cultural substance from the non-Jews among whom he lives. Wherever he moves he finds himself in a non-Jewish environment, the environment of the all-powerful majority. It controls the government, the economy, the law, the political parties, and the dominant culture. The Jew is influenced by it, whether he wishes to be or not, whether he knows it or not. Jewish life is set apart, having no roots in the all-pervading majority environment. To remain Jews, Jews can draw only on their past and on Jewish tradition.

This produces a constant duality in the life of the Jew who wishes to preserve his Jewishness. There is a gap between the Jewish sphere and the civic sphere and, in some countries, often a contradiction. After all, the culture of a people is not merely its language, its storehouse of memories of the past, or even its "religious idea" or religious customs. The culture of

DAVID BEN-GURION. An early leader of the Zionist movement, he settled in Palestine in 1906. With the formation of the newly independent State of Israel in 1948, he served as its first prime minister. (Werner Wolff, Black Star)

a people is the totality of the human and social experience of the entire community, an experience deriving from nature, tradition, the economic, legal, and social systems, and from free public controversy. In this sense, there can be no such thing as Jewish culture in the Diaspora. At the most there can be a cultural ghetto. It may have a religious, social, and spiritual character, but it is a ghetto nonetheless, limited and separate . . .

In Israel, the barrier between the Jew and the individual as a person has been abolished. One can be a complete person and a complete Jew, for the prevailing environment is one created by Jews. Our life in Israel has become once again, as in biblical days, a complete and comprehensive experience, comprising within a state framework that is Jewish all the living values of the individual and the nation . . .

The profound differences between the Jews of Israel and the Jews overseas are likely to become deeper as the state advances toward the consolidation of its independence. But let us be clear about our use of the word "differences." I do not mean it in the sense of conflict but of differences in character, for the reasons I have just given. But such differences do not mean that one can live without the other. I do not think they can.

I believe that each needs to sustain the other, though the respective needs are not of the same order. Jewry in the Diaspora, notably in the two great centers, the United States and the Soviet Union, has traveled far along the path of assimilation; and, even though its Jewish consciousness is still alive, it is doubtful whether, without Israel, it may not perish to euthanasia or suffocation. Similarly, without strong bonds with Diaspora Jewry, it is doubtful whether Israel can survive or fulfill its mission of redemption. . . .

We in Israel and those outside must take active measures to preserve the unity of the Jewish people, for the future of both is at stake. This unity, to be effective, must be rooted in a Jewish consciousness which can be felt by all sections of Jewry, Israeli and non-Israeli, religious and non-religious. This consciousness must draw its sustenance from the ancient springs of the Jewish people and must be linked to the mission of modern Israel. Unity can therefore be guaranteed by a three-pronged effort.

The first effort will be the spread of Hebrew education. A language common to all sections of Jewry, to Israel and the Diaspora, can be the single most important factor in achieving and preserving a common Jewish consciousness. . . .

The second is an increased awareness on the part of all Jews of the vision of messianic redemption. Like the Torah of Israel, which preached the national ideal for the Jewish people but which also uttered ideals embracing mankind, so the messianic vision was both Jewish and universal. The redemption of Israel was bound up with the redemption of the world. This Jewish national ideal combined with a universal human ideal, one of the outstanding themes of Jewish prophecy and most of the books of the Bible, was never more topical than today. . . .

Third, the needs of both demand that there shall be a strengthening of the bonds between Diaspora Jewry and the State of Israel. The most urgent call is for the youth of overseas Jewry and for the young professional class, graduates in the humanities and the natural sciences, to join the builders and defenders of Israel and thus play a personal part in the creative work of redemption.

For those who wish to remain in the lands in which they live, the ties can be strengthened by visiting Israel, sending their children to undertake a period of study here, participating in Israel's economic development. This will give a deeper meaning to their Jewish consciousness and at the same time it will heighten the effectiveness of Israel as the major instrument for the preservation of Jewish integrity. . . .

—From David Ben-Gurion, "The Facts of Jewish Exile," *Harper's,* Vol. 231, No. 1384 (September, 1965), pp. 47–51.

OTHER THINGS TO READ

Bamberger, Bernard J., *The Story of Judaism:* Chap. 47, "Emancipation and Anti-Semitism"; Chap. 48, "The Birth of Political Zionism"; Chap. 49, "American Judaism, 1880–1914"; Chap. 51, "The Effects of the First World War"; Chap. 53, "Progress in Palestine"; Chap. 54, "American Judaism, 1918–1932"; Chap. 55, "The Greatest Tragedy"; Chap. 56, "The Greatest Tragedy—Second Phase."

Elbogen, Ismar, *A Century of Jewish Life:* Book 4, Chap. 3, "The Jews of America at the Beginning of the Twentieth Century"; Book 5, Chap. 5, "The Jewish National Home in Palestine"; Chap. 6, "Hitler's Total War against the Jews."

Feuer, Leon I., and Azriel Eisenberg, *Jewish Literature since the Bible,* II: pp. 228–235, 263–268 (conflicting views on Zionism); 236–238 (the Dreyfus Affair).

Friedlander, Albert H., *Out of the Whirlwind: A Reader of Holocaust Literature.*

Lehman, Emil, *Israel—Idea and Reality.*

Levinger, Lee J., *A History of the Jews in the United States:* Chap. 17, "The Third Wave of Immigration: From Russia"; Chap. 18, "The Cultural Institutions of the Russian Jews"; Chap. 22, "Between Two Wars"; Chap. 23, "The Second World War and Its Aftermath."

Lowenthal, Marvin, "Theodor Herzl," Chap. 8, in Simon Noveck (ed.), *Great Jewish Personalities in Modern Times.*

Masserman, Paul, and Max Baker, *The Jews Come to America:* Chap. 12, "The Russian Jews in America"; Chap. 16, "Zionism in America."

Philipson, David, "The Pittsburgh Rabbinical Conference," *The Central Conference of American Rabbis Yearbook,* Vol. 45 (1935), pp. 190–206.

Plaut, W. Gunther, *The Growth of Reform Judaism:* Chap. 9, "Germany: Dream and Nightmare"; Chap. 10, "Zion: The Great Debate."

Sachar, Howard, *The Course of Modern Jewish History,* Chap. 13, "The Rise of Zionism"; Chap. 14, "The Growth of Jewish Socialism"; Chap. 15, "The Great Migration and Settlement in America"; Chap. 16, "Russian Jewry's 'Liberal' Tradition in America"; Chap. 17, "The Jews of Eastern Europe between the Wars"; Chap. 18, "The Palestine Mandate"; Chap. 20, "The Onslaught of Nazism"; Chap. 21, "Europe *Judenrein*"; Chap. 22, "The Birth of Israel."

Schwartzman, Sylvan D., *Reform Judaism in the Making:* Chap. 13, "1885–1935—A Half-Century of Change."

Standard Jewish Encyclopedia: "Anti-Semitism," pp. 121–129; "Theodor Herzl," pp. 894–896; "Germany," pp. 743–747; "Hungary," pp. 932–934; "Israel," pp. 974–996; "Rumania," pp. 1623–1624; "Russia," pp. 1624–1629; "Abba Hillel Silver," pp. 1720–1721; "Stephen Samuel Wise," pp. 1917–1918; "Zionism," pp. 1964–1968.

Universal Jewish Encyclopedia: "Anti-Semitism," Vol. 1, pp. 341–409; "Germany," Vol. 4, pp. 541–584; "Theodor Herzl," Vol. 5, pp. 337–342; "Hungary," Vol. 5, pp. 483–503; "Palestine," Vol. 8, pp. 361–373; "Rumania," Vol. 9, pp. 247–265; "Russia," Vol. 9, pp. 278–286; "Abba Hillel Silver," Vol. 9, pp. 536–537; "Stephen S. Wise," Vol. 10, pp. 543–544; "Zionism," Vol. 10, pp. 645–667.

SUGGESTED ACTIVITIES

1. As though you were Rabbi Stephen S. Wise, prepare a speech proposing changes in the

Reform Judaism of 1935. What response would you give if you were Kaufmann Kohler?

2. Have the class conduct a meeting of the Central Conference of American Rabbis to consider changes in the Pittsburgh Platform for the Reform movement today. What specific recommendations would your class have to offer?

3. Prepare a chart comparing the situation of the Reform movement in 1885, 1935, and today in terms of the following: (a) population of the Jews in the United States, (b) immigration of Jews to the United States, (c) nature and number of American Reform members, (d) major Reform practices, (e) major Reform beliefs, (f) Reform attitudes toward Jewish tradition, (g) Reform views on Palestine, and (h) current Reform problems. On the basis of your findings, prepare an article summarizing some of the major changes that have taken place.

SUBJECTS FOR RESEARCH

1. What activities of personal diplomacy did Theodor Herzl carry out to achieve his objectives? Why didn't they succeed?

2. What forms of antagonism developed between the so-called "German" and "Russian" Jews in America? What effect did this have upon the development of Judaism in the United States?

3. What attitude did the socialist-minded Jews from Eastern Europe take toward Judaism? How, then, did they express their identification with Jews in the United States?

4. How did the German National Socialist Party originate and why did it gain wide support? What efforts did the Jews of Germany make to combat it? Why did they fail?

5. What roles did Rabbis Stephen S. Wise and Abba Hillel Silver play in the establishment of

the State of Israel? To what extent did they and their fellow Zionists see in a Jewish Palestine something more than simply a "haven of refuge" for persecuted Jews?

FILMSTRIPS TO SEE

If You Will It—The Life and Work of Theodor Herzl (Jewish Agency), presenting the highlights of the life and activities of the founder of modern Zionism.

Rabbi Stephen S. Wise: A Twentieth Century Prophet (UAHC), picturing the role and achievements of this leading modern Reform rabbi.

Dr. Leo Baeck: Man of Faith (UAHC), describing the experiences of this great German Jewish spiritual hero of the Nazi period.

300 Years: Memorable Events in American Jewish History (UAHC), depicting the major happenings in the background of the American Jew.

Jews in the Soviet Union, in two parts (UAHC), portraying modern Jewish life in Russia against the background of the past.

A LIVE ISSUE

In recent years, the Reform movement has become much more involved in social action. To a large extent, as we shall see, this was encouraged by the greater emphasis on social justice and peace of the Guiding Principles of Reform Judaism, adopted in 1937.

Though Reform Jews are in general agreement with the social ideals of their faith, controversy arises from time to time over a particular stand the movement may take in translating them into reality, as for example in connection with foreign policy or civil rights. Some claim that this goes beyond the bounds of religion and intrudes in areas that should be left up to the individual's conscience.

The Basic Problem: The fundamental question, then, concerns the role of religion in social issues. Some maintain that Reform Judaism's task is chiefly to determine the broad ethical goals for which the individual and society should strive. But others insist that this is inadequate since, to be effective, religious ideals must be converted into ac-

tion. Hence, they defend the movement's right to support specific measures of political, economic, and social reform.

Some Important Questions: (1) What justification is there for religion in general and Reform Judaism in particular to involve itself in political, economic, and social issues? (2) What is the proper role of the Reform movement in matters of social action? (3) Should it confine itself chiefly to broad statements of ethical principle and leave their application up to the individual? (4) Or should it express its support for particular reforms and take whatever action is necessary to secure them? (5) How best, too, can the movement deal with differences of opinion among its members over social issues?

What Do You Think? As you read over the material dealing with social justice and the statements of the Guiding Principles, bear these questions in mind. What conclusions do you come to about Reform Judaism's role in social action?

16. REFORM ADOPTS ITS GUIDING PRINCIPLES

An Appeal for Caution

Tall, erect, and white-haired, Rabbi David Philipson, then seventy-three, was an impressive figure as he stood before his colleagues of the Central Conference of American Rabbis in June of 1935 and reminisced about the historic meeting in Pittsburgh. He recalled how the platform was adopted and some of the reactions to it, including the criticism of the Conservatives to which his revered teacher and friend, Isaac M. Wise, published this reply in *The American Israelite:*

> . . . **The future of American Judaism belongs to the men of those very principles which were announced in the Pittsburgh Conference. Be not mistaken, gentlemen, there is only one way backward and that leads to the grave. We live in a young country and have entered upon a new phase of public life; we must advance; we must prepare the forms of Judaism for posterity, for the world about us.**

Now, fifty years later, said Philipson, some were convinced that the Pittsburgh Platform was outmoded and needed to be revised or even repudiated. That, he said, was for the conference to decide, but he cautioned:

> . . . **Whatever is done let it be done with deliberation and with a deep consciousness of our responsibility as the heirs of a great liberal tradition and as the instruments of a continuing revelation of God's truth with the passing of time. Let us beware lest we listen to the siren voices of sentimental reactionism or the advocacy of a political [Zionist] program.**

1936 and the Draft of a New Platform

When the conference reconvened the following year, word was out that a special Commission to Redraft the Principles of Judaism had been appointed and that it was ready to report on a draft it called the Guiding Principles of Reform Judaism.

Two days after the convention began, the president introduced the subject. The commission, he said, had encountered considerable difficulty because of conflicting points of view, especially over Zionism. Some, he added, also opposed the very idea of adopting a new platform for fear that it might crystallize Reform at that stage in its development. Nevertheless, he went on, the commission had succeeded in producing a draft, which he now asked the chairman, Rabbi Samuel Cohon, a professor at the Hebrew Union College, to present.

The document that the chairman then read was divided into three main sections. The first and longest described Reform's essential beliefs and concentrated upon its view of God, man, and the Jewish people. In connection with the Jewish people, it stressed both the need for unity and support for Palestine as "a haven for the oppressed" and "a Jewish cultural and spiritual center."

The second section dealt with Jewish ethics, relating them to both the individual and society. The document then concluded with a section devoted entirely to Reform practice that emphasized the observance of the Sabbath and holidays; worship and ceremonies in home and synagogue; more intensive Jewish education; and greater cultivation of Hebrew, Jewish symbols, music, and art.

The heated discussion that followed brought out some of the main differences between the commission's draft and the Pittsburgh Platform. Not only was it much longer and far more detailed, but it also grappled with certain problems that had not existed fifty years before. The chairman said:

> Since 1885 . . . a radical shift has taken place in the realm of thought. American Jewish life has grown in complexity. New problems press upon us. We have people to guide and we cannot guide them by convictions which we have outgrown in part.

Moreover, he added, the new principles approached Reform from a more moderate position than the Pittsburgh Platform and tried consciously to avoid attacking other interpretations of Judaism.

As the discussion continued, it was evident that the rabbis were far from agreed on either the need for a new platform or the particular draft the commission had drawn up, and the debate went on far into the night. Finally the conference endorsed the proposal to produce a new platform and instructed the commission to revise its draft.

PROFESSOR SAMUEL COHON. Member of the faculty of the Hebrew Union College, he served as chairman of the committee that produced the Guiding Principles. (HUC, American Jewish Archives)

Reform Gets a New Platform

By the time the rabbis gathered in Columbus, Ohio, the following June, the commission had completed its work. During the course of the year, it had solicited opinions from every member of the conference and considered not only many individual suggestions but two additional sets of principles drafted by others. Then, at the second session of the 1937 Convention, the chairman of the commission moved that the revised version of the Guiding Principles of Reform Judaism be adopted.

Many members immediately voiced their objection. A few still argued against adopting any new platform whatsoever, and some preferred one of the other sets of principles that had been rejected by the commission. However, the greatest opposition came from those who considered the section on Palestine too "Zionistic."

As the debate moved to a close, a substitute motion was introduced to thank the commission for its work but to refrain from adopting any platform. However, before the results of the vote could be announced, the president adjourned the meeting for lunch. When the members reassembled, he announced that the vote had been 81 to 81. "I am going to break the tie," he said, "by voting against the motion that would prevent us from adopting a new platform."

The convention now proceeded to consider each statement of the Guiding Principles, and it approved all of them with only minor changes. Rabbi David Philipson then arose and moved that the new platform be accepted:

> Though I was not in favor of a new Declaration of Principles and there are certain things in it that do not please me, if the younger men of the Central Conference want it, I will move its adoption.

The motion was promptly passed. Reform finally had its new platform.

A Reaffirmation of Reform's Position

The Guiding Principles opened with the following brief preamble in which the rabbis reaffirmed Reform's position on religious change:

> In view of the changes that have taken place in the modern world and the consequent need of stating anew the teachings of Reform Judaism, the Central Conference of American Rabbis makes the following declaration of principles. It presents them not as a fixed creed but as a guide for the progressive elements of Jewry.

Thus the movement acknowledged that the twentieth century had produced dramatic changes and that its belief in the developmental character of Judaism compelled it to provide a set of principles that would relate to the new and different circumstances of the times, thereby enabling the modern Jew to live by his faith.

Yet, in line with the liberal character of Reform, the Guiding Principles were in no sense to be considered a "creed," or set of beliefs and practices binding upon each member. As the very name signified, they were to serve merely as a "guide," retaining freedom of conscience for each individual.

Then, in keeping with the original draft, the three principal sections dealing with the movement's beliefs, ethics, and practices followed.

JEWISH RALLY AT MADISON SQUARE PARK. It was held to compel the opening of Palestine, then under British control, for the rescue of Hungarian Jews. (Photoworld)

MAP OF REFORM·DEVELOPMENTS IN AMERICA

THE CCAR ORGANIZED
IN 1889
DETROIT

"GUIDING PRINCIPLES"
ADOPTED IN 1937
COLUMBUS

ORGANIZATION OF A
REFORM SOCIETY IN 1858

SINAI CONGREGATION
FORMED IN 1861
CHICAGO

ADOPTION OF REFORM BY
2 CONGREGATIONS, 1854-1855
•
OPENING OF ZION COLLEGE
IN 1855
•
FORMATION OF THE UAHC
IN 1873
•
FOUNDING OF THE HUC
IN 1875
CINCINNATI

PHILADELPHIA

ADOPTION OF REFORM
BY THE KENESETH ISRAEL
CONGREGATION IN 1856
•
PHILADELPHIA RABBIN-
ICAL CONFERENCE
1869

BALTIMORE

ORGANIZATION OF A REFORM
SOCIETY IN 1842, LEADING
TO THE CREATION OF THE
HAR SINAI CONGREGATION

CLEVELAND CONFERENCE
OF 1855
•
FIRST MEETING OF THE
CCAR IN 1890
CLEVELAND

PITTSBURGH RABBINICAL
CONFERENCE OF 1885
PITTSBURGH

FORMATION OF A REFORM
CONGREGATION IN 1850
ALBANY

NEW YORK
FORMATION OF THE
EMANU-EL CONGREGATION
IN 1845
•
FIRST CONFIRMATION IN
THE U S IN 1846
•
JIR ORGANIZED IN 1922

CHARLESTON
ORGANIZATION OF A REFORM
SOCIETY IN 1824
•
BUILDING OF A TEMPLE
WITH AN ORGAN, 1841

The Guiding Principles of Reform

Part I: Judaism and Its Foundations

1. The Nature of Judaism

[Text]

NATURE OF JUDAISM: Judaism is the historical religious experience of the Jewish people. Though growing out of Jewish life, its message is universal aiming at the union and perfection of mankind under the sovereignty of God. Reform Judaism recognizes the principle of progressive development in religion and consciously applies this principle to spiritual as well as to cultural and social life.

Judaism welcomes all truth, whether written in the pages of Scripture or deciphered from the records of nature. The new discoveries of science, while replacing the older scientific views underlying our sacred literature, do not conflict with the essential spirit of religion as manifested in the consecration of man's will, heart, and mind to the service of God and of humanity.

[Digest]

Reform believes that Judaism:

a. is the product of the Jews' past,

b. develops through growth and change,

c. is concerned with the improvement of all people,

d. seeks to achieve God's Kingdom for mankind,

e. is in harmony with scientific truth, and

f. accepts the results of biblical science.

Here the Guiding Principles did not really differ from the Pittsburgh Platform. Both saw Judaism as the product of "progressive development" and considered its goal to be the establishment of God's Kingdom on earth. Neither found any conflict between Judaism's teachings and the discoveries of modern science or biblical research. But, as we shall see, the use of such expressions as "the Jewish people" and "our sacred literature" already hinted at certain striking differences in their respective points of view about the nature of the Jews and about tradition.

2. The Jewish Conception of God

[Text]	[Digest]
GOD: The heart of Judaism and its chief contribution to religion is the doctrine of the One, living God, who rules the world through law and love. In Him all existence has its creative source and mankind its ideal of conduct. Through transcending time and space, He is the indwelling Presence of the world. We worship Him as the Lord of the universe and as our merciful Father.	Holding belief in God to be central in Judaism and the Jew's great contribution to mankind, Reform conceives of Him as: a. one, just, and loving, b. the ruler and creator of all, c. the example and source of righteousness, and d. dwelling both in the world and beyond it.

Agreeing with the Pittsburgh Platform on the importance of the Jews' belief in God, the Guiding Principles gave it even greater emphasis. In part, this represented a reaction to the continuing conflict over science and religion and the rise of certain new atheistic philosophies, including communism. But it was also Reform's response to the growing influence of many secular American Jewish movements often in competition with religion, among them the Jewish Center and Zionism, as well as scores of fraternal, philanthropic, and self-protective organizations. Though recognizing their merit, Reform Judaism nevertheless felt compelled to stress both here and elsewhere the essential role of religion in Jewish life, centering upon belief in God.

3. Judaism's View of Man

[Text]

MAN: Judaism affirms that man is created in the divine image. His spirit is immortal. He is an active co-worker with God. As a child of God, he is endowed with moral freedom and is charged with the responsibility of overcoming evil and striving after ideal ends.

[Digest]

Reform believes that every person:

a. possesses the quality of Godliness,

b. is endowed with an everlasting soul,

c. is free to conduct himself for good or evil, and

d. as God's co-worker on earth, must constantly strive for the good.

Beyond referring to the immortality of the human soul, the Pittsburgh Platform had little to say about the nature and responsibilities of man, largely because in the 1880's progress seemed assured with the spread of democracy. But, by the middle 1930's, the world was witnessing the enslavement of more and more people to the will of the state under the corrupting and brutal regimes of fascism and communism. All the more urgent, therefore, was the Guiding Principles' reaffirmation of Judaism's belief in the sacredness of the individual, his right to make moral choices in life, and his need to do so.

4. The Nature of Torah

[Text]	[Digest]
TORAH: God reveals Himself not only in the majesty, beauty, and orderliness of nature but also in the vision and moral striving of the human spirit. Revelation is a continuous process, confined to no one group and to no one age. Yet the people of Israel, through its prophets and sages, achieved unique insight in the realm of religious truth.	Reform believes that the Torah is: a. one of the important ways by which God has revealed Himself to man,
The Torah, both written and oral, enshrines Israel's evergrowing consciousness of God and of the moral law. It preserves the historical precedents, sanctions, and norms of Jewish life and seeks to mould it in the patterns of goodness and of holiness.	b. a unique source of religious truth, c. composed of both biblical and rabbinic teachings,
Being products of historical processes, certain of its laws have lost their binding force with the passing of the conditions that called them forth. But as a depository of permanent spiritual ideals, the Torah remains the dynamic source of the life of Israel. Each age has the obligation to adapt the teachings of the Torah to its basic needs in consonance with the genius of Judaism.	d. the continuing source of the Jew's standards and ideals, and e. subject to reinterpretation and modification as new conditions arise.

In the process of rejecting Orthodoxy, the Pittsburgh Platform left the impression that Reform had abandoned all of the historic Jewish sources except the Bible. But fifty years more of Jewish experience in a menacing world brought new appreciation for the entire tradition and the conviction that both the Oral and Written Law had much to offer the modern Jew.

5. The Jewish People

[Text]

ISRAEL: Judaism is the soul of which Israel is the body. Living in all parts of the world, Israel has been held together by the ties of a common history and, above all, by the heritage of faith. Though we recognize in the group-loyalty of Jews who have become estranged from our religious tradition a bond which still unites them with us, we maintain that it is by its religion and for its religion that the Jewish people has lived. The non-Jew who accepts our faith is welcomed as a full member of the Jewish community.

In all lands where our people live, they assume and seek to share loyally the full duties and responsibilities of citizenship and to create seats of Jewish knowledge and religion. In the rehabilitation of Palestine, the land hallowed by memories and hopes, we behold the promise of renewed life for many of our brethren. We affirm the obligation of all Jewry to aid in its upbuilding as a Jewish homeland by endeavoring to make it not only a haven of refuge for the oppressed but also a center of Jewish culture and spiritual life.

Throughout the ages it has been Israel's mission to witness to the Divine in the face of every form of paganism and materialism. We regard it as our historic task to cooperate with all men in the establishment of the Kingdom of God, of universal brotherhood, justice, truth, and peace on earth. This is our messianic goal.

[Digest]

Reform believes that the Jews:

a. are a people united by many common ties,

b. have been preserved chiefly by their religion,

c. seek to be devoted citizens and faithful to Judaism wherever they live,

d. are obliged to assist in the upbuilding of Palestine, and

e. have a historic mission and messianic goal of establishing God's Kingdom on earth.

Whereas the Pittsburgh Platform had spoken of the Jews simply as a "religious community," the Guiding Principles now defined them as a "people" bound together by broad group loyalties. In so doing, the Reform Jew acknowledged his common identity with all Jews, the non-religious as well as those subscribing to other interpretations of Judaism. From this flowed his obligation to support the upbuilding of Palestine. Not only was it a humanitarian responsibility to desperate fellow Jews under the Nazis but, by the very ties that bound him to the whole Jewish people, it was his plain duty as a Jew.

251

Part II: Ethics

The second section of the Guiding Principles dealt with ethics, and here, too, it went into considerably more detail. The Pittsburgh Platform had merely issued a general plea for justice between rich and poor, but conditions a half-century later seemed to demand still greater social responsibilities on the part of Reform Jews. America was still plagued by many serious and unjust economic and social conditions; much of Europe was threatened by fascism and communism; and the world was again being menaced by war. The Guiding Principles reflected all this by insisting that the Reform Jew urgently address himself to the pressing social issues of the day as they concerned America and the world.

6. Reform and Ethics

[Text]

ETHICS AND RELIGION: In Judaism, religion and morality blend into an indissoluble unity. Seeking God means to strive after holiness, righteousness, and goodness. The love of God is incomplete without the love of one's fellow men.

Judaism emphasizes the kinship of the human race, the sanctity and worth of human life and personality, and the right of the individual to freedom and to the pursuit of his chosen vocation. Justice to all, irrespective of race, sect, or class, is the inalienable right and the inescapable obligation of all. The state and organized government exist in order to further these ends.

[Digest]

Reform believes that Jewish ethics:

a. grow directly out of the Jews' religion,

b. are indispensable in their worship of God,

c. stress concern for all human beings,

d. emphasize individual freedom and worth,

e. demand justice for all races, sects, and classes, and

f. require moral and ethical conduct by governments as well as individuals.

The condition of the sharecropper was a national scandal in 1937; so was the treatment of various minorities, including the Negro and those of Spanish descent in the Southwest. Even worse, however, was the situation of those who were enduring unspeakable tortures in the prisons and concentration camps of Italy, Germany, Poland, and Russia. In protest, the Guiding Principles insisted that this violated the elemental teachings of religion.

7. The Demands of Social Justice

[Text]

SOCIAL JUSTICE: Judaism seeks the attainment of a just society by the application of its teachings to the economic order, to industry and commerce, and to national and international affairs. It aims at the elimination of man-made misery and suffering, of poverty and degradation, of tyranny and slavery, of social inequality and prejudice, of ill will and strife.

It advocates the promotion of harmonious relations between warring classes on the basis of equity and justice and the creation of conditions under which human personality may flourish. It pleads for the safeguarding of childhood against exploitation. It champions the cause of all who work and of their right to an adequate standard of living, as prior to the rights of property.

Judaism emphasizes the duty of charity and strives for a social order which will protect men against the material disabilities of old age, sickness, and unemployment.

[Digest]

Reform holds that social justice demands:

a. the application of religious ethics to economic, national, and international conditions,

b. the elimination of poverty, tyranny, and prejudice,

c. the maintenance of fairness and justice to every group,

d. an adequate standard of living for all,

e. the practice of charity, and

f. special protection for children, the aged, and the ill.

The effects of the Great Depression of 1929 had lingered on. About fifteen million American wage-earners were still without work, and more than one-third of the nation lacked adequate food, shelter, and clothing. From the standpoint of Judaism, declared the Guiding Principles, that these and other social ills should exist in the wealthiest nation on earth was indefensible.

253

8. The Necessity for Peace

[Text]

PEACE: Judaism, from the days of the prophets, has proclaimed to mankind the ideal of universal peace. The spiritual and physical disarmament of all nations has been one of its essential teachings. It abhors all violence and relies upon moral education, love, and sympathy to secure human progress. It regards justice as the foundation of the well-being of nations and the condition of enduring peace. It urges organized international action for disarmament, collective security, and world peace.

[Digest]

Reform believes in the establishment of world peace through:

a. moral education and sympathy for humanity,

b. abhorrence of all violence,

c. disarmament,

d. justice among the nations, and

e. international organization to prevent war.

By now, the League of Nations had shown itself powerless to halt the aggression of the three Axis powers. Japan had invaded Manchuria and China; Italy was attacking Ethiopia; and, in addition to supporting the fascist forces in Spain, Hitler Germany was threatening to overrun Austria, Czechoslovakia, and Poland. Gradually the Western democracies were beginning to realize the peril, but they were still hopeful that somehow World War II could be avoided because the development of new weapons on both sides, notably heavy bombers, promised frightful devastation of cities, with enormous loss of life.

Only in connection with the Messianic Age had the Pittsburgh Platform even mentioned peace, but, to a world seemingly on the brink of war, it was clearly a matter of immediate and desperate concern.

Part III: Religious Practice

Religious practice was the subject of the third and final section of the Guiding Principles, indicating the profound change that had taken place within the movement during the previous half-century.

However, fifty years of American Jewish life had taken their toll, and by 1937 assimilation had become a serious problem. Belief alone had proved incapable of preserving the Reform Jew, and religious practice, together with other forms of Jewish activity, seemed urgently needed to promote a stronger sense of Jewish identification and deeper emotional attachment to Judaism.

9. Religious Practice

[Text]

THE RELIGIOUS LIFE: Jewish life is marked by consecration to these ideals of Judaism. It calls for faithful participation in the life of the Jewish community as it finds expression in home, synagogue, and school, and in all other agencies that enrich Jewish life and promote its welfare.

The home has been and must continue to be a stronghold of Jewish life, hallowed by the spirit of love and reverence, by moral discipline and religious observance and worship.

The synagogue is the oldest and most democratic institution in Jewish life. It is the prime communal agency by which Judaism is fostered and preserved. It links the Jews of each community and unites them with all Israel.

The perpetuation of Judaism as a living force depends upon religious knowledge and upon the education of each new generation in our rich cultural and spiritual heritage.

Prayer is the voice of religion, the language of faith and aspiration. It directs man's heart and mind Godward, voices the needs and hopes of the community, and reaches out after goals which invest life with supreme value. To deepen the spiritual life of our people, we must cultivate the traditional habit of communion with God through prayer in both home and synagogue.

Judaism as a way of life requires, in addition to its moral and spiritual demands, the preservation of the Sabbath, festivals, and holy days, the retention and development of such customs, symbols, and ceremonies as possess inspirational value, the cultivation of distinctive forms of religious art and music and the use of Hebrew, together with the vernacular, in our worship and instruction.

[Digest]

Essential to the preservation of Jewish life are the following religious demands:

a. participation in the Jewish community,

b. religious observance and morality in the home,

c. worship and full participation in synagogue activity,

d. sound religious education,

e. observance of the Sabbath and Jewish holidays,

f. religious customs, symbols, and ceremonies,

g. religious art and music, and

h. Hebrew in worship and study.

A Comparison of the Pittsburgh Platform		
	The Pittsburgh Platform—1885	**The Guiding Principles—1937**
Jewish Tradition	Judaism is a developing religion and, though it must preserve its connection with the past, it no longer regards all of biblical or rabbinical law as binding.	Reform recognizes that Judaism is a developing religion in which the Written and Oral Law must be adapted to the needs of each generation.
Judaism's God-Idea	Judaism presents the highest conception of God.	Central to the Jewish faith and its most important contribution to religion is its conception of God.
The Jewish People	Jews are no longer a nation but a religious community.	Jews are bound together by common history and religion, and the non-religious among them must still be considered members of the Jewish people.
The Mission of Israel	Jewry welcomes the aid of other faiths in helping to fulfill its mission of bringing the teachings of the one God to all mankind.	The Jews' mission is to bring to all people knowledge of God and, in cooperation with them, to achieve the establishment of the Messianic Age.
Messianic Belief	Reform no longer expects the coming of a personal Messiah but believes that the approaching Messianic Age of truth, justice, and peace must be achieved by all mankind.	In cooperation with all peoples, the Jews seek to establish a Messianic Age of justice, truth, and peace upon earth.
Palestine	A return of the Jews to Palestine is not sought.	All Jews should aid in the rebuilding of Palestine as the Jewish homeland.

The Guiding Principles concluded with the following appeal to all Jews to renew their devotion to Judaism and its goal of establishing God's Kingdom on earth:

> These timeless aims and ideals of our faith we present anew to a confused and troubled world. We call upon our fellow Jews to rededicate themselves to them and, in harmony with all men, hopefully and courageously to continue Israel's eternal quest after God and His Kingdom.

Catastrophe for European Jewry

The world events that have taken place since their adoption demonstrate the soundness of the Guiding Principles.

The most immediate was the catastrophe that befell the Jews of Europe as Nazi anti-Semitism engulfed one European country after another. First came the sudden German occupation of Austria and portions of Czechoslovakia. Then, on September 1, 1939, the Nazis invaded Poland and, when Great Britain

256

and the Guiding Principles

	The Pittsburgh Platform—1885	The Guiding Principles—1937
The Hereafter	Reform rejects all notions of heavenly rewards, punishments in hell, and resurrection. Rather, it believes only in the immortality of the soul.	Man possesses an immortal soul.
Judaism and Science	Judaism and science are not in conflict, and biblical stories of miracles and the like are simply legends of earlier times.	Judaism welcomes all truth, and the discoveries of modern science are not in conflict with its essential teachings.
Religious Practice	All laws regulating diet, dress, and priestly purity are abolished, and only those observances in keeping with modern life are to be maintained.	Jews are expected to maintain a Jewish home and participate fully in the activities of the synagogue, religious school, and Jewish community. The practice of Judaism also demands prayer, observance of the Sabbath and holidays, symbols and ceremonies, and the use of Hebrew.
Social Justice	It is the duty of the Jew to participate in regulating the relations between rich and poor on the basis of justice and righteousness.	Judaism strives for a just society in which unemployment, poverty, tyranny, slavery, and hatred are abolished and children, the aged, and ill are protected.
World Peace		Judaism seeks a peaceful world founded on justice and strives for strong international organization to prevent war.

and France came to its aid, World War II was launched. Within a year the Germans had conquered Norway, Denmark, Holland, Belgium, Luxemburg, and France, and the very next year, while their air force was savagely battering England, they invaded Russia.

Most of the Jews of Europe were now in Nazi hands. Step by step, they reduced the Jews to beggary and starvation, and then they began what Hitler termed "the final solution of the Jewish problem," the secret and systematic extermination of every European Jew.

The Jews of each community were rounded up, and some were immediately mowed down by machine guns in front of huge pits into which their bodies fell. Most, however, were shipped off in freight cars to concentration camps where they were either beaten, starved, or worked to death, or exterminated by poison gas, with their bodies burned in huge ovens. In all, between four-and-a-half and six million Jews were eventually destroyed.

As word of the mass exterminations leaked out, Jews everywhere made frenzied efforts to rescue as many as possible, raising huge sums of money to ransom them from the Nazis and transport them to safety. But most countries, including the United States, were reluctant to accept them. Palestine, where the Jewish homeland was being developed by the British under the supervision of the League of Nations, seemed the only answer, but restrictions now adopted by the British government enabled only a limited number to enter.

The Establishment of the State of Israel

By the outbreak of World War II, Palestine had already endured more than twenty years of violence at the hands of Arab nationalists who objected to the establishment of a Jewish homeland. Now, encouraged by Hitler, they engaged in widespread rioting and murder. Meanwhile, several attempts on the part of the British to partition the country had failed, and, in an effort to appease the Arabs, they decided to limit all further Jewish immigration to a total of 75,000.

As a result, the Jews of Palestine were caught in a dilemma. On the one hand, they were compelled to support the British in warding off the Nazis who were sweeping through North Africa and threatening the Suez Canal and Palestine itself. But, on the other hand, they were also determined to resist the policies of the British that would shut off immigration to hundreds of thousands of Jews facing extermination. So, while joining with the British forces in defending the Middle East against the Germans and their Arab collaborators, the Jews of Palestine also managed to smuggle in thousands of so-called "illegal" immigrants despite the blockade designed to prevent it.

Meanwhile, except for a small minority of anti-Zionists who formed the American Council for Judaism in 1943, the Reform move-

ment overwhelmingly supported the Jews of Palestine. A considerable number became actively identified with Zionist organizations, and many more contributed to the aid of Palestinian Jewry through the United Jewish Appeal and other fund-raising efforts.

With the end of World War II, "illegal" immigration to Palestine was stepped up to rescue a quarter of a million survivors languishing in the refugee camps of Europe. The violent reaction of the Arabs convinced the British that they could no longer cope with the situation. They now turned over control of Palestine to the newly-formed United Nations which, despite bitter Arab opposition, finally voted to partition the country. Thus, on May 14, 1948, as the British forces were leaving and Egyptian fighter-bombers flew menacingly overhead, the Jews proclaimed the establishment of the State of Israel. Immediately, the armies of five Arab countries launched an attack on the Jews, promising to drive them into the Mediterranean. Fighting largely with only crude weapons, the Jews finally repulsed them and forced them to plead for an armistice.

Though Arab terrorism has continued and the Jews have had to fight three wars for survival, the State of Israel has nevertheless flourished. By 1967, the year in which it amazed the world by its brilliant six-day victory over Egypt, Syria, and Jordan, it had a Jewish population of more than two million who enjoyed an expanding industrial economy and a highly creative Hebrew culture.

New Responsibilities for American Jewry

After World War II, little of Jewish life remained in most of Central and Eastern Europe. In Germany, no more than thirty thousand Jews survived; in Poland, only about twenty thousand, and half that number in Austria.

The nearly two and a half million in the Soviet Union were also rapidly being assimilated under official Communist Party policy that closed most of the synagogues, forbade religious instruction of the young, and prohibited Jews from associating with world Jewish causes, including Zionism.

Thus, the only remaining major centers of Jewish life were in Israel and the United States. However, in the 1950's and 1960's the State of Israel had numerous problems of its own, chief among which was the continuing hostility of the Arab world, the pacification of those in its expanded territory, and the absorption of many thousands of poverty-stricken and culturally-deprived Jewish refugees from Arab lands.

As a result, American Jewry found itself called upon to accept many new responsibilities. Reform Jews were soon playing a leading role in promoting the United Jewish Appeal, Bonds for Israel, and many other causes, as well as undertaking specific projects of their own in Israel, including the planting of several forests, the maintenance of the Leo Baeck High School in Haifa, and the operation of the Hebrew Union College Biblical and Archaeological School in Jerusalem.

With European Jewish life largely destroyed, the American Jewish community was also thrown upon its own resources for survival, prompting it to expend much greater energy toward raising the general level of Jewish knowledge and culture. Thus, the Reform movement intensified its own program of religious education with the expansion of the use of Hebrew, the introduction of additional religious school classes during the week, full high school programs, youth group summer camp activities, and a far greater number of courses for adults.

Moreover, in keeping with the Guiding Principles, it embarked upon developing deeper Jewish commitment on the part of its members through more religious observance.

The extent to which this has been carried out is quite evident when we analyze the practices of the Reform Jew today.

QUESTIONS FOR DISCUSSION

1. How do you account for the opposition of certain Reform rabbis to the adoption of the Guiding Principles? What were their major arguments? How did those in favor of the Guiding Principles reply to them and why?

2. Where did the Guiding Principles reaffirm the basic doctrines of the Pittsburgh Platform? In what ways were the two platforms different? How do you account for this?

3. Why did the rabbis at both Pittsburgh and Columbus insist upon belief in God as central in Judaism? Do you agree? Why? How do you explain the differences in the two statements concerning God?

4. How do the Pittsburgh and Columbus platforms differ in connection with: (a) the value of Jewish tradition? (b) the concept of a Jewish people? (c) the objectives of social justice? (d) Reform religious practice? (e) Jewish resettlement in Palestine? How do you account for this?

5. In what respect does your congregation follow the Guiding Principles? Where does it differ? To what extent do events since 1937 account for this?

6. What provisions of the Guiding Principles would you retain today? Which would you revise and why? What major changes would you suggest in the Guiding Principles to bring them up to date?

SIGNIFICANT DOCUMENTS

A Survivor's Description of a Nazi Extermination Camp in Treblinka, Poland, 1942

As a rule, two transports arrive daily: one in the morning and one toward evening.

NAZI TROOPS MARCHING. (From European)

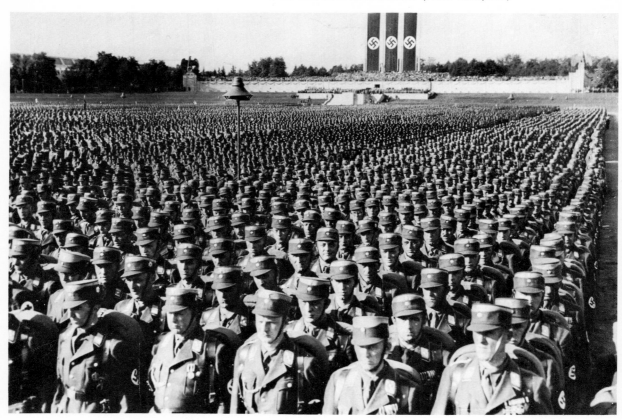

NAZIS PARADE BEFORE HITLER. They are at the Nuremburg stadium. (Photoworld)

BERLIN JEWS ARRESTED. Taken by Nazi police. (Keystone)

PRISONERS. Inmates of a German concentration camp. (From European)

CREMATORIA. These furnaces were designed for disposing of human bodies at Buchenwald. (Keystone)

CLEANING STREETS. Here Jewish children in Galicia are compelled to clean the streets. Note the Austrian soldiers overseeing the work. (Photoworld)

LIBERATED INMATES. These are freed prisoners from a Gestapo concentration camp. (Photoworld)

GERMAN CONCENTRATION CAMP. Here former union leaders and people in professions were imprisoned. (From European)

At the height of the "action," several transports arrived daily. Each train consists of a few score freight cars. Part of the cars halt at the siding directly across from the arrival square, while the remaining cars are shifted to the side to wait until the first part is taken care of.

The cars are quickly emptied. The tortured and greatly excited human throng breathe with relief when let out on the square. They are immediately taken over by the Jewish auxiliary guard, headed by the *kapos* [Jewish overseers], who give them orders in Yiddish. The women and children are told to enter the barracks immediately, while the men remain in the square.

Looking around, they see a high pillar with a poster bearing a large inscription: "*Achtung Warschauer*" (Attention, People of Warsaw), despite the fact that transports of Jews from many other towns of the [Polish] general government, from Germany, and the states of Western Europe are also brought to Treblinka. "Do not worry about your fate"—continues the poster—"you are all going eastward for work; you will work and your wives will take care of your households. Before leaving, however, you have to take a bath and your clothing must be disinfected. You have to deposit your valuables and money with the cashier, for which you will get receipts. After the bath and disinfection, you will receive everything back undamaged."

In the first period of murder in Treblinka, an S. S. [Nazi storm trooper] officer with an angelic, confidence-inspiring face used to come to the square and deliver a speech along the same lines to those assembled. When, however, transports began to arrive from various parts and the crowds had to be liquidated quickly, the Germans cancelled that speech as superfluous.

To make the Jews believe that actual classification according to trades would take place at the arrival square, in order to assign occupational groups for labor, they posted small signs with inscriptions: tailors, shoemakers, carpenters, etc. It goes without saying that no such segregation ever took place.

The *kapos* quickly arrange the men in rows of ten, asking them to take off their shoes, undress completely, and prepare for a bath. Everybody is permitted to take along a piece of soap and his documents. In the meantime the sorting service men take away the clothing to the sorting place. Women and children also have to undress completely.

Then comes the last act of the Treblinka tragedy. The terrorized mass of men, women, and children starts on its road to death. At the head, a group of women and children is driven, beaten by the accompanying Germans, whips in hands. Ever quicker the group is driven; ever heavier blows fall upon the heads of the women, mad with fear and suffering. The cries and laments of the women, together with the shouts and curses of the Germans, shatter the silence of the forest. The people finally realize that they are going to their death.

At the entrance of Death House No. 1 the chief himself stands, a whip in his hand; in cold blood, beating them, he drives the women into the chambers. The floors of the chambers are slippery. The people slip and fall; they cannot get up any more for new groups of forcibly driven victims fall upon them. The chief throws small children into the chambers over the heads of the women. When the execution chambers are filled to the brim, the doors are sealed and the slow strangulation of live persons by the steam issuing from the numerous vents in the pipes begins. In the beginning, stifled cries penetrate to the outside. Gradually they quiet down, and fifteen minutes later the execution is complete.

Now comes the gravediggers' [also Jews] turn. Shouting and cursing, the German overseers drive the diggers to work, which consists of getting the bodies out of the execution chambers. The gravediggers stand at the troughs near the valves. The valves open, but not a body falls out. Due to the steam all the bodies have been fused into a homogeneous mass cemented together with the perspiration of the victims. In their death agonies, arms, legs, trunks intertwine into a large, macabre entanglement.

To make it possible for the gravediggers to get out individual bodies, cold water from the nearby well is poured over that mass. Then one body separates from another and may be taken out. As a rule, the surfaces of the bodies are not deformed; only the faces and buttocks are purple. The gravediggers, constantly beaten and driven by the Germans, place the corpses in the troughs until the chambers are empty. The bodies lie piled up like slaughtered cattle; now the burying takes place.

Formerly (during the first half of August), the gravediggers had hand-carts to convey the bodies to the ditches, which had to be done at top speed. Lately, however, the chief disposed of that facility. *Ein Mann—zwei Leichen* (one man—two corpses), meaning that each gravedigger has to bury two corpses. He ties legs or arms of the body with the belt from his trousers and, running, pulls the body from the trough to the ditches, throws it in, and, again running, has to return for the next load.

Formerly, the graves were right at the death house so that the burying of corpses could take place quickly. As new victims were added, the grave-line moved ever further to the east and pulling the corpses to their place of eternal rest now takes longer. After a ditch is filled, the gravediggers quickly cover the bodies with earth and the digging machine nearby is already preparing the next ditch for the dead . . .

> —From Marie Syrkin,
> *Blessed Is the Match,*
> pp. 163–166.

On Reform Judaism and Palestine, 1943–1949

1. Resolutions on Zionism Adopted by the Central Conference of American Rabbis, 1943

RESOLUTION I

In 1935 at its Chicago Convention, the Central Conference of American Rabbis declared that it would take no official stand on Zionism. It decided that it was to be the prerogative of individual members to determine for themselves, within the framework of Reform Judaism, what their point of view on this subject might be. This was and is a salutary policy and should be continued.

Of late, however, some of our members have renewed the assertion that Zionism is not compatible with Reform Judaism. The attempt has been made to set in irreconcilable opposition "universalism" and "particularism." To the members of the Conference [as it is often called], this appears unreal and misleading. Without impugning the right of members of the Conference to be opposed to Zionism, for whatever reason they may choose, the Conference declares that it discerns no essential incompatibility between Reform Judaism and Zionism, no reason why those of its members who give allegiance to Zionism should not have the right to regard themselves as fully within the spirit and purpose of Reform Judaism.

RESOLUTION II

While members of the CCAR [Central Conference of American Rabbis] are fully within their rights in espousing whatever philosophy of Jewish life they may accept, nevertheless the American Council for Judaism, because of the special circumstances under which it came into being, has already endangered the unity of the Conference. Its continued existence would become a growing threat to our fellowship.

The American Council for Judaism was founded by members of the CCAR for the purpose of combating Zionism. The Zionist movement and masses of Jews everywhere, shocked by the rise of this organization at a time when Zionists and others are laboring hard to have the gates of Palestine reopened for the harassed Jews of Europe, could not avoid judging this event in the light of past controversies or seeing in it an example of what they had come to consider the constant opposition of Reform Judaism to Zionist aspirations. This impression does grave injustice to the many devoted Zionists in the CCAR and to the Conference itself.

Therefore, without impugning the right of Zionists or non-Zionists to express and to disseminate their convictions within and without the Conference, we, in the spirit of amity, urge our colleagues of the American Council for Judaism to terminate this organization.

—From the *Central Conference of American Rabbis Yearbook,* Vol. 53 (1943), pp. 92–94.

2. Declaration Establishing the State of Israel, 1948

PROCLAMATION OF THE STATE OF ISRAEL

The Land of Israel was the birthplace of the Jewish people. Here their spiritual, religious, and national identity was formed. Here they achieved independence and created a culture of national and universal significance. Here they wrote and gave the Bible to the world.

Exiled from Palestine, the Jewish people remained faithful to it in all the countries of their dispersion, never ceasing to pray and hope for their return and the restoration of their national freedom.

Impelled by this historic association, Jews strove throughout the centuries to go back to the land of their fathers and regain their statehood. In recent decades they returned in their masses. They reclaimed the wilderness, revived their language, built cities and villages, and established a vigorous and ever-growing community, with its own economic and cultural life. They sought peace yet were prepared to defend themselves. They brought the blessings of progress to all inhabitants of the country.

In the year 1897 the First Zionist Congress, inspired by Theodor Herzl's vision of the Jewish state, proclaimed the right of the Jewish people to national revival in their own country.

This right was acknowledged by the Balfour Declaration of November 2, 1917, and reaffirmed by the Mandate of the League of Nations, which gave explicit international recognition to the historic connection of the Jewish people with Palestine and their right to reconstitute their national home.

The Nazi holocaust which engulfed millions of Jews in Europe proved anew the urgency of the reestablishment of the Jewish state, which would solve the problem of Jewish homelessness by opening the gates to all Jews and lifting the Jewish people to equality in the family of nations.

The survivors of the European catastrophe, as well as Jews from other lands, proclaiming their right to a life of dignity, freedom, and labor and undeterred by hazards, hardships, and obstacles, have tried unceasingly to enter Palestine.

In the Second World War the Jewish people in Palestine made a full contribution in the struggle of the freedom-loving nations against the Nazi evil. The sacrifices of their soldiers and the efforts of their workers gained them title to rank with the peoples who founded the United Nations.

On November 29, 1947, the General Assembly of the United Nations adopted a resolution for the establishment of an independent Jewish state in Palestine and called upon inhabitants of the country to take such steps as may be necessary on their part to put the plan into effect.

This recognition by the United Nations of the right of the Jewish people to establish their independent state may not be revoked. It is, moreover, the self-evident right of the Jewish people to be a nation, like all other nations, in its own sovereign state.

Accordingly, we, the members of the National Council, representing the Jewish people in Palestine and the Zionist movement of the world, met together in solemn assembly today, the day of the termination of the British Mandate for Palestine, and by virtue of the natural and historic right of the Jewish people and of the resolution of the General Assembly of the United Nations, hereby proclaim the establishment of the Jewish state in Palestine to be called Israel.

We hereby declare that as from the termination of the mandate at midnight, this night of the 14th to 15th of May 1948, and until the setting up of the duly elected bodies of the state in accordance with a constitution, to be drawn up by a Constituent Assembly not later than the first day of October 1948, the present National Council shall act as the Provisional State Council and its executive organ, the National Administration, shall constitute the Provisional Government of the State of Israel.

The State of Israel will be open to the immigration of Jews from all countries of their dispersion; will promote the development of the country for the benefit of all its inhabitants; will be based on the precepts of liberty, justice, and peace taught by the Hebrew prophets; will uphold the full social and political equality of all its citizens, without distinction of race, creed, or sex; will guarantee full freedom of conscience, worship, education, and culture; will safeguard the sanctity and inviolability of the shrines and holy places of all religions; and will dedicate itself to the principles of the Charter of the United Nations.

The State of Israel will be ready to cooperate with the organs and representatives of the United Nations in the implementation of the Resolution of the Assembly of November 29, 1947, and will take steps to bring about the economic union over the whole of Palestine.

We appeal to the United Nations to assist the Jewish people in the building of its state and to admit Israel into the family of nations.

In the midst of wanton aggressions, we yet call upon the Arab inhabitants of the State of Israel to return to the ways of peace and play their part in the development of the state, with full and equal citizenship and due representation in all its bodies and institutions, provisional or permanent.

We offer peace and amity to all the neighboring states and their peoples and invite them to cooperate with the independent Jewish nation for the common good of all. The State of Israel is ready to contribute its full share to the peaceful progress and development of the Middle East.

Our call goes out to the Jewish people all over the world to rally to our side in the task of immigration and development and to stand by us in the great struggle for the fulfillment of the dream of generations —the redemption of Israel.

With trust in Almighty God, we set our hand to this declaration, at this session of the Provisional State Council, in the city of Tel Aviv, on this Sabbath eve, the fifth of *Iyar* [אִיָּיר, the eighth Hebrew month], 5708, the fourteenth day of May, 1948.

Provisional Council of the
Government of Israel

A Noted Reform Rabbi's Observations on the New Emphases in Worship, 1949

. . . Many of us believe that our synagogues and our homes must be illumined with more Jewish pageantry and drama and prayer and thrilling festival celebration, because these constitute the cement that keeps a religious community together. More Hebrew, more poetry, more congregational singing, more lay participation in the service: these are emotional techniques dictated by the discoveries of individual and social psychologists—practitioners of reason in our day . . .

. . . The ideals of religion are abstract, noble, universal. It is the language of the prayers and the ceremonies of the sanctuary and the home which can give Jews and Jewesses a feeling of participation and can impart a unique color to their shared life. Reform Judaism in the future must not depend upon theology or morality alone. We are wise in introducing dramatic pageantry, music, and art into the synagogue because man is not merely a reasoning but also a feeling creature. Unlike Orthodox Jews, we do not view the past as entirely sacred. We look upon it as a treasure chest in which are contained wonderful jewels and some old and useless remnants. We choose the jewels and discard the relics. We clothe the naked bones of ideal and doctrine with the radiant flesh of pageantry and practice.

Reform Judaism has been psychologically unwise not only with regard to ritual but also with reference to discipline. It has

RABBI JOSHUA LOTH LIEBMAN. One of Reform's gifted leaders, a brilliant orator and writer, he served Temple Israel in Boston. (Solari, Boston, Mass.)

been too often like an open prairie exposed to all the winds of anarchy and license. No religion can survive with vitality unless it presents to its worshipers a minimum code of conduct which binds the group together into a disciplined fellowship. We do not want a creed of belief so much as a pattern of action. We desire not coercion but persuasion—wise, self-chosen discipline which will make Reform Judaism understandable and meaningful in the realms of worship, study, and action.

—From Joshua L. Liebman,
''New Trends in Reform Jewish Thought,''
in *Reform Judaism: Essays by*
Hebrew Union College Alumni,
pp. 59–62.

Reform Judaism—Then and Now

OTHER THINGS TO READ

Bamberger, Bernard J., *The Story of Judaism:* Chap. 54, "American Judaism, 1918–1932"; Chap. 55, "The Greatest Tragedy"; Chap. 56, "The Greatest Tragedy—Second Phase"; Chap. 57, "The State of Israel"; Chap. 58, "American Judaism, 1932–1945."

Central Conference of American Rabbis Yearbook: Vol. 47 (1937), pp. 94–114 (adoption of the Guiding Principles).

Elbogen, Ismar, *A Century of Jewish Life:* Book 4, Chap. 3, "The Jews of America at the Beginning of the Twentieth Century"; Book 5, Chap. 5, "The Jewish National Home in Palestine"; Chap. 6, "Hitler's Total War against the Jews."

Feuer, Leon I., and Azriel Eisenberg, *Jewish Literature since the Bible,* II: pp. 263–315 (various writings on the development of Zionism); 316–322 (an early appeal to German Jewry under the Nazis).

Gittelsohn, Roland B., *Modern Jewish Problems:* Chap. 10, "What Is Zionism?"

Learsi, Rufus, *The Jews in America: A History:* Chap. 19, "The Long Truce Abroad"; Chap. 20, "Rage of the Heathen"; Chap. 21, "War and Postwar Trials"; Chap. 22, "New Pride, New Care"; Chap. 24, "Of Today and Tomorrow."

Lehman, Emil, *Israel—Idea and Reality:* Unit 4, Chap. 2, "Upheaval from Within and Without"; Chap. 3, "Shadows and Agonies"; Unit 5, Chap. 1, "A Nation Restored."

Levinger, Lee J., *A History of the Jews in the United States:* Chap. 22, "Between Two Wars"; Chap. 23, "The Second World War and Its Aftermath"; Chap. 24, "A Bird's-Eye View of American Jewry"; Chap. 25, "How the Jew Keeps His Judaism in America"; Chap. 29, "American Jews and World Jewry"; Chap. 32, "The Future of the American Jew."

Marcus, Jacob R., *The Rise and Destiny of the German Jew:* Chap. 4, "Adolf Hitler and Nazi Anti-Semitism."

Masserman, Paul, and Max Baker, *The Jews Come to America:* Chap. 12, "The Russian Jew in America"; Chap. 16, "Zionism in America."

Plaut, W. Gunther, *The Growth of Reform Judaism:* pp. 96–100 (Columbus Platform); Chap. 9, "Germany: Dream and Nightmare"; Chap. 10, "Zion: The Great Debate"; Chap. 12, "The Changing Environment."

Sachar, Abram L., *A History of the Jews:* Chap. 29, "Europe between the Wars"; Chap. 30, "The Western Hemisphere in the Twentieth Century"; Chap. 31, "The Epic of Palestine"; Chap. 32, "World War II and After"; Chap. 33, "The New State of Israel."

Schwartzman, Sylvan D., *Reform Judaism in the Making:* Chap. 13, "1885–1935—A Half-Century of Change"; Chap. 14, "Reform's Present Principles."

Schwarz, Leo W., *The Root and the Bough* (an anthology of writings from the Nazi period).

Standard Jewish Encyclopedia: "American Council for Judaism," p. 90; "Germany," pp. 743–747; "Israel," pp. 974–996; "National Socialism (Nazism)," pp. 1395–1396; "Reform Judaism," pp. 1584–1586.

Universal Jewish Encyclopedia: "Germany," Vol. 4, pp. 541–564; "Judaism in America (Reform Judaism)," Vol. 6, pp. 242–243; "Zionism," Vol. 10, pp. 645–667 (including the American Council for Judaism).

SUGGESTED ACTIVITIES

1. Prepare the script for a television documentary on Reform Judaism and Zionism.

2. Prepare a chart indicating the particular ways in which the program and practices of your congregation reflect the teachings of the Guiding Principles.

3. Through reports of appropriate committees, have the class develop a new Reform platform in line with the needs of the movement today.

SUBJECTS FOR RESEARCH

1. Using the 1937 yearbook of the Central Conference of American Rabbis (Vol. 47), read the

contents of the set of Reform principles offered by Rabbi Samuel Schulman. How did it differ from the platform proposed by the commission, and why was it rejected?

2. Why has Reform Judaism been so consistently opposed to the adoption of a ''creed''? What is the difference between it and a platform or set of ''guiding principles''?

3. The criticism has sometimes been voiced that Reform Judaism makes no demands upon its members. On the basis of the Guiding Principles, how would you reply to this charge? What are its requirements for being a worthwhile Reform Jew?

4. What were the particular circumstances that led to the formation of the American Council for Judaism in 1943? How do you account for its attitudes toward Zionism, and why did the Reform movement officially reject them?

5. What responsibilities for world Jewry did the American Jewish community accept following World War II? How, for instance, did American Jewry contribute to the establishment and maintenance of the State of Israel?

FILMSTRIPS TO SEE

The Anatomy of Nazism (Anti-Defamation League of B'nai B'rith), describing major phases of the operation of fascism in Hitler Germany and its effect upon the Jews.

Dr. Leo Baeck: Man of Faith (UAHC), depicting the life and activities of this great German Jewish spiritual hero of the Hitler period.

Eliezer Ben-Yehuda (Jewish Agency), portraying the life of this zealot for the revival of the Hebrew language in Palestine.

Israel (*Life*), picturing some of the major problems facing the State of Israel in recent years.

Jews in Morocco (UAHC), showing the background and various aspects of the life of Eastern Jews, most of whom presently live in the State of Israel.

The Leo Baeck School in Israel (UAHC), presenting highlights of the activities of this important Jewish liberal institution in Israel.

A LIVE ISSUE

Reform practice, as we shall see in this chapter, tends to vary from congregation to congregation. Not only does this cause a certain amount of confusion, but it sometimes leads Reform Jews to conclude that religious practice is largely a matter of personal preference.

All this has prompted some Reform Jews to propose a uniform "Guide to Reform Practice." The movement today, they contend, suffers from the chaos growing out of its earlier emphasis upon "individualism," and only a guide can overcome this. Actually, several have already been produced and adopted by a number of temples.

But others are strongly opposed to such a guide, fearing that it will work to the serious disadvantage of the movement.

The Basic Problem: Those who object claim that a guide can easily become a rigid "code" that will undermine the liberal spirit of the movement, stifle its creativity,

and "freeze" reform at its present stage of development, thereby transforming it into a kind of "orthodoxy."

Not so, argue the advocates of a guide. Since it is that and nothing more, it remains subject to change, and thus any fears of a "code" are really unfounded.

Some Important Questions: (1) To what extent do the present variations in Reform practice actually represent a weakness? (2) Should Reform strive for more uniform practice? (3) To what degree is this possible within a liberal religious movement? (4) How would a "Guide to Reform Practice" adopted by the movement improve the situation? (5) Do the risks involved outweigh the advantages?

What Do You Think? As you read about present-day Reform practice, how do you react to the proposal for a guide? Do you feel that the movement really needs one, and would you, as a Reform Jew, agree to abide by it?

17. PRESENT-DAY REFORM PRACTICE

A "Puzzlement"?

In the musical, *The King and I,* the king of Siam admits to his good friend Anna that he is often perplexed by the contradiction between things people say and do. "It's a puzzlement!" he complains.

Some are likely to feel the same way today about all the variations in Reform practice. In one congregation, for example, the worship may be almost entirely in English; in another it will be mainly in Hebrew. In many temples a cantor sings the responses; others have no cantor. In certain temples the men customarily wear a hat and *talit;* while in most others they wear neither. No wonder Reform sometimes seems a "puzzlement" even to its own members, causing some to urge that the movement adopt a guide to its practices.

Much of this is characteristic of a liberal form of Judaism that permits each of its congregations to determine its own practice. But, in recent years, the differences have tended to multiply as a result of the changing times and the varying backgrounds of the movement's expanding membership.

In spite of this, the great majority of Reform congregations do seem to maintain much

the same basic observances, which enable us to describe the movement's current practices. For purposes of organization, we have grouped them into nine broad areas—use of Hebrew in worship, music in the service, use of head covering and *talit,* women's religious rights, observance of the Sabbath, observance of the holidays, marriage practices, divorce laws, and funeral and mourning practices. We have also provided a brief chart summarizing the essential facts for each.

The Use of Hebrew in Worship

One of the problems Reform inherited from traditional Judaism was the all-Hebrew service that was no longer intelligible to most worshipers. The European rabbinical conferences of the 1840's established the principle that worship might be conducted in whatever language Jews understood. Nevertheless, in the interest of maintaining Reform's ties with the Jewish past and the Jewish people as a whole, they retained the use of Hebrew with the more important prayers.

For the most part, American Reform has adopted this practice, and the *Union Prayer*

Reform Judaism—Then and Now

FIRST JEWISH SERVICE. Held in Berlin after Hitler's defeat, this was the first service since 1938. (FPG)

BRUNSWICK SYNAGOGUE. (Darmstaedter)

TEMPLE EMANU-EL OF NEW YORK. Here a service is being conducted in this leading American synagogue. (N.Y. Herald Times)

INTERIOR OF ISAAC M. WISE TEMPLE. Here is the well-known Plum Street Temple where Isaac M. Wise himself conducted services. The ordination of rabbis from the Cincinnati School of the College-Institute is held here each year. (HUC, American Jewish Archives)

273

The Use of Hebrew in Worship

Traditional Practice	Why Reforms Were Sought	European Reform	American Reform
An all-Hebrew service.	Many no longer understood or enjoyed the all-Hebrew service.	Worship may be conducted in the vernacular, with the retention of important prayers in Hebrew.	Both Hebrew and English are used in the service. Many prayers are rendered differently into English. Today's trend includes greater use of Hebrew and the Sephardic pronunciation.

Book, used by practically all its congregations today, includes the Hebrew of most of the essential prayers, as well as an English rendition that is more than simply a translation. For instance, the Hebrew of the opening sentence of the prayer *Sim Shalom* (שִׂים שָׁלוֹם, Grant us peace) literally reads in English:

> **Establish peace, goodness, blessing, grace, lovingkindness, and mercy upon us and upon all who fear Thy name.**

However, the *Union Prayer Book* renders this as:

> **Grant us peace, Thy most precious gift, O Thou eternal source of peace, and enable Israel to be its messenger unto the peoples of the earth.**

The present trend within the movement, as encouraged by the Guiding Principles, is to use more Hebrew in the service, which in turn has stimulated greater attention to its study in the religious school. Furthermore, because the Sephardic (Spanish) pronunciation is used by the Jews of Israel, an increasing number of Reform congregations have adopted it in place of the former Ashkenazic (Central European) pronunciation. Many nevertheless continue to use Ashkenazic, arguing that historically Jews in different parts of the world have always pronounced Hebrew differently and that Hebrew for the purpose of prayer should be distinguished from the manner in which it is usually spoken on the streets of Israel.

Music in the Service

European Reform strongly objected to the traditional chanting of the liturgy, claiming that it often became unintelligible and made for confusion and irreverence in the synagogue. But, recognizing music's importance in worship, it introduced the organ and mixed choir and urged that cantors be given a sound musical training. It also produced many new congregational hymns and other forms of liturgical music, among which are the brilliant Sabbath and holiday services composed by famous cantor-musicians like Solomon Sulzer of Vienna and Louis Lewandowski of Berlin.

Music in the Service

Traditional Practice	Why Reforms Were Sought	European Reform	American Reform
Chanting of the entire service. Instrumental music and mixed choir prohibited. Only the cantor and a male choir permitted.	Worship was frequently unappealing and unintelligible. Most cantors were musically untrained. Many desired more inspiring music in worship.	Introduced instrumental music and the mixed choir. Recommended the musical training of cantors. Much new synagogue music produced by cantor-musicians.	Adopted instrumental music and the mixed choir. Cantors reintroduced in many temples. Formal training of cantors provided by the College-Institute. Publication of the *Union Hymnal* and *Union Songster.* Much new synagogue music currently being produced.

In general, the movement in America followed the pattern of European Reform, but it frequently eliminated the cantor. However, in recent years many congregations have engaged cantors to provide greater warmth in the service, and the movement has since established a program of cantorial training in the New York School of its seminary.

Over the years, the American Reform movement has published the *Union Hymnal* and *Union Songster,* two extensive collections of musical responses, hymns, and services. Currently, it has also begun to produce much new synagogue music that is more in keeping with the older traditional modes or musical themes.

Praying with Covered Head and Talit

Though traditional Jewish law does not require males to wear a head covering during prayer, the custom nevertheless developed in Babylonia during talmudic times as a mark of piety and respect. Still, in some places this practice was not followed, as for example in thirteenth-century France where even the rabbis are reported to have prayed bareheaded. Eventually, however, a head covering at prayer became universal, with the more observant refusing to appear bareheaded at any time.

For the most part, the European Reformers continued to worship with covered heads, and only among the more radical was any change introduced. The first group to do so was the Berlin Reform Society which in 1845 made the skull cap optional at services, but very few other European congregations ever abandoned it.

Quite the opposite has been the case in America. As far back as 1824, the Charleston Reform Society began conducting services without hats and, when the Har Sinai Reform

275

Praying with Covered Head and Talit

Traditional Practice	Why Reforms Were Sought	European Reform	American Reform
Males must wear a head covering in the synagogue and whenever engaged in prayer and study. The *talit* must be worn at all morning services and on Yom Kippur eve.	Covering the head appeared contrary to the usual manner of showing respect in the Western world. Modern Jews saw no need to wear any distinctive garb at worship.	Few temples abandoned the head covering and *talit*.	Praying bareheaded is the most widely followed practice. In some temples, the rabbi wears a head covering, and in a few the members do, too. An *atarah* or *talit* is worn by the majority of rabbis. In some temples, all males at the pulpit also wear a *talit*.

Society of Baltimore was organized in 1842, it also abandoned them on the grounds that in the Western world one showed respect by removing his hat. As time passed, many temples made the skull cap optional, and following the Pittsburgh Conference, which abolished all forms of religious garb, most did away with it entirely.

Traditional Jews probably reacted more strongly to this than to anything else in Reform. Many condemned it as completely "un-Jewish," and those who might otherwise have been attracted to the temple often found worshiping without a hat emotionally too uncomfortable. In recent years, however, an increasing number of Reform weddings have been conducted with covered heads, and in some temples the rabbi and, in certain instances, the members themselves wear a head covering at all services.

The *talit* has likewise reappeared in many Reform temples. Historically, of course, the practice goes back to the Bible which requires the wearing of "fringes upon the corners of one's garments" (for example, see Numbers 15:37–40 and Deuteronomy 22:12), and in traditional Judaism the *talit* is worn by all males at every morning service and on Yom Kippur eve.

Though Israel Jacobson eliminated the *talit* at weddings, and the Berlin Reform Society did away with it at its services, European Reform as a whole retained it. American Reform, however, gradually abandoned it, but in recent years it has found its way back into many temples in various forms. Today, for example, the majority of Reform rabbis wear a modified *talit* over their rabbinical robe in the form of a stole or *atarah* (עֲטָרָה, decoration). Some, however, prefer to wear an actual *talit*. And, in some congregations, all males are expected to put on a *talit* whenever they appear at the pulpit.

At the same time, some rabbis now prefer to conduct services with neither a robe nor the *talit*.

276

Religious Rights of Women

Traditional Practice	Why Reforms Were Sought	European Reform	American Reform
Men enjoy special religious privileges. Women must sit in a separate synagogue section. Women are not included in a *minyan*. Women are barred from conducting the worship or serving as witnesses in ritual matters. Special hardships for women in cases of the *agunah* and *chalitzah*.	Jewish women endured special hardships and religious inequalities. The inferior religious status of Jewish women was regarded as having originated in the Middle East. The Western world was gradually emancipating women.	*Agunah* and *chalitzah* abolished. Women permitted to serve as witnesses in all ritual matters. Full religious equality for women recommended but no official action taken.	*Agunah* and *chalitzah* abolished. Women enjoy full religious equality. They may sit with the men, conduct the service, be counted toward a *minyan,* and generally participate in all phases of synagogue life.

Women's Religious Rights

Traditional Judaism, as we have observed, grants greater religious privileges to men than to women, which explains why the following blessing appears in the morning service: "Praised be Thou, O Lord who hast not made me a woman."

As seen by the European Reformers, such notions originated in the Middle East, where females were generally looked upon as inferior, and they considered these outmoded in a Western world that was gradually emancipating women.

Consequently, the rabbinical conferences and synods sought to protect Jewish women from the hardships of certain traditional laws, such as those involving the *agunah,* the woman whose husband had disappeared, and *chalitzah,* where the childless widow was expected to marry her husband's brother.

They also sought to obtain full religious equality for them, but here they made comparatively little progress.

American Reform proved far more successful. Not only were women permitted to sit with the men at worship but eventually, at the 1891 convention of the Union of American Hebrew Congregations, a woman was accredited as a full delegate from her congregation. Gradually, all discrimination between the sexes has disappeared so that today women participate as equals in all phases of temple life, even to the extent of serving as trustees and officers of the congregation.

Observance of the Sabbath

The European Reformers struggled with many of the problems that grew out of the traditional observance of the Sabbath and in time per-

Observance of the Sabbath

Traditional Practice	Why Reforms Were Sought	European Reform	American Reform
Thirty-nine categories of "work" prohibited on the Sabbath, including riding to the synagogue, writing, turning on the lights, etc. Friday evening services at sundown; Saturday morning worship. Sabbath home and synagogue rituals.	Modern circumstances made many Sabbath restrictions outmoded. Working on the Sabbath was necessary for many also making it impossible for them to attend the customary services. Distances from the synagogue often made riding necessary.	Riding to the synagogue and essential work permitted on the Sabbath. Sunday morning services introduced in addition to Sabbath worship.	Riding to the synagogue and essential work permitted on the Sabbath. Adoption chiefly of late Friday evening services in addition to regular Sabbath morning worship. Special Sabbath home and synagogue rituals.

mitted Jews to play the organ on the Sabbath, ride to the synagogue, and carry on essential work. Though rejecting the more radical proposal to transfer the Sabbath to Sunday, they did permit congregations to carry on Sunday worship, which only a few, however, introduced.

Following the Pittsburgh Conference, many American Reform congregations adopted the Sunday morning service in addition to worship on Saturday, and in 1902 the Central Conference of American Rabbis even prepared a ritual for it. But, over the years, the late Friday evening service that Isaac M. Wise introduced in 1865 gradually replaced most Sunday worship.

With the adoption of the Guiding Principles in 1937, Friday evening worship came to feature a number of added observances, among them the kindling of the Sabbath candles, the chanting of the *Kiddush,* and the reading of the Torah. Following the service, most congregations also conduct an *Oneg Shabbat* (עֹנֶג שַׁבָּת , enjoyment of the Sab-

bath, or Sabbath social with refreshments) that often includes special lectures and discussions.

American Reform has largely disregarded the traditional Sabbath restrictions. Instead, it has sought to emphasize the spiritual significance of the day as a time of religious renewal, through worship in the home with the Friday evening ritual of welcoming the Sabbath and through services at temple. Some Reform families also carry on the ceremony of *Havdalah* (הַבְדָּלָה , division) on Saturday nights to mark the separation of the Sabbath from the rest of the week.

Observance of the Holidays

The Reformers of Europe recognized three main difficulties with traditional holiday observance. The first involved many of the minor holidays, chiefly fast days, which though long observed had lost much of their significance. Here, however, they took no official action.

278

Observance of the Jewish Holidays

Traditional Practice	Why Reforms Were Sought	European Reform	American Reform
Outside of Palestine an extra day of all major Jewish holidays was observed because of difficulties in establishing the correct date. Observance of numerous minor holidays, mostly fasts. Prohibition of marriages on so-called "unlucky days."	Scientific calculation of the calendar made extra days of the holidays unnecessary. Many minor holidays no longer meaningful. "Unlucky days" looked upon as superstitious.	All extra days of holidays, with the exception of Rosh Hashanah, eliminated. Most "unlucky days" abandoned.	All extra days of the holidays eliminated. All minor fast days abandoned. "Unlucky days" abolished. New rituals introduced into the observance of the major holidays. Wider celebration of Chanukah and Purim.

They were more successful in dealing with the other two problems. They did away with all the extra days of the major Jewish holidays, except for Rosh Hashanah, on the grounds that since science had now eliminated any possibility of error in the calendar these were no longer necessary. And they abandoned as mere superstition most of the so-called "unlucky days" on which weddings were prohibited.

Only in America did Reform finally give up the observance of the minor holidays and the second day of Rosh Hashanah. The movement here, moreover, has sought to enrich each of the major holidays with special ceremonies, such as the consecration of beginners in the religious school on the last day of Sukot, the observance of Confirmation on Shavuot, and the conducting of an extended memorial service on Yom Kippur. It has also encouraged the wider celebration of Chanukah and Purim, both regarded as minor holidays by traditional Judaism but whose celebration in America has become popular, especially with children.

Jewish Marriage Practices

By permitting weddings on minor fast days and during the so-called "unlucky periods," European Reform had already altered traditional practice. But it modified other marriage regulations by recognizing a death certificate issued by the state as sufficient to permit the *agunah* to remarry and by abolishing the whole institution of *chalitzah.* It also sanctioned the double-ring ceremony and encouraged the bride to take a more active part in the wedding by having her recite a marriage formula similar to that of the groom.

Building upon what Europe had already achieved, most American Reform congregations gradually dispensed with the use of the *chupah* or canopy, the *ketubah* or marriage contract, and the breaking of the glass and permitted the use of a wedding ring with precious stones. To add dignity and beauty to the ceremony, it introduced the use of candles and a single cup of wine instead of two, a more formal wedding procession, the wed-

Jewish Marriage Practices

Traditional Practice	Why Reforms Were Sought	European Reform	American Reform
Many marriage regulations requiring the use of a canopy, marriage contract, breaking of the glass, a plain gold ring, etc. Cases of the *agunah* and *chalitzah*. Prohibition of marriage on the so-called "unlucky days."	*Agunah* and *chalitzah* created special hardships for women. With emancipation, Jews also became subject to civil marriage regulations that sometimes differed from Jewish law. Women disadvantaged in the marriage ceremony. Many Jewish wedding practices regarded as outmoded.	*Agunah* and *chalitzah* abolished. Introduction of some reforms in wedding practices, such as permitting the double-ring ceremony and greater participation of the bride. Most "unlucky days" abolished.	*Agunah* and *chalitzah* abolished. Introduction of reforms in wedding practices, including permitting the double-ring ceremony and greater participation of the bride. Weddings permitted on all days except Sabbaths and major Jewish holidays. More dignified and meaningful rituals added to the ceremony. Recent reintroduction of certain traditional practices, such as the *chupah* and the breaking of the glass.

WEDDING CEREMONY. A Reform wedding ceremony is being conducted within the temple. (Joseph Davis)

ding sermon, and a bower of flowers for the traditional *chupah.*

In recent years, however, with the renewed interest in ceremonials, a number of traditional practices have been reintroduced. Thus, use of the *chupah* and the breaking of the glass have become quite common in Reform weddings.

Jewish Divorce Laws

After Jewish emancipation, traditional divorce laws became especially troublesome because a civil divorce alone did not enable a Jew to

Jewish Divorce Laws			
Traditional Practice	**Why Reforms Were Sought**	**European Reform**	**American Reform**
A religious divorce is required in addition to the civil decree. Only the husband can grant a divorce, or *get*.	With emancipation and provision for civil divorce, a Jewish divorce made for added difficulties. Jewish divorce laws worked a special hardship on women and often led to abuses.	Though there was much opposition to Jewish divorce as needless and unfair to women, no action was taken.	The practice of Jewish divorce was abolished. A *get* is unnecessary; all that is needed for remarriage is a civil decree.

remarry. Jewish law also demanded a religious divorce, and the fact that only the husband can grant this often made it impossible for the woman to remarry. Even today it is not unheard of for an Orthodox woman to be unable to obtain a *get,* or Jewish divorce, because her husband cannot be located or is unwilling to grant it without being given a sizable sum of money.

Arguing that divorce should be regulated entirely by civil law, the Reformers in Europe objected to the whole institution of the Jewish divorce, but they were never able to do away with it. However, at the Philadelphia Rabbinical Conference of 1869, American Reform proceeded to dispense with the *get* and to adopt the rule that a civil decree acceptable to both parties was sufficient for remarriage.

Funeral and Mourning Practices

Traditional Judaism has a great many laws and customs associated with death and mourning. Prompt burial of the dead, even on the day of death if possible, is required; so is clothing the corpse in a shroud or plain, loosely-sewn robe. Flowers are not permitted

at a funeral nor is internment in a mausoleum or tomb. Among traditional Jews it is also customary to place a small sack of Israeli soil in the coffin, halt the casket a number of times on the way to the grave, call upon the nearest relatives to fill in the grave, and have mourners pluck grass and throw it behind them as they leave the gravesite. And, as we have already noted, mourners are expected to observe numerous restrictions during the seven days of *shivah.*

The European Reformers did little to change existing funeral practices, but they succeeded in modifying many of the mourning customs. They prescribed an intense mourning period of only three days and freed the mourners from sitting on the floor or low stools. They also permitted them to wear shoes, bathe, shave, and greet visitors.

American Reform has largely adopted these changes and, though officially it recommends a mourning period of seven days, most Reform Jews generally observe only three. It is also customary for mourners to conduct a religious service in the home each evening and recite *Kaddish* for a full year at Sabbath and, in some congregations, at daily services. Thereafter they commemorate the anniversary

Funeral and Mourning Practices

Traditional Practice	Why Reforms Were Sought	European Reform	American Reform
Immediate burial is prescribed. A wide variety of funeral practices and prohibitions. A seven-day mourning period is required. Many specific regulations governing mourning.	Immediate burial may prevent members of the family from attending the funeral. A great number of funeral and mourning regulations appeared outmoded. The seven-day mourning period often worked a financial hardship on the family.	Many traditional mourning practices abolished. A three-day home mourning period prescribed.	Delay in burial permitted through embalming. Many changes introduced in funeral practices, including the use of flowers, etc. Many traditional funeral and mourning practices abandoned. A three-day home mourning period is generally followed.

of death by kindling a *yahrzeit* (a Yiddish and German word meaning anniversary) lamp in the home, reciting *Kaddish* in the synagogue on the anniversary date or nearest Sabbath, and making a memorial contribution to the temple. They also remember the dead at special memorial services conducted Yom Kippur afternoon and, in many congregations, on the last days of Sukot and Passover.

Unlike European Reform, however, the movement in America made numerous changes in funeral practices as well. Thus it permits a delay in holding the funeral, clothing the corpse in regular dress, and the use of flowers and plants at the funeral. And it allows for the practice of embalming, burial in a mausoleum, and even cremation.

The funeral itself is conducted in the temple or chapel of a funeral home where the rabbi offers prayers and a "eulogy," or funeral sermon. At the conclusion of the service, the casket is taken in a simple procession to the gravesite. There the service ends with the recitation of the *Kaddish,* and the family usually departs before the grave is filled in.

The Advantages of American Reform

In terms of religious practice, then, American Reform has gone considerably beyond the movement in Europe, both in departing from tradition and in introducing new observances and procedures. Not only did the pioneering spirit of America stimulate the movement to respond more promptly to the new conditions of the age, but the greater degree of freedom it enjoyed made it far less hesitant about abandoning practices it considered outmoded. Hence, to cite one example, while the European Reformers continued to issue a *get,* the movement in America simply dispensed with the whole practice of a Jewish divorce.

Reform in America has enjoyed still another advantage. Here local congregations have generally accepted the recommendations of the movement as a whole, which was rarely the case in Europe. Thus, though European Reform had long sanctioned religious equality for women, it was not until 1928 that one of the most liberal of all the temples, the Berlin Reform congregation, actually permitted a woman to deliver a sermon from the pulpit, and then only because an international Reform conference was being held in the city. "So revolutionary a step had not yet been taken by it [the congregation] in the course of its existence of eight decades," observes a leading Reform historian.

To a great extent, American Reform's achievements have come about through effective organization, something that was long lacking in Europe. Therefore, the current picture of Reform is far from complete without some understanding of the movement's organizations and the important role they play.

QUESTIONS FOR DISCUSSION

1. How do you explain the fact that practices often differ from one Reform congregation to another. Does this indicate a particular weakness in Reform Judaism? Why?

2. Why do some Reform temples carry on many more traditional practices than others? What position does your own congregation take toward adopting traditional observances? How do you account for this?

3. What significant changes has American Reform introduced in: (a) synagogue worship? (b) Sabbath observance? (c) observance of the Jewish holidays? (d) funeral and mourning customs? (e) religious rights of women? (f) marriage and divorce regulations?

4. In what ways do the practices of your temple agree with the decisions of European Reform? Where has the congregation found it necessary to go beyond them? Why?

5. What are some of the major differences in synagogue practice today between Orthodox and Reform Jews? In what way does each grow out of their respective interpretations of Judaism?

6. What changes in practice has your congregation introduced within the past five years? What do they reveal about current trends in Reform Judaism? How do you account for these?

SIGNIFICANT DOCUMENTS

Some Traditional Laws of Mourning, from the *Shulchan Aruch*, 1567

From Chapter 208

1. During the seven days of mourning the mourner is forbidden to do any work, to bathe or anoint himself, to wear freshly washed garments, to cut his hair, or to be present at any festivity. On the first day he is also forbidden to lay *tefilin*.

2. What is the law concerning work? During the first three days he is forbidden to work, even if he be poor and have nothing to eat. From the fourth day on he may work privately in his home. A woman also may work privately in her own home to earn enough for her sustenance. The sages say: "May poverty overtake his neighbors who force him to work," for it is their duty to provide for the poor, especially in his days of mourning . . .

From Chapter 209

1. The mourner is forbidden to bathe his entire body, even in cold water; moreover washing the face, hands, and feet with warm water is prohibited, but with cold water it is permitted. Bathing in warm water is forbidden the entire thirty days [of extended mourning]. Bathing the entire body even in cold water is forbidden in the thirty days if done for the sake of pleasure. A woman who must bathe before immersion [in

the *mikveh,* or ritual bath] is permitted to bathe in warm water after her seven days of mourning . . .

From Chapter 210

6. What is the rule concerning greetings? During the first three days of mourning, he [the mourner] should neither salute anyone nor respond to another's salutation, but he should inform them that he is a mourner. After three days until the seventh day he should not salute, but he may respond to another's salutation. From the seventh until the thirtieth day, he may salute another inasmuch as the other may receive greetings of peace, but others should not salute him, as he is not in a state of contentment. If, however, they saluted him, he should respond to their greeting. After the thirty days (of mourning) he is like other people in regard to salutation . . .

From Chapter 211

1. He is forbidden to sit upon cushions and pillows during the seven days, but he should sit only on the ground. In the case, however, of an invalid or of an old man to whom sitting on the ground is painful, it is permissible for them to sit on a small cushion. The mourner may walk and stand, and he is not required to sit except in the presence of those who come to comfort him, when it is obligatory to sit. It is also forbidden to sleep in a bed or on a bench, only on the ground, but he may put pillows or mattresses on the ground, as he is accustomed to lie in bed. Others permit him to sleep in the bed, and so it is the custom because their constitutions are weak and they are like sick in this regard. . . .

4. One is forbidden to wear a washed garment, even a shirt, during the seven days of mourning, even in honor of the Sabbath. It is even prohibited to use freshly washed sheets or bedspreads or (freshly washed) towels. In honor of the Sabbath, however, it is permissible to cover the tables with tablecloths that had been washed prior to the period of mourning . . .

12. One is forbidden to cut his hair during the thirty days of mourning. This refers not only to the hair on his head, but also the hair of any other place. If he is in mourning for a parent, he is forbidden to cut his hair until he be rebuked by his friends [for not having his hair cut]. The limit of the time in this case is the subject of controversy between the authorities. We are accustomed not to cut the hair during the entire twelve months unless it be necessary; for example, if his hair were a burden to him, or if he were to go among people of different beliefs and be looked upon with disdain on account of his hair. No actual rebuke is essential, but if his hair grew to a size which alters his appearance so that he is unlike other people to such an extent as to arouse comment, under such circumstances he is allowed to cut his hair, but only after the thirty days of mourning . . .

—From Hyman E. Goldin,
Code of Jewish Law,
Vol. 4, pp. 120, 122–126.

A Traditional Ketubah, as Currently Used

Ketubah

On the _____ day of the week, the _____ day of the Hebrew month _____ , in the year five thousand, seven hundred and _____ since the creation of the world, the era according to which we are accustomed to reckon here in the city of _____, state of _____, in the country of _____, how [name of the groom] _____, son of [name of his father] _____, surnamed [family name], said to this virgin, [name of the bride], daughter of [name of her father], sur-named [family name]:

"Be thou my wife according to the Law of Moses and Israel and I will cherish, honor, support, and maintain you in accordance with the custom of Jewish husbands who cherish, honor, support, and maintain their wives in truth.

"And I herewith make for you the settlement for virgins, two hundred silver zuzim [a zuz is worth about 25 cents], which belongs to you, according to the Law of Moses and Israel; and I will also give you your food, clothing and necessities, and live with you as husband and wife according to general custom."

And Miss [name of the bride], this virgin, consented and became his wife. The wedding outfit that she brought him from her father's house in silver, gold valuables, wearing apparel, house furniture, and bed-clothes, all this the groom, [name], accepted as the equivalent of one hundred silver pieces. And the groom, [name], consented to increase this amount from his own property by the sum of one hundred silver pieces, making in all the sum of two hundred silver pieces. And thus said the groom, [name]:

"The responsibility of this marriage-contract, of this wedding outfit, and of this additional sum, I take upon myself and my heirs after me, so that they shall be paid from the best part of my property and possessions that I have beneath the whole heaven, that which I now possess or may hereafter acquire.

All my property, real and personal, even the cloak on my shoulders, shall be mortgaged to secure the payment of this marriage-contract, of the wedding outfit, and of the addition made thereto, during my lifetime and after my death, from the present day and forever."

The groom, [name], has taken upon himself the responsibility of the marriage-contract, of the wedding outfit and the addition made thereto, according to the restrictions in all marriage-contracts and the additions thereto made for all daughters of Israel, in accordance with the regulations made by our sages of blessed memory. It is not to be regarded as a fictitious obligation or as a mere formula put into a document.

We have followed the legal formality of the symbolic exchange of possessions between the groom, [name of the groom], son of [his father's name], and the bride, the virgin, [name of the bride], daughter of [her father's name], and we have used a garment legally fit for the purpose to reinforce all that is stated above.

And Everything Is Valid and Confirmed.

Groom _____

Attested to [name of the witness]

Attested to [name of the witness]

—From Hyman E. Goldin,
HaMadrikh: The Rabbi's Guide,
pp. 17–20.

Major Decisions of the Augsburg Synod Regarding Marriage, 1871

1. It is proper that during the marriage ceremony, after the bridegroom has delivered the ring to his bride with the words: *"Hare at mekudeshet li"* [הֲרֵי אַתְּ מְקֻדֶּשֶׁת לִי, Behold, you are consecrated unto me], the bride in turn should also give to her future husband a ring with a few appropriate words.

2. The synod recommends that, in countries where the civil marriage is entrusted to the rabbi, he should, during the religious ceremony, ask the couple whether they are willing to marry one another.

3. Nobody can be declared unfit to be a witness at a marriage or divorce on account of his non-observance of certain ceremonies.

4. The synod declares that the custom of not performing marriage ceremonies on certain so-called unlucky days, in particular during the period from Pesach to Shavuot and during the so-called three weeks [before the ninth of *Av*], has no religious foundation at all, serves only to further superstition, and does not foster pious feelings. Hence this limitation is to be set aside, with the exception only of the week in which the ninth of *Av* is celebrated . . .

7. A final decision of the courts, concerning the identity of a deceased person, and a judicial decision, declaring the missing person to be dead, have also sanction for ritual cases [e.g., the *agunah*].

8. The biblical precept concerning *chalitzah* has lost its importance since the circumstances which made the levirate marriage necessary and *chalitzah* no longer exist. The idea underlying this observance has become estranged from our religious and social views.

9. The non-performance of *chalitzah* is no impediment to the widow's remarriage. In the interest of liberty of conscience, however, no rabbi, if requested by the parties, will refuse to conduct the act of *chalitzah* in an appropriate form . . .

—From the *Central Conference of American Rabbis Yearbook*, Vol. I (1890), pp. 112–113.

OTHER THINGS TO READ

Bial, Morrison D., *Liberal Judaism at Home* (Reform practice).

Doppelt, Frederic A., and David Polish, *A Guide for Reform Jews.*

Edidin, Ben M., *Jewish Customs and Ceremonies* (traditional).

Edidin, Ben M., *Jewish Holidays and Festivals* (traditional).

Freehof, Solomon B., *Reform Jewish Practice:* Vols. I and II.

Jewish Encyclopedia: "Bar Mitzvah," Vol. 2, pp. 509–510; "Burial," Vol. 3, pp. 432–438; "Cohen," Vol. 4, p. 144; "Divorce," Vol. 4, pp. 624–628; "Fasting and Fast Days," Vol. 5, pp. 347–349; "Funeral Rites," Vol. 5, pp. 529–530; "Marriage," Vol. 8, pp. 335–347; "Mourning," Vol. 9, pp. 101–103; "Phylacteries," Vol. 10, pp. 21–28; "Talit," Vol. 11, pp. 676–678; "Woman, Rights of," Vol. 12, pp. 556–558.

Philipson, David, *The Reform Movement in Judaism:* Chap. 13, "The Latest Developments in Europe."

Plaut, W. Gunther, *The Growth of Reform Judaism:* Chap. 14, "Practice in Transition"; Chap. 15, "Synagogue in Transition"; Epilogue "Reform Judaism after 1948."

Plaut, W. Gunther, *The Rise of Reform Judaism:* Chap. 7, "Worship Reform"; Chap. 8, "Sabbath and Holiday Observance"; Chap. 9, "The Personal Life"; pp. 252–255 (status of women); 260–265 (a guide for Reform Judaism).

Schauss, Hayyim, *The Jewish Festivals* (traditional and Reform).

Schauss, Hayyim, *The Lifetime of a Jew* (tradtional and Reform).

Schwartzman, Sylvan D., *Reform Judaism in the Making:* Chap. 15, "The Practices of Modern Reform Judaism."

Schwarz, Jacob D., "Reform Jewish Practice," *Reform Judaism: Essays by Hebrew Union College Alumni:* pp. 221–249.

Silverman, Lou H., *"The Union Prayer Book,"* Chap. 3 in Bertram W. Korn (ed.), *Retrospect and Prospect.*

Singer, Howard, *With Mind and Heart* (Conservative).

Steinberg, Milton, *Basic Judaism.*

Standard Jewish Encyclopedia: "Bar Mitzvah," pp. 234–235; "Burial and Burial Societies," pp. 375–376; "Divorce," pp. 567–568; "Fast," pp. 668–669; "Marriage," pp. 1272–1273; "Talit," p. 1784; "Tefilin," p. 1808; "Women," pp. 1924–1925.

Universal Jewish Encyclopedia: "Bar Mitzvah," Vol. 2, pp. 73–75; "Burial and Burial Customs," Vol. 2, pp. 594–602; "Cohen," Vol. 3, p. 233; "Divorce," Vol. 3, pp. 577–580; "Fasting and Fast Days," Vol. 4, pp. 249–252; "Funeral," Vol. 4, pp. 477–480; "Marriage," Vol. 7, pp. 369–376; "Mourning," Vol. 8, pp. 28–31; "Phylacteries," Vol. 8, pp. 522–528; "Talit," Vol. 10, pp. 159–160; "Women," Vol. 10, pp. 564–566.

SUGGESTED ACTIVITIES

1. Prepare a class booklet on the subject: "A Recommended Guide for Reform Practice in Our Congregation."

2. Conduct a debate on the subject: *"Resolved, that Reform should adopt many more traditional observances."*

3. Create a series of charts, slides, or transparencies comparing Reform and Orthodox practice in connection with: (a) a wedding, (b) a funeral, (c) a Friday evening service, and (d) a *Bar Mitzvah.*

SUBJECTS FOR RESEARCH

1. What are the origins of such traditional practices as: (a) the wearing of a head covering at worship? (b) the wearing of the *talit?* (c) the use of *tefilin* during morning prayer?

2. Study the Doppelt-Polish volume, *A Guide for Reform Jews* and compare its recommendations with the practices currently carried on by your own congregation. Where are they similar and where are they different?

3. What does a modern Conservative *ketubah* contain? What might you, as a Reform Jew, find objectionable in it? Why?

4. What explanation does Orthodoxy give for the following marriage practices: (a) the breaking of the glass? (b) the canopy? (c) the use of a plain gold wedding ring? (d) placing the ring on the index finger? (e) leading the bride around the groom seven times? Why do some Reform Jews object to these practices?

5. What are the minor fast days that traditional Judaism observes? Why and how are these commemorated? Why did Reform see fit to eliminate them?

FILMSTRIPS TO SEE

Shavuot: Festival of Torah and Confirmation (UAHC), describing both the ancient and current Reform observance of the Festival of Weeks.

David Einhorn: Father of the Union Prayerbook (UAHC), picturing the life and activities of this American Reform pioneer upon whose work Reform's prayer book is based.

The Story of the Sabbath (Jewish Education Committee of New York), portraying the traditional observance of the Sabbath in home and synagogue.

Torah in Jewish Life (Jewish Education Committee of New York), depicting the historical role of the Torah in traditional Judaism.

The Jewish Wedding in Art (UAHC), tracing Jewish wedding customs from their earliest origins to the present, in color reproductions of paintings by Rembrandt, Delacroix, Renoir, Chagall, and others.

The Sabbath at Home (UAHC), portraying the Sabbath customs and ceremonies in the Jewish home over the centuries through paintings, woodcuts, illuminated manuscripts, etc.

A LIVE ISSUE

Reform organization, as we shall see in this chapter, provides many benefits. But it can also produce problems as well.

For instance, there is the matter of its positions on certain controversial issues to which some temple members object. Others complain about the politics or bureaucracy they see developing within the movement or deplore the conflicts that arise from time to time between the Union, Conference, and College-Institute.

In recent years, however, some Reform Jews have also begun to question whether organization does not interfere with the essential purposes of religion itself.

The Basic Problem: The chief difficulty, as they picture it, is that people can become so involved in the operation of synagogues and national religious bodies that this becomes of primary importance. The result is that people can come to view their religious obligations chiefly in terms of fund-raising or other organizational considerations rather than in the larger concerns of Judaism itself.

Some Important Questions: (1) To what extent is religious organization necessary? (2) How would Reform Judaism suffer were there no local congregations or national organizations? (3) What practical problems, however, do they create? (4) Is greater concern with organization than with Judaism itself a serious problem within Reform? In what respect? (5) How might the movement overcome some of its other organizational difficulties?

What Do You Think? As you read this chapter, what do you see as some of the important benefits and shortcomings of Reform organization? What improvements, starting with the operation of your own congregation, would you therefore recommend?

18. THE ORGANIZATION OF THE MOVEMENT

The Need for Reform Organization

What would your temple be like without Reform organization? You would probably have no rabbi because there would be no seminary to train him. And, were the congregation to engage an Orthodox or Conservative rabbi, imagine the controversy over beliefs and practices!

Lacking a Reform rabbinical association, your temple would have no prayer book. The congregation would either have to produce its own or use the traditional *siddur,* or prayer book, for daily, Sabbath, and festival services, *machzor* for the High Holy Days, and *Haggadah* (הַגָּדָה, a retelling, or ritual for Passover). What problems this would create!

Nor without some organization of Reform congregations, would this book or a great many others be available for your use. Picture, if you can, your religious school without suitable texts and materials.

Yet these are only a few of the benefits your temple enjoys as a result of Reform organization, and it all starts with your own congregation.

How Reform Congregations Operate

Within the wide limits of Reform Judaism, every congregation in the movement is free to determine its own policies, practices, and procedures. This in turn explains why those of some other Reform congregation may be different from yours.

A temple may also engage any rabbi of its choice as long as he qualifies by previous length of service, and the rabbi is at liberty to select the congregation he wishes. However, in order to be eligible for a larger congregation, he must first have gained sufficient experience by serving a smaller one or assisting an older colleague for a number of years.

Once elected, he carries on a great many activities in behalf of the congregation. He conducts the services, officiates at weddings, funerals, and other religious observances, and counsels with those who are troubled or ill. He supervises the educational program, generally doing some of the teaching himself, particularly with confirmands, high school youths and adults; engages in a wide variety of civic activity; and works with many orga-

289

nizations and agencies devoted to the promotion of Jewish life and the improvement of society. And, as the term "rabbi" (רַבִּי, my teacher) implies, he is also obliged to improve his own Jewish knowledge through regular study.

Every congregation maintains itself financially and determines its own program of activities. Meeting at least once a year, the members elect the officers and a board of trustees to conduct the congregation's affairs. The officials are assisted by various committees that oversee important phases of the temple's operation, such as its program of religious education and worship, as well as its finances and facilities. However, in matters of major consequence, such as engaging a rabbi or building a new sanctuary, the entire membership generally must make the decision.

Affiliated with most temples are Sisterhoods, Brotherhoods, and youth groups that carry on numerous activities in behalf of the congregation. The Sisterhood, for instance, usually operates the temple gift shop, the Brotherhood may be in charge of adult education, and the youth group will often sponsor certain holiday celebrations and affairs for the religious school.

Every local congregation contributes to the support of its national Reform organizations. Two of them, the Hebrew Union College-Jewish Institute of Religion and the Union of American Hebrew Congregations, receive most of their funds from the Maintenance of Union Membership (MUM) program, which provides them with a specified percentage of the congregational dues paid by each member, and the Reform Jewish Appeal (RJA), the annual campaign to which congregants also contribute. The third, the Central Conference of American Rabbis (CCAR), is supported mainly by membership dues and the sale of its publications, notably the *Union Prayer Book, Union Hymnal,* and *Union Songster.*

Where Reform Rabbis Are Trained

The overwhelming majority of Reform rabbis today have received their training at the Hebrew Union College-Jewish Institute of Religion, known as the College-Institute for short.

The College-Institute conducts rabbinical training at three schools. The one established in Cincinnati in 1875 by Isaac M. Wise is the oldest and largest, with a campus containing several dormitories, a classroom building, library, museum, gymnasium, and other facilities. The library, with nearly a quarter of a million volumes on Jewish subjects and featuring many rare books and manuscripts as well as outstanding collections in the fields of Jewish music and philosophy, is considered one of the greatest in the world. The Cincinnati campus also houses the American Jewish Archives which specializes in the collection and study of documents relating to the history and development of American Jewry.

The second school, located in New York, was originally the Jewish Institute of Religion, founded in 1922 by Rabbi Stephen S. Wise. Acclaimed as one of the leading rabbis of the times for his fight against political corruption in New York and his defense of Jewish rights all over the world, Wise was convinced that the unity of American Jewry required the creation of a single seminary that would prepare rabbis for all interpretations of Judaism. Hence he created the Jewish Institute of Religion which, in 1950, was merged with the Hebrew Union College.

The California School, established in 1954, is the youngest of the three. Located in Los Angeles, it quickly outgrew its original quarters, and starting in 1969 the construction of a new campus was commenced near the University of California. Students complete the first two years of their rabbinical training at the California School before transferring to Cincinnati for the remainder of their studies.

The Training of a Reform Rabbi

What is involved in training a Reform rabbi? Let's take the case of Rabbi B. who was recently ordained at the Cincinnati School.

Many things led to his decision to become a rabbi, among them the influence of his home life, the activities of his temple youth group, a close association with his own rabbi, and his experiences as a member of the Hillel Foundation on the campus of his university. Convinced that he wanted to devote his life to the rabbinate, he applied for admission to the College-Institute and received his acceptance.

Before actually starting the rabbinical program, however, he spent a full year at the college's Jerusalem School to improve his knowledge of Hebrew and of Judaism generally. Then the following fall, he began the regular program of classes in Cincinnati, receiving instruction in such subjects as the Bible, rabbinic literature, Jewish history and thought, as well as training in actually conducting services, preaching, teaching, and counseling.

During his years at the College-Institute, B. also gained considerable practical experience for the rabbinate. In addition to teaching in one of the local religious schools and preparing students in Hebrew for *Bar* and *Bat Mitzvah,* he participated in a number of regional youth conclaves and retreats and spent several summers working with Reform young people at one of the Union camps. In his last two years, he served as the student-rabbi for a small congregation located about two hundred miles from Cincinnati.

Meanwhile he also managed to find time to participate in various school functions. In addition to serving as an officer of the Student Association, he wrote regularly for its literary magazine and took part in a number of joint faculty-student activities, including several dramatic productions.

Finally, at the end of his sixth year of study, B. and the other members of his class were ordained at a special Sabbath morning service in the historic Plum Street Temple where Isaac M. Wise himself had officiated. There, in the presence of a large congregation that included the families and friends of the graduates, the president of the College-Institute placed his hands on the head of each member of the class in the act of *semichah* (סְמִיכָה, "laying on" of hands or ordination), blessed him, and pronounced him a "rabbi in Israel." In addition, each graduate received his Doctor of Jewish Studies degree.

REFORM RABBI. Here a Reform rabbi is wearing his rabbinical robe and *talit.*

Reform Judaism—Then and Now

THE CINCINNATI SCHOOL. This is the Cincinnati campus of the Hebrew Union College-Jewish Institute of Religion.

THE JERUSALEM SCHOOL. The Hebrew Union College Biblical and Archeological School in Jerusalem. (HUC, American Jewish Archives)

DISPLAY OF REFORM BOOKS. Published by the Union of American Hebrew Congregations, these are part of its work.

CAMPERS. Here, at one of the many Union camps, campers are enjoying arts and crafts activities.

Other Activities of the College-Institute

Though the primary task of the College-Institute is to prepare rabbis, that is by no means its only function. It also trains cantors and directors of religious education to assist the rabbi and conducts courses for temple administrators, religious school principals and teachers, and professional Jewish communal workers.

However, from the very beginning, scientific Jewish research has been a major interest of the school. Its faculty is renowned for its scholarship in many fields, ranging from the languages of the ancient Middle East to contemporary Jewish history, and ranked among the finest scholarly publications today are its *Hebrew Union College Annual* and *American Jewish Archives.* Outstanding authorities in Talmud, Jewish theology, and Bible have

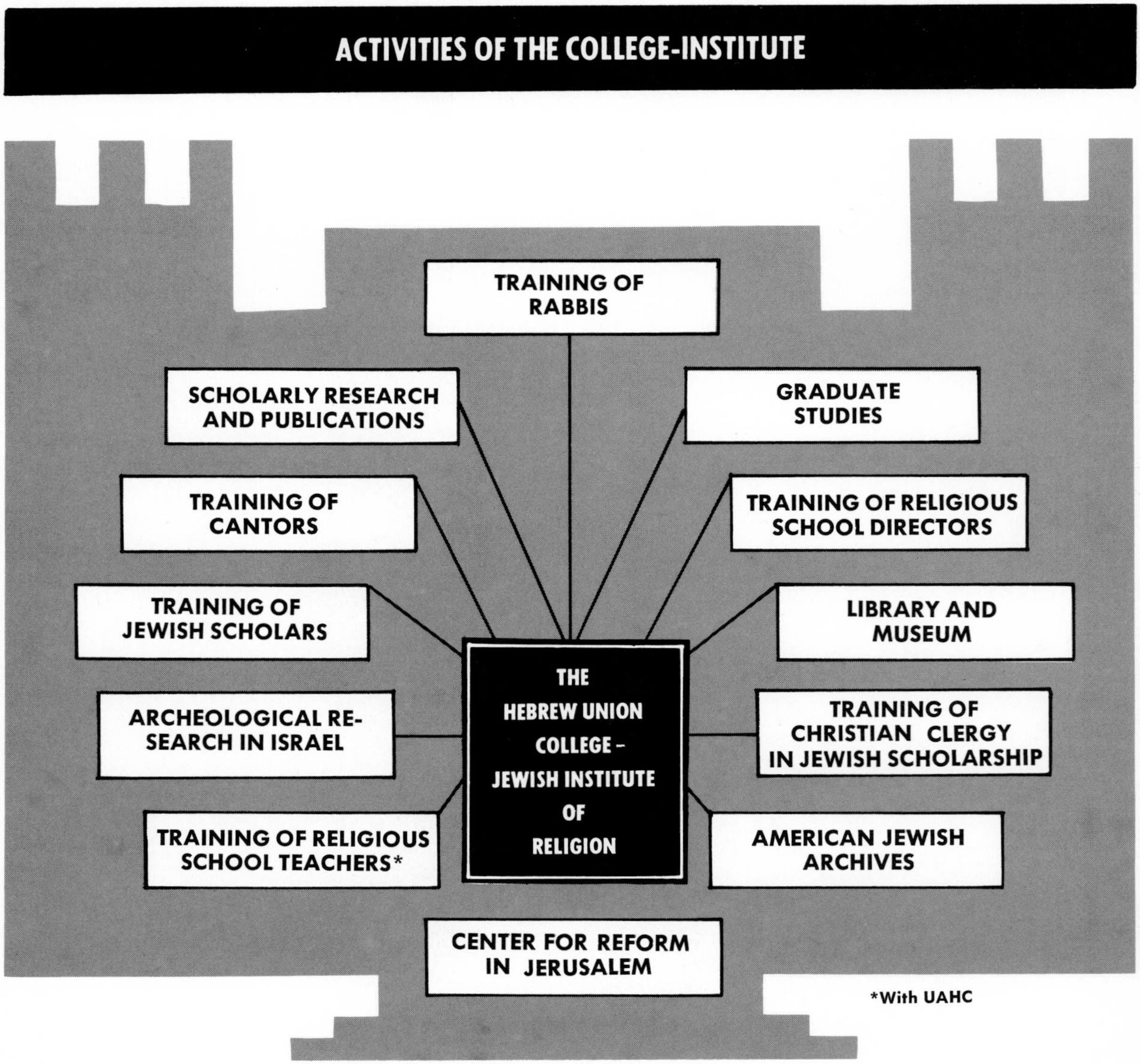

ACTIVITIES OF THE COLLEGE-INSTITUTE

TRAINING OF RABBIS

SCHOLARLY RESEARCH AND PUBLICATIONS

GRADUATE STUDIES

TRAINING OF CANTORS

TRAINING OF RELIGIOUS SCHOOL DIRECTORS

TRAINING OF JEWISH SCHOLARS

LIBRARY AND MUSEUM

ARCHEOLOGICAL RESEARCH IN ISRAEL

THE HEBREW UNION COLLEGE – JEWISH INSTITUTE OF RELIGION

TRAINING OF CHRISTIAN CLERGY IN JEWISH SCHOLARSHIP

TRAINING OF RELIGIOUS SCHOOL TEACHERS*

AMERICAN JEWISH ARCHIVES

CENTER FOR REFORM IN JERUSALEM

*With UAHC

headed the school in the past. Its former president Dr. Nelson Glueck was a world-famous archeologist who located many ancient copper mines and King Solomon's seaport.

Its current president is Alfred Gottschalk, a well-known scholar and former dean of the California School.

Hence, an important phase of the school's work is the training of Jewish scholars, and among the members of its faculty are many of its own graduates. In recent years, too, an increasing number of Christian ministers and priests have taken work at the school in pursuit of a doctorate in Judaic studies, with the result that its graduates now serve on the faculties of some of the leading Christian seminaries in the United States.

In 1963, the College-Institute established a branch school in Jerusalem, primarily for the purpose of biblical and archeological research. Today, scholars from all over the world study there and take part in its archeological explorations. One of the best-known of these has been the excavation of Gezer, an ancient Canaanite city, located about midway between Jerusalem and the seacoast, that was originally captured by the Pharaohs and later presented to King Solomon as part of the dowry of his Egyptian bride.

The Jerusalem School also serves as an important center for Reform Judaism, enabling many Israelis who have had no contact with it to participate in lectures and discussions and to attend Reform Sabbath and holiday services.

The Union of American Hebrew Congregations

The work of the College-Institute has been made possible largely by the support of its patron organization, the Union of American Hebrew Congregations, or Union as it is commonly called. The unfortunate experience with Zion College finally convinced Isaac M. Wise that his seminary needed the financial support of as many congregations as possible. Therefore in 1873, two years before the college was created, he organized a union of congregations pledged by its constitution "to establish (and maintain) a Hebrew Theological Institute."

Beyond this, the Union was assigned three other important tasks:

—To provide for and advance the standards of Sabbath schools for the instruction of the young in Israel's religion and history and the Hebrew language;

HOUSE OF LIVING JUDAISM. Located on Fifth Avenue in New York, these are the national headquarters of the Union of American Hebrew Congregations and its affiliates.

Reform Judaism—Then and Now

—To aid and encourage young congregations by such material and spiritual support as may be at the command of the Union; and

—To provide . . . such other institutions which the common welfare and progress of Judaism shall require, without however interfering in any manner whatsoever with the affairs and management of any congregation.

Within two years the new Union more than doubled its original membership of twenty-four congregations. By the beginning of World War I it had about 200 member-congregations, roughly 300 by 1940, and in the late 1960's it had once again doubled its membership with about 700 affiliated temples.

Directing the Union is its president, currently Rabbi Maurice N. Eisendrath, a widely-known figure in American Jewish life.

The organization operates under policies established by its member-congregations, whose representatives meet every other year in a General Assembly of Delegates, otherwise called the Biennial Convention. Between conventions, the president takes counsel with a National Board of Trustees and a smaller Executive Committee to insure that policies and programs are carried out in the best interests of the movement.

In 1951, the Union moved its headquarters from Cincinnati to New York where, in the ten-story House of Living Judaism, more than a dozen different departments carry on the work. To render direct assistance to local temples, the Union also operates sixteen regional offices under the supervision of councils representing the congregations of each area.

The Union continues to carry on the duties prescribed by its original constitution almost a century ago, but the size and interests of the movement as well as changing conditions have greatly expanded its activity.

GROWTH OF THE REFORM MOVEMENT IN THE UNITED STATES

Congregations	24	103	172	205	254	284	400	688
FAMILIES	2,700	9,000	17,000	31,000	60,000	59,000	155,000	260,000
Year	1873	1900	1910	1920	1930	1940	1950	1968

The Union's Services to Its Congregations

Congregations benefit in many ways from the Union's services. It offers them valuable information on all phases of synagogue operation, from congregational constitutions, record-keeping, and membership campaigns, to the construction of a new sanctuary and the maintenance of a temple cemetery. Each congregation receives the results of synagogue research as well as experimental worship services and new ceremonial objects, such as the lovely Union Chanukah *menorah* (מְנוֹרָה, candelabrum) and the *kiddush* cup. In addition, the Union's publication, *Dimensions,* provides every temple member with the latest thinking on current religious issues.

In recent years, the organization has likewise helped establish more than a hundred new congregations and provided them with every assistance until they were capable of carrying on by themselves.

However, its most important contribution has been in the field of religious education. Over the years, its Department of Jewish Education has produced a model religious school curriculum, with hundreds of textbooks and materials, including teacher's guides, filmstrips, recordings, the magazine *Keeping Posted,* and many other publications that are used by more than a thousand schools throughout the world, many of which are not Reform. It promotes teacher training through special courses of study, workshops, institutes, and a national program of teacher certification. It also provides for youth and adult education through the preparation of numerous books, pamphlets, programs, and courses, and the promotion of numerous activities from coast to coast in more than a half-dozen year-round camps.

In all phases of its work, the Union draws heavily upon the best professional resources available. Matters of synagogue construction, for example, receive the counsel of a committee of some of America's finest architects. Similarly, the Union's own affiliates, the National Association of Temple Administrators and the National Association of Temple Educators, assist it in meeting the administrative and educational needs of both individual congregations and the movement as a whole.

The Wider Role of the Union

But the Union's role in Jewish affairs has extended far beyond the Reform movement. For almost a century it was the principal spokesman for the American Jew in protesting against the mistreatment of Jews everywhere, particularly in Russia and Rumania. It helped organize the Hebrew Sheltering and Immigrant Aid Society, the present HIAS, to assist in the resettlement of newcomers from Eastern Europe. It actively fought all forms of discrimination against Jews in the United States and sought to eliminate violations of the separation of Church and State, especially the teaching of Christian doctrine and practice in the public schools.

Today, two of its main concerns are social action and interfaith understanding. Working with local temple social action committees, the Union prepares books, pamphlets, films, discussion manuals, and projects that seek to apply the ethics of Judaism to the issues of poverty, civil rights, religious liberty, and world peace. At the same time, its Religious Action Center, established in Washington in 1961, cooperates with leading religious and civic groups to influence the governments of the United States and other nations to support particular measures in behalf of peace and social justice.

Development of better religious understanding is the objective of the Union's Department of Interfaith Activities. In cooperation with similar agencies of the Protestants and Roman Catholics, it engages in mutual religious dialogue and projects, such as visits to churches and synagogues, to promote wider understanding among the followers of the various faiths. Another important phase of its program is to provide as many non-Jews as possible with accurate information about Jews and Judaism. Here, in addition to producing appropriate television and radio programs, conducting interfaith weekends for youth, and promoting institutes on Judaism for Christian ministers, religious school teachers, and laymen, it publishes a series of pamphlets, called *Popular Studies in Judaism,* that supply authentic information about Jewish beliefs and practices and Jewish literature and institutions.

Sisterhoods—Brotherhoods—Youth

The House of Living Judaism is also the headquarters of the Union's three most important affiliates, the National Federation of Temple Sisterhoods (NFTS), the National Federation of Temple Brotherhoods (NFTB), and the National Federation of Temple Youth (NFTY).

The national Sisterhood organization was founded in 1913, and today comprises more than 600 temple women's groups throughout the world, with a total of some 110,000 members. Beyond supplying local Sisterhoods with all types of assistance and materials that range from program suggestions to an annual Jewish art calendar, the NFTS regularly carries on certain important national and international projects.

For example, in 1925, it built the first dormitory on the Cincinnati campus of the College-Institute and some years later succeeded in raising considerable sums toward the construction and enlargement of the Union's House of Living Judaism. In 1931 it founded the Jewish Braille Institute through which Sisterhood members prepare Jewish books for the blind. And its annual sale of Uniongrams contributes to student aid to the College-Institute and support of the Union's work in the religious school and with youth. A recent project is the building of a synagogue in Ben-Shemen Children's Village in Israel.

The National Federation of Temple Brotherhoods, formed in 1923, likewise renders valuable assistance to its 500 local Reform men's clubs and encourages them to undertake important activities in behalf of temple attendance, youth and adult education, religious observance in the home, and service to the aged. And, as its chief national project, NFTB sponsors the Jewish Chautauqua Society.

Originally established in 1893 by one of the early graduates of the Hebrew Union College to provide lectures on Jewish subjects for Jews, the Jewish Chautauqua Society now concentrates on bringing information about Judaism to college campuses. Each year it sponsors lectures and classes on some 500 college campuses and at about 400 church camps. To date it has also donated an average of fifty volumes dealing with Judaism to more than a thousand colleges and universities and produced more than a dozen films about Jewish practice and belief.

Youngest of the three affiliates is the National Federation of Temple Youth, which was founded in 1939. It currently consists of about 500 local youth groups, with a total membership of some 25,000 high-school-age youths, and carries on a program devoted to performing *mitzvot,* commandments, that call for service to others and Jewish religious and intellectual growth among its own membership. Thus, in addition to regular social and organizational activities, each youth group conducts a full program of study, worship, and service to the congregation and community, for which it receives the *Na-aseh Venishma* (נַעֲשֶׂה וְנִשְׁמַע, "We shall Do and We Shall Hearken") Award, a title derived from the promise of Israel at Sinai to obey God's commands (Exodus 24:7).

NFTY also sponsors annual regional and subregional conclaves and a variety of exciting summer activities that include leadership training institutes, workshops in the Jewish arts, study in Israel or in the "Torah Corps," and service in one of the "*Mitzvah* Corps" that operate in the slums of an American city or in some underdeveloped country. In recent years its major national project has been the annual campaign for the Leo Baeck School

in Haifa, the only full-time high school in Israel offering young people a liberal Jewish education.

The Central Conference of American Rabbis

Of the three major American Reform organizations, the last to be established was the Central Conference of American Rabbis, or-

ACTIVITIES OF THE UNION OF AMERICAN HEBREW CONGREGATIONS

SERVICE TO REFORM CONGREGATIONS

ORGANIZING NEW CONGREGATIONS

INTERFAITH ACTIVITIES*

PREPARATION OF CEREMONIALS AND RITUALS*

INFORMATION ON JUDAISM*

NATIONAL FEDERATION OF TEMPLE YOUTH

THE UNION OF AMERICAN HEBREW CONGREGATIONS

SOCIAL ACTION*

RELIGIOUS EDUCATION*

REGIONAL OFFICES AND CAMPS

PATRON OF THE COLLEGE-INSTITUTE

NATIONAL FEDERATION OF TEMPLE BROTHERHOODS

NATIONAL FEDERATION OF TEMPLE SISTERHOODS

*With CCAR

299

ganized in 1889 by Isaac M. Wise and some thirty colleagues. Two of its main purposes were to develop "authoritative norms, guiding principles, and precedents" for the movement through annual meetings whose proceedings would be reported in a yearbook and to create a fund to protect "any unfortunate colleague or his family from becoming humiliated as objects of charity."

These are still among its more important functions. Meeting annually and publishing the proceedings in its yearbook, the Conference determines major Reform principles and practices and expresses its position on current Jewish issues as well as on the leading reli-

gious, social, and international problems of the day. And, in addition to maintaining a relief fund for members, it has since established a rabbinical pension fund and placement system which it conducts jointly with the Union.

Between conventions, the Conference, which now numbers almost a thousand members, carries on its work through elected officials, a permanent executive vice president, and a variety of standing committees. Among them is one responsible for providing Reform chaplains for the armed forces; another supervises the publication of the *CCAR Journal,* a periodical of scholarly and profes-

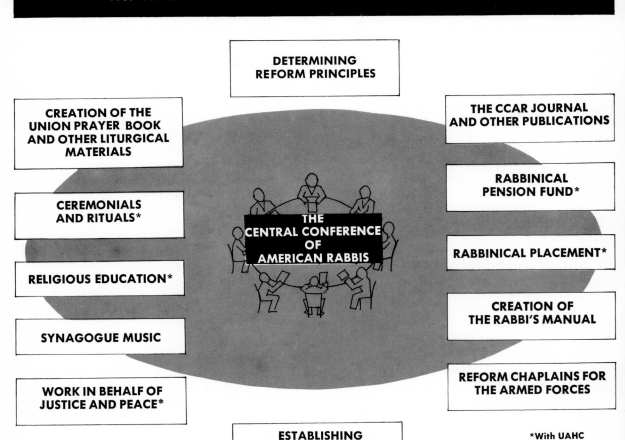

ACTIVITIES OF THE CENTRAL CONFERENCE OF AMERICAN RABBIS

DETERMINING
REFORM PRINCIPLES

CREATION OF THE
UNION PRAYER BOOK
AND OTHER LITURGICAL
MATERIALS

THE CCAR JOURNAL
AND OTHER PUBLICATIONS

CEREMONIALS
AND RITUALS*

THE
CENTRAL CONFERENCE
OF
AMERICAN RABBIS

RABBINICAL
PENSION FUND*

RELIGIOUS EDUCATION*

RABBINICAL PLACEMENT*

SYNAGOGUE MUSIC

CREATION OF
THE RABBI'S MANUAL

WORK IN BEHALF OF
JUSTICE AND PEACE*

REFORM CHAPLAINS FOR
THE ARMED FORCES

ESTABLISHING
REFORM PRACTICE*

*With UAHC

sional interest; and a third is devoted to issues involving the separation of Church and State. Through various joint commissions with the Union, the Conference is also involved in the movement's programs for religious education, social action, and interfaith cooperation.

From the very beginning, another of the Conference's chief concerns has been the preparation of materials for Reform worship, and over the years it has produced many essential works. Foremost among them have been the two volumes of the *Union Prayer Book,* one of which is designed for weekday, Sabbath, and festival services, and the other for the High Holy Days. The Conference also publishes the *Union Hymnal* and *Union Songster* for congregational singing, the *Union Home Prayer Book* for private and family devotions, the *Union Haggadah* for the Passover seder, and the *Rabbi's Manual* for conducting weddings, funerals, and other important religious rites.

A World Organization

By belonging to a Reform congregation, then, every member enjoys all the benefits of the movement's national organizations. But he is also linked with other Reform movements in about twenty-five different countries throughout the world by his association with the World Union for Progressive Judaism.

The World Union was formed in July, 1926, at an international Reform gathering in London called by Miss Lily Montagu, Rabbi Israel Mattuck and Dr. Claude G. Montefiore, all prominent Reform leaders of England. At this meeting, representatives from the United States, Germany, Czechoslovakia, France, Sweden, and India, as well as those from England, agreed to establish a permanent World Union for Progressive Judaism. At a second meeting two years later the organization adopted three objectives: (1) to preserve Judaism by enabling it to respond to

SISTERHOOD CONVENTION. The National Federation of Temple Sisterhoods is an important affiliate of the Union and engages in many national projects for the movement.

modern conditions and stimulating all Jews to participate in religious life, (2) to encourage the growth of Reform everywhere in the world, and (3) to promote cooperation among the existing Reform movements.

Since then, the World Union has conducted an international conference every two years at which it reviews the religious needs of Jews throughout the world and adopts plans for promoting Reform Judaism in particular countries. By placing rabbis and supplying prayer books and educational materials, it has thus far been successful in establishing Reform movements in South Africa, Australia and New Zealand, Central and South America, India, Israel, and several countries in Europe.

Since its creation, the World Union has undertaken two additional projects. One has been the establishment of Reform seminaries in Paris and London to train rabbis for service in foreign lands. The other has resulted in the creation of an international youth federation, called the World Union of Progressive Jewish Youth Section—generally known simply by the initials WUPJYS—through which Reform youth can meet and plan religious and social programs for European Jewish young people.

What of the Future

With effective organization, the Reform movement has been able to overcome many of its earlier weaknesses. So much so that the other interpretations of Judaism in the United States soon followed its example. Thus, the Conservative movement today operates with a rabbinical school of its own, the Jewish Theological Seminary, a union of congregations known as the United Synagogue, and a rabbinical association called the Rabbinical Assembly. The Orthodox also have similar organizations.

Yet judging from the various "live issues" that exist, Reform continues to face problems. Some, such as the opposition of the ultra-Orthodox and the difficulties with Sabbath observance, have been inherited from the past. Others, such as the proposal for merger with Conservatism and the question of a guide for Reform practice, are of more recent origin.

Other problems also have begun to appear as a result of the scientific, intellectual, and social revolutions that are producing so many changes in present-day life. Here, in common with other religions, Reform faces many new and difficult challenges, among them some that involve the future of Judaism and the Jews.

Thus the question remains whether, having dealt successfully with so many problems of the past, Reform will also be able to cope with those of today and tomorrow.

QUESTIONS FOR DISCUSSION

1. How is your own temple organized? How does this kind of organization help achieve the various purposes for which the congregation exists? What improvements, if any, would you recommend and why?

2. How does your congregation benefit from each of the various national Reform organizations? What difficulties would your temple face without them?

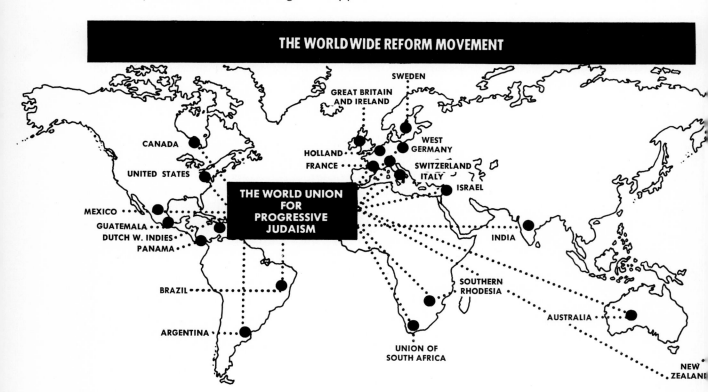

THE WORLDWIDE REFORM MOVEMENT

THE WORLD UNION FOR PROGRESSIVE JUDAISM

SWEDEN
GREAT BRITAIN AND IRELAND
CANADA
HOLLAND
WEST GERMANY
FRANCE
SWITZERLAND
ITALY
ISRAEL
UNITED STATES
MEXICO
GUATEMALA
DUTCH W. INDIES
PANAMA
INDIA
BRAZIL
SOUTHERN RHODESIA
AUSTRALIA
ARGENTINA
UNION OF SOUTH AFRICA
NEW ZEALAND

3. What are some of the principal duties of Reform rabbis? What activities, for instance, does your own rabbi carry on? How did his training at the College-Institute prepare him for this?

4. How do the Union of American Hebrew Congregations and the Central Conference of American Rabbis seek to carry out the purposes for which they were originally organized? What other functions, if any, should they be carrying on today?

5. Why is the World Union for Progressive Judaism of importance to the Reform movement today? Of what benefit is it to you and your congregation? To the Jews of other countries?

6. What problems faced by the movement in Europe have American Reform organizations succeeded in overcoming? What other problems do you see Reform facing today? How do you account for these?

SIGNIFICANT DOCUMENTS

The Spirit of the College-Institute, by Nelson Glueck, Its Sixth President, 1964

We are a liberal institution of higher learning in Judaism. Born and bred in the American scene, the College-Institute shares in the spirit of free inquiry and study which marks American colleges and universities. Unlimited academic freedom blends harmoniously with fidelity to Jewish institutions, as these have been shaped in Reform Judaism in the past 150 years. Nothing in the Jewish past or present is alien to our interest. We cherish the right of the free conscience to study Judaism, and we impose the need to study as an obligation on candidates for the Reform

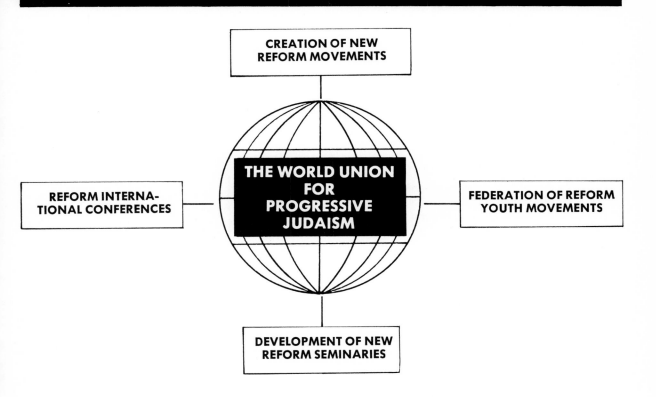

ACTIVITIES OF THE WORLD UNION FOR PROGRESSIVE JUDAISM

CREATION OF NEW REFORM MOVEMENTS

REFORM INTERNATIONAL CONFERENCES

THE WORLD UNION FOR PROGRESSIVE JUDAISM

FEDERATION OF REFORM YOUTH MOVEMENTS

DEVELOPMENT OF NEW REFORM SEMINARIES

rabbinate. We have confidence that the accurate and affirmatively critical and free study of our tradition will ensure its survival and enhance its sanctity. We are dedicated to God and to Israel.

—From the *Hebrew Union College-Jewish Institute of Religion Catalogue,* 1967, p. 3.

Objectives of the Union of American Hebrew Congregations, from Its Revised Constitution, 1946

Preamble

The congregations represented in this Union of American Hebrew Congregations affirm their faithful attachment to Judaism and their adherence to its liberal interpretation, and unite to discharge their responsibilities under the protection of benign Providence.

Objects

a. To encourage and aid the organization and development of Jewish congregations.

b. To promote Jewish education and to enrich and intensify Jewish life.

c. To maintain the Hebrew Union College.

d. To foster other activities for the perpetuation and advancement of Judaism.

Congregational Autonomy

Nothing contained in this Constitution or the By-laws shall be construed so as to interfere in any manner whatsoever with the mode of worship, the school, the freedom of expression and opinion, or any of the other congregational activities of the constituent congregations of the Union.

—From the *71st–73rd Annual Report of the Union of American Hebrew Congregations,* p. 287.

The Functions of the Central Conference of American Rabbis, from the Opening Address of Its First President, Isaac M. Wise, 1890

. . . The united rabbis of America have undoubtedly the right—also according to talmudical teachings—to declare and decide, anyhow for our country with its peculiar circumstances unforeseen anywhere, which of our religious forms, institutions, observances, usages, customs, ordinances, and prescriptions are still living factors in our religious, ethical, and intellectual life and which are so no longer and ought to be replaced by more adequate means to give expression to the spirit of Judaism and to reveal its character of universal religion.

It is undoubtedly the duty and right of the united rabbis to protect Judaism against stagnation and each individual rabbi against the attacks frequently made upon every one who proposes any reform measure. Let the attack be made hereafter on the Conference and let the honor of the individual be preserved intact. All reforms ought to go into practice on the authority of the Conference, not only to protect the individual rabbi but to protect Judaism against presumptuous innovations and the precipitations of rash and inconsiderate men. The Conference is the lawful authority in all matters of form.

The united rabbis of America have undoubtedly the right and the duty to produce a uniform form of worship for all our houses of worship. This cannot be done at once, as disintegration has spread its roots too far, and must not be done by adapting texts and forms from abroad, as Israel lends to many and borrows from none. It must be done gradually and originally—a beginning will be made to it in this meeting—with the consent and to the satisfaction of all and can be done lawfully and effectually by the Conference only.

All work done in contribution to such ritual must, of course, correspond with the principle that Judaism is universal religion and contains nothing contrary to it. In order to develop Judaism for this, its mission, it must be provided with such ritual from which every intelligent person can utter his Maker's praise and adoration, can render thanksgiving to Him who is the source of all that gladdens the heart of man, and pray to Him who is the Father of all, in prose or in verse, from the Psalms of David and the Prophets, the typical prayers of the ancient sages and Hebrew poets, or the original composition of our own contemporaries, if it only has the character of universal religion and the eloquence of genuine piety.

The united rabbis have furthermore the duty to provide a catechism [course of study] for the Sabbath schools on the same principle with the ritual. This also must be done after mature deliberation, with the consent and to the satisfaction of the whole Conference, to imprint it with the authority of the entire rabbinate of America. Hitherto, we have given a number of such textbooks resting on the authority of individuals, which critical minds do not consider the authorized expression of Judaism; and, in fact, some of these books are good and others are not, some are good yet and others are antiquated. Some make concessions to superannuated Orthodoxy and others to the sectarian views of our Christian neighbors, and others again to some predominating philosophy. We ought not allow the rising generation to depend on individual views and opinions in so important a matter as is American Judaism to us and the cause of humanity.

The united rabbis in conference assembled should annually give fresh impulses and new encouragement to the study of the literature of Israel, especially by giving out select subjects for investigation and research to individuals or committees to be worked up in essays, treatises, reports, sermons, or lectures, to be published in the *CCAR Yearbook,* in magazines, or pamphlets and books. Unless the literature of Israel become the common property of the American rabbinate, it cannot fully perform its duty to American Judaism and cannot successfully unfold the spirit of universal religion contained therein.

Whatever advances the spirit of Judaism in its true character as universal religion, it is the right and duty of the united rabbis in conference assembled to do, and to do it well, in the name of God and Israel, for the sake of our country and our people, for the triumph of truth, humanity, and righteousness . . .

—From the *Central Conference
of American Rabbis Yearbook,*
Vol. 1 (1890), pp. 19–21.

The Purpose of the World Union for Progressive Judaism, from Its Constitution, 1928

Name

The name of this organization shall be the "World Union for Progressive Judaism" (hereinafter referred to as the "World Union").

The term "Progressive" shall include all forms of Judaism which are in harmony with the principles of the Preamble, whether designated "Liberal," "Reform," "Progressive," or by any other name.

Purpose

The objects of the World Union are:

To further the development of Progressive Judaism; to encourage the formation of Progressive Jewish religious communities or congregations in the different countries of the world and to promote their cooperation; to stimulate and encourage the study of Judaism and its adaptation and application to modern life without changing the fundamental principles of Judaism, and to awaken an active interest in Progressive Judaism among those Jews who, for one reason or another, do not participate in Jewish religious life.

In furtherance of these objects the World Union will, as far as possible, keep its members informed of the developments of thought and the progress in Judaism throughout the world; and in those countries in which there are no Progressive congregations, the World Union may, through such representatives and organizers as the Governing Body, from time to time, appoint, cooperate with, and assist residents of the said countries in organizing such congregations . . .

—From W. Gunther Plaut,
The Growth of Reform Judaism,
p. 92.

WORLD UNION CONFERENCE. The first official conference of the World Union for Progressive Judaism after its formation was held in Berlin in 1928.

OTHER THINGS TO READ

Central Conference of American Rabbis Journal: latest issue.

Central Conference of American Rabbis Yearbook: latest edition.

Cohon, Samuel S., "The History of the Hebrew Union College," *Publications of the American Jewish Historical Society,* Vol. 40, Part 1 (September, 1950), pp. 17–55.

Dimensions (published by the Union of American Hebrew Congregations): latest issue.

Feuer, Leon I., and Azriel Eisenberg, *Jewish Literature since the Bible, II:* pp. 187–190 (the Union and the role of the congregation).

Gumbiner, Joseph H., *Isaac Mayer Wise, Pioneer of American Judaism:* Chap. 12, "Building a Union of Congregations"; Chap. 13, "The Hebrew Union College"; Chap. 14, "The Central Conference of American Rabbis."

Hebrew Union College-Jewish Institute of Religion Catalogue: latest edition.

Jewish Encyclopedia: "Conferences of American Rabbis," Vol. 4, pp. 215–217; "Hebrew Union College," Vol. 6, p. 311; "Union of American Hebrew Congregations," Vol. 12, pp. 344–345.

Learsi, Rufus, *The Jews in America: A History:* Chap. 14, "Trends and Leaders."

Levinger, Lee J., *A History of the Jews in the United States:* p. 254 (the Union); Chap. 25, "How the Jew Keeps His Judaism in America."

Masserman, Paul, and Max Baker, *The Jews Come to America:* pp. 187–197 (founding of the Union, College, and Conference).

News and Views (published by the World Union for Progressive Judaism): latest issue.

Philipson, David, *Centenary papers and Others:* "The Principles and Achievements of the Central Conference of American Rabbis," pp. 191–228. [Also found in *Central Conference of American Rabbis Yearbook,* Vol. 23 (1913).]

Philipson, David, *The Reform Movement in Judaism:* pp. 357–358 (founding of the Conference); pp. 377–381 (founding of the Union, College, and Institute); pp. 428–434 (founding of the World Union).

Plaut, W. Gunther, *The Growth of Reform Judaism:* Chap. 2, "Congregational Union in America"; Chap. 3, "Rabbinic Union in America"; pp. 50–59 (Hebrew Union College, Jewish Theological Seminary); 86–96 (Jewish Institute of Religion, World Union for Progressive Judaism).

Schwartzman, Sylvan D., *Reform Judaism in the Making:* Chap. 16, "How Reform Is Organized."

Standard Jewish Encyclopedia: "Central Conference of American Rabbis," p. 420; "Maurice N. Eisendrath," p. 606; "Nelson Glueck," p. 761; "Hebrew Union College-Jewish Institute of Religion," pp. 876–877; "Union of American Hebrew Congregations," p. 1855; "Stephen Samuel Wise," pp. 1917–1918; "World Union for Progressive Judaism," p. 1929.

Universal Jewish Encyclopedia: "Central Conference of American Rabbis," Vol. 3, pp. 88–92; "Hebrew Union College," Vol. 5, pp. 282–283; "Jewish Institute of Religion," Vol. 6, pp. 132–133; "Union of American Hebrew Congregations," Vol. 10, pp. 344–345; "Stephen S. Wise," Vol. 10, pp. 543–544; "World Union for Progressive Judaism," Vol. 10, pp. 575–576.

SUGGESTED ACTIVITIES

1. View one of the movies produced by the national Federation of Temple Brotherhoods. On the basis of the information it offers, do you think it would be helpful to Christians your age? If so, arrange to show it in a nearby church school and conduct an open discussion afterwards.

2. On the basis of the constitution of your congregation, draw up an organizational chart showing how the temple operates and what duties each officer, committee, and employee of the congregation performs.

3. Conduct a campaign in your school for the Reform Jewish Appeal. Prepare a series of posters, pamphlets, or slides describing the work of the Union and the College-Institute, especially as it affects your religious school and temple.

SUBJECTS FOR RESEARCH

1. What activities are carried on by your temple's Sisterhood, Brotherhood, and youth group? How do these benefit the congregation?

2. Examine a copy of the latest catalogue of the College-Institute. What subjects does an individual training for the Reform rabbinate today have to study? Why is each necessary?

3. How and why was the Jewish Institute of Religion merged with the Hebrew Union College in 1950?

4. Compare the *Union Prayer Book,* Vol. I, published in 1924, with the present edition. How do you explain some of the differences?

5. What contributions has each of the following made to Reform: (a) Rabbi Stephen S. Wise, (b) Claude G. Montefiore, (c) Miss Lily Montagu, (d) Rabbi Leo Baeck, (3) Rabbi Maurice N. Eisendrath, and (f) Dr. Nelson Glueck?

FILMSTRIPS TO SEE

Within the Family of Liberal Judaism (UAHC), describing the roles of the Reform national organizations in relation to the local congregations.

Isaac Mayer Wise: Master Builder of American Judaism (UAHC), picturing the life and achievements of this great creator of American Reform organization.

The Leo Baeck School in Israel (UAHC), presenting highlights of the activities carried on by this important Liberal Jewish institution in Israel.

Rabbi Stephen S. Wise: A Twentieth Century Prophet (UAHC), portraying the life and contributions of this dynamic Reform Jewish leader and founder of the Jewish Institute of Religion.

Nelson Glueck, Rabbi: Archeologist and Biblical Scholar (UAHC), presenting some of the major accomplishments of this distinguished president of the College-Institute.

Call for the Question: The Synagogue in the Community (UAHC), depicting the temple's role in social action.

A LIVE ISSUE

Though the Guiding Principles describes Reform's essential religious beliefs, much debate has since arisen over the matter of its theology, particularly, as we shall see in this chapter, its conception of God.

In spite of the difficulty of trying to describe God in even the most general terms, most people in the movement hold that Reform as a rational faith must present some reasonable conception of Him. Failure to do so, they contend, is not only to divorce reason from religion but to make God so remote from man as to eliminate any meaningful relationship with Him.

The Basic Problem: If Reform theology must be revised, what conception of God should the movement adopt? Many different answers, as we shall see, have been proposed, but which is most suitable for Reform remains to be decided. This, in turn, will also affect solutions to other theological questions, such as the nature of God's role in the world and the function of prayer.

Some Important Questions: (1) In view of the arguments of some, how is it possible for human beings ever to comprehend the nature of God? (2) Why, nevertheless, is it necessary for Reform Judaism to develop some conception of God? (3) What are some of the difficulties with the theology contained in the Guiding Principles? (4) What other God-concepts are currently being proposed? (5) How does each seek to cope with the critical theological issues that have arisen in recent years?

What Do You Think? The problem of Reform theology is a difficult one, but as a religious movement it obviously demands some view of God. As you read about the subject in this chapter, what conclusions do you as a Reform Jew find most satisfactory?

19. REFORM JUDAISM—PROGRESS AND PROMISE

Some Impressive Achievements

> **It ought today no longer be denied that Reform Judaism . . . came as a saving force at a time when religion was at a decline and apostasy had become almost epidemic among the higher classes . . .**

So stated Kaufmann Kohler before the Central Conference of American Rabbis in 1925, and we may well share his appreciation for the contributions of Reform.

The fact is that for a movement that did not exist before the 1800's, it has certainly accomplished a great deal in a relatively short time. For here in brief are some of its more impressive achievements:

—A liberal Jewish religious movement with well over a million members.

—A series of national and world organizations to promote its work.

—More than a thousand rabbis, and numerous cantors, synagogue administrators, educators, school principals, and teachers.

—A full-scale program of Jewish religious education, with appropriate resources for every age-level, from the young to the aged.

—A wide variety of liturgical materials, including prayer books, hymnals, and holiday rituals.

—A great number of important contributions to Jewish scholarship through scientific study of the past and present.

—Many new forms of synagogue art, architecture, music, ceremonials, and congregational procedures.

To these must be added Reform's record of leadership in the struggle for civic morality and social justice. For instance, during an early strike against the US Steel Corporation, Rabbi Samuel Goldenson, a noted Reformer of Pittsburgh, actually went into the coal mines to see conditions for himself. He then

Leading Twentieth-Century Reformers in Europe and America

Key Reform Events	European Reformers	American Reformers
1869—Leipzig Synod. 1871—Augsburg Synod. 1873—Formation of the Union of American Hebrew Congregations. 1875—Founding of the Hebrew Union College.	*Claude Montefiore* (1859–1938), philanthropist, scholar, leader of British Reform, and an organizer of the World Union. *Lily (Lillian H.) Montagu* (1873–1965), leader of British Reform and an organizer of the World Union. *Leo Baeck* (1874–1956), last head of the Berlin Reform Seminary and spiritual hero of the Nazi period.	*David Philipson* (1862–1949), member of the first class of Hebrew Union College, Reform historian, and rabbi in Cincinnati. *Stephen S. Wise* (1874–1949), New York rabbi, world Jewish leader, and founder of the Jewish Institute of Religion. *Judah L. Magnes* (1877–1948), organizer of the New York Jewish Kehillah, founder and first president of the Hebrew University in Jerusalem. *Samuel Goldenson* (1878–1962), rabbi in Pittsburgh and later New York, noted scholar, and prominent in social action.
1883—First class graduated from Hebrew Union College. 1889—Formation of the Central Conference of American Rabbis. 1892—Publication of the *Union Prayer Book*.	*Israel Mattuck* (1883–1954), American-educated rabbi of London's Liberal Synagogue and chairman of the World Union.	*Abraham Cronbach* (1882–1965), professor at the College-Institute, a leader in behalf of social justice and world peace. *Solomon B. Freehof* (1892—), rabbi of Pittsburgh, leading scholar, author of many Reform responsa, and honorary life president of the World Union.

Key Reform Events	European Reformers	American Reformers
		Abba Hillel Silver (1893–1963), eloquent rabbi of Cleveland, outstanding leader of the American and World Zionist movement.
		Edward L. Israel (1896–1941), rabbi of Baltimore, and leader in social action, who served briefly as head of the Union.
1899—Formation of the Union of Liberal Rabbis in Germany.		*Nelson Glueck* (1900–1971), biblical archeologist and scholar, president of the College-Institute.
		Maurice N. Eisendrath (1902—), rabbi in Toronto, American Jewish leader and president of the Union.
1909—Organization of the Jewish Religious Union in England.		
1922—Founding of the Jewish Institute of Religion.		
1926—Formation of the World Union for Progressive Judaism.		
1950—Merger of the College-Institute.		
1955—Creation of the Liberal Rabbinical Seminary in Paris.		
1963—Founding of the College-Institute's Jerusalem School.		

supported the claims of the miners against the employers, among whom were some of his most prominent members.

Similarly, Rabbi Stephen S. Wise resisted enormous pressure against his helping to put an end to the power of the notorious Tammany Democratic machine that controlled New York City. And at the threat of losing his life, Rabbi Samuel Mayerberg persisted in exposing political corruption in Kansas City. Among other notables in the field of social action were Rabbi Edward L. Israel of Baltimore, whose work included the arbitration of numerous labor disputes, and Dr. Abraham

Cronbach, a professor at the College-Institute, whose personal concern for the socially oppressed inspired an entire generation of Reform youth.

Numerous, too, have been the movement's efforts to advance Jewish life in the United States and elsewhere. It was Reform Jews who helped establish the American Jewish Historical Society, the Jewish Publication Society, the National Council of Jewish Women, the American Jewish Committee, the Synagogue Council of America, and many other organizations. The first Jew to be commissioned as a chaplain in the American armed forces was Reform. A Reform rabbi, Benjamin Frankel, established the first Hillel Foundation on a university campus, and another, Judah L. Magnes, was the first president of the Hebrew University. The original, monumental *Jewish Encyclopedia* was largely the work of Reform scholars, and the editor-in-chief of the latest English translation of the Bible issued by the Jewish Publication Society is a faculty member at the College-Institute. The list could go on and on.

Also of prime importance has been Reform's influence upon the modern Jew's religious life. As Kohler himself noted, "The Reform movement roused Orthodoxy from its medieval slumber, warning it that in adhering to its ghetto form and spirit it will lapse into utter stagnation and decay." Thus, not only did Reform give rise to Conservative Judaism but it inspired the development of modern forms of Orthodoxy as well.

In a variety of practical ways, moreover, Conservatism and modern Orthodoxy have tended to follow Reform's example. Both have introduced decorum into the synagogue, provided translations of the prayers, and adopted weekly preaching, the late Friday evening service, and the ceremony of Confirmation. They have likewise patterned their national organizations and programs of religious education after those of Reform.

But it is Reform's conception of Judaism and Jewish life that has had the greatest impact on the thinking of the modern Jew.

Reform's Fundamental Principles

The Jew, declares Reform, cannot close his eyes to the realities of life today. At the very least he must reckon with the enormous effect of emancipation and Western culture and the need for an expression of Jewish life that comes to grips with both. To this end Reform holds that five of its fundamental principles are indispensable: the primary role of religion, the progressive nature of Judaism, the purpose of Jewish life, Jewish self-preservation, and support of liberalism.

The Primary Role of Religion

The first principle, which insists upon the primary role of religion in Jewish life, may be summed up as follows:

> **Religion is central to the Jew. Without it the causes he champions are bound to suffer and his very survival is endangered. For lacking a sense of devotion to God and His demands, the Jew soon loses his sense of purpose, and the quality of Jewish life deteriorates.**

Ever since emancipation, Jews have put forward various secular interpretations of Jewish life. We have only to recall how popular were socialism and Jewish nationalism during the movement's earlier days, and today other forms of secularism have arisen to challenge Judaism. Among them are those that center upon Hebrew and Yiddish culture, Jewish philanthropy, the State of Israel, even social action itself.

Though the Reform Jew looks upon all these as legitimate Jewish concerns, he sees them simply as facets of his religion. Histori-

312

cally he observes how, in the absence of a genuine religious commitment, some of the most worthwhile Jewish causes failed to live up to their high purpose. How quickly, for example, the prophetic call to social righteousness was forgotten and how soon former Jewish states in Palestine collapsed when the people's devotion to Judaism grew slack. Jews after all are human, and lacking the moral and spiritual motivation of Judaism, their endeavors quickly succumb to the same ills that befall those of other peoples.

Religion, then, says Reform, is the vital element in a sound program of Jewish life.

The Progressive Nature of Judaism

That Judaism is a progressive faith is Reforms' second important principle.

> In line with an advancing conception of God and His demands, Judaism continues to develop as the Jews respond to the changing circumstances of each age. Not only has this proved necessary in the past, as scientific study of the Bible and rabbinic literature confirms, but it is no less essential to the vitality of Judaism in the modern world.

From the Reform point of view, the Jewish religion has never been static. It has repeatedly undergone fresh interpretation as it has reacted to changing conditions. Thus older forms of worship involving supplication for rain and crops and ancient norms of conduct imposing heavy penalties for certain ritual infractions ultimately gave way to vastly different practices. In our own time new discoveries about the cosmos, with its millions

RADIO TELESCOPE. Located in Australia, it is capable of receiving waves from deep space. (Wide World Photos)

313

of galaxies that reveal the same constancy of physical law, have advanced the Jew's conception of God far beyond what was conceivable when the earth was thought to be the center of a comparatively small universe.

Indeed, as Reform insists, changing circumstances and advancing knowledge make religious progress a necessity.

The Purpose of Jewish Life

Third, the main purpose for the existence of the Jews is to fulfill a religious role that may be summed up as follows:

> Growing out of its ancient covenant with God, the Jewish people has undertaken to serve as His agent in society by seeking to become the living example of personal and social righteousness, justice, mercy, and peace and by alerting the world to their demands. In performing this mission, the Jews continually strive to achieve the establishment of the Messianic Age when God's ways will prevail on earth for the benefit of all mankind.

In essence, then, Reform reaffirms the teachings of the prophet Isaiah in which God refers to the Jewish people in these terms:

> Behold My servant whom I uphold,
> My chosen [people] in whom My soul takes
>   pleasure.
> I have put My spirit upon him;
> He shall make the right go forth to the
>   nations. . . .
> I, the Lord, have called you in
>   righteousness,
> And have taken you by the hand,
> And kept you, and set you for a covenant
>   with the people [of the earth],
> For a light unto the nations—
> To open the blind eyes,
> To bring out the prisoners from the
>   dungeon,

> And those who sit in darkness out of the
>   prison-house. . . .
> You are those who witness in My behalf,
>   says the Lord,
> And My servant whom I have chosen,
> That you may know and believe in Me, and
>   understand
> That I am He;
> Before Me there was no God,
> Neither shall there be any after Me . . .
> Look unto Me and be saved,
> All the ends of the earth!
> For I am God, and there is none else.

> (Isaiah 42:1, 6–7; 43:10; 45:22)

Indeed, says Reform, in an age of such frightful weaponry, the Jews' mission is all the more critical. For, without a determined effort to promote universal peace founded on justice, modern man may ultimately destroy himself.

Jewish Self-Preservation

If the Jews' mission is indispensable, then so obviously is their self-preservation. Hence the fourth Reform principle asserts:

> The perpetuation of the Jews, both in the Diaspora and the State of Israel, is essential and demands that each individual strive to maintain a vigorous Jewish life. To this end it is his obligation to support those institutions that contribute to the physical and spiritual preservation of Jewry and to cultivate that distinctive way of life that incorporates Jewish study, observance, and moral and ethical conduct.

Acknowledging that Judaism cannot exist without Jews, Reform stresses the need for the survival of a distinctive Jewish people. This, in turn, requires the Jews' protection from anti-Semitism, their relief and rescue when under attack, and the upbuilding of Jewish communities everywhere, including the State of Israel. In the face of growing assimilation today, the preservation of Jews urgently calls for the development and maintenance of a strong sense of Jewish identity and deep convictions about the worthwhileness of Jewish existence.

But self-perpetuation from the Reform point of view does not imply segregation. The Jew's mission, as we have seen, demands the fullest involvement with society. Nonetheless, his obligations to humanity begin with concern for his own people, very much as an individual's responsibilities start with his own family. Indeed, the Jew's devotion to fellow Jews prepares him for his wider duties to the whole of mankind.

Support of Liberalism

The movement, finally, is committed to the support of liberalism, which the dictionary defines as:

> . . . that philosophy which advocates the freedom of the individual, democratic systems of government, non-violent modification of human institutions to assure unrestricted development in human endeavor and governmental guarantees of individual rights and civil liberties.

So, for its fifth principle, Reform Judaism holds:

> Long experience reveals that the true progress of mankind, as well as the welfare of the Jewish people and the pursuit of its mission, requires the greatest possible freedom for every human being. To this end, Reform Judaism is committed to the cause of liberalism which insists upon equal rights and opportunities for all people, just social and economic conditions,

> and complete freedom of thought and religion. It demands no less of a liberal spirit among Jews themselves that will insure freedom of expression, belief, and practice for all members of the Jewish people.

Once more Reform draws upon its own experience in Europe where, in spite of Jewish emancipation, it often found itself the victim of political reaction, government interference in religious affairs, and continuing anti-Semitism, as well as repression by a type of Jewish community life that denied Judaism any opportunity for religious progress. In sharp contrast was the situation in America, with its unparalleled commitment to religious freedom. Little wonder that to Reform an expanding liberalism remains indispensable to both Jews and Judaism.

A Capacity for Dealing with Problems

In the course of our study of Reform Judaism we have encountered a great many "live issues." Perhaps you do not realize just how many, and so they are listed again below, grouped this time into four main categories:

1. Concerning Jews and Judaism in General

—What need is there for religion in Jewish life today?

—Is Jewish isolation necessary?

—How can assimilation be avoided?

—Who is a Jew?

—Should there be one organization to represent all of American Jewry?

—What is the future of the Diaspora?

2. Concerning Reform as a Movement

—How should Reform respond to Orthodox opposition?

—Is a merger between Reform and Conservatism desirable?

—To what extent should the movement involve itself in social action?

—Does Reform suffer from too great a concern with organization?

—Is the movement's program of religious education relevant?

3. Concerning Reform Practices

—Are both *Bar Mitzvah* and Confirmation needed?

—Should Reform have more traditional rituals or less?

—How should the Sabbath be observed by Reform Jews?

—Does Reform need a Guide to Practice?

4. Concerning Reform Beliefs

—Is there a genuine conflict between religion and science?

—Should Reform change its stand on separation of Church and State?

—Should Reform follow a moderate, evolutionary approach to religious change or one that is radical?

—What can Reform Jews believe about God?

SPECIAL MUSICAL SERVICE. Frequent today are such services conducted by Reform young people. (Jack Warner)

By no means do these exhaust the list. We could cite many other issues that the movement currently faces, including the question of introducing certain newer forms of worship like the rock service, revising the *Union Prayer Book,* establishing Reform all-day schools, and the like.

What becomes clear is the willingness of Reform Jews to deal with problems, among them some of the shortcomings of the movement itself. It is this capacity that has contributed so much to its vitality.

At a time when individual freedom is so much under attack, Reform Judaism's encouragement of open discussion and debate promises to be a source of continuing strength to the modern Jew.

Reform's Response to Change

If Reform progress may be measured by its record of achievement, its commitment to fundamental principles, and its capacity for dealing with problems, still another of its valuable assets is its receptivity to change—particularly so today when change is so much a part of our lives.

For a vastly different kind of world is emerging today. New views of man, society, and the universe have followed in the wake of the continuing "explosion" of knowledge and the sweeping changes in technology and communications. This, in turn, has challenged people to take a fresh look at some of their accepted standards and to reassess a number of their religious beliefs. Complete faith in the progress of man, for example, and in the ultimate establishment of God's Kingdom on earth has been severely strained by the existence of atomic weapons that can destroy the entire planet. For Jews in particular, the Nazi holocaust has raised doubts about belief in God's goodness and justice and in His capacity to prevent human catastrophe. Some

MARTIN BUBER. A religious philosopher known especially for his concept of the "I-Thou" relationship. (HUC, American Jewish Archives)

have even come to question His existence. Where was God, they ask, at Auschwitz and Buchenwald, where so many Jews were mercilessly slaughtered?

The result has been much theological debate leading to the expression of a number of different conceptions of God among Reform Jews. One, for instance, insists that He remains unlimited, all-powerful, and personal Being historically experienced by the Jewish people. Another describes Him as man's highest, everlasting concern, but utterly unknowable and indefinable. We catch a glimpse of Him, only as we seek to relate ourselves to Him through deed and prayer.

A third view holds that God is simply the creative Force or Power in the universe that makes for goodness and righteousness, toward which He impels us to strive. Still another position regards God as real, though by

American Reform Developments—from 1871

Important Happenings in World and Jewish Life	Major European Reform Events	Reform Developments in America
1871—Unification of Germany and of Italy.	**1871**—Augsburg Synod. **1872**—Founding of the Liberal Rabbinical Seminary in Berlin.	**1873**—Formation of the Union of American Hebrew Congregations. **1875**—Founding of Hebrew Union College. **1883**—First graduation from Hebrew Union College. **1885**—Pittsburgh Rabbinical Conference. **1889**—Formation of the Central Conference of American Rabbis. **1892**—Publication of the *Union Prayer Book.*
1881—Beginning of pogroms against Russian Jews. Start of mass immigration to the United States.		
1894—Beginning of the Dreyfus Affair (to 1906).		
1897—Formation of the World Zionist Organization.	**1899**—Formation of the Union of Liberal Rabbis in Germany.	
1903—Kishinev pogrom.	**1903**—Founding of the Union Israélite Libérale in Paris. **1908**—Establishment of the Union for Liberal Judaism in Germany.	
1909—Tel Aviv founded.	**1909**—Organization of the Jewish Religious Union in England.	**1913**—Organization of the National Federation of Temple Sisterhoods.
1914—Start of World War I (to 1918).		**1914**—Publication of the *Union Hymnal.* **1916**—Publication of the *Rabbi's Manual.*

Important Happenings in World and Jewish Life	Major European Reform Events	Reform Developments in America
1917—Balfour Declaration issued. Start of the Russian Revolution.		
		1922—Founding of the Jewish Institute of Religion.
		1923—Organization of the National Federation of Temple Brotherhoods.
	1926—Formation of the World Union for Progressive Judaism.	
	1929—Adoption of a common Reform prayer book in Germany.	
1933—Control of Germany seized by Hitler. Start of persecution of the Jews.		
		1937—Adoption of the Guiding Principles of Reform Judaism.
1939—Start of World War II (to 1945).		**1939**—Organization of the National Federation of Temple Youth.
1948—Founding of the State of Israel.		**1950**—Merger of the Hebrew Union College with the Jewish Institute of Religion.
		1951—Dedication of the Union's House of Living Judaism.
	1955—Creation of a Liberal rabbinical seminary in Paris.	
	1956—Establishment of the Leo Baeck School in London.	
		1962—Opening of the Union's Religious Action Center.
		1963—Founding of the College-Institute's Jerusalem School.

no means either perfect or all-powerful, else the world itself as His creation would have to be perfect. The fact that the universe is still incomplete and imperfect, observe supporters, should lead us to conclude that, though far more perfect and complete than man, God must still strive to attain His own perfection.

Each view in turn offers somewhat different answers to a series of other theological questions such as: What role does God play within an orderly universe? What is the purpose of prayer? Does God respond to prayer and, if so, how? What is the source of our religious knowledge, and how do we know it to be "true"? How valid today are Judaism's historic standards of "right" and "wrong"? What religious duties, or *mitzvot,* does God require of us?

Just as Reform is seeking to respond to the theological demands of the times, so it is also in the process of developing new forms of religious expression for this rapidly changing world. But this does not surprise us. Reform's capacity to respond to change is one of its most basic characteristics. And, as a famous British historian maintains, it is this very quality that confirms the soundness of a civilization or a society.

A Grave Situation, But—

Nevertheless there are some in the movement who have misgivings about Reform's future. One Reform spokesman, for instance, puts it this way:

> **Our movement has many organizational successes to its credit . . . But we know in our hearts that we have not succeeded in making American Jews pious, worshipful, happy, or prophetic . . .**

Another, citing the warning of Professor Oscar Janowsky that the cultural and spiritual life of American Jewry in general has become "shrunken and shallow," calls attention to an increasing amount of assimilation among Reform Jews. Nor, asserts an experienced Reform Hillel Foundation director, is the movement "winning substantial members of the college generation to a deep and serious commitment to Judaism."

By no means, of course, is Reform alone in feeling the effects of the current situation. Every segment of Jewish society shares this. But it does present a very special challenge to Reform Judaism which came into being to foster a vigorous Jewish way of life in the modern world. Obviously there is a great deal it must do to overcome present-day conditions.

Nevertheless, Reform remains optimistic about the future. From the perspective of its own history it recalls the deep despair about Judaism's future that was constantly voiced during its earlier days. Not only was this characteristic of traditional Jews who saw disaster in every change, but Reform leaders themselves would often give way to pessimism. So in a letter to a close friend written in 1840, Abraham Geiger was moved to say:

> **. . . And now, my dear friend, as regards Judaism's great strides forward, I am greatly dejected once again, and I do not know whether it is possible to breathe new life into these historical ruins . . . I must admit that at times I totally despair of this situation! . . .**

And in the aftermath of the Cleveland Conference, Isaac M. Wise so despaired of the Jews' future in America that he penned these words in his diary:

> **. . . We are swaying in mid-air, as it were, without support. Strife, contention, and disunion are rife among us.**

Yet, in both instances, the greatest achievements of the movement were still to come— in Europe, with the rabbinical conferences and synods and the formation of a Reform seminary; in America, with the unification of the movement, the creation of its national organizations, the development of the *Union Prayer Book,* and the remarkable growth of Reform membership.

Judging from the past, then, Reform has good reason to hold out hope for the future, deriving added confidence from other sources as well.

Reform Optimism . . . and—

In part, that optimism of Reform springs from a century and a half of success in coping with problems as vexing as those of our own day, of developing fundamental principles, introducing religious change, and producing numerous practical achievements.

It also has confidence in the future of Western civilization and its capacity to promote the spiritual progress of man. Reform Judaism, as Dr. Ellis Rivkin, a leading Jewish historian, sees it, looks upon the present situation as full of promise for the Jew.

> [It is enabling the Jew to] man the spiritual frontiers of the global society that is being born . . . secured by the knowledge that the economic and technological prerequisites for an age of humanity are at hand.

Indeed, as he affirms, Western civilization offers enormous "opportunity for religious creativity not the death knell of Judaism."

But beyond this is the faith that Reform draws from its pioneers, men like Jacobson and Geiger, Einhorn and Wise, and all the others, who were determined to wrest triumph from the trials of their own day. So, in the very words spoken by Isaac M. Wise himself, Reform finds its continuing sense of purpose and its faith for the future:

> What the Reform group proposes it proposes for the welfare of the future generations. It wishes to prevent the endless desertions [from Judaism] . . . It wishes to banish the hideous indifference that has taken hold of a large portion of the Jewish community. It wishes to inspire the Jews with new love for their religion—and, with such intentions, it does not fear . . . but trusts in Him [God] who grants His best blessings to every just and sincere undertaking.

QUESTIONS FOR DISCUSSION

1. How would Jewish life today be different had Reform never come into existence? How important are Reform's contributions to (a) American Jewish life? (b) world Jewry? (c) the advancement of the Jewish religion? (d) your own life as a Jew?

2. What are the chief principles of the Reform Jew? How do they differ from those of the traditional Jew? Of what importance are they to you?

3. What reasons does Reform Judaism advance for (a) a religiously-centered Jewish life and (b) the preservation of the Jewish people? What would be the effect on Jewish life if Judaism were eliminated? In what ways would society as a whole suffer if the Jews were to disappear as a people?

4. How do you explain the decline in religious commitment on the part of some modern Jews? To what extent are the following responsible: (a) modern science? (b) various secular Jewish causes? (c) Western culture? (d) theological conflicts? (e) intermarriage? (f) the establishment of the State of Israel? How might a greater sense of religious commitment be achieved among Reform Jews today?

5. How do you account for the fact that so many theological problems have arisen in the modern world? What are the main issues for the modern Jew in connection with: (a) belief in God? (b) the role of prayer? (c) standards of right and wrong? (d) the Jews as a "chosen people"? and (e) the sacredness of the Jewish tradition? What answers seem most satisfactory to you?

6. What problems do you personally find in connection with current Reform practice? Why? In what ways would you modify the *Union Prayer Book?* How would you change worship and holiday practices in your congregation?

SIGNIFICANT DOCUMENTS

Religion in the American Jewish Community, by Oscar Janowsky, 1964

A striking development of the past two decades has been the increasing identification of American Jewry as a religious community . . .

The trends of recent decades reveal that the non-religious conception of Jewishness has become a far less significant force in the Jewish community. Today, perhaps two-thirds of American Jews are affiliated with congregations. Except for a small fraction, the Jewish schools have come under congregational influence; that is, Jewish education is under religious auspices. Symbolic of this development is the increasing tendency to employ the term "religious school" instead of "Hebrew school." In fact, this is more than symbolic, for there is today greater emphasis in Jewish schools upon prayer and ritual.

The reader of this book will recall that Jewish art in America is basically synagogue art and Jewish music synagogue music. The Yiddish schools which formerly shunned "religion" have moved closer to the traditional ways. The anti-religious enclaves, which were vociferous during the early years of this century, have dwindled and are heard no more. Recent surveys have shown . . . that today American Jews regard themselves as primarily a religious group. The image of the American Jewish community is assuming a definite religious complexion.

However, when the adjective "religious" is applied to the Jewish community, its meaning must be properly identified. The Protestant Reformation and the rise of national states tended to confine "religion" to theology, ethics, and ritual. Many Americans therefore employ the term in this limited sense. But the American Jewish community is far more embracing. . . .

Moreover, when Jews say that they regard Jewishness as primarily religious, it does not necessarily imply a commitment to a body of doctrine or a code of ritual. For some it *is* a confession of deep faith and strict observance. Others are non-observant in the ritualistic sense and they are neither rejected nor misprized by synagogue and temple. Many turn to the synagogue only on special occasions, such as the High Holy Days or *Bar Mitzvah.* Synagogue affiliations may be no more than a formality, an expression of "togetherness," or a means of finding companionship. For such Jews, religion is a symbol of identification rather than an expression of faith in Divine Providence.

—Oscar I. Janowsky,
The American Jew: A Reappraisal,
pp. 389–391.

Some Trends within Reform, by Leon I. Feuer, President of the Central Conference of American Rabbis, 1965

During the past several years the air has been filled with alarums about the fate of American Jewry. We are told that extinction is staring us in the face, perhaps within two or three generations. We are warned that our birthrate is falling, that the curve of our exogamy rate is swinging up to frighteningly high proportions, that Jews by one route or another in unknown but substantial numbers of thousands are leaving the encampment of Israel. Need I remind you that prophecies of doom from within, and premature and often exultant threats of destruction from without, are not novel in our experience. It would be folly not to take a realistic view of the inadequacies of our American Jewish situation and to do everything within our power to broaden the knowledge, to deepen the religious commitment, to make more attractive and meaningful our ritual observance, and thus to fortify the survival motivations of our people. Moreover, I am personally convinced that we in the Conference must hold the line on the question of marriage outside the faith, that we must continue our historical policy of discouraging intermarriage. At the same time it would be fallacious, retrogressive, and in my view utterly futile to resort to measures which distortedly reflect the mood of panic.

Such measures are being advocated and often from voices within our own ranks. . . . Some among us are offering the nostrum of parochial schools. Others are enamoured of neo-Orthodox or some type of halachically [governed by Jewish law] controlled revival and multiplication of rituals, on the theory that drama and quaintness and sheer quantity will work better than evolution and rational adjustment. Do not mistake me! I am by no means anti-ritualist or anti-halachah— quite the contrary—but it has not been demonstrated to my satisfaction nor does the contemporary experience of Orthodox and Conservative Judaism here or elsewhere prove that the pioneers of our Reform movement were wrong, or for that matter that historic Judaism generally was wrong, in attempting to relate ceremonial practice in some revitalizing manner to contemporary thought and culture. Shall we turn orthodox when the winds of change are sweeping through the orthodoxies of other faiths?

There are those who would have us draw other circles of self-segregation about ourselves, educing what seems to me to be misleading and artificially concocted conclusions from societal data about the ethnic, religious, and regional pluralism of American society. They would have us try to structure patterns of living in our environment derived from the *Kehillah* [the European organized Jewish community], *shtetl* [the small Jewish community in Eastern Europe], and other *Galut* [Diaspora] nationalist models of earlier and totally dissimilar environments and historical periods. To employ a Yiddishism—it will not help at all. . . .

I also find disturbing some of the theological trends in our midst, especially those which seem to take their cue, their concepts, and even their vocabulary from the neo-Orthodox Christian emphasis upon personal encounter, confrontation, and dialogue between Divinity and individual soul. We are being offered doctrines of personal salvationism which try to serve as the counterpoise between the existential reality of this moment and, what is in the final analysis for these theologians, the despair of ultimate unknowableness. Here, too, we are grasping at intellectual, if comprehensible, straws for glamorizing Judaism by dressing it up in the fashionable vocabulary of the hour. . . .

There is a certain paradoxical and almost poignant aspect to this backward-looking obsession with the techniques of survivalism. Here we are in a dramatically hopeful hour in religion's career on this planet. The Catholic and Protestant Churches are struggling mightily and also against fierce reactionary opposition to open windows on the world, while some of us are tugging to turn back into the rooms of our past or even to escape into the garret of dust-laden antiquities. Ministers and rabbis and priests are marching with locked arms in the streets and singing the songs of freedom in jails, and this is certainly one of the factors which is today exciting and challenging our young people and making them feel perhaps for the first time in their lives that Judaism is more than a series of tales told and retold in Sunday school classrooms, that it has something to say to them about the personal dilemmas and social problems of the world in which they are living. Can we not, do we dare not to grasp the nettle of this spiritual power which is within our reach?

The advancing religious forces of American life, and perhaps some day of the entire world, will be slowly and painfully but steadily recovering the essential meaning of religion as we have understood it, the religion of the Old Testament, the word of God which burns in the bosom and cannot be contained, the revelation which made man through Israel beloved and chosen for partnership with God. This advance guard of the other faiths is resuscitating and trying to relive in action the moments when Moses stood on Sinai and Amos at Beth-El. While some of us worry about whether Judaism will survive!

—Leon I. Feuer, "The President's Message," *Central Conference of American Rabbis Yearbook,* Vol. 75 (1965), pp. 11–13.

Four Current Reform Views of God, 1967

I

. . . If someone were to suggest, or even to prove, that this world of ours must have been given the first push, as it were, by some Prime Mover, or that Evolution (with a capital "E") makes the wheels go round, or that life would be impossible without some Life Force (of which we may capitalize the "L" and the "F"), I would be very grateful for the information. I would find it to be very helpful and useful. But I could not *pray* to it, any more than I could pray to the law of gravity. I can only pray to something I can address because it ad-

dresses me. And, since some*thing* is not very likely to address me, we had better come out in the open and admit that we are referring to some*one.*

That is why the tradition speaks of God as a Person. Of course, the tradition does not mean to imply that God has flesh and bones, arms, hands, and a nose. But tradition does speak of God's will, and of God's love, and of God's concern. And to have a will, love, and concern means that one is so constituted as to have them; and, in our human language, that kind of constitution is called "personality." . . .

Above all, the people of Israel have encountered Him again and again in their millennial history. Four thousand years of Jewish life would be the cruelest joke ever perpetrated (and by whom?) if Jews had risked and sacrificed their security, their worldly goods, their very lives, and the lives of their children out of loyalty and devotion to a God who did not exist, who did not redeem them from Egypt, who did not meet them at Sinai, who did not share with them the vicissitudes of exile, and who did not hold out to them the promise of ultimate redemption. . . .

—From Jakob J. Petuchowski, "Symposium: The God We Worship"—A Traditional View, *Dimensions,* Vol. II, No. 1 (Fall, 1967).

II

We cannot *conceive* of the God of biblical faith; we cannot define Him conceptually in a neat, dogmatic formula or in an elaborate theological system. To say of Him that He is omniscient, omnipotent, and all-good—and apply to Him literally our human understanding of the categories of knowledge, power, and goodness—is to falsify Him. We cannot say this is what He is precisely in His own essence and nature. Once we do this, it is no longer the living

God of whom we speak but an idea or—if you will—an idol of our own making.

A God who is truly God, as Buber so wisely said, cannot be expressed but only addressed. And if we open ourselves to Him totally and unreservedly, if we penetrate beneath the surface into the depths, we shall hear Him calling to us in the most ordinary and mundane aspects of our life. We shall hear Him and, through our prayer, respond to His divine address.

—From Bernard Martin, "Symposium: The God We Worship"—An Existentialist View, *ibid.*

III

What glorious overtones modern science has thus added to the ancient watchword of our Jewish faith! As God is one, so the universe is one, life is one, man is one! That which is spiritual in man—his soul—has evolved out of his protozoan beginnings no less than his spine, his hands, or his brain. And such evolutionary development was possible precisely because there was soul within the universe from its beginning. God, to the naturalist, is the Soul of the universe. God is the creative, spiritual Seed of the universe—the Energy, the Power, the Force, the Direction, the Thrust—out of which the universe has expanded, by which the universe is sustained, in which the universe and mind find their meaning.

I must insist—with all the emphasis of which I am physically and intellectually capable—the religious naturalist neither denies God nor diminishes Him. He simply enlarges his concept of nature enough to include God. It is not belittling God to talk of Him as a Life Force or as the creative, indefinable Soul of the universe. It is not subjecting God to subhuman form. To the contrary, it is precisely the person who insists on talking about God within a human vocabulary and in terms of human analogy who is belittling God.

—From Roland B. Gittelsohn, "Symposium: The God We Worship"—A Naturalist View, *ibid.*

IV

The God we worship, above all else, must be real. Man has known Him through a variety of ways, but in each instance He is as real as the universe itself. Being a rational creature, distinguished from other animals by his capacity to think, man cannot suddenly deny his mind when he thinks about God—certainly not as a Jew. God must make sense. . . .

There is one traditional understanding of God which requires a reexamination. Men have generally described Him as being omnipotent and omniscient. There is much in our experience which justifies a doubt about these characteristics of God. It appears that instead of the absolute view of Deity we are nearer to the truth if we view Him as nonabsolute. In the first place, the evolutionary nature of the universe and of life suggests that the world is imperfect, incomplete. It is true that the Bible records that on the sixth day God finished making the world. But the world is not finished at all, it is terribly incomplete. Furthermore, it reveals in its long evolutionary process many blunders, cruelties, and much waste. A perfect, all-powerful God ought to do better than that!

In fact, there is no need for God to be absolute in power to be God. God is better understood as a becoming, even as is the universe and man. God struggles against evil and learns to overcome it. Man can help God and God can help man. They are co-workers in the building of the kingdom. Man needs God and God needs man.

—From Levi A. Olan, "Symposium: The God We Worship"—An Organicist View, *ibid.*

OTHER THINGS TO READ

Bamberger, Bernard J., *The Story of Judaism:* Part 8, "Problems and Opportunities."

Blau, Joseph L., *Modern Varieties of Judaism:* Chap. 6, "Was Emancipation a Mistake? Mid-Twentieth-Century Appraisals."

Central Conference of American Rabbis Journal: latest issues.

Cronbach, Abraham, *Judaism for Today.*

Enelow, Hyman G., *The Faith of Israel.*

Fackenheim, Emil L., *Paths to Jewish Belief.*

Gittelsohn, Roland B., *Man's Best Hope.*

Janowsky, Oscar I. (ed.), *The American Jew: A Reappraisal.*

Keeping Posted (published by the Union of American Hebrew Congregations): latest issues.

Kohler, Kaufmann, *Jewish Theology Systematically and Historically Considered* (Reform).

Korn, Bertram W. (ed.), *Retrospect and Prospect.*

Levinger, Lee J., *A History of the Jews in the United States:* Chap. 24, "A Bird's-Eye View of American Jewry"; Chap. 25, "How the Jew Keeps His Judaism in America"; Chap. 28, "How American Jews Are Organized for Many Purposes"; Chap. 32, "The Future of the American Jew."

Noveck, Simon (ed.), *Contemporary Jewish Thought.*

Noveck, Simon (ed.), *Great Jewish Thinkers of the Twentieth Century.*

Plaut, W. Gunther, *The Growth of Reform Judaism:* Part 3, "Reform in Transition"; "Epilogue."

Sachar, Howard M., *The Course of Modern Jewish History:* Chap. 24, "The Growth of the American-Jewish Community"; Chap. 25, "The State of Israel."

Schwartzman, Sylvan D., *Reform Judaism in the Making:* Chap. 17, "This Is Reform Judaism."

Standard Jewish Encyclopedia: "American Jewish Committee," pp. 94–95; "American Jewish Historical Society," p. 95; "American Jewish Joint Distribution Committee," pp. 95–96; "Martin Buber," pp. 367–368; "Hillel Foundations," pp. 905–906; "Mordecai Kaplan," pp. 1104–1105; "Jewish Publication Society of America," pp. 1045–1047; "Judah Leon Magnes," pp. 1246–1247; "National Council of Jewish Women," p. 1394; "Abba Hillel Silver," pp. 1720–1721; "Stephen S. Wise," pp. 1917–1918; "Zionist Organization of America," p. 1971.

"Symposium on the Prayer Book," *Central Conference of American Rabbis Journal,* Vol. 14, No. 4 (October, 1967), pp. 11–49.

"Symposium: The God We Worship," *Dimensions,* Vol. II, No. 1 (Fall, 1967), pp. 20–27.

Universal Jewish Encyclopedia: "American Jewish Committee," Vol. 1, pp. 242–247; "American Jewish Historical Society," Vol. 1, p. 253; "American Jewish Joint Distribution Committee," Vol. 6, pp. 170–176; "Martin Buber," Vol. 2, pp. 569–570; "Abraham Cronbach," Vol. 3, p. 425; "Samuel Goldenson," Vol. 5, pp. 19–20; "Hillel Foundations," Vol. 5, pp. 363–367; "Edward L. Israel," Vol. 5, pp. 618–619; "Jewish Publication Society," Vol. 6, pp. 138–140; "Jewish Theological Seminary," Vol. 6, pp. 143–147; "Mordecai M. Kaplan," Vol. 6, p. 311; "Judah Leon Magnes," Vol. 7, pp. 276–277; "National Council of Jewish Women," Vol. 8, pp. 116–118; "Abba Hillel Silver," Vol. 9, pp. 536–537; "Stephen S. Wise," Vol. 10, pp. 543–544; "Zionism" (in the United States), Vol. 10, pp. 658–662.

Vorspan, Albert, *Giants of Justice.*

Vorspan, Albert, *Jewish Values and Social Crisis: A Casebook for Social Action.*

Vorspan, Albert, and Eugene J. Lipman, *Justice and Judaism.*

SUGGESTED ACTIVITIES

1. Have the class act as the temple board of trustees in proposing improvements in congregational worship and religious practice.

2. Prepare a large chart with three columns. In the first, list the various issues that confront Reform Judaism today. In the second, describe the nature of the problem. Then, after assigning all of the problems to class committees, enter their proposed solutions in the third column.

3. On the basis of your knowledge of American Jewish life today, produce an article for a newsmagazine describing some of the trends you observe and the needs that seem most important to you.

SUBJECTS FOR RESEARCH

1. What role did Reform Jews play in the establishment of (a) the Jewish Theological Seminary? (b) the Zionist Organization of America? (c) the National Council of Jewish Women? (d) the Jewish Publication Society? (e) the American Jewish Committee?

2. Study the lives of each of the following Reform rabbis: (a) Sidney Goldstein, (b) Samuel Mayerberg, (c) Stephen S. Wise, (d) Edward L. Israel, and (e) Abraham Cronbach. What contributions did each make to the cause of social justice?

3. What are some of the important theological issues among American Protestants today? How do they differ from those confronting the Reform Jew?

4. What effect has the present-day situation in American Jewish life had upon the Conservative and Orthodox movements? How does this compare with the effects upon Reform?

5. As reported in the ''President's Message'' found in the latest volume of the *Central Conference of American Rabbis Yearbook,* what are some of the major problems the Reform movement currently faces?

FILMSTRIPS TO SEE

Martin Buber: The Life of Dialogue (UAHC), describing the life and thought of this modern Jewish religious thinker who has had such a profound influence on current theology.

Grant Us Peace: The Lifework of Arthur J. Goldberg (UAHC), picturing the contributions of this noted Reform Jew in behalf of justice and peace in today's world.

Within the Family of Liberal Judaism (UAHC), portraying the activities of the major American Reform organizations in connection with the work of the local temple.

Rabbi Stephen S. Wise: A Twentieth Century Prophet (UAHC), depicting the life of this outstanding Reform leader, his struggle against political corruption, and his contributions to American and world Jewish life.

BIBLIOGRAPHY

Abrahams, Israel. *Jewish Life in the Middle Ages*. New York: Atheneum, 1969.

American Jewish Yearbook, 1936–7. Philadelphia: Jewish Publication Society.

Bamberger, Bernard J. *The Story of Judaism*. New York: Union of American Hebrew Congregations, 1957.

Ben-Gurion, David. "The Facts of Jewish Exile," *Harper's,* Vol. 231, No. 1384 (September, 1965), 47–51.

Bentwich, Norman. "Solomon Schechter," in Simon Noveck (ed.), *Great Jewish Personalities in Modern Times.* New York: B'nai B'rith, 1951.

Bial, Morrison D. *Liberal Judaism at Home* (Revised Edition). New York: Union of American Hebrew Congregations, 1971.

Blau, Joseph L. *Modern Varieties of Judaism.* New York: Columbia University Press, 1966.

Browne, Lewis (ed.). *The Wisdom of Israel.* New York: Modern Library, 1956.

Caplan, Samuel, and Harold U. Ribalow. *The Great Jewish Books.* New York: Horizon, 1952.

Carlyle, Thomas, *The French Revolution.* New York: Modern Library, 1937.

Central Conference of American Rabbis Journal. "Symposium on the Prayerbook," Vol. 14, No. 4 (October, 1967), 11–49.

Central Conference of American Rabbis Yearbook. Selected volumes, 1889–1967. "Results of the European Conferences and Synods," Vol. 1 (1890), 85–117; "Major Decisions of the Augsburg Synod Regarding Marriage," Vol. 1 (1890), 112–113; "Neutrality Resolution," Vol. 45 (1935), 102–103; 110–112; "Adoption of Guiding Principles," Vol. 47 (1937), 94–114; "Resolution on Zionism," Vol. 53 (1943), 92–94.

Cohen, A. *Everyman's Talmud.* New York: Dutton, 1949.

Cohon, Samuel S. "The History of the Hebrew Union College," *Publications of the American Jewish Historical Society,* Vol. 40, Part 1 (September, 1950), 17–55.

Cronbach, Abraham. *Judaism for Today.* New York: Twayne, 1954.

Davis, Moshe. *The Emergence of Conservative Judaism,* Philadelphia: Jewish Publication Society, 1963.

Dimensions. "Symposium: The God We Worship," Vol. II, No. 1 (Fall, 1967), 20–27.

Doppelt, Frederic A., and David Polish. *A Guide for Reform Jews.* New York: Bloch Publishing Co., 1957.

Edidin, Ben M. *Jewish Community Life in America.* New York: Hebrew Publishing Co., 1947.

————. *Jewish Customs and Ceremonies.* New York: Hebrew Publishing Co., 1941.

————. *Jewish Holidays and Festivals.* New York: Hebrew Publishing Co., 1940.

Elbogen, Ismar. *A Century of Jewish Life.* Philadelphia: Jewish Publication Society, 1944.

Enelow, Hyman G. *The Faith of Israel.* New York: Union of American Hebrew Congregations, 1917.

Fackenheim, Emil L. *Paths to Jewish Belief.* New York: Behrman, 1960.

Feldman, Abraham J. *Reform Judaism: A Guide for Reform Jews.* New York: Behrman, 1956.

Felsenthal, Emma. *Bernhard Felsenthal, Teacher in Israel.* New York: Oxford University Press, 1924.

Feuer, Leon I. *Jewish Literature since the Bible,* Vol. I. New York: Union of American Hebrew Congregations, 1937.

————. "The President's Message," *Central Conference of American Rabbis Yearbook,* Vol. 75 (1965), 11–13.

————, and Azriel Eisenberg. *Jewish Literature since the Bible,* Vol. II. New York: Union of American Hebrew Congregations, 1941.

Fleg, Edmond. *The Jewish Anthology.* New York: Harcourt, Brace & Co., 1925.

Bibliography

Freehof, Solomon B. *Recent Reform Responsa.* Cincinnati: Hebrew Union College Press, 1963.

───────. *Reform Jewish Practice.* Vols. I and II. New York: Union of American Hebrew Congregations, 1964.

───────. *Responsa Literature.* Philadelphia: Jewish Publication Society, 1959.

───────. *What Is Reform Judaism?* "Popular Studies in Judaism," Series. New York: Union of American Hebrew Congregations, 1950.

Freimann, A., and F. Kracauer. *History of the Jews of Frankfort.* Philadelphia: Jewish Publication Society, 1929.

Freidlander, Albert H. *Out of the Whirlwind: Reader of the Holocaust Literature.* New York: Union of American Hebrew Congregations, 1968.

Gebhardt, Carl. *Uriel Acosta, An Example of a Human Life.* Helen Lederer (trans.). Cincinnati: Hebrew Union College-Jewish Institute of Religion, 1958.

Gittelsohn, Roland B. *Man's Best Hope.* New York: Random House, 1961.

───────. *Modern Jewish Problems.* New York: Union of American Hebrew Congregations, 1964.

───────. "Symposium: The God We Worship," A Naturalist View, *Dimensions,* Vol. II, No. 1 (Fall, 1967), 24–25.

Goldin, Hyman E. *Code of Jewish Law,* Vol. 4. New York: Star Hebrew Book Co., 1928.

───────. *HaMadrikh: The Rabbi's Guide.* New York: Hebrew Publishing Co., 1939.

Graetz, Heinrich. *History of the Jews,* Vols. 5 and 6. Philadelphia: Jewish Publication Society, 1891–1898.

Gumbiner, Joseph H. *Isaac Mayer Wise, Pioneer of American Judaism.* New York: Union of American Hebrew Congregations, 1959.

Guttheim, James K. "Address to the Conference of Rabbis of Southern Congregations" (sermon). New York: Bloch Publishing Co., 1886.

Guttman, Julius. *Philosophies of Judaism.* David W. Silverman (trans.) New York: Doubleday, 1966.

Hebrew Union College-Jewish Institute of Religion Catalogue, 1970.

Heller, Bernard. *The Odyssey of a Faith.* New York: Harpers, 1942.

Heller, James G. *Isaac M. Wise, His Life, Work and Thought.* New York: Union of American Hebrew Congregations, 1965.

Hertzberg, Arthur. "The American Jew and His Religion," in Oscar I. Janowsky (ed.). *The American Jew: A Reappraisal.* Philadelphia: Jewish Publication Society, 1964.

Herzl, Theodor. *The Jewish State.* New York: Scopus Publishing Co., 1943.

Hess, Moses. *Rome and Jerusalem.* Meyer Waxman (trans.). New York: Bloch Publishing Co., 1918.

Hirsch, Samson Raphael. *The Nineteen Letters of Ben Uziel.* Bernard Drachman (trans.). New York: Funk & Wagnalls, 1899.

Janowsky, Oscar I. (ed). *The American Jew: A Reappraisal.* Philadelphia: Jewish Publication Society, 1964.

Jelenko, Edward W. "Samson Raphael Hirsch," in Simon Noveck (ed.). *Great Jewish Personalities in Modern Times.* New York: B'nai B'rith, 1951.

Jewish Encyclopedia. 12 Vols. New York: Funk & Wagnalls, 1901.

Jospe, Alfred. "Moses Mendelssohn," in Simon Noveck (ed.). *Great Jewish Personalities in Modern Times.* New York: B'nai B'rith, 1951.

Kley, Edward, and S. Gunzberg. *The German Synagogue,* Vol. I. Berlin: Maurer, 1817–1818.

Knox, Israel. "Isaac Mayer Wise," in Simon Noveck (ed.). *Great Jewish Personalities in Modern Times.* New York: B'nai B'rith, 1951.

Kohler, Kaufmann. "A Revaluation of Reform Judaism," *Central Conference of American Rabbis Yearbook,* Vol. 34 (1924), 223–224.

───────. "David Einhorn, the Uncompromising Champion of Reform Judaism," *Central Conference of American Rabbis Yearbook,* Vol. 19 (1909), 215–270.

───────. *Jewish Theology Systematically and Historically Considered.* New York: Ktav, 1968.

───────. *Studies, Addresses and Personal Papers.* New York: Bloch Publishing Co., 1931.

Korn, Bertram W. (ed.). *Retrospect and Prospect.* New York: Central Conference of American Rabbis, 1965.

Learsi, Rufus. *The Jews in America: A History.* Cleveland: World, 1954.

Lefkovitz, Maurice. "Samuel Hirsch," *Central Conference of American Rabbis Yearbook,* Vol. 25 (1915), 174–190.

Lehman, Emil. *Israel—Idea and Reality.* New York: United Synagogue Committee, 1962.

Lessing Gotthold. *Nathan the Wise,* in George Kohut (ed.). *A Hebrew Anthology,* Vol. II. New York: Bloch Publishing Co., 1913.

Levinger, Lee J. *A History of the Jews in the United States.* New York: Union of American Hebrew Congregations, 1961.

Lewis, Theodore N. "Journal of a Rabbi" (book review), *Reconstructionist,* Vol. 33, No. 13 (November 3, 1967), 29–30.

Liebman, Joshua. "New Trends in Reform Jewish Thought," *Reform Judaism: Essays by Hebrew Union College Alumni.* Cincinnati: Hebrew Union College Press, 1949.

Locke, John. "First Letter on Toleration," *Four Letters on Toleration.* London: A. Murray, 1870.

Lowenthal, Marvin L. *The Jews of Germany.* Philadelphia: Jewish Publication Society, 1936.

——————. "Theodor Herzl," in Simon Noveck (ed.). *Great Jewish Personalities in Modern Times.* New York: B'nai B'rith, 1951.

Mandelbaum, David G. "Change and Continuity in Jewish Life," in Marshall Sklare (ed.). *The Jews, Social Patterns of an American Group.* New York: Free Press, 1958.

Marcus, Jacob. "Israel Jacobson," *Central Conference of American Rabbis Yearbook,* Vol. 38 (1928), 386–481.

——————. *The Jew in the Medieval World.* Cincinnati: Sinai Press, 1938.

——————. *Memoirs of American Jews, 1775–1865,* Vol. 1. Philadelphia: Jewish Publication Society, 1955.

——————. *The Rise and Destiny of the German Jew.* New York: Union of American Hebrew Congregations, 1934.

Martin, Bernard. "Symposium: The God We Worship," An Existential View, *Dimensions,* Vol. II, No. 1 (Fall, 1967), 22–23.

Maslin, Simeon. *Selected Documents of Napoleonic Jewry.* Cincinnati: Hebrew Union College-Jewish Institute of Religion, 1957.

Masserman, Paul, and Max Baker. *The Jews Come to America.* New York: Bloch Publishing Co., 1932.

May, Max B. *Isaac Mayer Wise.* New York: Putman, 1916.

Mendelssohn, Moses. *Jerusalem* (Vol. II, pp. 89, 96), in Walter Jacobs, "Moses Mendelssohn and the Jewish-Christian Dialogue," *Central Conference of American Rabbis Journal,* Vol. 13, No. 3 (October, 1965), 48–49.

Morgenstern, Julian. *As a Mighty Stream.* Philadelphia: Jewish Publication Society, 1949.

News and Views. New York: World Union for Progressive Judaism, 1968–1970.

Noveck, Simon (ed.). *Contemporary Jewish Thought.* New York: B'nai B'rith, 1963.

——————. *Great Jewish Personalities in Ancient and Medieval Times.* New York: B'nai B'rith, 1951.

——————. *Great Jewish Personalities in Modern Times.* New York: B'nai B'rith. 1951.

——————. *Great Jewish Thinkers of the Twentieth Century.* New York: B'nai B'rith, 1963.

Olan, Levi A. "Symposium: The God We Worship," An Organicist View, *Dimensions,* Vol. II, No. 1 (Fall, 1967), 26–27.

Petuchowski, Jakob J. "Symposium: The God We Worship," A Traditional View, *Dimensions,* Vol. II, No. 1 (Fall, 1967), 20–21.

Philipson, David. *Centenary Papers and Others.* Cincinnati: Ark Publishing Co., 1919.

——————. "Geiger the Reformer," *Central Conference of American Rabbis Yearbook,* Vol. 20 (1910), 246–283.

——————. *Max Lilienthal, American Rabbi.* New York: Bloch Publishing Co., 1915.

——————. "The Pittsburgh Rabbinical Conference," *Central Conference of American Rabbis Yearbook,* Vol. 45 (1935), 190–206.

——————. *The Reform Movement in Judaism,* rev. ed. New York: Ktav, 1967.

Pilch, Judah. *Fate and Faith.* New York: Bloch Publishing Co., 1963.

Plaut, W. Gunther. *The Growth of Reform Judaism.* New York: World Union for Progressive Judaism, 1965.

——————. *The Rise of Reform Judaism.* New York: World Union for Progressive Judaism, 1963.

Polsky, Howard. "A Study of Orthodoxy in Milwaukee," in Marshall Sklare (ed.). *The Jews, Social Patterns of an American Group.* New York: Free Press, 1958.

Postgate, R. W. *Revolution from 1789–1906.* New York: Harper, 1962.

Randall, Jr., John Herman. *The Making of the Modern Mind.* New York: Houghton Mifflin, 1940.

Bibliography

Reichler, Max. "Reform Judaism and World Jewry," *Reform Judaism: Essays by Hebrew Union College Alumni.* Cincinnati: Hebrew Union College Press, 1949.

Reznikoff, Charles, and Uriah Z. Engelman. *The Jews of Charleston.* Philadelphia: Jewish Publication Society, 1950.

Rivkin, Ellis. "The Jew in American Society," *Central Conference of American Rabbis Yearbook,* Vol. 77 (1967), 200–226.

Roth, Cecil. *A Bird's-Eye View of Jewish History.* New York: Union of American Hebrew Congregations, 1954.

Sachar, Abram L. *A History of the Jews.* New York: Knopf, 1965.

Sachar, Howard M. *The Course of Modern Jewish History.* New York: World, 1958.

Schauss, Hayyim. *The Jewish Festivals, From Their Beginnings to Our Own Day.* New York: Union of American Hebrew Congregations, 1938.

——————. *The Lifetime of a Jew, Throughout the Ages of Jewish History.* New York: Union of American Hebrew Congregations, 1950.

Schwartz, Jacob D. "Reform Jewish Practice," *Reform Judaism: Essays by Hebrew Union College Alumni.* Cincinnati: Hebrew Union College Press, 1949.

Schwartzman, Sylvan D. *Reform Judaism in the Making.* New York: Union of American Hebrew Congregations, 1962.

Schwarz, Leo W. *The Root and the Bough.* New York: Rinehart and Co., 1949.

71st–73rd Annual Report of the Union of American Hebrew Congregations.

Sherman, C. Bezalel. "Demographic and Social Aspects," in Oscar I. Janowsky (ed.). *The American Jew: A Reappraisal.* Philadelphia: Jewish Publication Society, 1964.

Shinedling, Abraham I. (trans.). "A Call to Detroit—1869," *The American Jewish Archives,* Vol. 19, No. 1 (April 1967), 37–40.

Silverman, Joseph. "Samuel Adler," *Central Conference of American Rabbis Yearbook,* Vol. 19 (1909), 415–423.

Silverman, Lou H. "The Union Prayer Book," in Bertram W. Korn (ed.). *Retrospect and Prospect.* New York: Central Conference of American Rabbis, 1965.

Singer, Howard. *With Mind and Heart.* New York: United Synagogue Committee, 1961.

Singer, Simeon. (trans.). *The Standard Prayerbook.* New York: Bloch Publishing Co., 1946.

Sklare, Marshall. "Aspects of Religious Worship in the Contemporary Synagogue," in his (ed.) *The Jews, Social Patterns of an American Group.* New York: Free Press, 1958.

Standard Jewish Encyclopedia. Garden City, N.Y.: Doubleday and Co., 1959.

Steinberg, Milton. *Basic Judaism.* New York: Harcourt, Brace & World, 1947.

——————. *The Making of the Modern Jew.* New York: Behrman, 1948.

Syrkin, Marie. *Blessed Is the Match.* Philadelphia: Jewish Publication Society, 1947.

Union of American Hebrew Congregations Annual Reports. Selected volumes, 1875–1967.

Universal Jewish Encyclopedia. 10 Vols. New York: The Universal Jewish Encyclopedia, 1939.

Vorspan, Albert. *Giants of Justice.* New York: Union of American Hebrew Congregations, 1960.

——————. *Jewish Values and Social Crisis: A Casebook for Social Action.* New York: Union of American Hebrew Congregations, 1968.

——————, and Eugene J. Lipman. *Justice and Judaism.* New York: Union of American Hebrew Congregations, 1959.

Weisberg, Harold. "Ideologies of American Jews," in Oscar I. Janowsky (ed.). *The American Jew: A Reappraisal.* Philadelphia: Jewish Publication Society, 1964.

Wiener, Max. *Abraham Geiger and Liberal Judaism.* Philadelphia: Jewish Publication Society, 1962.

Wise, Isaac M. "Opening Address," *Central Conference of American Rabbis Yearbook,* Vol. 1 (1890), 19–21.

——————. *Reminiscences.* Cincinnati: Leo Wise and Co., 1901.

Wolf, Lucien. *The Legal Sufferings of the Jews in Russia.* London: Unwin, 1912.

World Union for Progressive Judaism Directory, 1969.

Zuckerman, Nathan. *The Wine of Violence.* New York: Association Press, 1947.

INDEX

Index

Index

Index

New Testament, 22, 29
New Zealand, 7, 301
Nuremberg Laws, 235–236

O
Occident, The, 163, 179, 180, 181
Oneg Shabbat, 278
Olath Tamid, 197
Organ, 5, 70, 71, 73, 93, 98, 102, 111, 117, 118, 124, 129, 131, 144, 162, 179, 180, 212, 274
Organization, problem of, 288, 316
Orthodox, 3, 4, 5, 8, 11, 65, 66, 79, 80, 81, 82, 83, 84, 85, 86, 87, 93, 95, 98, 111, 112, 130, 140, 144, 145, 147–148, 150, 162, 163, 165, 174, 178, 182, 205, 302, 312, 316, 323

P
Pale of Jewish Settlement, 174, 175, 208
Palestine, 20, 24, 54, 58, 73, 97, 98, 102, 179, 182, 194, 195, 216, 230, 231–232, 245, 251, 257, 258, 265–266
Paris, 50, 52, 125, 150, 153, 301, 311, 319
Passover, 4, 64, 69, 89, 99, 282
Peace, 254, 257
Perozbul, (Prozbul), 81–82, 106
Pharisees, 29, 30
Philadelphia Rabbinical Conference, 183, 191–192, 193, 194, 195, 198, 212, 246, 281
Philippson, Ludwig, 103, 104, 107, 113–114, 116, 124, 159, 164, 174, 175, 196, 212
Philipson, David, 145, 199, 210, 233, 243, 245, 310
Pinsker, Leon, 230
Pirke Avot, 80
Pittsburgh Conference, 207–208, 210, 213, 214, 215, 216, 217, 218, 230, 246, 276–278, 318
Pittsburgh Platform, 10, 214–218, 225–226, 227, 228, 229, 230, 233, 243, 244, 247, 248, 249, 250, 251, 252, 254, 256, 257
Pius VI, Pope, 36
Plum Street Temple, 273, 291
Poland, 21, 51, 254, 256, 258
Polygamy, 54, 82
Popular Studies in Judaism, 298
"Positive historical Judaism," 126, 134, 135, 207
Poznanski, Gustav, 162, 179, 212
Prayer book, traditional, 98
"Progressive" Judaism, 6–7
Progressive revelation, 141, 142
Prophets, 9, 17
Protestant Reformation 21, 23, 40
Protestants, 4, 36, 39

Protocols of the Elders of Zion, 229
Prussia, 34, 50, 72, 83, 84, 95, 130
Purim, 24, 279

R
Rabbinical Assembly, 302
Rabbinical robe, 5, 83, 84, 276, 291
Rabbinic seminary, Reform, 85, 104, 113, 115, 116, 119–120, 124, 173, 178, 182–183, 201–202
Rabbi's Manual, 301, 318
Raphall, Morris J., 179
Reason, Age of, 35–36, 37
"Reformed" Judaism, 6, 10
Reform Jewish Appeal, 7, 290
Reform Judaism, nature of, 10–11, 12–13, 201
Reform religious practice, 255, 257
Religion, centrality of, 142, 144, 312–313, 315
Religious Action Center, 297, 319
Religious education, 145, 158, 163, 168, 255, 257, 259, 295, 297, 304, 305, 316
Renan, Ernest, 146
Responsa, 11, 13, 17, 20
Resurrection, 192, 194, 217
Revolutions of 1848, 128, 135, 150, 152, 193
Riesser, Gabriel, 112–113, 128, 212
Roman Catholics, 4, 20, 21
Rome, 20, 22, 145, 146
Rothschild, Lionel, 146
Rumania, 129, 229
Russia, 50, 146, 148, 153, 174, 175, 184–185, 195, 208, 227, 229, 259, 318, 319

S
Saadia, 21
Sabbatai Zevi, 21, 24, 41
Sabbath, 24, 56, 92, 98–99, 102, 111, 123, 124, 127–128, 130, 131, 144, 192, 202, 255, 257, 277–278, 302, 316
Salomon, Gotthold, 73
Salon Jews, 42, 67
Schechter, Solomon, 207
Schott, Leopold, 114, 115, 116
Schulman, Samuel, 232–233
Science and religion, 204, 208–209, 214, 257, 316
Scientific Journal for Jewish Theology, 112, 114, 115
Scientific study of Judaism (*Wissenschaft*), 95, 142
Secularism, 2, 248, 312
Seesen, 68, 69, 70, 71, 72, 73, 74–75, 125, 212
Semichah (Ordination), 291
Sermon, 5, 83, 84, 86, 98, 144, 162

UNION EDUCATION SERIES

Edited by

JACK D. SPIRO, *National Director of Education*
UNION OF AMERICAN HEBREW CONGREGATIONS
MYRNA POLLAK, *Associate Editor*
ABRAHAM SEGAL, *Director of Continuing Education*
MANUEL GOLD, *Director of Professional Education*
EDITH SAMUEL, *Editor of Keeping Posted*
RALPH DAVIS, *Director of Publications*